The End of K

'Measure for Measure,'
Incest, and the
Ideal of Universal Siblinghood

Marc Shell

The Johns Hopkins University Press
Baltimore and London

Copyright © 1988 The Board of Trustees of the Leland Stanford Junior University
All rights reserved
Reprinted and published by arrangement with Stanford University Press
Printed in the United States of America on acid-free paper

Originally published as a hardcover edition by Stanford University Press, 1988
Johns Hopkins Paperbacks edition, 1995
04 03 02 01 00 99 98 97 96 95   5 4 3 2 1

The Johns Hopkins University Press
2715 North Charles Street
Baltimore, Maryland 21218-4319
The Johns Hopkins Press Ltd., London

Library of Congress Cataloging-in-Publication Data will be found at the end of this book.

A catalog record for this book is available from the British Library.

ISBN 0-8018-5242-0 (pbk.)

For Stanley Cavell

Acknowledgments

For their help and encouragement I have the privilege to thank my students and colleagues at the State University of New York (Buffalo) and at the University of Massachusetts (Amherst). Carol Jacobs pointed out to me a main gist of my argument at an early stage in its development. I am also grateful to the late Jacques Ehrmann for support of my early work on Racine's *Iphigenia*; to Barry Weller, Bruce Jackson, Eugene Goodheart, and Diane Christian for their help with several research problems; and to Helen Tartar for her assistance in preparing the manuscript for publication. For permission to reproduce photographs I am indebted to the Chantilly Museum (Condé) and the Louvre Museum (Paris). Above all, I must thank Susan, Hanna, Jacob, Lieba, Brian, and Sophie—my wife, daughter, son, sister, brother, and mother.

M.S.

Contents

Preface

They passed no further, neyther could they discover the
land's end (which some holde to be there).

*Acosta's Naturall and Morall Historie of
the East and West Indies, 3.11.156.*

THAT AN ACT we relegate to the perverse periphery or to the holy
center of human life is essentially what we all practice—this would be
an outlandish thesis. It would suggest that an apparently alien act—
one that we claim to despise at the outermost limit of the sphere of
life, or to revere at the innermost limit, or to both despise and revere
as "taboo"—is really a familiar act. It would suggest that the line or
point marking the bounds of the conventions and laws we hold dear
actually defines those conventions and laws not only by opposition to,
or difference from, them but also by its essential sameness to them.

The taboo on incest—the fact that we regard it as both perverse and
holy—is interesting in its own right, but it is not my principal concern
in *The End of Kinship*. Instead I will focus on the ordinary sphere of
social life, defined by opposition to the center or periphery where incest is accepted or expected. We ordinarily suppose ourselves to live
free of incest by virtue of a kinship structure that allows us to distinguish—to believe that we can distinguish or that it makes sense to distinguish—between non-kin (those persons with whom we can have
sexual intercourse without violating the incest taboo) and kin (those
with whom we cannot). We might call this distinction one end, or generic intention, of kinship. Could it be, however, that the distinction
between nonkin and kin—or between chastity and incest—might be
called reasonably into question?

The End of Kinship is, in part, an exploration of one way to make
sense of this question. It is an exploration of the doctrine of Universal
Siblinghood, an idea that has informed the thought and life of the
West for millennia. We shall see that the doctrine of Universal Siblinghood, which is usually dismissed as being merely figural or lin-
guistically perverse, collapses the defining elements of society—the
perverse periphery and the holy center—into the sphere of ordinary
social life in such a way that incest is understood to pervade all human
intention and action. The teleological and ideological completion, or
end, of the distinctions that kinship establishes is thus its own undoing. The end of kinship is the ending of kinship.

A thesis that takes its ground from the outermost and innermost borders of the place where we live is inevitably outlaw and discomforting. We shall be tempted therefore to dismiss its claims, even to the point of calling them overly figural or excessively literal. Putting in question the law of the land involves trying to stand for a while at land's end, and talking about apparently extraterrestrial matters can involve putting into play terms that are, at first blush, inadequate or unpleasantly archaic. "Universal Siblinghood" is such a term, for it implies "a kind of incest" that makes for the ending of kinship. "Taliation," which indicates a return of like for like, is another. It implies an exchange of the kind that informs not only revenge (or retaliation) but also those commercial and sexual substitutions where one thing or person passes for another, as happens in incest. Just such a notion of reciprocity in likeness and likelihood—of taliation in Universal Siblinghood—Shakespeare had in mind when he named the play that we shall discuss *Measure for Measure*: "Like doth quit like, and Measure still for Measure."

The chapters in this book compose a commentary that expresses the ideas of its author in the interpretation of another work. Commentary elucidates a text and thereby elucidates a thesis of its own about the human problems by which the text is informed. It is an ancient medium of expression, and in certain circumstances it is the best one, but sometimes it is difficult to read. Special problems of exposition make repetition inevitable, and roadside stops are often few and far between. More importantly, a commentary assumes from the first what is only later shown to be or not to be the case: namely, that the text under discussion is—or will be made to be—as meaningful in its own way as people used to believe were the Holy Books (the commentaries on the Bible are legion) or philosophical works (a good commentary on Kant's *Critique of Pure Reason* still counts as an individual work in its own right). To classify *Measure for Measure* with such writings may seem presumptuous to believers or philosophers; however, I have chosen to discuss *Measure for Measure* not only because I believe it is a "great" work in its own right but because it has a pivotal place in the Western tradition. Wonder about whether and how a single dramatic work can, or can be made to, play out a crux of our tradition—a healthy skepticism one should welcome from any quarter—is the soundest place from which studious interpretation can take its bearings.

Why not speak about incest and taliation without the intermediation of speaking about or through *Measure for Measure*, or of speaking through a dummy? I might well have used another voice. And the voices of economist, anthropologist, psychologist, and political theorist, as well as of me, will sound here from time to time, sometimes for many pages. Yet it is one thesis of this book that literary commentary can offer unique access to the problems incest poses. By concerning itself with the figurative aspect of language and with literary works that are at once fictional and typical, it can provide a unique way to understand central issues. The particular literary work—*Measure for Measure*—discussed in the central chapters of this book brings to light a series of fundamental problems involving the classification of kin and kind, the tension between natural teleology and political teleology, and the opposition between celibacy and liberty. With its help we shall reexamine the nature of sexual and commercial exchange in human society and focus on what has been called, with what reason we shall henceforward put into question, one overall characteristic of human beings in society.

Introduction

French fourteenth-century miniature, showing Abelard conversing with Heloise. (*The Romance of the Rose*; Chantilly Museum, Condé.)

Your majesty, and we that have free souls, it touches us not.
Let the galled jade winch; our withers are unwrung.

HAM 3.2.233–34

Wʜᴀᴛ's ᴡʀᴏɴɢ with incest that its taboo should be, or should have been made, a quintessential characteristic of human beings or of human beings in society? A traditional answer would be that were incest allowed, disaster would ensue. Folktales, for example, claim that the earth would shake or darkness fall. Psychologists say that kin roles would become so confused no one would know who he or she "was." Political theorists argue that incest would upset authority and property relations within society. From a biological point of view, it has been argued that genetically those who breed in will die out.[1] And so on. Whatever the reasons with which one might justify or refute these positions, their threats of calamity are probably less explanations of the incest taboo than expressions of it. For even if some people knew some disaster story to be true, that would not account for the taboo among *all* people.

What, then, might explain the apparent universality of the taboo? Some modern thinkers say that humans have an instinctive aversion to sexual relations with people by whom or with whom they have been raised from childhood, or that the proximity found in the family itself makes for aversion.[2] Others (notably Freud) have argued that as individuals people *do* want to have incestuous sexual relations, but that civilization depends upon repressing that desire; thus familiarity leads, not to sexual contempt, but to incestuous desire and neurotic fear. From yet a third position, the incest taboo is interpreted as a social adaptation to past biological or sociological reality. Calculating from lifespan and breeding needs (the age at maturity and the time needed to suckle infants), one anthropologist has argued, for example, that among the original hominids incest was rare, if not impossible.[3] More to our present purpose, another anthropologist, remarking that human beings mature sexually before they are ready to leave home, claims that an incest taboo was necessary to minimize sources of rivalry and aggression within the stable family groups in which humans live.[4]

3

By seeing the incest taboo, however universal, as merely the outcome of historical factors, the last set of positions opens another question. Might the incest taboo have run its sociological course? Is it a holdover from our early history that we could get over—possibly for good rather than ill—if we could accurately distinguish and perhaps eradicate the political and social institutions that made it necessary?[5] The contemporary threat of the annihilation of all humankind by war (whose fundamental motivations, some say, include the repression the incest taboo may encourage and the aggression it seems powerless to prevent) is urgent enough to make us question, no matter what, our social and political structures. Is it possible that the disasters incest threatens are less than the disaster that if we do not love one another equally, we will die out?

Odd as it may sound to speculate about the withering of the incest taboo, the thought is not new. In fact, it centrally informs the major religious and philosophical traditions of the West, which have sought, by practicing Universal Siblinghood, to transcend altogether the distinction between kin and nonkin, thus between chastity and incest.

Kinship by Biological Consanguinity and by Sociological Fiction

Therefore shall a man leave his father and his mother.

Gen. 2:24

The commonplace Western view is that kinship by consanguinity is primary, or real kinship. Anthropologists and sociologists usually have lumped together all other kinds as pseudo-kinship (or kinship by extension),[6] which they then divide into subcategories such as figurative, fictive, artificial, and ritual.[7] However, the fundamental distinction between "real" kinship and "pseudo"-kinship—or between literal and figural structure—is the topic of a still-unresolved debate about whether kinship is essentially a matter of biology (whose terms include "genitor" and "genetrix") or sociology (whose terms include "father" and "mother").[8]

The Bastard and the Changeling. We like to think that consanguinity is easy to determine, yet nothing is harder than to make verifiable public assignations of biological parenthood. The possibility of being a bastard casts doubt on one's assigned father; the possibility of being a changeling casts doubt on both father and mother. Bastards and changelings indicate the indeterminability of biological parenthood; they suggest its fictional aspects, even in a society such as ours, which

4

believes that it really knows the facts of life and that the real facts of life are biological.[9]

"The end of Marriage," writes Burnet, "is the ascertaining of the Issue." To provide legitimate offspring who are "certain and better known," argues Alfonso el Sabio, is the purpose of marriage.[10] But can an individual man or his community ever be certain that he is the father of a particular child? Posthumus' enraged cry "We are all bastards" (CYM 2.5.2) or Leontes' assertion, fearing himself a cuckold, that "Many thousand on's / Have the disease and feel't not" (WT 1.2.205–6) may seem excessive or even neurotic. But society in general must be concerned about bastards because if kinship is basically consanguineous then compliance with the incest taboo depends upon knowledge of consanguinity. In many societies women are thus closely guarded by one or another mechanical, social, or internalized mechanism for ensuring chastity—by a chastity belt, for example, a well-patrolled harem, or some religious taboo against adultery.[11]

The emphasis placed on male procreation by the Christian religious and legal traditions may be a response to this fearful uncertainty about paternity. As James Joyce's Stephen Dedalus puts it:

Fatherhood, in the sense of conscious begetting, is unknown to man. It is a mystical estate, an apostolic succession, from only begetter to only begotten. On that mystery and not on the madonna, which the cunning Italian intellect flung to the mob of Europe, the church is founded, like the world, macro- and microcosm, upon the void. . . . Paternity may be a legal fiction. Who is the father of any son that any son should love him or he any son?[12]

A similar uneasiness about paternity informs the Greek tradition. The debate involving politics (Orestes) and family (Clytemnestra) in Aeschylus' *Oresteia,* for example, is ended by the argument of the virgin goddess Athena (born from the head of Zeus), who proclaims that, since "no mother gave me birth," only the male of the human species is the begetter.[13] Her argument, backed by Aristotle's view that in human reproduction "the male provides the form and the principle of the movement; the female provides the body, in other words the material,"[14] would no doubt have convinced the doubting Hamlet that he stood in a definitively closer relationship to his father than ever Priam's son stood to Hecuba (HAM 2.2.543–44).

To call any particular child some man's son or daughter—or any particular man someone's father—is a fiction insofar as all paternity is inevitably indeterminable. The Common Law in Rome and Germany held that a child whose natural father was not his social father had no

father at all, that he was "the son of no one" (*filius nullius*), much as
the Christian tradition regards Jesus seen as a mere man;[15] and the
German Civil Code provides that "an illegitimate child and its father
are not deemed to be related."[16] In contrast is the old British practice
of legally deeming a bastard to be the child of the master of the household in which it is born: "Who that bulleth my cow," says the English
proverb, "the calf is mine."[17] The fiction of assigning paternity where
the natural and social fathers are believed to be one (so that the child
is legitimate) and the fictions of denying or arbitrarily assigning paternity where they are believed to be two (so that the child is illegitimate)
are thus interrelated: the ultimate indeterminability of biological paternity makes us all equal, as interchangeably legitimate children, children of no one, and illegitimate children. And yet the societal need to
determine paternity, which Malinowski calls the sociological rule of
rules, requires us social beings either to maintain distinctions by accepting the fiction of biological paternity as the literal truth of things
(as we do in this culture) or by establishing persons to be *thought* of "as
of a father" (HAM 1.2.108)—as figural or sociological fathers.[18]

To introduce the indeterminability of parentage in terms of bastardy may seem to privilege wrongheadedly the male view, for the individual husband's concern that his wife's child is not his own (or the
child's concern that his legal father is not his biological one) and the
corresponding societal concern that the paternity of each child be established derive from the biological fact that in sexual reproduction
the man's role begins and ends with intercourse, but the woman's role
continues from conception through pregnancy and birth. But absolutely verifiable biological maternity is essentially as much a social fiction as is absolutely verifiable biological paternity.[19]

Just as uncertainty about the father begins after intercourse, so uncertainty about the mother begins with birth. Women, "thinking too
precisely on th'event" (HAM 4.4.41), may come to fear that their children are changelings just as men may come to fear that their children
are bastards.[20] Insofar as changeling affects both fathers and mothers
(or patrilineal and matrilineal societies), it is the archetypal sign of the
indeterminability of parenthood.[21]

Although "changeling" can mean any "person or thing (surrep-
titiously) put in exchange for another"[22] (like the "changeling never
known" Hamlet substitutes for the letter of his uncle-father Claudio,
HAM 5.2.53, or the adult changelings Mariana, Barnadine, and Ragozine in *Measure for Measure*), its principal meaning involves infants. All
infants are said to pass for like, much as they are all said to resemble

6

their parents; infants thus suggest teleologically the substantial sameness of all grown-ups. The archetypal changeling is "a child secretly substituted for another in infancy"[23] in such a way that the biological father, mother, and child do not know of the taliational substitution. (*Measure for Measure* again provides an example of sorts, when grown-up Claudio is miraculously delivered, or changed, as his own infant son—"As like almost to Claudio as himself," 5.1.487.)

A changeling, then, is a child whose blood kin, in the eyes of *everyone*, are not its blood kin, and vice versa. In this limited sense a changeling differs from a kidnapped child, a child purposefully left to die, or a child accidentally lost.[24] A kidnapping like that in *Cymbeline*, for example, may eventually result in a sister's falling in love with a grown-up man she does not recognize to be her brother; however, some people know of the kidnapping, and they have reasonable (if reasonably small) grounds to be wary of any amatory attachment that the grown-up sister or brother might develop.[25] (Similarly, in a case of child-theft like the one in the Judgment of Solomon, the two women who claim maternity are, presumably, aware of the actual kinship of the child, and the tale hangs by the questionable figure that the woman who loves the child is the consanguineous genetrix [1 Kings 3:16–28].) The exposure and finding of a baby girl in *The Winter's Tale* eventually results in her falling in love with the unrecognized kin of someone more or less akin to her; however, some know about the exposure and finding, and hence about the mystery of her parentage and its attendant dangers.* In Sophocles' *Oedipus the King*, Jocasta likewise had grounds to be more wary of her attachment to Oedipus, since she had no proof of her son's death, and Oedipus' adoptive parents, Polybus and Merope, should have warned him that he was a foundling. Finally, such loss of a daughter as occurs in *Pericles of Tyre* may eventually result in unrecognized incest. In *Pericles* 1.1 it almost does; however, the father and daughter both know enough of the history of their separation to be wary.

Archetypal changelings differ in degree, if not in kind, from all these kidnapped, exposed, or lost children because no one knows that anything or anyone is out of place. The one possible exception, the thief, is often not human, as in King Henry IV's ambiguous wish that his riotous son and the honor-drunk son of his enemy Henry Percy had been secretly changed in infancy: "O that it could be proved /

---

*In the love between Perdita, the foundling daughter of King Leontes, and Florizel, the son of Leontes' nearest friend, Shakespeare conflates the theme of the foundling with that of the changeling (WT 3.3.117 and 4.4.687–89).

That some night-tripping fairy had exchanged / In cradle clothes our children where they lay" (1H4 1.1.86–88; compare the thief in MND 2.1.120–37). But if it is impossible to know for sure that anyone is out of place, how could such a changing be "proved"? Nowadays we make footprints from babies' feet in order to eliminate substitutions in the hospital, but for the foundling Oedipus—whose foundling status, if not actual parentage, was relatively easy to determine—even the most remarkable form of pedal identification apparently did not ensure that Jocasta would recognize him grown up.

One might object that what really matters is not that biological parentage be established but that parents and society believe it has been. (This objection assumes that no social disaster would ensue if there were bastards, changelings, or incest, so long as no one knew. In contemporary society, in fact, we discount disaster stories as myths and say any genetic mutations that might result from unwitting incestuous encounters are unlikely in a society as populous as ours. We thus deny adopted children the right to know who their biological parents are.) Yet the position that pseudo-kinship is real kinship insofar as it is believed to be real, although it reduces to sheer mystification the tension between the fictional aspect of blood kinship and any literal substrate, sidesteps the awesome question to which our literatures and religions draw our attention and from which, perhaps, they have sprung. "Who, really, are my parents?" That is both Oedipus's query and Jesus's.

The possibility of supposititious substitutions in the bedroom and the cradle thus affects us all, both men and women—in patriarchal or matriarchal, patrilineal or matrilineal, societies.[26] What way, but by privileging one or another kind of pseudo-kinship, is there to eliminate changeling and bastardy—which represent the general ambiguity and indeterminability of all kinship relations that make incest an unseen and ever-present threat? What way is there to ensure that we know our kin but to put down biology (call it reality) and set up sociology (call it fiction) as our standard?

Kinds of Sociological Kin. Most sociological kinships are identical to biological ones in that they, too, divide the human world into two groups of people—those who are kin and those who are not—and group kinfolk together on the basis of some common measure or something consubstantial. "Children are everywhere thought to be of the same substance as their parents," says one anthropologist, "because they are produced by them: 'like breeds like' in every system of thought."[27] "Like father, like son" is the taliational key to kinship that Aristotle proposes in the *Politics*,[28] and it is the focus of Leontes' first questions about whether the biological children of his wife are also his own (WT 1.2.122 and 1.2.128–35, cf. 2.3.97–107). Yet the substance, or quality, that makes people akin varies from culture to culture and is ambiguous even within a culture. Which is more fundamental, for example, my likeness to my supposed genitor or my likeness to God, who created me in his image? Which substance is most fundamental: the genes I share with my genitor, the love between my adoptive parent and myself, the milk I sucked from my mother, the blood I commingled with my blood brother, the food I shared at a communal feast, or the dust from which all things (including myself) are made?

In our political and epistemological traditions, most sociological kinships involve a distinction between kin and nonkin, and many involve an incest taboo much like that for biological kinship. Milk kinship (relating persons nursed at the same breast), nominal kinship (relating people who share the same name, that is, people who are called kin, however the name may have been acquired), legal adoption, steprelationship, kinship by marriage, and kinship by spiritual alliance, all can involve an incest taboo.[29] The kinship that obtains among godparents and godchildren (the gossipred) similarly outlaws as "spiritual incest"* either intra- or intergenerational sexual intercourse.[30]

Unlike consanguinity, the standards of sociological kinship can often be known with absolute certainty by virtue of a public ceremony or similarly visible fact. In this sense, at least, the sociological kinships are superior to biological kinship. Indeed, in some societies sociological kinship provides a diriment, or nullifying, impediment to marriage although consanguineous kinship does not. (The Eskimos, for example, virtually ignore the "facts of life" and heed only kinship by residence.)[31] In our own social tradition, sexual intercourse with pseudo-kin has often been regarded as a more serious violation of the incest taboo than sexual intercourse with biological kin; the Western Church, for example, paid special attention to gossipred.

Moreover, certain kinship institutions in the West—including some blood brotherhoods, friendship societies, religious orders, and political associations—have challenged the essential division of human beings into kin and nonkin that informs the kinds of kinship we have mentioned.[32] Blood brotherhoods, for example, attempt to replace ordinary biological and sociological kinds of kinship with a structure

---

*In its specific theological and legal sense, "spiritual incest" refers either to sexual intercourse involving such gossipred kin as godsons and goddaughters or to sexual intercourse involving such universal kin as Brothers and Sisters. The use here of "spiritual incest" to refer to sexual relations between godsibs is the first of three technical meanings I shall employ.

that is both potentially transgenerational and universalist. They already suggest those extraordinary forms of kinship, at once peripheral and central to society, in which every human being is sibling to every other one. The principal example of such forms, although there are others, is the kinship organization hypothesized and to some extent practiced by traditional Christianity and specifically by the celibate Catholic orders.

Siblings In and Out of Incest: A Literary Topology

One way or another, the idea of Universal Siblinghood has influenced the Western tradition for millennia, at least since the time of Pythagoras,[33] calling into question our relegation of incest to the perverse periphery or holy center of human life. The association of monachist institutions with the fear and practice of physical incest is, indeed, a crucial topos in Christian literature. In joining an order, an individual gives up earthly kin relations (in which some people are family and others are not family) and takes on heavenly kin relations (in which all people are explicitly Siblings and God is at once parent, spouse, sibling, and child).[34] This give-and-take of kinship can be seen in two opposed but closely interrelated literary plots. In the first, a lay person, for whom some people are kin and some are not, tries to escape from the desire to commit sibling incest or the guilt of having done so by entering a nunnery or monastery. Here all people are equally kin or not kin and making love to one's sibling is no worse or better than making love to any other person in the Universal Siblinghood.[35] By entering the nunnery or monastery a protagonist thus ascends from earthly incest into Universal Siblinghood in the order. In the second plot, a monk or nun leaves the convent and commits physical incest with a biological sibling, thus descending from Siblinghood in the convent into physical incest outside it. Taken together, the typologies of ascending from earthly incest and descending into it help to define the ideological significance of and the social need for such apparently fictive places or topoi as heaven on earth, the Garden of Eden, and the family as the young child is sometimes supposed to see it, places where the ordinary concerns of sexually mature human beings in society seem to have all but disappeared.

Since the eighteenth century, at least, "spiritual kinship" has connoted romantic soul-mating, but in the technical sense I use here the term concerns the relationship between a nun or a monk and any other person in the world, which establishes a kinship in God and outlaws as "spiritual incest" sexual intercourse between them. According to major Church authorities, for anyone to sleep with or marry a person consecrated to God was incestuous.[36] The creed of Christianity maintains, moreover, that all human beings are siblings, or at least that everyone human is essentially convertible to the same siblinghood. "All ye are brethren" (Matt. 23:8). By universalizing kinship in this way the doctrine of spiritual kinship puts into question, not merely the status of consanguinity as the standard for kinship, but also the distinction between kin and nonkin and thus between incest and chastity on which all the other structures of kinship rely and, some say, on which society itself is founded.

Descent from Chastity to Incest.   In the West, most theoretical and fictional works about incest have focused on the recognition of consanguinity rather than put into question the literalist standard of consanguinity, the absolute knowability of consanguineous parents, or the distinction between kin and nonkin. (We never doubt that Oedipus is Jocasta's son, do we?)

Since this focus on consanguinity appears to allay our own concerns about kinship, it is socially reassuring. Recognition of consanguineous kin thus plays an articulating and major role in both tragedies and comedies.[37] The plots of relevant tragedies commonly involve a protagonist who mates with someone he wrongly believes not to be kin; then the actual kinship is revealed. The tragic recognition scene shows that an act thought to be chaste was incestuous. Sophocles' *Oedipus the King* is the principal ancient example; modern examples are likely to involve sibling incest: German "tragedies of fate,"[38] Goethe's *Wilhelm Meister*, Horace Walpole's *Mysterious Mother*,[39] Dineson's *Caryatids*, Voltaire's *Zaïre*, and Diderot's *Natural Son*. The plots of relevant comedies generally involve a protagonist who wishes to mate with someone he wrongly believes to be kin, and the comic recognition scene shows that an act thought to be incestuous is chaste. Examples of comic concern with sibling incest include Lessing's *Nathan the Wise*, Goethe's *Siblings*, and Beaumont and Fletcher's *A King and No King*.[40]

Such tragedies and comedies present kinship as knowable, although initially it may be unknown.[41] Yet Western literature has also hinted at the absolute indeterminability of human parenthood—at the fact that none of us can really know who his parents are—in at least two notable figures. The first is the "orphan" hero, who leaves what he takes to be his family home (sometimes because of doubts about his parentage) and in consequence makes love with unrecognized kin. Oedipus, the adopted child of Polybus and Merope, originally left Corinth, for example, because "a drunken man, accused me in his drink / of being bastard."[42] The second figure is the "parentless child," who, fearing that any sexual intercourse might be incestuous, leaves not only his family home but all human families to become a child to some god or goddess and a Sibling to all human beings. When this "child of adoption" to god or goddess descends from heavenly Siblinghood to the world of earthly ties, however, his fears or desires are fulfilled in enactment, for in this typology he unknowingly falls in love with, or makes love to, a person of his earthly family.

Thus, in many literary works, whenever a nun or monk has sexual intercourse ouside the convent, it turns out that the lovers are consanguineous brother and sister. Their act of sexual intercourse is not only spiritual or figural incest, insofar as everyone (including a sibling) is a Sibling to a nun or monk, but also literal incest. By such incest, these works indicate one generic end, or intent, of a religious order insofar as the order emulates a kinship group: to incorporate and transcend incest. In the convent, intercourse with a sibling is no better—or worse—than with any other human being; and the multiple kin relations expressed or implied in terms for monks' and nuns' ties to God, Christ, and each other would be incestuous in an ordinary family.

Many of the saintly founders of the Catholic orders were actual, loving brothers and sisters who became Siblings and thereby embraced "spiritual incest," meaning the relationships that obtain among the members of the Holy Family of God, where the Parent is also Child, Spouse, and Sibling. The multiple kinship relations Jesus himself had to members of his earthly family are stressed by such theologians as the Franciscans and such secular writers as Marguerite of Navarre; they emphasize that Jesus is at once Parent, Spouse, Sibling, and Child of Mary and that, even when he denies his earthly family, he retains his position as Father, or Son, of himself (and, by analogy, Father of all humankind).[43] Such emphasis on incest in the Holy Family may have parallels in the New Testament authors' choices of which details of Jesus' genealogy and birth to report: the human genealogy of Jesus includes the incestuous sons of Tamar and her father-in-law Judah, and magi—priests said to be born of incestuous unions among a people (the Persians) supposed to practice incest without guilt—greeted the newborn God Jesus with gifts.[44]

The relationship between Jocasta and grown-up Oedipus is thus sublated in Christianity in a gamut of spiritual kinship relations within the Holy Family.* In the prelude to the final beatific vision in Dante's

---

*The Christian topos that Jesus stands in a quadrifold kinship relation to everyone is an idealist transcendence of a common situation in Greek epic and tragedy. In the *Iliad*, Andromache speaks thus to her doomed husband: "Hector, you are my father and my

Divine Comedy, Saint Bernard calls the Virgin Mary "the daughter of her own son"[45]—a holy mystery, since the incest involved is either chaste or somehow beyond the distinction between chastity and its opposite. The saintliness of some Christian saints is associated with overcoming incestuous desires or incestuous acts—as for Saints Albanus, Julian, and Gregory.[46]

Modern works have also linked incest and sainthood. In *The Cenci*, Stendhal claims that being the child of an incestuous union can lead to becoming a saint.[47] And in Lope de Vega's *The Outrageous Saint*, a brother's rape of his sister is identified with the Roman soldier's spearing Christ; the brother is redeemed by identifying with the figure of Christ, who appears and explicitly points out the connection: "See my chest, stuck with a spear, / And yours which only broods on ways of dishonoring your sister."[48]

The popular association of incest and the Catholic orders—such that whenever in story a monk or nun finds a mate outside the convent, the mate is sure to be a sibling—can be seen in many literary examples. A brief rehearsal of some of their plots, in this and the following section, can suggest how this extreme, yet representative, incest story informs our tradition and how literary plotting expresses the meaning, or telos, of biological and spiritual sexuality.

In Friedrich von Schiller's *Bride of Messina*, Beatrice, who has spent most of her life in a nunnery and does not know her blood kin, leaves the cloister for just a few hours to attend the funeral of the Duke of Messina. "I ventured from the convent fold / Into the alien crowds." She falls in love at first sight with Don Manuel, the son of the Duke of Messina. The chorus at first believes that Don Manuel's violation of sexual propriety has been merely spiritual incest in the technical sense of intercourse between religious and lay persons: "A theft of things divine you perpetrated, / The bride of heaven by your sin you desecrated, / For dread and sacred is the cloister's vow."[49] It turns out, however, that Beatrice is the daughter of the Duke, so that the near-Sister is also her lover's sister and the spiritual incest is also literal.[50]

---

lady mother, you are my brother and you are my husband" (Book 6, lines 429–30). In Aeschylus' *Oresteia*, Electra speaks similarly to Orestes: "To call you father is constraint of fact, / and all the love I could have borne my mother turns / your way, while she is loathed as she deserves; my love / for a pitilessly slaughtered sister turns to you. / And now you were my steadfast brother after all" (*Libation Bearers*, lines 239–43). The Christian culmination of this tradition sanctifies such manifold kinship relations by raising them from earth to heaven. Nietzsche thus writes that "Sophocles with his Oedipus strikes up the prelude to a victory hymn for the *saint*" (8, trans. Lebeck, *Birth*). (For full bibliographical citations of works cited in the footnotes, see the Bibliography, pp. 247–79.)

In another example, Matthew Lewis's *The Monk*, a foundling orphan Brother discovers that the woman he has raped is his sister, a reluctant novice in the Sisterhood of St. Clare.[51] Similarly, François de Rosset's "Incestuous Love of a Brother and Sister" tells of a brother who holds an ecclesiastical benefice at the time he and his sister consummate their affair. In Balzac's *Vicar of Ardennes* (*Le Vicaire des Ardennes*)—a *roman* of his youth signed with the pseudonym Horace de Saint Aubin—Melanie, who thinks herself the sister of Joseph, is willing to yield to her brother's incestuous advances in the name of happiness. Joseph becomes a priest, however, to escape his urges. When he learns that Melanie is his cousin, not his sister, they marry, even though she still does not know their true consanguineous relation. Thus, although she wrongly believes she is committing literal incest, he actually commits spiritual incest. In Roger Martin du Gard's *Thibault*, Jacques writes a novel—*The Little Sister*—in which the hero rejects normal family and civil ties and seems to consummate an incestuous affair with his sister after she has left the Sisterhood where she was an inmate.[52] And in Lope de Vega's *The Cowherd of Morana*, a jealous brother imprisons his sister in a convent after he has discovered her love affair with someone else. She escapes, however, and disguises herself as a cowherd. The brother and the cowherd accidentally cross paths, and they fall in love. Before their love can be consummated, however, they recognize each other.[53]

Ascent from Incest to Chastity.   The polar opposite to the movement from nonkinship (or universal kinship) into kinship is the movement from kinship into nonkinship. Here siblings who want to commit incest or actually have committed incest join a convent and become Siblings. In the convent, incest with one's sibling is not better—or worse—than intercourse with any other human being: desired or enacted incest here is not only transcended but also incorporated.

In folk literature, sibling incest is often averted thus.[54] The principal literary example is Chateaubriand's novella *René*.[55] In *René*, Amelia, when she decides to enter a Sisterhood, expresses the hopes that her brother René will find a wife in whom "you will believe that you have found again your sister" and that "the same tomb might unite us again one day."[56] René, who realizes neither that he is in love with his sister nor that she is in love with him, suspects that she wishes to take vows in order to escape "a passion for a man that she dare not avow." He cannot bring himself to acknowledge that he is himself the man Amelia loves until a moment of peculiarly Christian tragedy: the instant between his sister's death to the world (the first part of the ceremony for becoming a nun is a service for the dead) and her rebirth as a Sister by spiritual marriage (the second part is a marriage service to Christ).[57] At that instant the brother overhears his sister begging God to forgive her "criminal passion."[58]

At this intersection of repressed sibling love and expressed Sibling love—between spiritual death and spiritual marriage—René gives romantic expression to his love for his sister:

As these words whispered by Amelia escaped from the coffin, the awful truth dawned on me; my reason wandered. I let myself fall on the shroud of death, pressed my sister in my arms, and cried out: "Chaste spouse of Jesus Christ, receive my last embraces through the iciness of trespass and the profoundness of eternity that separates you already from your brother."[59]

Like Hamlet's outburst during *The Mousetrap*—"You shall see anon how the murderer gets the love of Gonzago's wife" (HAM 3.2.253–54) —René's exclamation puts a halt to the ceremony. Soon afterwards, Sister Amelia tells him that "for the most violent love, religion substitutes a sort of burning chastity in which the lover and the loved are one," develops a burning fever, and dies.[60]

Other literary works in which a woman or man enters a convent for fear of, or in repentance for, an incestuous love affair include Pierre de Longchamps's *Memoirs of a Nun*, Elemir Bourges's *Twilight of the Gods*, Georges Rodenbach's *The Carillonneur*, Johann Gottlob Pfeil's *The Savage Man*, and Goethe's *Wilhelm Meister*.[61] Related plots include the history of Heloise and Abelard, in which spiritual incest (physical intercourse between religious and lay people) leads to the castration of Brother Abelard and the Sistering, or enclaustration, of Heloise; and a tale in the *Heptameron* of Marguerite of Navarre in which a man and woman in feudal service to the same Lord and Lady are so desperate at being barred from marrying each other that he joins the Franciscans and she joins its sister order, the Clares—the two lovers thus becoming one flesh in Christ.[62] The topos, adapted to Protestantism, even informs the first American novel, William Hill Brown's *The Power of Sympathy; or the Triumph of Nature*; in it Harrington says of his sister Harriet, to whom he is drawn by the "link of nature": "In Heaven—there alone is happiness—there shall I meet her—there our love will not be a crime."[63] The relationship between brothers and sisters inside and outside the Catholic orders calls to mind a secular attempt to deal with the societal dilemma of incest through the political goal of universal fraternity in liberty and equality.

The Romantic Siblinghood of Humankind

From the late eighteenth century on, Romanticism attempted to re-define the older Christian notion of universal brotherhood. The most important of its redefinitions was not the "cult of fraternal love" between individual brothers and sisters (whose theoretical treatises include Lord Byron's depiction of contemporary sibling love and Karl Marx's depiction of primitive sibling love),[64] the focus on elective affinities (the relation of things to each other not in the blood so much as in the spirit," said to take precedence over societal rules involving marriage, adultery, and incest)[65] or the old notion that we are all consanguineous insofar as "it's said that we all come from the same stock."[66] It was the hypothesis of a universal relationship making us brothers and sisters all, which would erase and rise above such categories as particular brother and sister, particularized affinities, and common biological descent. Such fraternity was an issue throughout the eighteenth century; for example, the secular idealists and egalitarian democrats of the French Revolution made universal brotherhood crucial to their version of democracy.[67] Their objective was to take us from Fatherland or Motherland to a secular Promised Land.

Modern social theorists have argued from connections between genealogy and classification, or between kin and kind, that all group bonds are related to bonds of kinship. In "kind" and its cognates resides the classificatory metaphor that underlies all political theory: thus Wilson McWilliams, discussing American notions of democratic fraternity, writes that "when human relations have meaning to men, we judge them to be at least akin to kinship,"[68] seeing kinship ties as original to the associations presupposed by friendship or politics. The Romantic era seemed haunted by a disturbing and logically inescapable conclusion that sexual relations between people whose human relations are at least akin to kinship are themselves at least akin to incest, that is, they constitute "a kind of incest" (MM 3.1.138). If we are all kind of akin, then our sexual relations are all kind of incestuous.

The ideal of universal fraternity—which seems at first to be not only a politically reassuring notion (insofar as it seems democratic) but also a psychologically and socially reassuring one (insofar as its realization appears to require no change in sexual arrangements)—thus raises the specter of incest. One reaction to the fear of this incest was the Catholic orders' asocial doctrine of spiritual incest in celibacy. Another reaction was the call to practice universally physical incest.

From the Greek Plato to the American John Humphrey Noyes, thinkers have argued that incest—whether welcomed or feared—is the essential basis and political end of an abolition of heredity or hierarchy such as that advocated by democratic republicanism. The Marquis de Sade, for example, developing a hint in Plato's *Republic* that the people must all believe they are akin if there is to be a republic,[69] suggests in his political tractate "French People, Yet Another Effort Is Needed If You Want To Be Republicans" that incest would be a positive benefit to the republic of the "liberty, equality, fraternity" that Frenchmen said they wanted to establish: "Incest extends the ties of family and consequently encourages the citizens' love of country."[70] Sade turns on its head the Augustinian argument that exogamy is good because it extends the bounds of property and love.[71] "I dare to claim," he writes, "that, in a word, incest must be the law of any government of which fraternity is the base."[72] Other French ideologists, beginning with Montesquieu, had come to see that their version of the doctrine of universal brotherhood entailed a kind of incest and thus had hypothesized a guiltless incestuous sexual intercourse beyond the antiegalitarian distinction of (good) chastity from (bad) unchastity.[73]

Yet the revolutionary government, and many revolutionary thinkers, attacked the spiritual and celibate form of incest found ready to hand in the Catholic orders, finding transcendent spiritual incest by participation in the Holy Family repressive and teleologically genocidal. They charged that even sincere monks and nuns were unable to sublimate their desires (and thus desired to enact physically their spiritual incest); argued that most religious celibates were, in any case, insincere;[74] and confiscated the property of the Orders and executed their members. Francis Poulenc reminds us of the result in his opera *Dialogues of the Carmelites*, in which a sister becomes a Sister to die for Christ.[75]

Physical consummation of incest within Universal Siblinghood was incorporated into plans for some late-eighteenth- and nineteenth-century egalitarian communities, notably the community envisioned by Robert Southey and Samuel Taylor Coleridge for the banks of the Susquehanna at about the turn of the century, and it was actually incorporated into plans for John Humphrey Noyes's Oneida Community, founded in 1848. Southey's and Coleridge's community, planned in the wake of the French Revolution (they visited France in the 1790's), was to be based on aspheritism (the abolition of private property) and pantisocracy (universal equality in rank and social position).[76] In devising their American utopia, Southey and Coleridge tentatively hypothesized a community where sleeping with a sister would be neither worse nor better than sleeping with any other woman, so that all intercourse would be at once chaste and unchaste.

Coleridge, for example, argues that sibling love initiates all genuine society. From "pure" sibling love, says Coleridge, develops first conjugal love and then love of other human beings: "By the long habitual practice of the sisterly affection preceding the conjugal, this latter is thereby rendered more pure, more even, and of greater constancy. To all this is to be added the beautiful Graduation of attachment, from Sister, Wife, Child, Uncle, Cousin, one of our blood, and so on to mere Neighbour—to Townsman—to our Countrymen."[77] Coleridge extends sibling love to love of one's countrymen (one's tribal or national "brothers"), but he does not extend love of one's own sibling to include love of *all* human beings, that is, to a consistently equal and universal Siblinghood in which all people are alternately (1) neither siblings nor aliens, and (2) both siblings and aliens. Coleridge knows that such Universal Siblinghood is a logical precondition for his community, but he withdraws from supporting it because he sees that the realization of Universal Siblinghood must result either in incest or in celibacy. He therefore dropped the utopian ideals and excepted the sister from the group of all human beings.[78]

Coleridge felt the contradiction between sibling and Sibling love as well as did the extravagantly rebellious Percy Bysshe Shelley, who tried to fulfill in poetry the old dream of incestuous pantisocracy and himself probably violated the ordinary incest taboo.[79] What Coleridge wanted to know, however, was not how the taboo could be violated but whether it could be *eliminated* altogether—that is, whether the incest taboo could be both erased and raised to the point where all women are sisters and all men are brothers, and all sex equally incestuous and chaste. He writes:

Among common minds, aye, among any *but* very uncommon minds, who enquires whether any one can do that which no one does do—. Add to this all the moral Loveliness of the Disposition of the two affections [sisterly and conjugal], which the better part of our nature feels—tho' only a few speculative men develop that feeling, and make it put forth in its distinct form, in the understanding.—A melancholy Task remains—namely to show, how all this beautiful Fabric begins to moulder, in corrupt or bewildered (*verwilderte*) Nature—the streets of Paris and the Tents of the copper Indians, or Otaheitans.—Of this elsewhere, when we must. It is a hateful Task.[80]

To avoid the need to define the withering of the incest taboo, Coleridge developed a theory of "spiritual incest"—of how a brother might love a sister both chastely *and* sexually. Proposing a thesis of what John Dryden, in another context, had called "Incest in our very souls,"[81] Coleridge writes that he would hazard the impeachment of *heresy*, rather than abandon [his] belief that there is a sex in our SOULS as well as in their perishable garments: and he who does not feel it, never truly loved a Sister—nay, is not capable even of loving a Wife as she deserves to be loved, if she indeed be worthy of that holy name.[82]

To be in one's "family of the soul"[83] is, however, not the same as to be in one's family of the perishable body. With a member of the former family, it turns out, one is allowed to have sex in the bodily sense; with a member of the latter family, one is not.*

The English romantic turn against the revolutionary notion of universal fraternity, whatever its sexual and political motivation, is in part justified by the doctrine's tendency to abstraction, which was the Hegelian and Victorian position against it. The Victorian James Fitzjames Stephen, in his *Liberty, Equality, and Fraternity,* thus criticizes the ideology of fraternity as a hypocritical substitution of the abstractly general for the particular: "Love for Humanity, devotion to All or Universum, and the like, are . . . little, if anything, more than a fanatical attachment to some favorite theory about the means by which an indefinite number of unknown persons (whose existence it pleases the theorist's fancy to assume) may be brought into a state which the theorist calls happiness."[84] Similarly, Aristotle accuses the Universal Siblinghood set forth in Plato's *Republic* of being watered-down kinship, saying that "it is better for a boy to be one's own private nephew than a son in the way described."[85] But more than this might trouble us about the notion of universal kinship. For it is better to be an outsider in a particularist kinship system, where there are human kin and human aliens, than to be an outsider in a universalist kinship system, where there are only humankind and animals. The universalist doctrine "All men are my brothers" can turn out, in secular context, to mean "All my brothers are men; all others are animals." Such a formulation metamorphoses a human being who cannot, or will not, be a member of the happy brotherhood into a dog (the fate of Shylock), just as Coleridge metamorphoses a cat into a member of his family.[86]

By the same token, the tradition that there are different human groups enjoins us to marry someone enough unlike ourselves not to be classified as kin but enough like ourselves to be classified as a human being; we must marry outside our families but inside our species.[87] In the universalist tradition, however, all who are not kin are

---

*But who or what is a soul-sibling and, at the same time, also a sexual soul-mate? Coleridge seeks to defuse this problem by including his pet cat, among other apparently nonhuman creatures, in his particular family. (See my "Family Pet.") In this way, instead of abandoning his doctrine of universal fraternity as endorsing either incest or celibacy, Coleridge adopts as his own a doctrine that entails spiritual bestiality.

essentially animals; there is no middle ground between family and species because the family of Man is the species. The twist is that, in accord with this universalist thinking, the only nonincestuous form of physical love is with an animal other than the human kind, unless the beast one loves could be made human, as in the tale of Beauty and the Beast. Beauty, the young maiden, nicely exemplifies the dilemma universalism creates: she shies away from marriage with the Beast she loves because, following Westermarck's species "law of similarity,"[88] he is so much unlike her, being a "kind" of animal other than her own; by contrast, she also shies away from exclusive love of her father because, in accord with Westermarck's familial "law of dissimilarity," he is her kin, so much like her as to be inside her immediate family.* Only the transformation by a kiss of the Beast into a human husband allows for a satisfactory conclusion.

In nationalist politics, where the kiss that undoes the bestial difference is hardly available, the secularized universalist position that "Only my brothers are men; all others are animals" has a murderous consequence. Pondering the French revolutionary slogan "Fraternity, or death!" (which, since a free *frater* is a *liber*, is also the American revolutionary slogan "Liberty, or death!"), Chamfort, a turncoat French republican, commented: "'Fraternity or Death?' Yes: be my brother or I will kill you."[89] Thus fraternal equality in celibacy is replaced by fraternal equality in death, and the wonderful promise of universal brotherhood turns into the individual and fatal fraternity of Cain and Abel.[90]

America

> Every history of the creation, and every traditionary account, whether from the lettered or unlettered world, . . .
> all agree in establishing one point, *the unity of man*; by which I mean that men are all of *one degree*, and consequently that all men are born equal, and with equal natural right, in the same manner as if posterity had been continued by *creation* instead of *generation*.[91]

In the United States, where fraternity is "the first objective, ethically . . . of the democratic way of life,"[92] the link between a radically egali-

---

*An equivalence of the two men in Beauty's life—one too unlike her, the other too like her—is hinted in the bargain of her life in exchange for, or on behalf of, her father's and in the two suitors' rivalrous mortal sicknesses, which force Beauty to choose between tending one or the other. In broader terms, the Beast (or the family pet) may be a disturbingly necessary transitional love object between parent and spouse, and bestiality may thus be intermediary between filial and spousal love. (See my "Family Pet.")

tarian democracy and incest potentially plays a remarkable ideological role. Perhaps the best instance is John Noyes's nineteenth-century Perfectionist Society, a long-lived and commercially successful "new Canaan" centered in Oneida, New York. To judge from their own writings, the Perfectionists seem to have realized on earth Coleridge's dream of Pantisocracy. Noyes explains his society's system of pantogamy—or universal marriage—by arguing that free sex without shame is possible within a holy community where "all things are lawful unto me" (1 Cor. 6 : 12) and by stressing the corresponding view that free sex, including incest, is a sign of the liberty that grace confers.[93] Noyes counters the usual objection to "amative intercourse between near relations"—that "breeding in and in" deteriorates offspring—with an unusual genetic theory of his own.[94] And he grounds his argument for universal physical love, hence incest, on the premise of Universal Siblinghood that the monastic orders use when they argue against any physical love whatever. "Love between the children of God," writes Noyes, "is exalted and developed by a motive similar to that which produces ordinary *family affection.*"[95] Where all human beings are siblings, siblings and spouses are one and the same. "In plain English," wrote Ellis in 1870, "according to the doctrine of the Oneida community, a man may have sexual intercourse with his grandmother, mother, daughter, sister, or with all of them, and be blameless. The world calls this incest, and brands it as a crime of the darkest dye . . . but at the Oneida Community it is regarded . . as perfectly lawful and right."[96]

Incest also impinges on the politics of universal brotherhood as professed by another American founder of a utopian community. George Lippard established the radical Brotherhood of Union, which seems almost an attempt to live out the monastic ideal of fraternity in a largely secular American context. Yet Lippard also wrote a Gothic novel, *The Monks of Monk Hall: A Romance of Philadelphia* (1845), which depicts a parson attempting the virtue of a woman whom he thinks is his daughter, but who turns out not to be.[97]

Remarkably, Herman Melville's *Pierre: or, The Ambiguities* moves from the commonplace romantic topos of individual brother-sister incest[98] toward the incorporation and transcendence of incest and its taboo in a secularized Universal Siblinghood. Melville's warning is apt: "And believe me you will pronounce Pierre a thorough-going Democrat in time; perhaps a little too Radical altogether to your fancy."[99]

At the novel's outset, Pierre and his mother Mary, whom he calls "sister" and who is compared to the Virgin Mary, express "a venerable faith brought from over the sea," having taken the Holy Sacrament together.[100] Saddlemeadows, their idyllic and aristocratic family estate, "seemed almost to realize here below the sweet dreams of those religious enthusiasts, who point us to a paradise to come, when etherealized from all drosses and stains, the holiest passion of men shall unite all kindreds and climes into one circle of pure and unimpairable delight." Yet Pierre, a "youthful Magian,"[101] falls in love at first sight with Isabel; the ambiguity of their possible family relationship constitutes the key element in the novel. (Pierre fears she may be the unacknowledged daughter of his revered dead father, but the novel insists throughout on the ultimate undeterminability of her parentage.)

Together with Isabel, Pierre departs from ordinary family (his mother Mary and fiancée Lucy). Like the loving brothers and sisters who became saintly Brothers and Sisters, Pierre and Isabel divest themselves of mortal parents and rend all mortal bonds. "Henceforth, cast-out Pierre hath no paternity," the narrator tells us; says Isabel, "I never knew a mortal mother."[102] Now Pierre is a parentless child—like the foundling Billy Budd on the high seas in a ship entitled "Rights of Man," and like an abandoned Ishmael "driven out . . . into the desert, with no maternal Hagar to accompany him."[103] He pretends to take the Holy Sacrament of marriage with his ambiguous kinsperson, and in one of the novel's central love scenes he insists that he is brother no more: "Call me brother no more! How knowest thou I am thy brother? . . . I am Pierre, and thou Isabel, wide brother and sister in the common humanity."[104]

Instead of calling his mother "sister," Pierre now calls his Madonna-like sister "wife." With his sibling/spouse Isabel Pierre wavers ambiguously between consummating and not consummating the remarkable love that is the principal ambiguity of *Pierre*. Isabel, in describing her relationship with Pierre, says: "I am called woman, and thou, man, Pierre; but there is neither man nor woman about it. Why should I not speak out to thee? There is no sex in our immaculateness." Yet Pierre's love cannot be contained within the confines of ordinary brotherly love: "Sisters shrink not from their brothers' kisses. And Pierre felt that never, never would he be able to embrace Isabel with the mere brotherly embrace."[105] Does Pierre want to embrace Isabel as if she were someone other than the consanguineous half sister he usually takes her to be? As a genuinely married wife? As a nun? As a fellow child of the universe?

Pierre loves Isabel as a secularized kind of Sister: "Isabel wholly soared out of the realms of mortalness, and for him became transfigured in the highest heaven of uncorrupted love."[106] It is in the commercialized "Church of the Apostles" that the brother-husband and sister-wife set up their household. This church has been renovated as a secular business center in New York City, yet it recalls the community of Christian Apostles in much the same way that contemporary Blackfriars in London recalls the ancient community of mendicant Brothers.[107] Those who live at the church are suspected of having some mysterious ulterior object, vaguely connected with the absolute overturning of church and state, and the hasty advancing of some "great unknown political and religious Millenium."[108] Pierre himself begins to formulate a plan to further "the march of universal love" with which the Apostles are linked and which forms a keystone of their general ideology: "The great men are all bachelors, you know. Their family is the universe."[109]

Modelling himself ambiguously on the figure of God and literalizing the meaning of "Isabel" as "consecrated to God,"[110] Pierre begins to "gospelize the world anew."[111] He is himself the rock, the *pierre*, on which he plans to build a new church. The doctrinal and practical basis of Pierre's church is the transcendence of the distinction between vice and virtue,[112] a transcendence that involves erasing and rising above all distinctions between kin and nonkin. For Pierre all human beings are finally autochthonous Siblings "of the clod" and "children of Primeval gloom."[113] From this unity of man Melville figures the old theme of a simultaneously spiritual and physical incest.[114] Pierre, like Mohammed and the other holy figures that Melville culls from the Western tradition and its tributaries, would transcend the taboo on incest.[115]

In *Pierre* Isabel has come to American Pierre from a France that is at once post-Catholic and post-revolutionary. The brother-sister love at the Church of the Apostles borders on an apocalyptic vision of the millennial unity of man like the eternity of Universal Siblinghood hypothesized by the Catholic orders and like the temporal state of equal siblinghood—liberty, equality, fraternity—sought by the French Revolution. Yet transcending the distinction between good and evil, or chastity and incest, means an end to being human as we know it. (Isabel says to her brother Pierre, the Brother of all men, "Were all men like to thee, then were there no men at all,—mankind extinct in seraphim.")[116] By the novel's end Pierre identifies with a castrated or neutered Titan—an unmanned man who is no man at all.[117] In the secular and commercial context of Protestant America in the nineteenth century, Pierre's gospel is finally acted out as an individual fratricide (he kills his cousin Frederic), and his doctrine of transcendent neutrality to kinship is acted out as a suicidal neutering. The terrible cry of *Pierre* is "Civilization, Philosophy, Ideal Virtue!, behold your victim!"[118] Between liberty and death—which the optimistic American revolutionary Patrick Henry set forth as comedic alternatives—there is, tragically, no essential difference.

The Moment of Vacillation

I have tried to bring to light a literary tradition associating physical and spiritual kinship and to suggest the manifestation of this tradition in the politics of the modern world. The conclusions to draw from all this are many, but I am a little hesitant to draw (and unable to demonstrate) them before embarking on a major project of the following chapters. That project involves reconsidering the polarity or the opposition between ascent into kinship and descent from kinship (or between incest and chastity) just as though "the way of descent and the way of ascent were one and the same."[119]

Some literary works display an inescapable vacillation between such descents and ascents, a vacillation from which society as we know it begins in an archaeological sense. Such vacillation takes place in *Hamlet*, where the hero thinks both about descent into incest or parricide, which he both desires and fears ("Let not ever / The soul of Nero enter this firm bosom" 3.2.378–79) and also about ascent into universal kinship ("To a nunnery, go" 3.1.149).[120] In *Measure for Measure*, which most fully develops this vacillation, a novice Sister and a player-Brother fall in love at the moment the novice Sister accuses her brother of begging her to commit "a kind of incest" in order to save his life.[121] The play as a whole is informed by ambiguities about whether the novice Sister *can* save her brother without that "incest" and, ultimately, about whether the "Sister" will marry the "Brother." Such vacillation enables *Measure for Measure*, or its interpretation, to put into question the figure of incest, both physical (brother-sister) and spiritual (Brother-Sister).

The movements to and from absolute chastity and unchastity (incest), taken together, lend credence to a discomforting thesis: that there is no ultimately tenable distinction between chastity and incest, so that our ordinary understanding of marriage—as a middle way or as an adequate solution to the difficulties posed by society's exogamous need for an intersection of intratribal unity and intertribal diversity—is mistaken. Perhaps society *must* take marriage as the only means to avoid the supposed disaster of endogamy or incest; marriage alone, it seems, makes chastity possible, and insofar as the taboo on incest is the basis of society, only marriage makes society itself possible. We shall wonder, however, whether marriage is not itself tragically incestuous as well as comically chaste, or whether marriage merely incorporates rather than transcends the vacillation between kinship and nonkinship that we must take it to arrest. The vacillation between incest and chastity that *Measure for Measure* depicts—and the kind of incest and marriage by which its plot is informed—will enable us to move from fear of incest and awe of marriage to wonder about the political goal of universal fraternity in liberty and equality.

1
Civilization and
Its Discontents

Egon Schiehle, *Cardinal and Nun*, 1912.

And the end [*telos*] is the chief thing of all.

Aristotle, *Poetics*, 50a.22

THE COLLISION of two motive forces
powers the plot of *Measure for Measure*. On the one hand is the urge to
reproduce our own kind, no matter how; on the other is the urge to
set limits on how we reproduce or to arrest reproduction altogether.
In no other work that I know are these issues so extended to their
logical, dramaturgical, and anthropological limits.

The Natural Motivation to Reproduce

The world must be peopled.   ADO 2.3.238–39

The importance of the motive to reproduce our own kind is suggested by the high regard in which thinkers of the Reformation and
earlier held the divine precept "Be fruitful, and multiply" (Gen. 9:1,
9:7).[1] But in *Measure for Measure* the injunction to increase comes not
from God but from nature. Thus the Duke, attempting to convince
Angelo to show off his virtues, claims that nature's gifts to man are not
made without obligation or intending an obligation. Rather, they are
loans in return for which nature demands a profitable return.

> Nature never lends   (1.1.36)
> The smallest scruple of her excellence
> But, like a thrifty goddess, she determines
> Herself the glory of a creditor,
> Both thanks and use.

The Duke's remark is not directly about sexual procreation; the
"use" to which he refers is, primarily, the good works Angelo's virtue
may generate. Yet here and throughout *Measure for Measure*—as well
as in a tradition extending back to Plato and Aristotle—the product of
monetary generation, or use, and the product of sexual generation,
or a child, have been compared. (The Greek word *tokos*, "offspring,"

referred to both.)² Thus, granting that Nature's loan is life, the Duke's injunction might be paraphrased: For the life nature lends a man, that man is required to repay both the principal and the interest ("use")— that is, both his own life (by his eventual death) and the lives of his progeny.³ In Jesus' parable of the talents, a master who leaves money with his servants expects both principal and interest (Matt. 25:27); the topos of God as banker pervades Christian writings.⁴ In *Measure for Measure*, we find a comparable natural usury.

The injunction to increase, whether attributed to God or to nature, is problematic from a social point of view. In Genesis, for example, God's command to Noah and his family to "be fruitful, and multiply" is not qualified by any rules about how to reproduce; indeed, He is to all intents commanding them to commit incest. For Noah's family after the Flood, as for Adam's family after the Fall, incest was allowable to ensure the survival of the human species. Neither incest nor fornication, by both of which the human species may increase and multiply, were yet infractions of the divine law. They became so only later in biblical history.⁵

In *Measure for Measure*, nature makes the same inexorable determination that we shall reproduce, no matter how. And the modern liberal impulse is to sympathize with such fornicators as Lucio and Juliet or with Lucio's praising (and perhaps false) description of the Duke: "Ere he would have hanged a man for the getting a hundred bastards, he would have paid for the nursing a thousand" (3.2.113–15). Such sympathy has some merit from the viewpoint of nature. First, nature as creditor regards all reproduction as good; it does not care whether the "use" that people beget and that it gets is legitimate or illegitimate. Nature loves bastards, or natural sons.⁶ Second, any act of sexual union, including fornication, is part of the natural, purportedly inexorable, and (we hope) acceptable sequence of events. The liberal Lucio puts the process of getting bastards into this natural perspective:

> As those that feed grow full, as blossoming time (1.4.41)
> That from the seedness the bare fallow brings
> To teeming foison, even so her plenteous womb
> Expresseth his full tilth and husbandry.

Claudio the fornicator argues further that, under some circumstances, from the natural perspective a socially vicious act can be transformed into its opposite: "Nature dispenses with the deed so far / That it becomes a virtue" (3.1.133–34)—here, the virtue of both making and saving a life.

But can this attitude toward fornication be the policy of a political order? Understanding whether a political figure such as a duke could treat any and all natural human offspring as good or any and all acts of reproduction as only natural involves understanding the relationship between political control and sexual reproduction.

The Motivation to Limit or Ban Reproduction

"If animate nature can be said to operate under any rules at all," says the contemporary anthropologist Robin Fox, "the basic commandment must be simply, 'Go forth and multiply.'"[7] The Edenic simplicity of this injunction is, of course, fictional; the rules human beings follow are, for whatever reason, anything but simple. The contrast between the God of Genesis, who overlooks fornication and incest by the generations of Adam, and the God later in the Pentateuch, who sets out elaborate proscriptions along with penalties for their transgression, echoes the dilemma of Western civilization—perhaps of civilization anywhere.

Measure for Measure goes a step further. It does not ground in biblical proscriptions or divine commandment the Viennese rule prohibiting the way one may "increase and multiply." The play is noticeably silent, for example, about such laws as Deuteronomy 22:22–25 or Leviticus 20:10–16, which define as adulterous, incestuous, or bestial those sexual acts that transgress marital, familial, or species boundaries. Instead of relying on the Bible as the ultimate source for rules against fornication, *Measure for Measure* looks to politics and the teleological consequences of fornication for the political order. In the play, fear of those consequences explains the regulations of sexual activity that the Bible and similar rule books contain. By singling out Claudio among Viennese fornicators—and by presenting his punishment as meted out not so much for his sexual intercourse as for its "character," the pregnancy that "too gross is writ on Juliet" (1.2.143)— *Measure for Measure* encourages the spectator to see the political interest in controlling sexual acts as an interest in controlling the natural end of such acts, that is, in restricting reproduction itself.

Just as in *Measure for Measure* the injunction to reproduce comes less from God's command to "be fruitful, and multiply" than from nature's requirement of use (1.1.36–40), so the injunction against fornication comes less from the God of Leviticus and Deuteronomy than from the fact that, as *Measure for Measure* pursues the telos of sexuality, fornication leads to a natural sickness (venereal disease) that tends toward destroying the individual body and, more seriously, to a

31

political sickness (incest) that tends toward destroying the body politic —Claudio calls it "the body public" (1.2.148)—as we know it. These sicknesses—venereal disease and incest—focus the essential dilemma of the play.

Nature, in order to ensure that she is provided with sufficient use, provides us with lust or sexual desire, perhaps with too much for the good of individual human beings. We need to restrain the use of nature (1.2.119–20) because, as Claudio the sexual usurer puts it:

> Our natures do pursue, (1.2.120)
> Like rats that ravin down their proper bane,
> A thirsty evil; and when we drink, we die.

In meeting the natural obligation to reproduce our own kind we may consume ourselves.[8]

Lust has traditionally been characterized as disease unto death. Thus Augustine writes, "Why do you praise the disease of lust, when you see a man will die of it unless the restraint of celibacy or the conjugal remedy resists it?"[9] In *Measure for Measure*, the physiological counterpart to Augustine's theological disease is the disease of Venus— venereal disease.

Venereal disease was a new affliction in the late fifteenth century, when Shakespeare probably sets the action of *Measure for Measure*. The first large-scale epidemic of syphilis swept over Europe in 1494–95, and it has been estimated that a quarter of the population was infected. Only half a century later did the disease lose its acute virulence.[10] By the sixteenth century, fear of the disease of Venus provided adherents of chastity and celibacy with the argument that limiting sexual intercourse was a means of saving the individual body, if not the soul. (The soul is lost whether lust is enacted bodily or not.) Indeed, "the whole development of Puritanism can be viewed," says William Empson, "as a consequence of the introduction of syphilis."[11] But in *Measure for Measure* saving the individual body is not a sufficient— meaning sufficiently spiritual or noble—justification for banning fornication. Its insufficiency is indicated by the fact that venereal disease in *Measure for Measure* does not affect the relatively noble social class— Juliet, Claudio, Angelo, Mariana—although they too engage in illicit sexual activities. Some further justification is needed.

Venereal disease in *Measure for Measure* (e.g., at 1.2.28–55) is the almost comic (because bodily) counterpart of a political disease that tends toward destroying the whole fabric of society. That disease is incest, whose symptoms are fornication, or bastardizing.[12] If Shakespeare is a syphilographer suffering from sexual nausea, as some critics have implied,[13] it is because he graphically describes the political or social disease par excellence, incest.

As we shall now see, the natural end, or telos, of fornication is illegitimacy, the end of illegitimacy is incest, and the end of incest is the annihilation of the political order as that order exists in Vienna and perhaps everywhere. "The telos," writes Aristotle in the *Poetics*, "is the chief thing of all."[14] Fornication is outlawed in *Measure for Measure* because the prohibition of fornication is a bulwark of politics and of law itself.

The Generic Intent in Nature of Sexual Intercourse: Reproduction

The natural end of each and every sexual act of intercourse (whether within or without wedlock) in *Measure for Measure* is procreation; to use the terms of the play, nature intends each and every act of intercourse to be a useful (use-begetting) act. The play adapts to secular dramaturgy this conceptual collapse of natural intent into act, so that, as in a kind of shorthand, all intercourse outside wedlock is treated as bastardizing. This conflation of intent, or telos, with act explains why Isabella behaves and thinks as though she will conceive if she should sleep but one time with Angelo (3.1.188–90).[15]

This conflation of intent and act is not unusual in the Western tradition—indeed, it may be an essential characteristic of that tradition. Thomas Aquinas, for example, argues that the real intent of an action does not depend on whether or not the agent or actor wants or knows about its end: "For in those things which clearly act for an end, we declare the end to be that towards which the movement of the agent tends. . . . Nor does it matter, as to this, whether that which tends to an end be endowed with knowledge or not; for just as the target is the end of the archer, so it is the end of the arrow's flight."[16]

The Church Fathers' discussion of sexual intercourse is informed by precisely this understanding of intent. Similarly, in his discussion of what is uniquely wrong with fornication, Aquinas considers the intent of the individual fornicator (often the satisfaction of concupiscence), the actual result for the family or species of the individual act of fornication (sometimes reproduction, sometimes not) and the telos or general intent of fornication (always reproduction). For him, the last is paramount, and all acts of fornication should be treated as though reproduction were their result:

One copulation may result in the begetting of a man, wherefore inordinate copulation, which hinders the good of the future child, is a mortal sin as to the very genus of the act, and not only as to the inordinateness of concupiscence.

On the other hand, one meal does not hinder the good of a man's whole life, wherefore the act of gluttony is not mortal sin by reason of its genus. It would, however, be a mortal sin, if a man were knowingly to partake of a food which would alter the whole condition of his life, as was the case with Adam.[17]

Measure for Measure, in which Claudio and Juliet have eaten such life-altering food, adapts to secular legal or political thought just this collapse of individual intent (satisfaction of concupiscence) into generic telos (reproduction).

In the play Claudio is, in one sense, arrested for the mere act of satisfying concupiscence outside wedlock,[18] as though he and Juliet had been discovered fornicating in flagrante and the generic result of their intercourse (the living foetus in Juliet's womb) were insignificant. Yet almost everyone in the play knows that it is, in a more significant sense, for the telos of fornication rather than for fornication itself that Claudio is arrested: "It is for getting Madam Julietta with child" (1.2.66–67), for making a life in a false way (2.4.46–49). The law is ultimately concerned not to end acts of extra-marital sexual intercourse but rather to end the eventual use, or offspring, of those acts. The law

> . . . like a prophet   (2.2.94)
> Looks in a glass that shows what future evils,
> Either new, or by remisses new conceiv'd,
> And so in progress to be hatch'd and born,
> Are now to have no successive degrees,
> But ere they live, to end.

Claudio himself suggests that his offense is not so much lechery as impregnation:

> *Lucio.* Lechery?   (1.2.129)
> *Cla.*   Call it so.
>
>   • • •
>
>   . . . it chances
> The stealth of our most mutual entertainment
> With character too gross is writ on Juliet.
> *Lucio.*   With child, perhaps?

Claudio suggests that pregnancy—*grossesse*—is the incriminating sign of his past criminal intercourse with Juliet; likewise, the gentlemen's venereal disease is the sign of their past fornication (1.2.49–53). But does Juliet's pregnancy come by chance, as he implies, or by necessity?

"On whom it will, it will; / On whom it will not, so" (1.2.114–15), he says, paraphrasing bitterly Paul's letter to the Romans: "I will have mercy on whom I will have mercy, and I will have compassion on whom I will have compassion" (Rom. 9:15). The immediate antecedent of "it" in Claudio's paraphrase would appear to be the weight of "Authority" in 1.2.111–12, but in the context of the play "it" refers to the impregnation by which he believes his fornication chanced to be discovered, to the secular law that, having discovered it, is set on punishing him, and to the mercy he hopes God or His earthly representative will have.[19] But the rule of nature, for which the end of every act of intercourse is pregnancy, is no chance chain of events. Thus what Claudio calls chance, the unlucky sign of his misdeed, is rather the unavoidable telos of every act of fornication and the will of nature. In this sense Juliet's pregnancy is no accident; moreover, it is not only a sign of past sexual intercourse (1.2.142–44) but also, and more essentially, a sign of future illegitimate procreation. (Aristotle calls pregnancy the necessary sign, or *tekmērion*, of procreation—just as a flower is the promise of fruit.)[20] Similarly, the gentlemen's diseases are the signs of past fornication and of the future destruction of their lives.

This concern with generic telos rather than mere chance suggests how *Measure for Measure* meets one Aristotelian precondition for great plays: events are to be necessary, not accidental.[21] In one of the great tropes in the history of drama, Shakespeare takes as the internal telos of his plot the natural telos of sexuality. Aristotle associates the telos of dramatic plots with the telos of organic nature, and Shakespeare connects the two kinds of teloi in a brilliant ideological knot that combines, as we shall see in Chapter 6, the birth of Claudio's son (the telos of Juliet's pregnancy) with the deliverance of Claudio (the telos of the plot).

The Intent in Law of Fornication: Bastardy

In Shakespeare's Vienna, where all acts of fornication result in bastards, Juliet and Claudio are typical and the production of illegitimate children is widespread: "Nay, if there be no remedy for it, but that you will needs buy and sell men and women like beasts, we shall have all the world drink brown and white bastard" (3.2.2–3).[22] Even the genealogies of the "central couple" in the play—Pater's term for Isabella and Claudio—are cast into doubt.[23] Thus Isabella, relying on the tradition that kinship between father and consanguineous son shows in some essential likeness between them, is undecided whether Claudio is her father's son or a bastard.

35

When Claudio appears ready to give up his life rather than bargain for it dishonorably, Isabella exclaims that he speaks like her father and therefore is her father's son: "There spake my brother: there my father's grave / Did utter forth a voice" (3.1.85–86).[24] She is assuming that the business of fathers and sons alike is to protect the chastity of their daughters and sisters, and that when Claudio knows the terms Angelo has proposed he will, like a true brother or son, reject them. Yet Isabella's "there" raises the question of whether she feels or fears that Claudio elsewhere may speak as someone other than a brother.[25]

What motives might Isabella have for concluding that Claudio's apparent willingness to die for her chastity is proof that he is her father's son? Perhaps she hopes to strengthen Claudio's resolve to die, which she fears is weak; perhaps she hopes to strengthen her faith in her mother's chastity, hence in his fraternal obligation. Be that as it may, were Claudio not her dead father's son, she might be unable to realize her presumed goal, becoming a nun. If she were her father's only child, the traditional advice would be for her to marry rather than to join a nunnery. Thus Erasmus counsels marriage, not religious celibacy, for those whose kin are all either dead or celibate: "Your mother is departed . . . your syster is entred in to a hous of barren nunnys . . . the hope of your stocke is turned onely unto you."[26] If Claudio is Isabella's father's son, Claudio's child, when it is born, will be her father's grandchild and hence will free her to enter the convent.

Isabella's situation is like that of the sister in George Whetstone's *Promos and Cassandra* (a source of *Measure for Measure*), Antigone in Sophocles' play, or the historical Queen Elizabeth. In *Promos*, Isabella's counterpart is concerned that her brother is "the onely meane, Got wot, that should our house aduaunce," so that the corrupt magistrate, by executing him, would also slay her and all their house's potential progeny. The brother, for his part, reminds his sister that "I once gone, our house will goe to wrack."[27] Antigone—the daughter-sister of Oedipus—is the last of her father-brother's bloodline. ("Antigone" means "anti-generation.")[28] Likewise, the Tudor Queen Elizabeth died childless, leaving her throne to the Stuart King James one year before the first performance of *Measure for Measure*.

Although Isabella says and hopes, on the one hand, that Claudio is her paternal brother, she says and fears, on the other hand, that he is not and that her mother was an adulteress.[29] When Claudio hesitates in his resolve to die, Isabella cries out: "Heaven shield my mother play'd my father fair: / For such a warped slip of wilderness / Ne'er issued from his blood" (3.1.140–42).[30] Isabella's denunciations have emotional and perhaps structural resonance: she may wish to separate Claudio from the legitimate family of her beloved father—to de-familiarize Claudio—so as to make his execution emotionally more bearable for her.* Such methods of defamiliarization would not be needed if the novice Isabella were less the sister of Claudio and more a Sister in the Order of Saint Clare. A good Sister is supposed to de-familiarize all men equally by treating each one as a brother; an at-tempt to defamiliarize blood kin in just this way often underlay the intentions of saintly sisters who entered Sisterhoods.

The Intent of Bastardy: Property and Incest

What's wrong with illegitimacy? Illegitimacy leads to uncertainties about paternity, which lead in turn to two problems. First, the practice of law (in Vienna and elsewhere) depends upon judging a man by who his father is, just as the appropriate dispensation of patrimonies de-pends on ascertainable parentage and birth order.[31] Thus when Esca-lus pleads for mercy to Claudio, he refers to Claudio's "most noble fa-ther" (2.1.7). Pompey, ironically, makes the same argument to Escalus when he pleads for mercy to Froth, whose father is wealthy (2.1.121–24), and Escalus seems to accept it (2.1.192–94, 201–4). Laws of suc-cession and inheritance embody the legal significance of genealogy; at least one legal historian has claimed that "whatever ideological prob-lems bastardy litigation might ultimately raise, jurisdiction over land was always at its center."[32] (Comically, in *Measure for Measure* Pompey suggests that widespread illegitimacy raises the value of real property by increasing the population as quickly as possible; see 2.1.237–39.)

Second, if illegitimacy becomes widespread, then any man and woman risk incest when they satisfy natural desire by sexual inter-course. Tiresias' question in *Oedipus the King*—"Do you know who your parents are?"—reminds us that if one does not know with cer-tainty, one cannot be sure any given sexual union is not incestuous.[33] In fact, many of the central sexual unions contemplated in *Measure for Measure* are tinged with incest. Isabella accuses Claudio of having a kind of incestuous intention in proposing that she sleep with Angelo, for example (3.1.138–39). Perhaps, as Lucio at one point seems to im-ply, even the union between Claudio and Juliet is vaguely incestuous, for Isabella's obscurity about Claudio's paternity is matched by her obscurity about her kinship with Juliet:

---

*Richard Wagner's first opera, *The Ban on Love* (1836), was based on *Measure for Mea-sure*. In it, the heroine tries to make nothing of (*vernichten*) her kinship with Claudio.

Isab. Someone with child by him? My cousin Juliet? (1.4.45)

Lucio. Is she your cousin?

Isab. Adoptedly, as schoolmaids change their names
By vain though apt affection.

The Intent of Incest: Liberty and the Transformation of the Body Politic

And why may not I love Johnny?
And why may not Johnny love me?
And why may not I love Johnny?
As well as another body?
Mother Goose's Melodies [34]

As we have seen, the end of fornication is bastardy and the end of bastardy is incest. It is, in part, this teleology that explains Jonas of Orleans's argument that "all illicit carnal relations are incestuous." [35]

It is said nowadays that the avoidance of sexual relations with one's own kin is a hallmark of the human species. Yet in Shakespeare's time, as in our own, there was considerable skepticism about the universality of the taboo. Montaigne, for example, asserted that among some societies incest is practiced without shame, and Charron claimed that the incest taboo was a "mere custom." [36] But what were the grounds for the incest taboo adduced in Shakespeare's time, and how does the play reflect them? So long as we do not limit Shakespeare's understanding to what we know about the thinking of his forerunners and contemporaries, these will be useful questions.

The Bible. For many, it was enough to know that the Bible forbids incest. The friar in John Ford's *'Tis Pity She's a Whore* (1628)—the first English play in which unmediated sibling incest is an obvious theme—locates the ultimate source of the incest taboo in God's dislike of incest. He argues that, even if incest were natural (the ancient philosophers, Aquinas says, claimed that it was), [37] Heaven has forbidden it:

> . . . if we were sure there were no Deity,
> Nor Heaven nor Hell, then to be led alone
> By Nature's light—as were philosophers
> Of elder times—might instance some defence.
> But 'tis not so: then madman, thou wilt find
> That Nature is in Heaven's positions blind. [38]

In *Measure for Measure*, however, Heaven comes in, if at all, only *ex machina* at the end, and the play is silent about both the Old Testament laws that ban incest and about 1 Corinthians 5–6, in which Paul condemns fornication. By this avoidance, the play implicitly treats the Bible as a symptomatic rule book, comparable to the laws of Vienna, and draws our attention instead to the familial and social systems that biblical injunctions legislate. To do so is to examine the very grounds for the Old and New Testament prohibitions, and to subject those grounds to a searching scrutiny.

Love, Charity, and Property. Luther's argument that if consanguinity were not an impediment to marriage people would often marry without love, for the sole purpose of maintaining the familial patrimony, was an influential theory justifying the incest taboo in Shakespeare's time.[39] His appeal to exogamous love is connected with an earlier justification of the incest taboo that appeals to charity. Thus Augustine justifies exogamy because it provides a benefit at once social and religious: interfamilial marriage, according to Augustine, encourages the extension of charity and love from the narrow kinship circle to the larger civic community.[40] Augustine's notion of turning some others (members of another kinship group) into brothers (members of one's own kinship group) conflicts, to some degree, with Jesus' notion that all men are brothers, but it does have the same effect: enjoining a conversion of all men into kin. That is, it explains the incest taboo in terms of a desire to (re)make the human species into a single kinship group.

Both Luther's argument from love and Augustine's from charity would knit together the people of the world in a network of exchanges of spouses and property.[41] In a way, these arguments are forerunners of the contemporary theories of Marcel Mauss and Claude Lévi-Strauss, who understand the social basis of the incest taboo in terms of a societal need to exchange spouses (usually female) as gifts or commodities.

Genetics. In the Christian tradition, the genetic or sociobiological explanation of the incest taboo harkens back at least as far as Saint Gregory the Great in the sixth century. The idea that incestuous unions weaken the physiology and intellect of the human race by producing defective progeny was well known in Elizabethan England; for example, Robert Burton believed that incest should be prohibited for that reason.[42]

Respectus parentelae. One way or another, all the preceding explanations or justifications of the incest taboo are considered in Shakespeare's play. *Measure for Measure* most strongly draws our attention, however, to the fact that both the fear of the practice of incest and the practice itself are social diseases that lead, one way or another, to the death of the body politic as we know it. First, the fear of incest can lead to avoiding procreation altogether. This can happen both in a society where no one knows who his particular father is, so that any sex partner is potentially kin (secular Vienna), and in a society where everyone acknowledges only the universal Fatherhood of God, so that all human beings are Siblings (religious Vienna). In societies where parenthood is believed to be either inascertainable or divine, only secular or religious celibacy can provide a nonincestuous way of life. Second, the practice of incest shows a hugely consequential disrespect to one's parents, hence to parentarchal political order. The Roman *respectus parentelae*, the reverence due to near kin, is apparently one of the earliest and most constant arguments against incest advanced in Western culture.[43]

The widespread practice of incest would lead to a radical transformation of the body politic since such sexual liberty would restructure kinship relations by destroying the crucial distinction between generations. Teleologically, incest dissolves the *pater* (father) in the *liber* (son) and replaces the patriarchy with a radical egalitarian *liberty*.* It establishes what Tiresias calls "a grim equality between you and your children."[44] From this perspective the longterm familial and political consequence of incest is not so much the destruction through murder of a fatherly ruler by filial subjects (which is what happens in the Freudian fable of the Primal Horde) as the complete transcendence for everyone, including those who were fathers, of the distinction between parent and child or between ruler and subject. Everyone becomes at once both either parent and child or neither parent nor child. (In *Measure for Measure* the tendency of sexual license to homogenize the father in the brotherhood of man is suggested in the figure of Vincentio, who. as "father friar" or "brother father" [3.2.10, 11], wavers between the roles of parentarchal duke and either fraternal monk or universalist libertine.)† With the dissolution of generations must come the dissolution of genealogical inheritance and a corollary dissolution of the tie of property (or polity) to purported bloodlines. This would pave the way for the argument that since all people are equal members of a

---

*The *Oxford Latin Dictionary*, s.v. *liberi*, defines the word as "sons and daughters, children in connection w[ith] their parents." *Liberi* is the plural of *liber* (free). (Cf. Elyot's and Chapman's use of *libertine* to mean "any man of bonde ancestour" and "an urban freeman" [Elyot, *Image Governaunce*, 34; Chapman, *Iliad*, 16.50].) According to the dictionary, the association of freedom with sonship is obscure. The present book is, in part, an attempt to clarify that association.

†"Friar," from Latin *frater*, means "brother."

single family all property should be held in common. From that point of view, the parentarchy's fear of sexual and propertal communism would explain the incest taboo.[45]

Liberty is the cause and the object of fear and desire in *Measure for Measure*. Claudio says that his act of fornication, which gives rise to the action of the play, came "from too much liberty" (1.2.117). What is "liberty"? On the one hand, it is libertinism in the sense of licentiousness, but on the other, it is also both liberty in a strictly political and sexual sense, and libertinism in an uncomfortably related theological and sexual sense.

In dealing with the first of these alternate senses of liberty, *Measure for Measure* is preeminently a play in political theory. Virtually its first words are "Of government the properties to unfold" (1.1.3). Not only does the play consider what it means to be a governor and to execute a law, it also unfolds the ground of Law in terms of the traditional rule of parent over child, and it subjects the rule to searching scrutiny.

During the Tudor and Stuart Renaissance, as throughout the history of the West, a ruler was viewed as a father and his people as his children.[46] Thus a child's beating his father is, according to the Elizabethan Nashe, tantamount to upsetting the natural order: "It is no maruaile if euery Alehouse vaunt the table of the world vpside downe, since the child beateth his father."[47] By the early seventeenth century the challenge to the patriarchy was growing into modern liberalism. In that century the proponents of absolute monarchy had such spokespersons as King James I, who in his *Trew Law* stressed the identity between the duty of a subject and that of a child,[48] and Robert Filmer, who in his *Patriarcha* finally provided both sides of the debate with a major rallying point. John Locke, among others, came to be the spokesperson for the proponents of liberalism. Locke criticized Filmer's conceptual reliance on a "strange kind of domineering phantom, called 'the fatherhood'"[49] and opposed to it his own idea of all men free and equal in the state of nature. For Locke, as Norman O. Brown puts it, "liberty . . . means equality among the brothers (sons)."[50] *Measure for Measure* explores the political and religious implications of the opposition between the parentarchal and liberal positions and presents an ideal transcendence of the distinction between parent and child.

The initial dilemma of the play is the "too much liberty" Claudio mentions. As Vincentio as Duke complains:

> . . . Liberty plucks Justice by the nose, (1.3.29)
> The baby beats the nurse, and quite athwart
> Goes all decorum.

The Duke is not a king, although princeliness, sovereignty, and royalty are attributed to him and, like a monarch, he compares himself to a father and his subjects to children (1.3.23–27). In fact, in the play the "King," whoever he may be, is absent.* He is sorely missed, for the tendency of incest, the telos of fornication, is to replace the patriarchial organization of Vienna—having the kingship and the papacy at its summit—with a society of equals in which everyone would be everyone else's liberal (i.e., fraternal) sibling. The political threat to Vienna is incestuous democracy—a republic of liberty, equality, and fraternity like the one the French Revolution once promised. In such a state everyone is everyone else's sibling and no one is a father. In it the sons have already gone to war with the father and defeated him, or, in the words of the play, "all the dukes fall upon the King" (1.2.2–3).

The foreign wars that give *Measure for Measure* its international background—and for whose sake everyone, with the possible exception of Lucio and the certain exception of Thomas, wrongly believes the Duke has left Vienna—figure the domestic struggle between sons and father, here "dukes" and "King." The external (exogamous) wars that threaten Vienna parallel the internal (endogamous) wars between the proponents of liberty and patriarchy that already rage within its walls.[51] This reading does not contradict interpretations of the wars that find historical counterparts in the relations between the Holy Roman Emperor and the Turks, the conflict between the King of Spain and James I (his allies included), and the alliance between James I and the Archduchess Isabella; nor does it take issue with the claim that the Duke stands for Frederick III, Duke of Austria and Holy Roman Emperor, and the King for Corvinus, the sovereign of Hungary who conquered Vienna in 1485.[52] But Shakespeare rises above his historical material: the Duke is one of many dukes, opposed to a single King. The dukes will either homogenize the King with themselves (i.e., come into "composition" with him; 1.2.2), or they will fall upon him. Either the sons will turn the father into a son, or they will kill the king as part of a primal action of liberty. In this sense the international tension in the play (1.2.1–16) matches the national action.

The similarity of external and internal enemies is suggested by the name and role of Pompey, who wars against the patriarchal authority of Vienna, the seat of the Holy Roman Empire, much as his namesake (Pompey the Younger) warred against the Empire of Rome. Albert Cook has astutely called him "emperor of bawdry."[53] Escalus, in his trial of Pompey, threatens to "prove a shrewd Caesar" to him (2.1.245–

---

*Richard Wagner felt that absence, and in his *Ban on Love* a king finally appears and provides a royal presence.

46), and Lucio remarks: "How now, noble Pompey! What, at the wheels of Caesar? Art thou led in triumph?" (3.2.42–43).

In conclusion, if the ground of the law, the patriarchal King (Caesar), were to be swept away by fornication, hence illegitimacy and inevitably incest, then the homogenously liberal people would be able to "use their abuses in common houses" and Constable Elbow would "know no law" (2.1.42–43). The Duke wants to cut short the development of such an outlaw state. In familiar terms, he wants to contain fornication, hence illegitimacy and inevitably incest, in order to protect his patriarchal place and, to give him the credit he deserves, to protect Law itself as he sees it.*

At first blush, Claudio seems caught by a legal technicality—after all, he and Juliet acted in mutual consent. Yet the mutual intent of individuals does not alter the natural and political telos of their fornication. The law against fornication that Claudio and Juliet have broken has a unique social place, so that their act is willy-nilly an attack on the ground of the rigorously generational, political order. No parentarchal ruler—not Angelo, not the Duke—could countenance such a violation. (At no moment in the play is there any indication that the Viennese law against fornication or the Viennese rule for punishing it will be changed.)[54]

The crucial need for the polis to order sexual relations is similarly suggested in *A Midsummer Night's Dream*, in which Theseus, Duke of Athens, cannot directly oppose the patriarchal basis of his rule, perhaps also of the political order. When Hermia refuses to marry the man chosen by her father, for example, that father cries out the purportedly primordial claim of the entire political order:

> I beg the ancient privilege of Athens: (MND 1.1.41)
> As she is mine, I may dispose of her,
> Which shall be either to this gentleman
> Or to her death, according to our law.

Theseus mitigates the law by providing another option: joining a Sisterhood.

> Either to die the death, or to abjure   (MND 1.1.65)
> Forever the society of men.
> Therefore, fair Hermia, question your desires.
> Know of your youth, examine well your blood,

---

*That the law against incest is necessary to the state does not imply that it must be enforced by the state; it is of some interest, however, that during Elizabeth's reign prosecution for such offenses as adultery and incest began to be transferred from the church authority (the Courts Ecclesiastical) to the state (the Queen or King). (See Cleveland, "Indictments," p. 59.)

> Whether, if you yield not to your father's choice,
> You can endure the livery of a nun,
> For aye to be in the shady cloister mewed.
> To live a barren sister all your life.

If Hermia does not choose to marry the man her father has chosen, hence reproduce in the way that her father wills, she must choose between celibacy and death. In either case, she will not reproduce at all. (Compare Theseus' demand that Hyppolyta forswear the Sisterhood of Amazons.) As a man, Duke Theseus may wish to be merciful, but as a political figure, he cannot be lenient:

> . . . fit your fancies to your father's will;   (MND 1.1.118)
> Or else the law of Athens yields you up
> (Which by no means we may extenuate)
> To death, or to a vow of single life.

The choices in *Measure for Measure* are also execution and celibacy. Yet both are finally the same, for the universal counterpart of execution—human annihilation—is the telos of individual celibacy.

The Viennese Response

> The incest prohibition is not a prohibition like the others.
> It is *the* prohibition in the most general form, the one per-
> haps to which all others . . . are related as particular cases.
> The incest prohibition is a universal like language.
> Claude Lévi-Strauss[55]

In *Measure for Measure* Shakespeare makes fornication, to which nature drives us, not merely one legal offense among others but rather the typically human (perhaps also the civilized) offense,[56] and he makes the law against it, demanded by the parentarchal political order (perhaps the order from which civilization and its discontents arise), the typically human law. "The rules of kinship and marriage," writes Lévi-Strauss, "are not made necessary by the social state. They are the social state itself."[57]

The standard response to the incest taboo, we usually assume, is exogamous marriage. Through the enforcement of laws prohibiting extra-marital sexual intercourse, paternity and maternity might be ascertained and incest avoided. Yet given the purportedly high illegitimacy rate in Vienna (or even the mere possibility of bastardy anywhere), not even marriage is a sufficient guarantee against the threat of incest, since it is impossible to know with absolute certainty who are

44

one's own parents, or those of anyone else. (In these terms the only eligible bachelor for Isabella to marry, besides Jesus, is the foreigner Barnadine, who is Bohemian, but he is condemned to die.) Moreover, if one agrees with Aquinas that incest is not merely a determinate species of lust but lust in general, and if one believes that all sexual urges are essentially lust, then incest may be the antonomasia of, or general term for, all sexual relations, whether within or without marriage. Aquinas argues:

Incest (*incestum*) takes its name from being a privation of chastity. But all kinds of lust are opposed to chastity. Therefore it seems that incest is not a species of lust, but is lust itself in general.[58]

In this view, which is not far from the Freudian grounding of sexual impulses in incestuous wishes, all sexuality is essentially incestuous, so that a successful eradication of the desire for incest, assuming that were possible, would mean the complete annihilation of sexual desire and the human species.

How, then, does one respond to the Law of Laws, the incest taboo? On the one hand, one can break the law or allow it to be broken (as do Claudio and the Duke, at least initially); on the other hand, one can obey the law and enforce obedience to it (as do Angelo and Isabella, at least initially). Yet both of these responses lead, each in its own way, to the destruction of society. In the first case, the practice of incest brings about a savage condition in which men copulate freely, or at least the breakdown of political or parentarchal society. In the second case, the enforcement of the law against incest, by ending procreation, leads to the annihilation of humankind. If incest is unavoidable in sexual practice, its taboo is genocide, or execution universalized.*

Genocide. The telos of Claudio's proposed execution, then, is universal genocide. The annihilation of humankind is invoked explicitly by Pompey and Lucio (2.1.227–40, 3.2.98–99) and implicitly by Claudio in his bitter comparison of sex to ratsbane (1.2.120–22). Angelo himself unwittingly hints at human annihilation when he defends the death sentence as a deterrent against fornication:

> Those many had not dar'd to do that evil (2.2.92)
> If the first that did th'edict infringe
> Had answer'd for his deed.

---

*"Genocide" ordinarily refers to the destruction of one or another group of human beings and not to the destruction of the entire human genus. Where familial or tribal distinctions between groups are transcended in favor of a universal siblinghood, however, there is essentially only one group, and "genocide" refers to the destruction of all human beings.

Angelo means the man who first infringed the edict against fornication when, some fourteen or nineteen years earlier,[59] the Duke began to ignore transgressions of the law against fornication; however, his words also refer to Cain, who committed the original act of fornication—incest with his sister.[60] Had Adam's or Noah's children not dared to commit fornication, there would have been no one to have "dar'd to do that evil" because the human species would have been annihilated.*

Celibacy. *Measure for Measure* hints at some ways other than marriage and genocide to avoid illegitimacy, hence, purportedly, anarchic disorder. These include castration (Pompey asks Escalus whether he means "to geld and splay all the youth of the city," 2.1.227–28),[61] externally enforced celibacy (consider the "secret holds" of the prison, 4.3.86), and homosexuality (the segregation of the sexes in the prison allows only homosexual relations; see Pompey's joke about serving Abhorson, 4.2.54–55). The problem with castration, externally enforced celibacy, and homosexuality, of course, is that, although they prevent the production of illegitimate offspring, they violate nature's injunction to reproduce. In *Measure for Measure*, such ways to restrain sexual desire remain part of the background; instead, the play focuses on religious celibacy (as practiced by the Sisterhood that Isabella is about to join and by the Brotherhood that the Duke pretends to join) and voluntary secular celibacy (as practiced by Angelo and perhaps also by the Duke before either statesman meets Isabella).

The way religious celibacy would incorporate and transcend the dilemma of physical incest is the subject of the next chapter. It is fitting to remark here, however, that Saint Jerome believed the divine injunction "Be fruitful, and multiply" would cease, when the Edenic "virginal order" would be restored, a restoration that would put an end to the dilemma of incest once and for all.[62] Western monachal institutions, as we shall see, would realize such virginity here and now.

---

*Lévi-Strauss, imagining a world without a taboo on incest, writes that "the multiple rules prohibiting or prescribing certain types of spouse, and the prohibition of incest, which embodies them all, become clear as soon as one grants that society must exist. But society might not have been." (*Elementary Structures*, p. 490.)

2

Children of Adoption

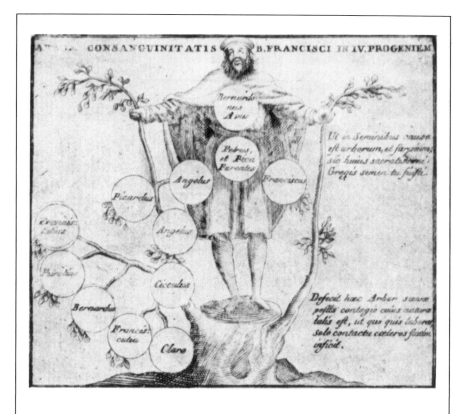

The genealogy of Saint Francis. (Petrus Rodulphius, *Hist. seraph. religionis*, fol. 3.)

By that meanes becommeth he the dear brothere, sister, and mother of Christ, . . . a cytizen of heaven with the Apostles and Prophetes, yea, the chylde of adopcyon and heyre togyther with Christ in the heavenly inherytaunce. . . . No soch chyldren left Socrates behynd hym, neyther yet Demosthenes, nor Plato, nor Cicero, with all their plesant wysdome and eloquence.

John Bale[1]

CHRISTIAN ETHICS has been a major concern in the criticism of *Measure for Measure*, yet Christian monachal institutions have rarely been considered an essential element in the play.[2] Despite the fact that the friar disguise was rare in Elizabethan drama and was generally attacked as silly, few critics have speculated about why Shakespeare should have changed the merchant disguise used by the incognito kings who may have been his sources for Vincentio's device.[3] Likewise, some have seen Isabella's novitiate as signifying only a desire for chastity, even though the chaste women who are her counterparts in the sources are not nuns.[4] Shakespeare's use of the orders in the play has even been considered anti-monachal satire.[5]

Shakespeare's attitude toward the orders cannot have been independent of his own religious beliefs, but his religion is a vexed question. His father John may have been a recusant Catholic, and some have argued that, for at least a portion of his life, Shakespeare himself was Catholic.[6] (The birth of his son Hamnet fewer than nine months after his public marriage to Anne Hathaway, for example, has been used to argue for an earlier, clandestine marriage, presumably performed by a Catholic priest.)[7] Moreover, there were two sixteenth-century nuns named Shakespeare in the Benedictine convent at Wroxall, just north of Stratford: Joan Shakespeare, who was sub-prioress at the time of the Dissolution and who lived until 1576 (the year William Shakespeare was twelve); and Isabella Shakespeare, who was prioress in the early years of the century.[8] (The latter may be among the sources for the name of *Measure for Measure*'s Isabella, although there are other possibilities.)

If Shakespeare was raised a Catholic, he would have been especially sensitive to the confrontation between Catholicism and Protestantism. In our play, quasi-Brother Vincentio's proposal to quasi-Sister Isabella echoes that confrontation: the Reformation had ended clerical celibacy, and Luther himself married a nun. I cannot presume to argue definitively one way or another the question of Shakespeare's religion, but the evidence does suggest that he may have been intellectually closer to the Catholic than to the Protestant position on the celibate orders.

Thus we should not be surprised that in *Measure for Measure* an examination of sexuality implies a searching and sympathetic depiction of the monachal orders. Indeed, the role of the orders in *Measure for Measure* is crucial to what the play suggests about the organization of human sexuality. It exposes, not the Catholic Church, as in a Protestant satire, but the psychological, historical, and theological grounds of monachal relationships by reinterpreting the religious orders in light of the awesome tension between nature and law, incest and chastity.

The Sexual Dimension of the Religious Orders

> We see, then, that savages have an unusually great horror
> of incest or are sensitive on the subject to an unusual de-
> gree, and that they combine this with a peculiarity which
> remains obscure to us—of replacing real blood-relationship
> by totem kinship. This latter contrast must not, however, be
> too much exaggerated, and we must remember that the
> totem prohibitions include that against real incest as a spe-
> cial case. Freud, *Totem and Taboo*[9]

Totemic tribes that enjoin exogamy (marriage outside the tribe) and allow for the existence of other totemic tribes can thereby avoid incest. However, a tribe that believes its totem to be universal and all other human beings to be part of itself (or, teleologically speaking, potential converts to its universalist doctrine) makes exogamy impossible and all intercourse incestuous. Christianity calls for the universal brotherhood of man and, in its proselytizing character, claims to treat as brothers even those who believe themselves to be non-Christians. The Christian monachal orders are microcosms of a potentially Universal Siblinghood in which kinship has a special significance. Freud remarks that terms like "Sisters in Christ" have analogues in societies where kinship terms "do not necessarily indicate any consanguinity, as ours would do: they represent social rather than physical relationships."[10] But the monachal use of such terms assumes more than the replacement of "physical" relationships by social ones: it assumes the conflation of social or theological with biological relationships.

As, according to Freud, social taboo parallels individual obsessional neurosis,[11] so the anti-fornication, or anti-incest, taboo that underlies the laws of Shakespeare's Vienna parallels the neurosis that can underlie both the fear of incest and the desire to engage in a sacred incest. The very term "taboo" means both "sacred, consecrated" and "dangerous, forbidden." [12] "Isabella," like "Elizabeth," means "consecrated to God" (from Hebrew *elishabet*); [13] as a Sister, one who violates the taboo on incest by marrying the Son of her Father, Isabella is both sacred and taboo. (According to Freud, a nun's virginity is in itself a kind of taboo act.) [14] "Anyone who has transgressed one of these prohibitions . . . acquires the characteristic of being prohibited," writes Freud; [15] Lucio acknowledges a taboo on Isabella as "a thing enskied" (1.4.34).

Familial Sisterhood and Universal Sisterhood. However sexually inexperienced Isabella may be, a Clarist novice such as Isabella would probably not be totally innocent of contact with, or speculation about, sex. [16] It is pointless to follow Lucio's lead in greeting her ambiguously as "virgin, if you be" (1.4.16), for she undoubtedly lacks the practical sexual experience of such other nuns as Aemilia, the abbess at Ephesus in *The Comedy of Errors*, or Thaisa, the mother who joins Diana's vestal virgins in *Pericles*. (Both women have had earthly husbands.) Yet Isabella must have the knowledge of secular love that everyone acquires by wondering about sexual conduct and kinship relations within an earthly family. In the course of the play, Isabella responds to that universally available knowledge; since she conducts her life somewhere between the earthly family that a novice plans to leave and the heavenly family that a novice plans to join, her response distinguishes her among women.

The play amply documents Isabella's theoretical knowledge of the facts of life. She raises the question of Claudio's legitimacy (3.1.140) and all too promptly understands the nature of Claudio's offense, associating it with Juliet (1.4.45). [17] But her distinctive sensitivity to the general Viennese malaise about legitimacy and incest is better reflected in the fact that she immediately links his act with kinship terms by referring to "my cousin Juliet" (1.4.45). Even Isabella's apparently reassuring response to Lucio's immediate question, "Is she your cousin?"—she says, "Adoptedly, as schoolmaids change their names / By vain though apt affection" (1.4.46–48)—is discomforting because the exchange reminds us that no one, especially in licentious Vienna, can know absolutely who his consanguineous parents are. Beyond the epistemological question of legitimacy, the interchange of names between Isabella and Juliet suggests an incestuous conflation of Claudio's sister and his lover; had Juliet been adopted by law rather than in name or by affection, intercourse with Claudio might also have been incest, since the canon laws frequently barred relatives by legal adoption from sexual commerce. [18]

Isabella's reference to adoption is loaded in another way, as well. It echoes the terms used to describe God's relationship to Christian believers: "We ourselves groan within ourselves, waiting for the adoption, to wit, the redemption of our body" (Rom. 8:23, cf. Rom. 8:15). The fact that Isabella is on the verge of publicly declaring her allegiance to a heavenly family as a Sister reminds us of her status—and the status of all the play's characters—as children by adoption of God.

By fornicating and bastardizing, secular Vienna has reached an extreme of exogamy, where the threat of unrecognized blood relationship has become so pervasive that if one wishes to be chaste one must marry out or marry not at all. Thus Barnardine the native Bohemian and foreigner to Vienna is for Isabella (or any other Viennese woman) the only certainly eligible bachelor in the city—and he is condemned to die.

The theme of ubiquitous incest similarly informs *Hamlet*. Claudius, like Cain, has killed his brother and, like Henry VIII, has married his sister-in-law—incestuously, Hamlet insists (HAM 3.3.90). Yet for Hamlet (as, we speculate, for Isabella) the problem is more pervasive—any person who marries becomes "a breeder of sinners" (HAM 3.1.122). That is why he counsels his beloved Ophelia (in the sources she is his collactaneous sister)[19] to enter a nunnery: "I say we will have no more marriage. Those that are married already—all but one—shall live. The rest shall keep as they are. To a nunnery, go." (HAM 3.1.147–49.) If Isabella had Hamlet's remarkable self-knowledge, she might well recoil like him from the taint of any implication whatsoever in human sexuality: "I am myself indifferent honest, but yet I could accuse me of such things that it were better my mother had not borne me" (HAM 3.1.122–24).

Much Ado's Beatrice touches on the distinctive source of Isabella's reaction when she says, with a clever pun on Isabella's chosen profession: "I'll none. Adam's sons are my brethren, and truly I hold it a sin to match in my kindred." (ADO 2.1.63–64.) The pun on "none" and "nun" also appears in Angelo's injunction to the novice Isabella, "Be that you are, / That is, a woman; if you be more, you're none" (2.4.133–34), and in the dialogue between Hamlet and the "gravemaker" who is digging a grave for Ophelia:

Hamlet. What man dost thou dig it for?   (HAM 5.1.121)
Clown. For no man, sir.
Hamlet. What woman then?
Clown. For none neither.
Hamlet. Who is to be buried in 't?
Clown. One that was a woman, sir; but, rest her soul, she's dead.

In *Hamlet*, as in *Antigone*, not death to the world and spiritual marriage to Jesus (i.e., entering a nunnery, which in some orders entailed a service for the dead before rebirth and marriage to Jesus), but becoming nothing in death homogenizes the members of the domestic household.* In *Measure for Measure*, by contrast, from the virtual inevitability of incest and lack of restraint that she sees almost everywhere in the secular world, Isabella seeks refuge in an institution where, more subject to a Mother Superior than to the memory of a conceivably adulterous mother and more subject to Brothers than to a lecherous brother, she hopes to transcend sexual desire and specific familial blood ties. She seeks to become a "chylde of adopcyon" (Rom. 8: 23, trans. John Bale) to God.

To take vows in a Sisterhood is radically to change one's relationship to everyone in the world, including the members of one's blood family. "If any one comes to me and does not hate his own father and mother and wife and children and brothers and sisters, yes, and even his own life," said Jesus, "he cannot be my disciple" (Luke 14: 26; Rev. Stand.).[20] Pope Innocent IV's description of how Saint Clare divorced her earthly family before joining the heavenly one is thus typical of Christian monachal tradition:

> Meditating on this verse of the Prophet, "O daughter, hear, see, and listen, forget your people and the house of your father, because the King has desired your beauty," the Blessed Clare of saintly memory . . . turned her back to fleeting, and transitory things. Divesting herself of herself, her parents, and of all things, and making herself a daughter of the celestial Kingdom, she elected and named as her spouse the poor Jesus Christ.[21]

Before entering a Christian Sisterhood and becoming a child of adoption to God, a woman is allowed to distinguish brothers from others

---

*In *Hamlet*, ambiguous family relationships become inseparable from ambiguous political relationships. This conflation is summed up in the figure of Gertrude, who stands to the political ruler in the same mixture of relations as a nun stands to God, being not only ambiguously sister and wife of Claudius but also mother of the potential king Hamlet. In one of Shakespeare's sources (Belleforest, *Histoires tragiques*, 5th series, 3d story, chap. 1), she is also the daughter of a king, from whom she receives the kingdom as a kind of dowry. Thus she is "imperial jointress to . . . the state" both as a woman who has a "'joint' tenancy in an estate" (cf. Coke, *On Littleton*, L.1; C.5; 36.D) in such a way that he who would be king of the state must marry its queen, or kill her—thus being in the same position as Jocasta—and as a woman who conjoins the various successive parts of the royal family and hence of the state. Tellingly, on entering Gertrude's chamber, Hamlet compares himself to Nero: "Let not ever / The soul of Nero enter this firm bosom" (HAM 3.2.378–79). Nero's incest with his mother, Julia Agrippina Minor, conflated in his person two of her relations as mother, sister, wife, and daughter of emperors; he enacts both the incest Hamlet may fear he desires and the matricide Hamlet may fear he will commit. See my forthcoming essay "Hoodman Blind."

and to treat them differently; indeed, for family purposes of marriage a laywoman is obliged to distinguish between a blood brother and other men, just as for state purposes of war she is obliged to distinguish between fellow citizens and aliens. As a novice in the Sisterhood of the Clares Isabella at the beginning of the play has presumably begun to learn how to transcend the distinction between brothers and others in both familial and political realms. (A member of an order must put into practice the Christian prescription that Christians should be "no more strangers and foreigners, but fellow citizens with the saints" [Eph. 2: 19], hence above earthly international wars.) She should have begun to think and act as though all men were equally her brothers.*

Sharing Hamlet's recognition of the pervasive taint of familial sexual sin, Isabella is in the position of Antigone, caught between horror at sexual transgression and pious duty to a family constituted (actually for Antigone, potentially for Isabella) by such transgression.[22] But her attempt to flee from the urban brothel-in-potentia to the Sisterhood, from mother and father to Mother Superior and Pope, merely relocates the problem of incest from the consanguineous family to the Christian Family, for the Christian rejection of blood family makes all sexual intercourse sibling incest. This is quintessentially true for a monk or a nun, and it is official Church doctrine that "concubinage or marriage with a person consecrated to God" is not merely fornication but incest.[23] The rejection of parenthood entails that all humans—parents, siblings, spouses—become wholly "children of your Father which is in heaven" (Matt. 5:45).[†] To Tiresias' formal and political

---

*The commandment to divorce one's earthly family is to be interpreted literally. (One purpose of "dying to the world," as do Catholic celibates, is to signal that divorce.) According to Saint Anthony, remembering one's relatives is a temptation of the devil (Athanasius [?], *Vita Antonii*, PL, 73:36, and Sulpicius, *Dialogues*, 1:22). The fifth-century abbot Saint John Cassian reports that the abba Apollos refused to go to his father's funeral, pleading that he himself had been "dead to this world for twenty years"; the same Apollos refused to help his brother save an ox in a swamp (Cassian, *Conferences*, 24:9). Herbert Workman cites a similar story of religious flight from consanguineous kin recorded in the *Patrologia*: "Pior, an Egyptian monk, for fifty years refused to see any member of his family, even when they came to visit him. When, on her appeal, his bishop at length bade him visit his sister, he obeyed, but took care, writes his admiring biographer, to keep his eyes closed all the time" (*Monastic Ideal*, pp. 59–60, drawing on *Verba Seniorum*, PL, 73:759, and Palladius, *Historia Lausiaca*, 39, PG, 34:991–1262).

†One parallel in Shakespeare to the Catholic ceremony in which a woman takes leave of her earthly family ("dies to the world") and enters the heavenly family ("is reborn") by becoming the wife, sister, daughter, and mother of God is the scene in which Coriolanus, banished by the Romans and "servanted to others" (i.e., to the Volscians; COR 5.2.84), attempts to cast off his "father" Menenius Agrippa and claims that he no longer knows "wife, mother, child" (COR 5.2.71 and 5.2.83; cf. 5.3.10). Compare

question "Who is your father?," then, all Christians should answer "Father."

Brother and Sister Saints

That Shakespeare has the sister in *Measure for Measure* enter a Sisterhood involves the theme of homogeneous liberty (equality and fraternity) that is crucial to monachism and its essential opposition to the political order. That Shakespeare then has his sister-in-training leave the Sisterhood on behalf of a brother suggests that she still loves, or can love, her brother unequally—either more than others or differently from others—and at the same time it foreshadows the possibility of a reinstatement of political, or parentarchal, heterogeneity. What might mediate between the positions of homogeneity in liberty and heterogeneity in parentarchy is, from a general sociological viewpoint, the practice of sibling incest of the sexual kind. But no one is allowed to practice such incest in an unmediated way. In theory, therefore, the love of blood relatives might combine with the fear of earthly incest and make for an individual's decision to join a monastic order or even to found one.

Historically, earthly sibling love and heavenly Sibling love have often been joined in the same persons. In Christian hagiography, a saintly person's intense earthly sibling love is often followed by an extraordinary Sibling love of all human beings, just as if each and every human being had become a brother or sister.[24] The *Acts of the Saints* includes more than 150 men and women who were brother and sister as well as Brother and Sister.[25] Sibling celibates appear from the very beginning of Christian monachism: Saint Anthony, traditionally the first Christian monk, placed his sister in a nunnery when he left the world for the ascetic life.[26] More strikingly, brother-sister liaisons played an important role in the historical beginnings of the Christian orders, for the sister of each of the three great cenobitical founders, Saint Pachomius, Saint Basil, and Saint Benedict, helped to preside over a community of nuns that followed an adaptation of her brother's rules for monks.[27]

Earthly sibling and Christian Sibling love figured in the lives of many great saints. Saint Benedict—founder of the order in which Isa-

---

Volumnia's remark that Coriolanus is no longer akin to his Roman mother, wife, and child, and other repetitions of the same motif (5.3.178–80, 5.3.101–3). Coriolanus claims that he has no family at all and allies his rejection of ordinary kinship with the atheist or arrogantly isotheist hypothesis that "a man [is] author of himself / And [knows] no other kin" (5.3.36–37).

bella Shakespeare was prioress and in which Clare once served, and author of the strict *Regula monachorum*—visited his sister, Saint Scholastica, once a year. On the last of these visits, according to Saint Gregory the Great's biography, Scholastica entreated Benedict to stay the night. When he adamantly refused, she fell to prayer until a sudden storm arose, so that she had her way. The consummation of that night, spent all in spiritual conversation, could be seen as the incorporation and transcendence of any earthly attraction, physical or otherwise, that might have existed between the brother and sister. Three days later, Scholastica died; in the course of time, Benedict joined her in a single grave.[28]

Legends about Gregory the Great's own life involve incest and the wonderful atonement for incest. As Hartmann von Aue tells the story, Gregory was the child of a brother-sister union and unknowingly married his own mother. When he became Pope (the first monk ever to do so) he forgave his mother's incest and his own, restored Benedictine discipline, and enforced the rule of celibacy for the clergy.[29] This Christian solution—repentance and atonement—to the Oedipal situation suggests that the Catholic orders made possible an atonement for the desire for incest or unchastity, even when the actual act was not in question. The Holy Family atones for the earthly one by making all even.

Some brother and sister saints voiced explicit concern for their siblings' sexuality, at times in terms that border on identification and possessiveness. In his *Rule, or Book on the Institute of Virgins and on the Contempt of the World, for Sister Florentine,* Saint Leander identifies his sister's virginity with the goal of the entire Church: "It is above the skies that we must seek the true wealth, the gift of holy virginity. . . . What all the saints hope one day to be, what the entire Church expects to become after the resurrection, thou art already. . . . Christ is already thy spouse, thy father, thine inheritance, thy ransom, thy Lord, thy God."[30] Yet exhorting his saintly sister as Sister to marry the Son of her Father, Leander expresses a more specific self-interest in safekeeping her virginity: "Ah, well-beloved sister, understand the ardent desire which inspires the heart of thy brother to see thee with Christ. . . . Thou art the better part of myself. Woe to me if another take thy crown."[31] In the monastic life into which he sends her, Florentina's earthly crown will be Leander's as much as any man's.

In an epitaph composed for the tombstone of his sister Saint Irene, Saint Damasus expressed a similar proprietary interest: "A witness of our love (our mother), / upon leaving the world, / had given thee, my blood sister, to me as a pure pledge."[32] Such concern with a sibling's

chastity was not confined to men. When Saint Lioba, a Sister, sought
to serve her cousin Saint Boniface, she wrote him, "God grant, unwor-
thy as I am, that I might have the honor of having you for my brother."
She closed the letter with the following suggestive verse:

> May the Almighty Judge, who made the earth
> And glorious in His kingdom reigns,
> Preserve your chaste fire warm as at its birth,
> Till time for you shall lose its rights and pains.[33]

The sixteenth-century Saint Teresa of Avila, who had nine beloved
brothers, ran away from home with one brother, Rodrigo, at the age
of seven, and with another, Antonio, at the age of twenty, to a Carmelite convent.[34] Originally Teresa had wanted Antonio to become a
Brother and herself a Sister,[35] but in her *Life* she seems to forget Antonio as brother from the moment she enters the Sisterhood. In her
Meditations on the Song of Songs (1566), Teresa seeks to replace the fraternal love she once had for Antonio by "spiritual marriage" and rebirth into a family where earthly kinship distinctions do not exist. Just
such a transcendence of consanguinity was Teresa's essential goal for
the Discalced Carmelite Order that she helped to found. Teresa writes,
"For the love of the Lord refrain from making individual friendships,
however holy, for even among brothers and sisters such things are apt
to be poisonous."[36] Reminding her Sisters to "think of the brotherhood which you share with this great God" as "children of this God,"[37]
she exhorts them, and all Christians, "to make our actions conform to
our words—in short, to be like children of such a Father and the
brethren of such a Brother."[38] Saint John of the Cross, an ideological
mainstay of Teresa's order, wrote in his *Precautions*, "You should have
an equal love for or an equal forgetfulness of all persons, whether
relatives or not, and withdraw your heart from relatives as much as
from others."[39] In precisely this way Teresa erased and raised herself
above differences between family and nonfamily. The saintly Teresa,
who verges in her *Life* on confessing to spiritual incest—a biographer,
pressing too hard, might conclude that she made love with a certain
Dominican Brother[40]—came to accept the ordinary taboo on sexual
intercourse with a brother only when she accepted the extraordinary
taboo on sexual intercourse with any human being.

As everloving Brothers and Sisters, such loving brothers and sisters
came close to marriage without violating the law against physical incest.
A few Catholic orders allowed closer physical communication between
siblings or Siblings in "double cloisters"—monasteries and nunneries
standing side by side. Among the Faremoutiers, who first developed

double cloisters in the seventh century, Saint Cagnoald ruled the monks in one wing and his sister, Saint Burgundofara, ruled the nuns in the other.[41] The Order of Fontevrault and the Brigittines adopted the same organization.[42] (For the mortification of the flesh, at times monks and nuns at Fontevrault would sleep in the same bed.)[43] The only order founded in England, the Order of Saint Gilbert of Sempringham, was a double cloister of cohabiting Brothers and Sisters.[44]

Saintly Sibling Love in Possible Sources of 'Measure for Measure'

Measure for Measure primarily reflects insight into a psychological dimension of monachism rather than direct influence from the biographies of the sibling or incestuous saints I have described (although a good case could be made for influence by Hartman's story of Gregory). Yet other saintly men and women whose names or biographies critics have cited as Shakespeare's sources have similarly ambiguous relations with blood kin.

Saint Bernard. The name Barnardine in *Measure for Measure* may derive from an incidental name—Bernardine—in Erasmus's *Funus*, which partly concerns the behavior of friars at a dying man's bedside.[45] (Compare the Duke's *ars moriendi* speech, 3.1.5–41.) Erasmus's "Bernardine" may in turn refer to the Order of Saint Bernard—the Bernardines.[46] "Barnardine" may just as well recall Bernardine of Siena, Bernardine Ochino, or Bernard of Vienne, however, and such echoes probably say little about the play.[47] Yet the spiritual affinity between brothers and sisters in *Measure for Measure* does recall the love of Saint Bernard of Clairvaux for his sister Humberlina, as well as his remarkable sermons on sibling love—both typical of the Christian monachal tradition.

After Bernard left home with his brother Andrew to enter the austere monastery of Citeaux, the story goes, Humberlina came, richly dressed, to visit them. Andrew greeted her, "Why so much solicitude to embellish a body destined for worms and rottenness, while the soul, that now animates it, is burning in everlasting flames?" Humberlina answered, "If my brother Bernard, who is the servant of God, despises my body, let him at least have pity on my soul. Let him come, let him command; and whatsoever he thinks proper to enjoin I am prepared to carry out."[48] Some time thereafter she entered a convent.

In Bernard's famous sermons *On the Song of Songs*, sisterly virginity and the theme "my sister as my wife" (*soror mea sponsa*) are sexualized, in a manner familiar from other sibling saints.[49]

The Blessed Isabella. The name of Shakespeare's Isabella, a novice in the Clares, has been connected with the Blessed Isabella of France, also associated with the Clares.[50] One critic has even conjectured that Shakespeare may have seen a manuscript of the "Isabella Rule" belonging to the Clares' abbey in London.[51] But critics who have associated the Blessed Isabella with Shakespeare's heroine have mistakenly believed she was associated with a sect of the Clares that was unusually strict in sexual discipline. Therefore, they have postulated that the special "restraint" on the Order of Clares that Shakespeare's Isabella seeks to join (1.4.4) must be sexual, paralleling Claudio's forced "restraint" (1.2.120) after his liberty with Juliet.

The sect of Clares with which the Blessed Isabella was associated and for which she formulated the "Isabella Rule" was not especially strict in its regulations for dealings with men, however. She founded a relaxed sect, called the Urbanist Clares from the name of Pope Urban II, who, along with Pope Alexander IV, ratified the relaxed rule; it was Saint Collette who reintroduced sexual strictness in the Colletine Clares.[52] Moreover, there is little if any textual evidence for the contention that the Clares as depicted in *Measure for Measure* are particularly strict in sexual matters. According to the rules that Sister Francisca enunciates, the scene in the nunnery (1.4) could open as follows: "The Prioress, asleep, the nuns entertaining smart visiting ladies and priests, some secular music."[53]

Instead, the unique regulation of the Clares was the "privilege of poverty" that Clare herself convinced Pope Innocent IV to grant her Sisters in 1253. This privilege gave a Sister the unique right to own absolutely nothing, not even communally as part of a collective.[54] (Isabella may refer to the dispensation in her first line of the play, "And have you nuns no farther privileges?" [1.4.1].) In the language of the Church, a privilege is not a restraint per se, but a license or permission—the term refers to a special ordinance issued by the pope.[55] The regulations of the Clares require that a postulant sell all her goods and distribute the proceeds to the poor. In the words of a modern account of the order, this radical gesture, which renounces the very basis of secular political organization, "with a single blow undoes all earthly ties and liberates the heart for a unique love."[56] (We will return to Clare's privilege later in this chapter.)

The Blessed Isabella was renowned for a love less unique, her affection for her brother, Saint Louis IX, the virgin King of France. Louis describes the strong feelings between himself and his sister, telling how he used to roll up in bedclothes the young Isabella. She was betrothed several times, but all her betrothals were canceled; some cancellations required payment of a forfeit, or "ransom," by her brother. (In exchange, she ransomed her brother from Muslim captivity, with the aid of the Order of Ransom.)[57] At one point the Blessed Isabella refused a proposal of marriage from Emperor Frederick II and informed the Pope himself of her "vow of virginity."[58]

For Isabella there was a definite tension between two tendencies: that of rejecting consanguineous bonds and loving all human beings equally with the unique love of a Sister, and that of accepting consanguineous bonds and loving some men, such as a brother or a husband, differently from others. The Blessed Isabella did not become a nun, although a story that she did circulated in the sixteenth century.[59] Instead, she lived as a laywoman in a house adjacent to the convent she founded; that is, she steered a middle course, virtually cohabiting with her saintly, virginal brother. (Ironically, some historians have erroneously called the siblings husband and wife.)[60]

St. Clare and St. Francis. In *Measure for Measure* the order whose garb Vincentio assumes is probably that of Saint Francis, the brother order to Isabella's of Saint Clare (1.4.5). (The name of Isabella's tutor, Francisca, is also reminiscent of St. Francis.)[61] Clare and Francis were not blood relations, but a deep, lifelong affection existed between them. At the age of eighteen, Clare heard a sermon by St. Francis and determined to devote herself to his mode of life. After testing her resolution, he himself received her vows at the altar and invested her with the Franciscan habit when, arrayed as a bride, she married Christ in spirit. He established her in a convent with a version of the Franciscan "Form of Life." After his death, for the rest of her life she fought to maintain the order's closeness to his spirit, despite pressure from Church authorities to mitigate its austerity.[62]

Sigmund Freud, in his discussion of how some people "find happiness . . . among the path of love . . . by directing their love, not to single objects, but to all men alike," calls Saint Francis of Assisi the man who "went furthest in exploiting love for the benefit of an inner feeling of happiness." Franciscan "readiness for universal love of mankind," says Freud, is, "according to one ethical view, . . . the highest standpoint which men can achieve."[63] Yet Francis's love for every being universally seems inextricably linked with love for his Sister in particular, as his remarkable poem "Brother Sun and Sister Moon," suggests.[64] Genealogists, bending the truth, even go so far as to present the two as close blood kin, even as brother and sister.[65] Franciscan theologians, moreover, often portray maleness and femaleness joined together, not in what we normally assume to be their closest union (marriage), but in roles that would normally be impediments to that union (namely, mother and son, or brother and sister).⁶⁶ What Francis and Clare could never permit in physical relations becomes a blessing in spiritual relations. In *The Soul's Journey into God*, Bonaventure likewise put the balance of all the soul's relationships into its one, supposedly whole, relationship with God as Christ—a spiritually incestuous relationship, since the soul becomes the daughter, spouse, and sister of God.⁶⁷

I do not wish to argue that the biographies of these sibling saints were sources for Shakespeare, but to point out a connection between the "ardent passion" of Isabella for Claudio that Walter Pater remarks and her vocation as a nun.⁶⁸ In the play, Isabella and Claudio trade almost overtly sexual statements. Isabella, for example, tells Claudio that he may live, but only by a method that "Would bark your honour from that trunk you bear, / And leave you naked" (3.1.71–72). Claudio responds: "If I must die, / I will encounter darkness as a bride / and hug it in mine arms" (3.1.82–84), foreshadowing what Angelo intends to do with Isabella in the darkness. These undercurrents of sibling love surface in Isabella's accusation that Claudio wants to commit "a kind of incest" (3.1.138); thereafter the brother and sister never again speak to each other, as though, even after the last act of pardon and atonement, they both fear a reemergence of the abhorred theme.

Such passion echoes the affection of brother and sister saints and the sibling love prominent in the rhetoric of the orders. The erotic libertine feelings of an earthly kind that a religious celibate must, in the words of a contemporary Augustinian Sister of Meaux, "damn well sacrifice"* may often historically have been directed, not only toward the opposite sex in general, but toward siblings of the opposite sex in particular. Be that as it may, the Catholic orders seem associated with ambiguous sorts of love—that is, incest—which they translate from earthly sexuality to a heavenly unification of all loves and all kinship in a single relation with Christ and a single, universalizing relation with all humans. How close these relations are to the indiscriminate libertine sexuality that threatens Viennese social organization in *Measure for Measure* appears in the fact that the members of one Christian order, the Brethren of the Free Spirit, were physical as well as spiritual libertines.

---

*"You can't sublimate it. You can't suppress it. You simply have to damn well sacrifice it." Quoted in Bernstein, *Nuns*, p. 109.

A Libertine Order: The Brethren of the Free Spirit

Ubi spiritus, ubi libertas.

Motto of the Libertine Brethren[69]

Similar motivations and appeals to grace are involved when a religious celibate overcomes sexual desire and loves everyone equally as Universal Siblings and when a religious libertine overcomes the restrictions of law and conscience after the Fall and loves everyone equally, including siblings. Both celibates and libertines hypothesize a Universal Siblinghood in which sleeping with a brother is no worse than sleeping with any other man. One seeks liberty from physical desire; the other, liberty from rules that restrict physical intercourse. But for both, in the words of Saint Paul (2 Cor. 3:17), "Where the Spirit of the Lord is, there is liberty."

The second Clementine decree, promulgated at the Council of Vienne in 1311 by church officials aiming to suppress the Brethren, describes in almost these very words the third "error" of the heretical Brethren of the Free Spirit, a lay order founded in the twelfth century that exhibited both the ascetic and the libertine aspects of Universal Siblinghood. According to the Council, the Brethren's error was this doctrine: "Those who have achieved this state of perfection and absolute freedom are no longer subject to obedience and law or obligated to follow ecclesiastical regulations, for where divine spirit rules, there is liberty."[70] The Brethren attempted to return to prelapsarian innocence by a harsh novitiate of absolute restraint followed by grace and absolute liberty.

Abiezer Coppe, a member of the Ranter sect, promulgated in England in 1650 a doctrine influenced by the Brethren. For the Ranters, as for the Brethren of the Free Spirit, "God dwelt inside them, as an inner light whose authority was above all laws. . . . Sin was thus made to disappear. The consequence was, for some Ranters, sexual license."[71] Coppe described the state beyond good and evil that was the Brethren's goal: "Be plagued back again into thy mother's womb, the womb of eternity: That thou maist become a little child, and let the mother *Eternity*, *Almightyness*, who is universal love, and whose service is perfect freedome, dresse thee, and undresse thee, swaddle, unswaddle, bind, loose, lay thee down, take thee up."[72] To such a child, dress and undress, incest and chastity, are alike—he knows no evil.

When the spirit of God is in one, one is God, or God's image in unfallen nature. One can truly say, "I belong to the liberty of nature, and all that my nature desires I satisfy. I am a natural man."[73] In the state of primal innocence or perfect grace, there is a perfect adequation or atonement between desires and acts, and the Pauline dictum "All things are lawful unto me" (1 Cor. 6:12) applies. According to one adept, "the Spirit of Freedom or the Free Spirit" is attained when one is "wholly transformed into God."[74] Such a person's guiding principle must be "Do what you want"—the single rule of Rabelais's anti-abbey of Thélème.[75] That injunction informs the principal extant theological work by a member of the Brethren of the Free Spirit. Marguerite Porete, in her *Mirror of Simple Souls*, writes, "Friends, love and do what you want."[76] Not to enact what one desires to enact would be in itself a sign of disunion with God.

The sect of the Free Spirit, founded at a time when Neoplatonism's influence was growing,[77] emphasized the soul's at-oneness with God. The Brethren's liberty was misinterpreted as mere libertinage, of course, but they attempted to synthesize Platonic Eros and Christian agape into an "Adamic eroticism"—"a sensuality above sensuality."[78] What this meant in practice is suggested by a hostile report: "Trithemius speaks of a girl, named Gisla, who, when asked if she was a virgin, replied that above the world she was, but in this world not."[79]

For at least one Brother of the Free Spirit, John Hartmann of Achmansteten, spiritual liberty meant "the complete cessation of remorse and the attainment of a state of sinlessness."[80] This entailed total transcendence of the post-Edenic taboo against incest:

The free man could do as he wished, including fornicate with his sister or his mother, and anywhere he wished, including at the altar. He added that it was more natural with his sister than any other woman because of their consanguinity. His justification lay in being perfectly free and bound by no law or ecclesiastical statutes and precepts; such a man was a Free Spirit in contradistinction to the gross men who were subject to existing authority of the church. His sister, far from losing her chastity, increased it as a result of their intercourse.[81]

The same liberty to have intercourse with mother or sister appears in the testimony of Conrad Kannler. As Leff retells it, Kannler said that "he could fornicate without sinning, and where a virgin was involved she remained chaste; he was similarly at liberty to have sexual intercourse with mother and sister, although he did not believe God would permit it for the imperfect." The followers of the sixteenth-century Belgian David Joris, a prominent member of a sect influenced by the Brethren of the Free Spirit, were said to have "incestuous orgies."[82]

It would be an error to dismiss the Brethren of the Free Spirit and similar groups as merely peripheral movements. Practicing incest in the name of Christian liberty may actually have been part of the oldest Christian doctrine. At least one biblical scholar suggests that the Corinthians' incestuous sexual intercourse, which Paul criticizes in 1 Cor. 5 ("such fornication as is not so much as named among the Gentiles, that one should have his father's wife," 1 Cor. 5:1), "was not a deed done secretly out of weakness but an ideological act done openly with the approval of at least an influential sector of the community."[83] Such a sect would have taken Paul's words about freedom from the law— "All things are lawful for me" (1 Cor. 10:23)—to indicate freedom from such rules as Lev. 18:8, "The nakedness of thy father's wife shalt thou not uncover."[84]

In the medieval era, the heresy of the free spirit, which spread among such lay orders as the Beguines and Beghards, came to inform the Women and Men of Intelligence and the Adamites. One of the Women of Intelligence, Bloemardinne of Brussels, "wrote much of the spirit of liberty and impious sexual love, which she called Seraphic."[85] The Adamites of Bohemia were an anarchist sect that foreshadowed Protestantism. (Consider the influence of both the Brethren and the Adamites on the Bohemian reformer Hus, a precursor to Luther who was influenced by the English Wycliffe.)[86] The Brethren may have understood an identification that helped drive or articulate the religious reformation: that of the polar opposition between and the sameness of incest on earth ("sin") and incest in heaven ("grace"). Did not Augustine warn, "Do not think that heresies could have arisen from a few narrow little souls. Only great men have brought forth heresies"?[87]

What characterizes a fraternal order such as the Franciscans or the Clares is its liberty from flesh or its razing the desires of the flesh and raising them to heaven. What characterizes a libertine order such as the Brethren of the Free Spirit is its graceful liberty of flesh. ("Now Libertines are named after the liberty of the flesh, which their doctrine seems to allow.")[88] But "grace is grace, despite of all controversy," says Lucio (1.2.24–25), recalling Rom. 11:6, "And if by grace, then is it no more of works: otherwise grace is no more grace." Although it might at first seem that between the two kinds of sexual freedom there is all the difference in the world, religious libertinism and religious celibacy are significantly linked in some Renaissance literature.[89] Moreover, the issues of liberty and libertinism—whether the connection between them be identity or opposition—resonate with the larger antinomian and Manichaean debates of the sixteenth century.[90] It was even claimed that the Protestant reformers' doctrine of faith implied both an essential connection of spiritual with earthly incest and a license for enacted earthly libertinism.

In England, the Family of Love, one of the best-known radical religious sects in the Elizabethan period, claimed that all members of the sect were "one Being" with their leader, who is "Godded man: and so bee all named Gods and Children of the most highest."[91] They assumed that all "are equal in degree among themselves; all Kings, and a kingdome of kings"[92] and announced a communist society where a new brother's "goodes shalbe in common amongst the rest of his brethren."[93] "The Family of Love," a comic play probably written by Thomas Middleton and performed by the Children of the Revels sometime between 1602 and 1607, contains a trial scene in which the Family's sexual freedom is institutionalized in law.[94]

The Mirror of the Incestuous Soul

The link between libertinism and celibacy, or incest and chastity, can be an upsetting one, and for that reason, perhaps, it often appears in the form of esoteric riddles. Incest has long been associated with the unspeakable solution to a perfect riddle, of course; the locus classicus is the story of Oedipus, who knows that the answer to the Sphinx's riddle is "man in general" (men generally crawl first, then walk, and finally hobble) but does not know that the answer to the oracle's riddle is "Oedipus in particular" (the man who killed his father and married his mother). Compare two similarly riddling late-medieval inscriptions from churches in Alincourt and Ecouis:

> Here lies the son, here lies the mother,
> Here lies the daughter with the father;
> Here lies the sister, here lies the brother,
> Here lies the wife with the husband;
> And there are only three bodies here.

> Here lies the child, here lies the father,
> Here lies the sister, here lies the brother,
> Here lie the wife and the husband,
> Yet there are but two bodies here.[95]

Like all epigrams, these should be considered together with the place where they are inscribed. The second appears in the exact middle of the collegial church of Ecouis, in the cross aisle. Its solution involves a local story: "The tradition is that a son of Madame d'Ecouis had by his mother, without knowing her or being recognized by her, a daughter named Ceclia, whom he afterwards married in Lorraine, she then being in the service of the Duchess of Bar. Thus Ceclia was at one and the same time her husband's daughter, sister, and wife. They were interred together in the same grave at Ecouis in 1512."[96] The riddle is about how a woman and man are, at one and the same time, wife and husband, sister and brother, and daughter and father; it is inscribed in a church, a religious institution devoted, like a nunnery, to transcending all relationships of consanguinity through a figure at once Son and Father. Similar epitaphs appear in other churches in Europe; Luther likewise retells such stories of incest.[97]

Shakespeare begins *Pericles of Tyre* with a similar riddle about a kind of incestuous self-consumption:

> I am no viper, yet I feed   (PER 1.1.65)
> On mother's flesh which did me breed.
> I sought a husband, in which labour
> I found that kindness in a father.
> He's father, son, and husband mild;
> I mother, wife, and yet his child:
> How they may be, and yet in two,
> As you will live, resolve it you.

During the course of *Pericles*, the hero discovers within himself the desire for father-daughter incest that he abhorred in Antiochus; the end of *Pericles* resolves, or atones for, that desire. The vital solution in *Pericles* requires a kind of resurrection—wife and daughter, believed dead, are reborn from their living deaths in a religious institution and a brothel. Dramatically, the solution to the riddle of Antiochus involves assigning to Pericles and Marina the roles of Antiochus and Antiochus's daughter; beyond the resurrection of the two women, the plot enacts a final rebirth, as Pericles calls it, of the father, Pericles, from the daughter, Marina. ("Thou that beget'st him that did thee beget" [PER 5.1.197].)[98] In this atonement, *Pericles* foreshadows kinship relations in all the other romances.

In Christianity, such atonement would be achieved by a wonderful transcendence of earthly incest in the Holy Family. It is depicted nowhere more clearly than in certain works of the devoutly religious sixteenth-century libertine Marguerite of Navarre, or Marguerite d'Angoulême.

Marguerite, who had been influenced by Marguerite Porete and the Brethren of the Free Spirit,[99] gave protection for a time to the Libertines, a pantheistic, antinomian sect attacked by Calvin in his pamphlet *Against the Fantastic Sect of the Libertines*.[100] (Lucio calls the Duke "fantastical" [3.2.89] and is himself described as a "Fantastic" in the Dramatis Personae.) The Libertines believed that everything is alike a manifestation of the Spirit of God, thus undoing the distinction between good and evil acts, since nothing can be truly outside God, hence truly bad. They were widespread in France by 1545, the year Calvin wrote his pamphlet, and their doctrines endured into the eighteenth century, when they influenced the "liberty, equality, and fraternity" of the French Revolution.[101]

Shakespeare may have known the works of such English libertines as John Champneis, who argue that God condones, for his chosen people, such "bodily necessities" as "theft, fornication, adultery, murder or any other sin."[102] He very probably knew the work of Marguerite of Navarre; her influence is suggested by his depiction of academic celibacy in *Love's Labor's Lost*, whose Princess is modeled on Marguerite of Valois, her grandniece,[103] and also by his apparent reliance in that play and in *Measure for Measure* on at least two of Marguerite's writings about physical and spiritual incest, *The Heptameron* and *The Mirror of the Sinful Soul*.[104]

In these works, Marguerite of Navarre expresses the relationship of religious celibacy to both earthly and spiritual incest. For example, the central tale in the *Heptameron* (the thirtieth of the third day) concerns a young man who unknowingly has sexual intercourse with his mother and then marries the offspring of this union—his sister, daughter, and spouse.[105] The mother had chosen for her young son "a schoolmaster, a man of holy life"; but "Nature, who is a very secret schoolmaster taught him a very different lesson to any he had learned from his tutor."[106] Neither the son nor the daughter ever learns of their blood kinship, and for them (if not for their knowingly incestuous mother) the tale ends happily: "And they [the son and daughter] loved each other so much that never were there husband and wife more loving, nor yet more resembling each other; for she was his daughter, his sister and his wife, while he was her father, her brother and her husband."[107]

In *The Mirror of the Sinful Soul*, Marguerite takes up a similar theme, but there the sin of earthly incest appears as the blessing of heavenly incest. The protagonist in the *Mirror* is a woman who compares herself with the Virgin Mary—the mother and sister of God the Son, and the daughter and spouse of God the Father. She acknowledges that her wicked desire for physical sex, even incest, can be overcome only by a liberating, graceful transformation, a raising, of the physical into the spiritual.

Love's Labor's Lost echoes Marguerite's two works in its treatment of the attempt to repress what Shakespeare calls natural "affects." *The Heptameron* says of the woman who knowingly slept with her son that "she must have been some self-sufficient fool, who, in her friar-like dreaming, deemed herself so saintly as to be incapable of sin, just as many of the Friars would have us believe that we can become, merely by our own efforts, which is an exceedingly great error." [108] The woman's presumption was trusting to her individual power to overcome lust "instead of humbling herself, and recognizing the powerlessness of our flesh, without God's assistance, to work anything but sin." [109]

The same position, that without grace flesh will out, is discussed during the founding of the "little academe" (LLL 1.1.13) in Shakespeare's Navarre in *Love's Labor's Lost*. The King of Navarre believes that he and his fellow courtiers are "brave conquerors—for so you are, / That war against your own affections" (LLL 1.1.8–9); it requires Berowne to say (if not to believe) that "every man with his affects is born, / Not by might master'd, but by special grace" (LLL 1.1.150–51). The courtiers of Navarre do not successfully keep to the rules they outline—including the rules that "no woman shall come within a mile of my court" (LLL 1.1.119–20) and that "if any man be seen to talk with a woman within the term of three years, he shall endure such public shame as the rest of the court can possibly devise" (LLL 1.1.128–31). The Sisterhood in *Measure for Measure* is like the little academe in *Love's Labor's Lost*: just as Isabella leaves the Sisterhood sometime after Lucio enters the nunnery to ask her to plead for her brother, so the courtiers in Navarre leave their little academe when "a maid of grace" (LLL 1.1.135) enters.* Finally, Costard's statement stands: "It is the manner of a man to speak to a woman" (LLL 1.1.206–7).

The Heptameron suggests that it is also the manner of men to commit incest. Incest of one kind or another is inevitable because without grace repression of incestuous desire is bound to be unsuccessful. There is a biographical dimension to Marguerite's concern with incest; her love for her brother, King Francis of France, is the subject of her greatest poetry. Saintsbury remarks that "it has been asserted that improper relations existed between the brother and the sister," [110] though the historical evidence is not conclusive on the side of either chastity or incest. Certainly sibling incest, whether physical or spiri-

---

*So, too, the "votaries" or "votarists" in the two plays are comparable (LLL 2.1.37, 4.2.132; MM 1.4.5). Although in *Measure for Measure* virginity is associated mostly with religious institutions, academic celibacy (which is foremost in *Love's Labor's Lost*) is at least hinted in the "science" of Old Escalus (1.1.5) and the learning of Angelo. Rejecting marriage is a traditional aspect of seeking secular wisdom as well as of religious righteousness. The wise man, according to Theophrastus, takes no wife (Jerome, *Adversus Jovinianum*, 1:49, in PL, 23:294; discussed in Dumm, *Virginity*, p. 49).

tual, informs her work. In *The Mirror of the Sinful Soul*, for example, she quotes and appears to draw forth the libertine implications for sibling lovers of such universalist passages in the New Testament as Matthew 12:50, "For whosoever shall do the will of my Father which is in heaven, the same is my brother, and sister, and mother."[111] When one rejects earthly kin and is reborn to do the will of God the Father, all men—including one's consanguineous kin—become equally members of one's new family. In this account, sexual desire for anyone who does the will of God is incestuous. Christian universalism as understood by Marguerite considers all sexual desires and acts to be incestuous and imposes on believers the torment of the soul that Marguerite's poem reflects.

Princess Elizabeth of England, in her translation of Marguerite's poem—originally titled *The Glasse of the Synnefull Soule* but significantly retitled *A Godley Medytacion of the Christen Sowle* (1544)—generally comprehends the tension in Marguerite's work between the desires for physical incest and for spiritual incest. In ancillary epistles Elizabeth hints that, for herself as for Marguerite, the solution to the desire for physical incest is a spiritual libertinism in God. If by physical incest one becomes at once the sister and wife of one earthly being (the quality and number of kinship relations varies from case to case), one becomes, by spiritual incest, at once the mother, daughter, sister, and wife of one heavenly being. The latter union is the spiritually incestuous one that Elizabeth seeks: "O what union is thys syth (through fayth) i am sure of thee, and nowe i maye call thee sonne, father, spowse, and brother. Father, brother, sonne, husband. O what giftes thou doest gyuve by the goodnes of those names. O my father: what paternite. O my brother: what fraternite. O my childe: what dilection. O my husband: O what comonction." Lest we miss the extraordinary quality of the poetess's love, which both incorporates and transcends incest, she asks of her unnamed quadrifold kin, presumably Jesus: "Is there any loue that maye be cmpared vnto this, but it hath some yuell condicion?"[112]

That the young Elizabeth should understand Marguerite's work on the transformation of physical into spiritual incest is not surprising: Elizabeth's mother Anne Boleyn had been executed for committing sibling incest,[113] and Elizabeth was heiress to the throne of England only because her father had committed sibling-in-law incest with Catherine of Aragon. Working from a copy of the *Mirror* that Marguerite of Navarre had given in friendship to Anne Boleyn, Elizabeth comes to English terms with the spiritual incest with God that informs this work of the unorthodox French spiritual: "Thou does't handle my soule (if so I durst say) as a mother, daughter, syster, and wife," and "Alas, ye, for thou hast broken the kindrede of myne olde father, callinge me daugther of adoption." [114]

This Renaissance riddling recalls one solution to the inscription in the center of the church at Ecouis: the doctrine of the Catholic Church concerning the adoption that makes God a brother, father, husband, and son. The feminine term for this four-sided relationship, "spouse of Christ," [115] emphasizes a woman's marriage with Christ the son in sibling incest, the sort of incest that Marguerite makes her poetical kingpin, that pervades the history of monachal orders, and that motivates the plot of *Measure for Measure*.

The Political Dimension of Monachism

Because it transcends earthly kin relations in a spiritual conflation where all are one, the spiritual liberty of the monachal orders tends to have the same effect on the earthly polity as does physical sexual liberty, with its threat of bastardy. Both attack the state by undermining the basis of political hierarchy and the ownership and transmission of property. [116]

Liberty and Property, or Communism. Isabella's entering a Sisterhood may solve, or sublimate, a sisterly fear of earthly incest or of the corrosive liberty that threatens Vienna. However, Sisterly (spiritual) incest threatens to dissolve parentarchal authority in Vienna as much as does the earthly kind because the essential kinship structure of the religious orders militates against the earthly patriarchalism of Vienna.

If we were all wholly children of one Father, we would be equal members of a state in which legal niceties like the ultimately essential Viennese one that treats men differently according to their different fathers would cease to exist. (Compare Angelo's stridently revolutionary, or liberal, claim to be able to do away with blood ties in administering justice to Claudio: "Were he my kinsman, brother, or my son / It should be thus with him" [2.2.81–82].) In such a state, no one would be superior to another in the way that a father (patriarch) is superior to a son (liberal); none could say with truth, "I and my Father are one" (John 10:30), with the exception of a man-god, like the son-father Jesus. There could be no visible, or ducal, authority.

Monachism, both in origin and in Tudor England, was, if only spiritually, an essentially revolutionary movement against political authority. Even before the formal establishment of eremitic communities in the early Church, both male and female ascetics would join together in a single residence in a family-like relationship. (The Pseudo-Clementian epistles "To Virgins" [fourth century] refer to Church members who lived in a "spiritual marriage" as brothers and sisters.)[117] The Church equivalent of political authority, in the persons of patriarchal critics like Eusebius of Emesa, viewed such practices with alarm because they furthered "either radical asceticism or radical libertinism."[118]

To the sexual radicalism of the orders there corresponded a propertal one. Just as the incest taboo can be related to the need to structure property relations, so the monachal injunction to commit spiritual incest often includes an injunction to end all merely human property relations. Saint Jerome, for example, writes, "Since you have been consecrated to perpetual virginity, your possessions are not your possessions [*tua non tua sunt*], because they now belong to Christ," and Saint Gregory praises his sister, Sister Macrina, who "found delight in temperance" and "thought it affluence to own nothing."[119] The fraternal orders do not merely endorse poverty; in some sense, they raze all property relations just as they raze all sexual relations. Saint John Chrysostom says, in his essay on virginity, "Now is not the time for matrimony and possessions; rather it is the time for penury and for that unusual way of life that will be of value to us in the time to come."[120] He succinctly expresses the politically threatening aspect of this rejection of possessions by calling virginity *isaggelos politea*, an extreme homogenization at once communist and incestuous.[121] In its essential form, monachal fraternity militates against any and all property ownership. This attitude makes property potentially a germ of conflict between monachal fraternity and patriarchal authority.

Elizabethans greatly feared political dissolution, which is implicit in such a rejection of ordinary kinship structure (the parentarchy) and ordinary economic structures (property), and they linked political dissolution with sexual liberty.[122] Bishop Stephen Gardiner, for example, relates the libertine position "all is for the flesh, women and meat with liberty of hand and tongue" to the political "dissolution and dissipation of all estates."[123] Apart from any connection between the monastic orders and liberty either sexual or political (propertal), few in Tudor England would have overlooked the connection between the monastic orders and a more specific threat of political chaos—revolt. In the general fear of Catholics and foreign Catholic infiltration, Catholic recusants (possibly including Shakespeare's father) were subject to arrest and severe punishment, and during Elizabeth's reign about two hundred Catholic priests were executed.[124] Monks had fig-

71

ured in such anti-Tudor plots as the Northern Rebellion and the Archpriest Controversy.[125] They had also been prominent among the opponents of Henry VIII, and one of the reasons he gave for dissolving the monasteries was a fear that monks would incite the commons to rebel.[126] (Ironically, one of the primary motivations historians now accept for the Dissolution is the very large amount of worldly property the crown gained thereby.)

While monachal resistance to the English king in the sixteenth century can be explained to some extent by specific historical circumstances, the strictly monachal doctrines that one should "Call no man father" and that one should own things only through a common God suggest how the resistance of liberal monks to parentarchal monarchs is a logical and ideological extension of fraternalism. In *Measure for Measure*, which explores the essential ideological basis of such a conflict as that in sixteenth-century England, the conflict between political authority (a parentarchal and royal duke) and fraternalistic liberty (Brothers and Sisters) is hinted in Brother Vincentio's claim concerning Duke Vincentio that "His subject am I not" (5.1.313).

Shakespeare's choice of the Clares rather than another order for his play highlights property relations, for the Clares' unique privilege concerned property. One sign of the potential subversiveness of the vow of poverty for which Clare struggled is that adherents of the original intents of Saint Francis were accused of heresy. Church authorities regarded his goal of mendicant poverty as appropriate for eremitic but not for conventual life, and Pope John XXII eventually passed legislation that effectively undermined it.[127] Clare's special privilege requires that her Sisters own nothing; this creates a potentially subversive association of monachal poverty with such begging as that of the mendicant orders and mere rogues.[128]

Our very word "beg" reflects a similar association. It derives from the names Beghard and Beguine,[129] which denote the men's and women's components, respectively, of a lay order established in the twelfth and thirteenth centuries, subject to no rule beyond the obligation to good works and (when members lived in a religious community) to chastity. The Beguines and Beghards originally had no vow of poverty, but they fell under the influence of the mendicant orders (which eventually subsumed many of their communities) and of various mystical and heretical movements. The name Beghard thus became associated with groups of wandering mendicants of a physically as well as spiritually libertine bent (hence "beggar"), who were often associated with the Brethren of the Free Spirit and similar groups.[130] At last their spiritual libertinism became too much for the Church authorities, and they were first restricted and finally persecuted.

In *Measure for Measure*, the enlightening Lucio characterizes the Duke as a beggar. "It was a mad, fantastical trick of him," Lucio says, "to steal from the state and usurp the beggary he was never born to" (3.2.89–90). In fact, the Friar/Duke tries to prepare Claudio for death by reminding him, as would any mendicant, that to live one must beg: "For all thy blessed youth / . . . doth beg the alms / Of palsied eld" (3.1.34–36). In *Measure for Measure*, moreover, begging is further compared, if not identified, with libertine fornication. Thus the debtor Master Caper, now a beggar (4.3.12), is in prison with fornicators, and Lucio follows his reference to the Duke's usurped beggary (which is ironically exact, since the Duke stands before him in the garb of a mendicant friar) with the accusations that the Duke would "mouth with a beggar" (3.2.177) and, with "your beggar of fifty," would "put a ducat in her clack-dish" (3.2.122–23). Lucio's association of sexual license with begging would be unnecessary (any harlot will mouth, any prostitute take a ducat, so there is no need to seek out beggars) if he did not intend to connect sexual license with begging.

Measure for Measure most clearly suggests the potential connection between begging and popular upheaval when Pompey describes (and may also show) the prison filled with clients of the whorehouse, now begging: "All great doers in our trade . . . are now 'for the Lord's sake'" (4.3.18–20). "For the Lord's sake" is the cry both of beggars and of libertine prisoners shouting from the windows of their prison.

Enter Lucio

Henry VIII, Robert Filmer, and others feared in certain religious and lay movements a tendency toward liberty. They believed that the public needed to believe, or they wanted the public to believe, in the "strange kind of domineering phantom" of the father, as Filmer's critic John Locke called it.[131] The absolutist king and his apologist were right in one sense: the struggle between liberty and absolute monarchy did involve the breakdown of the old family order and the development of a new political one.[132]

Libertine religious groups argued that where liberty is, there is the spirit of God—"Ubi libertas, ubi spiritus." They replaced patriarchal authority with a divine spirit that sanctions such liberal (if extreme) acts as incest, an act that in itself militates against the patriarchal social order. Eventually, political radicals in revolutionary France—intellectual descendants of the libertines[133]—attempted to bring "liberty, equality, and fraternity" to a new nation of free sons (*liberi*), and they beheaded the sovereign father. And political radicals in America, planning to overthrow a patriarchal king but fearing to destroy the developing idea of federalist patriotism, argued, not that liberty is where God is, but that one's fatherland is where liberty is. *Ubi libertas, ubi patria* was the motto of the American revolutionary James Otis.[134]

In *Measure for Measure*, both Isabella and Claudio represent the libertine or fraternal faction: Isabella, because as novice she is about to espouse Universal Siblinghood and become the spouse of God; Claudio, because as the producer of an illegitimate child he makes for a world in which everyone will be potentially a sibling. From this viewpoint, both siblings are in alliance against the state, and the play's Hegelian moment is the instant when the novice Isabella must decide whether she will serve as everyman's Sister, hence remain in the nunnery, or serve as Claudio's sister, hence leave the nunnery with the pimpish Lucio.

At the beginning of the play, before she meets Lucio, Isabella has presumably begun to raze the Old Testament prohibition against earthly incest by raising her family to heaven. Just as she is about to join the Christian Sisterhood, however, Lucio tells her that a fellow child of God the Father (a brother like all men) is in trouble with the law, and that the fellow also happens to be the child of her father and mother (a brother like no other man). When Isabella follows Lucio to plead before Angelo, she moves from an intended spiritual marriage with Christ, whose quintessentially incestuous birth is of questionable legal status, to serving her brother Claudio, whose legitimacy she comes to question. The novice leaves the liberal religious order and reenters the world of earthly familial relationships, including sister, mother, and wife. She moves away from homogeneity in liberty to political and patriarchal heterogeneity.

The Cathars of the Middle Ages renounced procreation and called sexual intercourse, even in marriage, "fornication." (It was to counteract their "Albigensian heresy" that the Roman church eventually imposed celibacy on the clergy.)[135] The Shakers renounced physical marriage in favor of a spiritual union (*syzygia*).[136] Unless we are, like them, truly universalist, incorporating and transcending both libertinism (in sex) and communism (in property)—that is, unless we are genuinely fraternal or liberal—Isabella's exit from the Sisterhood will make us glad for the sake of the parentarchal earthly order and for the sake of the propagation of the human race. We can sigh with relief that Isabella's exit from the nunnery figures "generation redeemed."[137] Many readers and spectators experience this comfortable gladness when Isabella leaves the nunnery in Act 1; at that point their feelings are in keeping with the gist of the play. But at that point the play has just begun, the dilemma is hardly stated, and the precise kind of generation that the play redeems is still unknown. It is the business of the rest of the play to bring that generation, indeed all human generation, under a new and discomforting scrutiny.

3
Individual Intent and Act

Marguerite of Navarre, holding a mirror in her hand.
(The Book of Hours of Catherine de Médicis; Louvre.)

My brother had but justice,
In that he did the thing for which he died:
For Angelo,
His act did not o'ertake his bad intent,
And must be buried but as an intent
That perish'd by the way. Thoughts are no subjets;
Intents, but merely thoughts.

MM 5.1.446–52

In the dramaturgical economy of *Measure for Measure*, as in Aquinas's account of fornication, the sexual act is teleologically conflated with its biological end, so that intercourse is always reproduction and fornication is always bastardizing, hence always eventually incest. *Measure for Measure* goes a step further: it conflates intent and act as well, with the result that the mere desire for sex is treated as essentially reproduction, hence as having immediate consequences for the moral standing of an individual and the social organization of the state.

The conflation of act with intent informs an essential political (or legal) and theological dilemma of the play: Should men be judged by their actions or by their intentions? Can they properly be judged at all? On the one hand, the dramaturgical logic of the play identifies intention with action, playacting out the intentions of Angelo and sentencing him as though he had actually enacted them. On the other hand, intent is finally separated from act when Isabella pardons Angelo's un-enacted "intents" on the grounds that they were "merely thoughts" (5.1.452).

Intent as Act

It is one tack of *Measure for Measure* that religious authority conflates intent with act and political authority separates them. Secular authority, on the one hand, can and must concern itself only with visible or audible action, such as the use, or acts, that the Duke requires of Angelo and the public marriage banns that Angelo requires of Claudio. Swinburne writes: "Mortal man cannot otherwise judge of men's meanings, than by their sayings, for the tongue is the messenger of the heart."[1] In much the same strain, in the seventeenth century James I wrote in *Basilicon Doron*, quoting Cicero, "Virtutis enim laus omnis in actione consistit" (The reward of virtue consists in action). He added, "It is not enough that ye have and retaine (as pris-

79

oners) within your selfe never so many good qualities and vertues, except ye employ them, and set them on worke, for the weale of them that are committed to your charge."[2] If what is within can be known only by what is without, people can and should be judged only by their actions or lack of action, for example, by their sexual activity or actual celibacy.

Religious authority, on the other hand, looks into and must govern the invisible, silent hearts of men. The Church, in the confessional, looks into people's hearts and discerns the intents upon which human beings—including the saintly Isabella or the good Duke—act. This means that the Church will judge people by the actions they desire or intend, consciously or not; it has already classified those desired actions, as Aquinas urges, by their telos, or impersonal intention as act. In separate requests for Isabella to sleep with Angelo, for example, Angelo intends fornication and Claudio may intend a kind of incest, but, regardless of their individual intentions, the generic telos of the requested sexual union is reproduction and the consequent destruction of the political order by illegitimacy and incest.

So long as we can conceptually separate intent from act in "secular" fashion, laws (such as those in the Old Testament) that forbid and punish acts of adultery and incest may restrain fornication without annihilating the human species. *Measure for Measure*, however, explores the awesome implications of conflating intent (or telos) with act. In its plot, individual intent (satisfaction of concupiscence) is connected with act (fornication) in the same way that sexual intercourse is connected with reproduction (natural "use") or fornication is connected with bastardizing and incest. All are conflated, so that illicit desire becomes one with illicit reproduction. Jesus argues that repressed (intended) sexual desire is no more acceptable than expressed (enacted) sexual desire because, morally speaking, repressed desire *is* the intended act. The general view of *Measure for Measure* has it that the religious and legal core of the play is the confrontation of justice with mercy; we shall see, however, how that core of the play involves rather the conflation of act (sexual intercourse) both with its individual intent (satisfaction of concupiscence) and with its generic intent (reproduction).

Razing the Old Commandment, or Raising the New Commandment. In the Sermon on the Mount, Jesus razes the Old Commandment against adultery given the Jews on Mount Sinai by raising it to a new level: "Ye have heard that it was said by them of old time, Thou shalt not commit adultery: But I say unto you, That whosoever looketh on a woman to lust after her hath committed adultery with her already in his heart"

(Matt. 5:27−28). Jesus here conflates desire (thought) with act. For him, a sinful intent is a sinful act, just as for nature each act of sexual intercourse is, to all intents, an act of procreation. This identification of intent with act makes the temptation to commit a crime the same as the attempt to commit a crime.* Under English common law, both the attempt and the crime itself are punishable by the same law, but Jesus would go one step further. When he presided over the "trial" of an adulteress (John 8), he acted on the most radical implication of this doctrine (assuming no one can completely avoid having intents) by appearing to offer no judgment at all.†

Jesus' words and actions challenge proponents of secular law and order, who must argue, along with Angelo in the middle of the play and Isabella at its end, that "'Tis one thing to be tempted . . . , / Another thing to fall" (2.1.17−18, cf. 5.1.448−51). According to him, being tempted to kill a man out of anger and actually killing him are one and are punishable (if at all) under the same law. ("Ye have heard that it was said by them of old time, Thou shalt not kill; and whosoever shall kill shall be in danger of the judgment: But I say unto you, that whosoever is angry with his brother without a cause shall be in danger of the judgment" [Matt. 5:21−22].) According to a variation of the same principle, intending to marry a woman and actually marrying her are one and the same. For Jesus, the intention of Claudio's "fast" marriage (1.2.136) might make his secret union with Juliet an actual marriage, but for Angelo the lack of public and visible enactment necessarily outlaws it. From Jesus' viewpoint, Claudio's child might be counted legitimate, but from Angelo's viewpoint, it is a bastard. (From Angelo's viewpoint, Jesus himself would be counted the illegitimate son of an adulteress rather than the extra-legal Son of God.)

*In his study of Dostoevsky and parricide, Freud to some extent concurs with the general gist of Matthew 5:27−28 that not action but only intent is what counts. "It is a matter of indifference who actually committed the crime," writes Freud. "Psychology is only concerned to know who desired it emotionally and who welcomed it when it was done. And for that reason all of the brothers are equally guilty" (Freud, "Dostoevsky and Parricide," p. 236).

†Some interpreters of the New Testament have tried to weaken or obscure Jesus' powerful, but discomforting, conflation of intent with act. Schweizer, for example, deflects attention from the discomforting aspect of the conflation when he says that the tale of the adulteress is intended merely "to protect the rights of women" (Schweizer, *Good News*, p. 121), who, according to the Law, were sometimes punished more severely for adultery than were men. Similarly, A. M. Hunter says the view that looking with lust upon a woman amounts to having sexual intercourse with her is intended to outlaw "not the involuntary waking of the sexual appetite but the deliberate intent to sin" (*Design*, p. 48). Yet Jesus himself, at least as Matthew and John report his words, clearly includes in his conflation of intent with act any act whatever (whether sinful or innocent) and any intent whatever (whether deliberate or involuntary).

The Implication of Jesus' Position. Jesus says that he has come not to abolish (erase) the Law, but to fulfill (raise) it. He suggests, however, neither that outlawed acts (adultery is a favorite example) are wrong nor that they should be punished. Instead, he presents the awesome argument that, since libertinism is essentially universal, one (or One) must (1) allow it, or else either (2) condemn all people to die or (3) grant some or all people a merciful pardon.

1. Allowing Universal Libertinism. From Jesus' argument that lust is essentially adultery it follows that humans must necessarily accept the widespread practice of adultery—hence relax or erase the laws against it—since men and women cannot always and invariably, at all points in their lives, repress their conscious or unconscious lust on seeing a woman. (Sisters, like the Clares, wear veils to help men, but that is not sufficient; in some situations, indeed, veils even arouse desire.) Such libertine acceptance of fornication has been the norm in Vienna for some fourteen or nineteen years, but it has worked ill, since celibacy and illegitimacy have been the results.

2. Enjoining Universal Genocide. Jesus' conflation of lust with adultery can also lead to the view that mankind should be annihilated. Since adultery is against God's law, since the desire for sex entails commission of the sex act, and since desire is universally human, therefore all men deserve execution (an Old Testament punishment for adultery). In this sense, Jesus "came not to send peace, but a sword" (Matt. 10:34). Vienna is threatened with this genocidal sword in the middle of the play when Angelo, relying on Viennese laws that confuse the Old Testament punishment for adultery with the one for fornication, plays the role of the heavenly swordsman and Claudio stands for mankind. We may think of Paul, swordsmanlike, condemning the incestuous Corinthians to death.

3. Forgiving Libertinism. A final consequence of Jesus' argument that intent is act is that, although the old law against adultery and the old punishment of adultery (execution) are just, no human being can punish any human being for adultery. Such punishment is unacceptable because the judge and jury, as well as the hangman, are, to all intents, also adulterers. The partly human Jesus suggests that *all* humans are, to all intents, adulterers; it follows that Angelo, if he is merely human (which the ironic Lucio doubts [3.2.99–101, 107–8, 167–68]), cannot sentence Claudio without violating Jesus' rule "He that is without sin among you, let him first cast a stone" (John 8:7). Escalus uses this argument (2.1.7–16), recalling Jesus' stern warning, "Judge not, that ye be not judged" (Matt. 7:1). Many readers of *Mea-*

sure for Measure take this to be the message of the play. But Angelo, if he is to carry out any laws at all—and how could there be a society without laws?—must reject the argument that sinners in intent cannot pass judgment on sinners in act. Angelo does what he must do. "What knows the laws," asks Angelo, "That thieves do pass on thieves?" (2.1.22–23). Not only must the law pass over actual crimes that leave no material trace (fornication without pregnancy, say), it must also pass over desired crimes that are not enacted (lust without fornication).

Jesus' argument seems, then, to lead inevitably to the acceptance of widespread libertinism or the relaxation of the earthly punishment of libertinism. Otherwise universal genocide would result, and even genocide would be wrong, since among fully human beings no one is pure enough to execute another for libertinism, not even the partly human Jesus. Only the Father, implies the Son, can properly punish his adulterous children. This is the revolutionary "new commandment" (1 John 2:7–8) that Jesus, though no scribe, figures in the dust at the trial of the adulteress (John 8:6), that scribbling being the only time Jesus (who is, like Socrates, the one who does not write) is reported by the official church apostles to have written.[3]

The position that we are all sinners is, according to most serious critics since Schlegel, the meaning of the play, and it always leads them to contemplate a sublime leap from justice to mercy. "The true significance of the work," writes Schlegel, "is the triumph of mercy over strict justice; no man being himself so free from errors as to be entitled to deal it out to his equals."[4] This is pleasant, but universal mercy is an impossible position for a political state. Shakespeare cannot rest content with the utopian, or incestuous, vision supposed by the conflation of intent with act and by the consequent demand for universal mercy.

The Partial Education of Angelo

At the beginning of *Measure for Measure*, the Duke suggests that each of the two men he will leave in charge of the state—Angelo and Escalus—has something in him that should come forth. Angelo, for example, has been unable, as underling to the Duke, to act upon or use his knowledge; the Duke's departure is an opportunity for him to do so. Angelo is pregnant with some hidden quality, and the Duke counsels him to give birth: "Thyself and thy belongings / Are not thine own so proper as to waste / Thyself upon thy virtues, they on thee"; and he warns Angelo, "Heaven doth with us as we with torches do, / Not light them for themselves; for if our virtues / Did not go forth of us, 'twere all alike / As if we had them not" (1.1.29–35, cf. Matt. 5:15–16).

The Duke refers not so much to the procreation of children or to the particular act of creation, as to action in general. He suggests that, just as Escalus is "pregnant" (1.1.11) in knowledge about the people, urban institutions, and justice, so Angelo has within himself some quality that should issue forth. Just what this quality is, of course, is unclear. Apparently, so far as the Duke is concerned, any issue—any "use"—from Angelo will be good, just as, so far as nature is concerned, any human procreation, legitimate or not, will be good.

> Nature never lends   (1.1.36)
> The smallest scruple of her excellence
> But, like a thrifty goddess, she determines
> Herself the glory of a creditor,
> Both thanks and use.

Like the puritanical Malvolio, as Maria in *Twelfth Night* makes him out to be, Angelo is made out by others (if not by himself) to be "crammed, as he thinks, with excellencies" (TN 2.3.150), but what he finally bears to the world is a monster. If Claudio's sexual use is illegitimate, so, too, we shall learn, is Angelo's moral use.

Perhaps some people, like the apostles' man-god Jesus, can successfully incorporate and transcend human desire and thus be without sin. (In the play, Brother Thomas and Sister Francesca may stand for such people.) The rest of us, however, are morally imperfect—especially if we accept the conflation of thought with act. Most of us could use some moral education. In *Measure for Measure* this education involves knowledge and place.

Knowledge. In *Measure for Measure* the first part of moral education is to recognize one's own lustful thoughts. Angelo, who substitutes in this unpleasant business for the Duke (he is the "King's player"),[5] gains such knowledge in theory from Escalus (2.1.8–16) and in practice from Isabella (2.2.163–87). It is Isabella who tells Angelo "Go to your bosom, / Knock there, and ask your heart what it doth know / That's like my brother's fault" (2.2.137–39); it is, moreover, her presence as woman that makes him do this—she later claims he was ignorant of his lust before he laid eyes on her (5.1.443–45).[6]

Before he learned from Isabella about his own lustful thoughts, the celibate Angelo's severe rulings arose in part from ignorance of what he was, even of where he came from. Lucio suggests that he acts as though he had been created, like Jesus, in an extra-human way: "They

84

say this Angelo was not made by man and woman, after this down-right way of creation" (3.2.99–101). Lucio further jokes that Angelo is a "motion ungenerative" (3.2.108) and an "ungenitured agent" (3.2. 167–68). Angelo seems impervious to the sexual desire that presumably all sexually generated beings must sometimes feel. Thus, for Angelo the apparent virtue of continence has involved no struggle to contain sexual desire within the realm of legitimate action or to transcend it; for him, the apparently virtuous adequation of conscious sexual desires with the enactment of those desires (an adequation that has resulted in his secular celibacy) has been facile because those desires in him seemed to him to be nil. But, as Lucio knows, Angelo is not what he seems, to others and himself, to be: "He's coming: I perceive't" (2.2.126).

The coming out of Angelo's repressed desires—the first part of his practical moral education—unpleasantly forces Angelo to recognize, perhaps for the first time, that he has desires in conflict with a moral or political law. In his psyche there thus develops a schism between what he consciously desires and what he feels he ought to do. Having been aroused by Isabella, for example, he can choose to act continently or incontinently, to obey his conscience or disobey it; but in either case his soul will be split.

In the past Angelo's sexual temper had not been stirred:

> Never could the strumpet   (2.2.183)
> With all her double vigour, art and nature,
> Once stir my temper . . .
>   . . . Ever till now
> When men were fond, I smil'd, and wonder'd how.

His meeting with Isabella has shown him that, after all, he is neither a physiological eunuch nor an impotent man, and that his past celibate life was the result not so much of his desire to serve the state as of a certain repression. His celibacy had been merely one response, albeit an extreme one, to the political or familial pressures that make not for an external (hence public) castration of the private parts but for an internal (hence private) castration of the mind. (Compare Rom. 2:29: "Circumcision is that of the heart, in the spirit.")

Dom Gregoire Lemercier, discussing his monks' treatment by a woman psychoanalyst, says: "There are eunuchs who are born such at the breast of their mothers; there are eunuchs who have become such through the acts of men; and there are eunuchs who have made themselves such for the sake of the Kingdom of Heaven [Matt. 19:12]. Psychotherapy reveals that many Brothers who had thought themselves eunuchs of the third class are in reality eunuchs of the first two classes."[7] Such a revelation is a precondition for becoming eventually one who has made himself a eunuch truly for the sake of the Kingdom of Heaven.[8] But it is not a sufficient condition; thus for Angelo self-knowledge is only the first part of the cure.

Place. Most critics argue that Angelo's basic fault is not hypocrisy but lack of self-knowledge.[9] It is precisely an increase in self-knowledge, however, that creates one precondition for his becoming a conscious hypocrite (i.e., acting out a virtuous part on stage). His new place, which creates the official stage from which he can seem to others to be virtuous, is the second precondition.

Angelo's ignorance of his own desires was one restraint on his actions, but that restraint is removed when he sees and hears Isabella. Will Angelo's newly discovered desire rule his conduct, so that he becomes incontinent? Or will the old law rule his conduct, so that he becomes knowingly continent?

For Angelo the option of incontinence is made more likely by the removal of a second restraint on his actions, his fear of punishment by authority or withdrawal of authority's approval. It is thus part of Angelo's moral education to have the ducal place, which, he believes, confers on him an invisible and all-seeing power. (In the *Republic* Plato relates how this power was once given to the tyrant Gyges in the form of a magic ring.)[10] In *Measure for Measure*, Angelo thinks that his actions are invisible (he is sure that no one will believe Isabella's account of the bargain he proposes [2.4.153–55]) and that the actions of everyone are visible to him (he is sure that he knows what is going on in the vineyard and the prison). That is how the office indicates the man.[11]

Insofar as these two restraints on his actions—ignorance of his desires and fear of external authority—are removed, Angelo is given a rare liberty to act out his intents. His desires, once repressed, can now be expressed freely without fear of external authority. Angelo can do what the Duke wanted him to: he can give birth to his intents as acts and thus become "unpregnant" (4.4.18) of his thoughts.

From one point of view, Angelo's new freedom is an extreme test of morality. (The test would be more extreme if a third restraint on action, bad conscience of the kind that Angelo suffers [4.4.18–32] but Plato's Gyges does not, had also been removed.) But from Jesus' point of view, it is really no test at all. From the first point of view, Angelo's choosing incontinence (lack of restraint) over continence (restraint) would be a sign of moral weakness or strength. For Jesus, however, moral weakness resides in the desire itself: Angelo's desire per se makes goodness impossible, whether Angelo represses or expresses that desire. If lust and adultery are the same, so too, if one continues to desire, are continence and incontinence. Only the self-mastering of desire is truly moral, as Theseus points out when describing a nun's life in *A Midsummer Night's Dream*: "Thrice blest they that master so their blood / To undergo such maiden pilgrimage" (MND 1.1.73–74). Dom Gregoire Lemercier associates such self-mastering with making oneself a eunuch for the sake of God; it could also be associated with Aristotelian moderation or the temperance of James I.[12]

The process of the play shows that what had kept Angelo from acting badly was not only ignorance of his desires but also fear of being seen by a master external to himself. When the substitute duke (Angelo) learns that the supposedly absent duke (Vincentio) was present, he is unhappy not so much that he acted badly as that he was seen acting badly:

> O my dread lord,   (5.1.364)
> I should be guiltier than my guiltiness
> To think I can be undiscernible,
> When I perceive your Grace, like power divine,
> Hath looked upon my passes.

The last act of the play constitutes a "confession" (5.1.370) of what Angelo desires, but it also indicates that Angelo has not learned how to live without such negative restraints as those represented for him by what he calls, more in need of an authority figure than in flattery, the god-like Duke. Angelo has not learned temperance.

Fearful Continence vs. Loving Temperance. The distinction between acting well out of fear and doing so out of love is precisely the distinction between contrition and attrition with which the Duke as Friar tests Juliet's repentance.

> . . . but lest you do repent.   (2.3.30)
> As that the sin hath brought you to this shame,
> Which sorrow is always toward ourselves, not heaven,
> Showing we would not spare heaven as we love it,
> But as we stand in fear—

At the end of the play, as in the middle, the "fornicatrix" Juliet is closer to true repentance (as she stands in love) than Angelo the fornicator (as he stands in fear).[13] (Similarly, in *Richard the Second*, the Duke of York accuses his treasonous son: "Fear, and not love, begets his penitence" [R2 5.3.54].)

Angelo's fear of the Duke is not Christian in the fraternal sense; he acts more like the slave of a Roman emperor than the free son (*liber*) of the Holy God as Father. Paul warns: "For all who are led by the

Spirit of God are sons of God. For you did not receive the spirit of slavery to fall back into fear, but you have received the spirit of sonship [or, according to the Vulgate, "the spirit of sons of adoption," *spiritum adoptionis filiorum*]. When we cry, 'Abba! Father!,' it is the Spirit himself bearing witness with our spirit that we are children of God." (Rom. 8:14–16; Rev. Stand.) "We wait for adoption as sons," says Paul, not as slaves (Rom. 8:23; Rev. Stand.). *Measure for Measure*, set in the seat of the Holy Roman Empire, explores the view that joining a fraternal order can turn slavery into filial freedom (liberty) under the Father. (Jesus, who is both an equal brother to all men and an equal son to God the Father, equalizes the sons with the Father.) Similarly the play explores the view that freedom may be found in being a "free dependant," like the Provost obedient to the Friar with the ducal ring (4.3.90), or in being mutually interdependent ("What's mine is yours, and what is yours is mine" is the marriage relationship the Duke ultimately proposes to Isabella [5.1.534]). But Angelo's fearful slavishness, connected to the patriarchal figurehead by earthly rather than heavenly sonship—or by the boundary in his consciousness between what he now knows he wants to do and what the father figure will let him do—keeps him from the freedom that universal fraternity, or liberty, might allow.

At the beginning of the play, Angelo is a self-ignorant man whose known desires are adequate to what he does. In the middle, he becomes an incontinent tyrant. At the end, he is a continent subject who is conscious of his "bad" desires but, if he will now act well, will do so only out of slavish fear: Angelo never gets to the point of being "good" for any reason other than the negative desire to be free from guilt or from espial by a father figure. The process of the play thus educates Angelo only partway toward making his known desires adequate with his acts, toward the Aristotelian moderation, temperance, or self-mastery by which the two parts of his split psyche—desire and law—might be rejoined in a higher union.[14]

James I, in the *Basilicon Doron*, says of the virtues that a man should make "Temperance, Queen of all the rest within you. I mean not the vulgar interpretation of Temperance, which only consists in *gustu & tactu*, by the moderation of these two senses; but I mean of that wise moderation, that first commanding your self, shall as Queen, command all the affections and passions of your mind."[15] In *Measure for Measure* Angelo is unsuccessful in temperately uniting desire with act, or in becoming, to quote Escalus's praise of the Duke, "a gentleman of all temperance" (3.2.231). Yet the play itself moves toward the conscious adequation of known intent and act, toward the mastering of one's own desire rather than the tyrannical enslaving of another human being (Angelo's attempted subjection of Isabella) or to another human being (Angelo's subjection to the Duke).

For Angelo and most all of humankind, belief in and fear of a visible and all-seeing external authority is necessary to restrain desire. In Vienna the Duke is called paternal, royal, even divine, because most people are morally weak; in order to behave well they need to personify authority in him, to mythologize him. At least two persons, however, probably have few illusions about the Duke: Escalus and Lucio. Escalus knows that the Duke as yet only contends to know himself (3.2.226–27). (The ancient advisor may be impotent sexually as well as politically, so that his need for a fictional authority is small. The incontinent Lucio, not without insight, accuses the Duke both of having illicit sexual desires and of acting on them (3.2.122–24). But society as a whole is composed of such childish men as the ignorant, celibate Angelo and the incontinent Froth, men who require and believe in the visible presence of the authoritative and parentarchal law. For them, liberalism is dangerous because through incest it destroys the law by making impossible the myth of the Parent that grounds the law.

However needful for Angelo and most all of humankind, parentarchal authority is essentially problematic, and not merely because it may be a mere fiction. Childish subjection to authority encourages, not the development of true moderation, but a continence in which one has bad intents but does not act on them because of fear. Such continence is not essentially good, since, as Jesus says, it is essentially the same as incontinence. Put another way, people who are subject to parentarchal authority are likely to act more out of fear or lack of fear than out of love. Perhaps the liberal Duke knows this and conducts his experiment in Vienna in the hope of making his presence as ducal patriarch unnecessary—in the hope of turning Vienna into a kind of liberal (even incestuous) democracy in which all would become educated about their desires and some become moderate. The case of Angelo, who is no worse than most men, shows that the experiment is a failure. The process of the play replaces Angelo's self-ignorance with self-knowledge, but it can replace his incontinence only with continence, not moderation. Because continence requires authority, Vincentio must eventually give up his liberal disguise as Friar and take up again his patriarchal place as Duke.

The Education of the Duke

> Oh, what may man within him hide,
> Though angel on the outward side!
> (3.2.264-65)

A parentarchal ruler should be visible to childlike subjects; to quote James I, "Kings being publike persons, by reason of their office and authority, are . . . set . . . upon a publike stage, in the sight of all people."[16] Vincentio, however, wants to give up his patriarchal role and become invisibly a member of the liberal community that a ruler should be seen overseeing:

> I love the people, (1.1.67)
> But do not like to stage me to their eyes:
> Though it do well, I do not relish well
> Their loud applause and *Aves* vehement.

Vincentio feels within himself the tension between authority and liberty (king and children) that informs the sexual and political life of Vienna. He wants to be of the people rather than, or as well as, above them—to be Son as well as Father. The ducal officer, in the words of the disguised King Henry V, still learning the art of governance, "is but a man, as I am" (H5 4.1.101-2).* Seeking a middle ground on which to transcend the tension between place (office) and man, Vincentio changes his own place to Brother of the Church and Angelo's place to father of the state.

Like Angelo, Vincentio is no angel. Critics have noted this, but they have condemned merely his past lack of action (e.g., his laxness in punishing fornicators and murderers) and present actions (his secret stratagems to save Claudio).[17] Vincentio's main weakness, however, is the all-too-human one Shakespeare introduces in his conversation with the doubting Friar Thomas: he has illicit, if natural, sexual intents, which are most likely hidden even from himself.[18] Vincentio's knowledge of his own intents and sexual activity is questionable. As confessant, Vincentio, with godlike assurance, says to Friar Thomas, "Believe not that the dribbling dart of love can pierce a complete bosom" (1.3.2-3). Yet doubting Thomas implies that Vincentio wishes to disguise himself to carry out some love scheme. As Friar, Vincentio tells Lucio, "I have never heard the absent Duke much detected for women" (3.2.118-19), yet Lucio, to the credibility of whose innuen-

---

*Vincentio disguises himself in the hood of the order of Friar Thomas so as not to stage himself to the people, just as Henry V, once the liberal Hal, disguises himself in the cloak of Sir Thomas in order to stage the troops to himself.

does we shall return, says that the duke "had some feeling of the sport" (3.2.115–16) and "would mouth with a beggar" (3.2.177).

In the same vein, Escalus tells Friar Vincentio that the Duke "contended especially to know himself" (3.2.226–27). Maybe this was "a very high tribute . . . during the Renaissance,"[19] but to consider only its meaning as compliment is to deflate the literal meaning of ancient Escalus's words: the Duke does *not* know himself. In ancient Greece the motto "Know thyself" was inscribed on the gates to the temple of Apollo at Delphi (echoed in Shakespeare's "Delphos," literally, "womb," from which the oracle's judgment is brought in *The Winter's Tale* [2.3.195]). There, it inspired Socrates to search for wisdom— unlike Vincentio, he knew that he did not know.[20] Apollo's oracle likewise encouraged the ignorant, know-it-all Oedipus to strive to know himself by seeking out his family origins. Before he falls for Isabella, Vincentio, like Angelo, knows himself no better than Oedipus before Oedipus knew his daughter Antigone to be his own sister.

Like Angelo, Vincentio seems to fall in love with Isabella at first sight.[21] Why? What does it mean to fall in love with a maiden made invisible by her hood and by the darkness of a prison cell? The Friar-Duke's earliest wooing of Isabella ("The hand that hath made you fair hath made you good" [3.1.179–80]) has a spiritual and a natural level, but to insist, as one critic does, that "at the 'natural' level the wooing constantly suggests the conventions of chivalric romance,"[22] is to obscure how and why Vincentio is naturally drawn toward the novice nun. Does the Duke, like his angelic substitute, "desire to raze the sanctuary"—that is, Isabella—precisely because she seems to be one of the "saints" (2.2.171, 181)?

Wordplay in *Measure for Measure* suggests that, at some psychological level, from his first sight of the veiled Isabella the Duke wants to have sexual relations with her. His very first words already require of her a "satisfaction" (3.1.154)—meaning a penance (as her father confessor) but foreshadowing the "satisfaction" (3.1.264), or sexual union, that Angelo will require and that Vincentio (also as confessor) will exact from Mariana in her stead.[23] The Friar-Duke says that "the satisfaction I would require is likewise your own benefit" (3.1.154–55), and he promises to "benefit" (3.1.200) Mariana as well. But by Elbow's memorable malapropism a "benefactor" is also a "malefactor" (2.1.50), and if means do not justify ends (as the complex teleology of the play suggests), Vincentio aims at a malefice. A similarly appropriate malapropism conflates "respect" with "suspect" (2.1.159–75). The Friar-Duke, who has often stilled Mariana's "brawling discontent" (4.1.9), asks her, "Do you persuade yourself that I respect you?" (4.1.53); but by Elbow's malapropism "respect" comes to mean "an obscene public thing."[24]

To be left alone with Isabella in the prison, Vincentio must reassure the seemingly suspicious Provost that "no loss shall touch her by my company" (3.1.177), when in fact he will use his disguise to woo Isabella in exactly the way Friar Thomas guessed he would.* Fornication between a father confessor and his spiritual daughter (or penitent) is "spiritual incest"; mediated by Vincentio-as-Friar's unrecognized intention to commit spiritual incest, the wooing of Isabella—overheard accusing her brother of "a kind of incest" (3.1.159)—by Vincentio-as-Duke begins.

In *Measure for Measure*, such ducal intentions, however unconscious, go hand in hand with—even lead to—actions. Angelo, the disguised Duke's right-hand man, acts out (gives birth to) Vincentio's desires and hence as substitute educates Vincentio by demonstration, without bringing the Duke into disrepute. During the course of the play the liberal desires of Vincentio thus come out from the "covent" (4.3.128), just as Isabella comes out of the convent.[25] As it progresses, Vincentio learns that his lax, or liberal, attitude toward carrying out the old law of Vienna matches his own lustful, or liberal, feelings.[26] He comes to know as his own the vice of fornication intended or actual: "Shame on Angelo, / To weed my vice, and let his grow!" (3.2.262–63).[27] Insofar as intent is (according to Jesus) act or is (in the play) substituted for act, the Duke's vice is an act of fornication, the fornication that he oversees his appointed substitute intending to enact or (as that substitute, Angelo, sees it) actually enacting. Only through his stand-in does the Duke come to learn where he stands.

That Angelo acts for Vincentio by taking his sexual as well as political place is one gist of Isabella's remarkable denunciation of some unnamed person who, like Angelo, seems to be good—seems, that is, either to himself (since he may be ignorant of his own desires) or to others (since he may keep his misdeeds invisible).

> Make not impossible　　　　　　(5.1.54)
> That which but seems unlike. 'Tis not impossible
> But one, the wicked'st caitiff on the ground,
> May seem as shy, as grave, as just, as absolute
> As Angelo.

---

*The Provost remains present during the Friar-Duke's "satisfaction," or "confession," of Juliet (2.3. cf. 2.2.25), just as Francisca probably remains present during the conversation between Isabella and Lucio. (See Lever's introduction in his edition of *MM*, p. xxvi, discussing stage directions in 1.4 and 3.1.)

Lucio and the Duke himself have used "shy" and "grave" to describe the Duke (3.2.127, 1.3.5). What is unlike is not impossible: Vincentio, for whom Angelo is the sexual surrogate as well as the deputied political substitute, is, to all intents, the principal caitiff in *Measure for Measure*, the one whose conscious and unconscious intents Angelo acts out. Insofar as intent and act are inextricably connected in the way that Jesus suggests, Vincentio is the whore-chaser that Lucio claims he is (3.2.127–85, 4.3.163–64). The accuracy of Lucio's claim, which enlightens us about the Duke's intentions by telling not impossible tales about his actions, is what makes Lucio so threatening a figure to Vincentio.

4
Taliation, Part One:
Punishment and Ransom

Illustration of *Measure for Measure*, 3.1. (Salaman, *Shakespeare in Pictorial Art*.)

Taliation. A return of like for like; retaliation; = *Talion.*

O.E.D.

And if any mischief follow, then thou shalt give life for life, eye for eye, tooth for tooth, hand for hand, foot for foot, burning for burning, wound for wound, stripe for stripe.

Exod. 21:23–25

According to the lex talionis (law of talion), a man must either give back what he has taken or make appropriate restitution for it. If he has taken a cow, for example, he must return that cow. When what he has taken cannot be returned, a substitute that somehow measures up to the stolen object must be found. *Measure for Measure* is about measuring up to such unreturnable goods as lost maidenheads and lost lives.

In the terms of the play, Claudio has stolen a maidenhead, and according to the lex talionis he must return it. Since once taken a maidenhead cannot be returned, however, a substitute like or commensurate with it must be found. The legal authority of Vienna, instead of demanding that Claudio do the impossible and return Juliet's maidenhead, determines that he must substitute his own head. This transaction, which involves a critical commensurability of head and maidenhead, would equal the return of Juliet's maidenhead and hence cancel out the original theft. That cancellation is the end or telos of punishment according to the lex talionis.

Angelo turns this proposed punishment—head for maidenhead—into a proposed ransom when he suggests that Isabella sleep with him. He demands that she exchange her maidenhead for the head of her brother (which Angelo will otherwise take), or substitute it for the maidenhead of Juliet (which her brother took). Depending on how one looks at it, the proposed ransom substitutes either maidenhead for head or maidenhead for maidenhead; it makes up for, or measures up to, the punishment and thus makes all even. This transaction is the taliation-through-unchastity that Angelo intends to take place and believes at the end to have taken place.

The Commensuration of the Destruction and Creation of Life

O, were it but my life . . . (3.1.103)

We have seen that the rule against fornication that Angelo prose-
cutes is not an accidental given or a stupidly puritanical, unnecessary
law; it is rather a bulwark of all laws insofar as fornication's telos is incest and the consequent destruction of political authority. What about
the specific penalty for fornication that Angelo pursues? Is it the mere
whim of a man or state?[1]

Angelo justifies taking Claudio's head in exchange for Juliet's maidenhead by adapting the lex talionis to an equation of lechery, or bastardizing, with murder. He argues that the illegal production of life
and the illegal destruction of life are commensurate:

> It were as good   (2.4.42)
> To pardon him that hath from nature stolen
> A man already made, as to remit
> Their saucy sweetness that do coin heaven's image
> In stamps that are forbid. 'Tis all as easy
> Falsely to take away a life true made,
> As to put mettle in restrained means
> To make a false one.

Given this equation between murder (taking a head) and bastardizing
(to all intents, taking a maidenhead), the nature of Claudio's punishment is intimately bound up with the teleology that makes sense of the
series of exchanges—measure for measure—informing the plot. The
identification of murder with bastardy, far from being an accidental
whim, is typical and necessary, a crucial aspect not only of the plot but
also of the world (our world) that the plot concerns.

Angelo's comparison between minting and begetting, or counterfeiting and bastardizing, is crucial to the political economy of Vienna,
where both monetary and sexual commerce involve the "figure" of
political authority. In *Measure for Measure*, the relationships of parent
to children and of sovereign to subjects are combined in the relationship of a sovereign seal (e.g., the one on the Duke's signet ring) to the
ingots or coins that it homogenizes by virtue of its stamp. An un-
minted or unsealed ingot is like "one ungot" (5.1.144), but Claudio's
crime is that he has gotten Juliet with child, a crime equated by both
Angelo and Isabella with the capital offense of counterfeiting coins.[2]
The gist of these associations is that the measure common to all men is
the political seal with which they are impressed; here the father's royal

seal is the common denominator that allows for sexual reproduction as well as commercial exchange without anarchy.

To quote William Fleetwood on kings and coining in his *Sermon Against Clipping* (1694):

For who are so fit as they, who are presum'd to be the Fathers of their People . . . to have this Charge committed to them, that is of such importance, and so universal a concern? The Heads of Princes are . . . stamped . . . publickly to vouch the true intrinsick worth of every piece, and tell Men that they there receive so much silver, and of such a fineness, and that that Image warrants it.[3]

Clipping destroys the currency in much the same way as does counterfeiting and is similarly punishable by execution. Like Robert Filmer, Fleetwood draws the analogy "king is to subject as father is to child," but he also adds "as image is to piece." The analogy encourages us to believe that without the king there would be no public voucher for intrinsic worth. The image of the father—the "phantom" of him, as John Locke puts it—is as necessary to the coinage, at least to the idea of the intrinsic worth of coinage, as it is to the law.[4] A crime against coinage, or a subversion of the official relation between image and piece, has the same anarchic effect as a crime against chastity, since both upset the relationship of father to children or of sovereign to subjects.

These political implications of the association of bastardizing with counterfeiting suggest one way that Angelo's justification for executing Claudio has import for the structure of the play as a whole. Isabella, too, comes to rely on the commensuration of bastardizing with killing to justify her decision not to ransom Claudio. She defends her decision not to redeem a man-to-be-killed with a bastard-to-be by adopting Angelo's position that the destruction of life is commensurable with (and even preferable to) the illegitimate procreation of life: "I had rather my brother to die by the law," she says, "than my son should be unlawfully born" (3.1.188–90). Likewise, when she later takes legal action against Angelo, Isabella relies on his identification of life with death, bastardizing with murder. At the gates of the city she denounces him as an "adulterous thief" (5.1.42)—both as an adulterer (hence bastardizer) and as a killer, or thief, of "a man already made" (2.4.44).

Of greater interest, however, is Isabella's remarkable response to Angelo's statement of the comparison of murder with bastardizing and counterfeiting, that is, of his justification for executing her brother.

She agrees that "'tis set down so in heaven, but not in earth" (2.4.50). In its earthly term, her statement seems a flat contradiction of fact: death for fornication *is* the law as set down on the part of the earth occupied by Vienna.[5] At no point in the play does anyone deny that this is the Viennese law as written or even suggest that the law should be changed. Moreover, in Giraldi Cinthio's *Hecatommithi* (1565), a recognized source of *Measure for Measure*, the earthly punishment for seduction is beheading.[6] In its heavenly term, Isabella's statement has puzzled the critics. Some claim that the New Testament would not be so unkind as to mete out death for fornication; Isabella, they say, must be either making a mistake about the New Testament or referring to certain cruel and unusual punishments in the Old.[7]

Yet Angelo's identification of bastardizing and murder is not set down in the laws of heaven as the Old Testament has them. Moses did not say that a man should die for fornication, only for adultery and for certain kinds of incest (Lev. 20:10–12). In cases of fornication the Old Testament says only that the man should marry the woman— which is what Isabella says when she first hears from Lucio about Juliet's pregnancy (1.4.49). Instead, the identification of fornication with murder (and hence the capital punishment for fornicators) "set down in heaven" is profoundly and perhaps inevitably Christian: it involves the conflation of intent with act, where, as Aquinas suggests, what matters is not the intent of the individual but rather the telos of the act. Aquinas writes that extramarital sexual relations "tend to injure the life of the offspring to be born of this union."[8] Such a tendency to harm life is distinguishable from murder only insofar as "one who is already an actual member of the human species attains to the perfection of the species more than one who is a man potentially."[9] Gregory the Great says similarly that the "deadly sin" of lust (cf. 3.1.110) is a capital vice, or deadly sin.[10] And in much corresponding Christian theology "the same penance is to be enjoined for adultery, fornication, and willful murder."[11] (The Essenes, an ancient religious sect with which Church Fathers associated Jesus and whose doctrines influenced official ecclesiastical jurisprudence, similarly identified the withholding of life with the destruction of it when they claimed that the renunciation of legitimate reproduction is equivalent to murder.)[12]

In agreeing with Angelo that bastardizing is murder and hence should be punished by execution, Isabella, finally, may be conflating all bastardizing with its ultimate, or teleological, consequence of universal incest. She thus recalls one of the rare passages in the New Testament that apparently specifies a particular punishment: Saint Paul's

injunction to his fellow Christians to kill or banish the incestuous Corinthians (1 Cor. 5:5).[13]

The commensuration of the destruction of human life with its creation informs both the language and the action of *Measure for Measure*.
Witness, for example, this exchange:[14]

Provost. Come hither, sirrah. Can you cut off a man's head?   (4.2.1)
Pompey. If the man be a bachelor, sir, I can; but if he be a married man, he's
his wife head; and I can never cut off a woman's head.

In the action, Barnardine the murderer and Claudio the fornicator
await the same capital punishment, and both are pardoned at the
same moment in the action. (Of this pardon, I will say more in Chapter 5.) When he first learns that Claudio has been arrested, Lucio asks,
"What, is't murder?" and then immediately "Lechery?" (1.2.129), as
if the two crimes were one. Likewise, Pompey can make amends
for being "an unlawful bawd" by becoming "a lawful hangman"
(4.2.14–16), the lives he lawfully takes being commensurate with the
lives he unlawfully aided to be got. As the Provost says (4.2.28), he
weighs equally with Abhorson (or "son-of-a-whore"),[15] the abhorrent
executioner.

Under the commensuration of birth and death, by the lex talionis
Claudio must pay his head for Juliet's maidenhead, or his life for the
illegal production of his natural child's life. Or, by the same token, Isabella can ransom him by paying her maidenhead for his head, or the
illegal production of a life (her son) for the redemption, or rebirth
from death, of a life (her brother). In *Measure for Measure*, punishment for producing a life that is illegal and ransom for a life that is
condemned or taken are the principal forms of human barter or exchange. Maidenhead is, in this commercial sense of measuring "being
born" (produced) with "being born again" (redeemed), the equal of a
man's head.

The Ransom as "a Kind of Incest"

Isabella's rejection of Claudio's plea that she yield Angelo her maidenhead in exchange for his head is the dramatic crux, or central dilemma, of *Measure for Measure*. It is a major difference between Shakespeare's play and his sources for the ransom plot (in which the maiden
usually gives in to the wicked magistrate), and it marks the end of the
first part of the play (in which it seems that Claudio must die, as in a
sad melodrama or tragedy) and the beginning of the second part (in
which the Duke oversees a comic kind of resolution).[16]

Isabella's rejection takes the form of a rhetorical question:

> Is't not a kind of incest, to take life   (3.1.138)
> From thine own sister's shame?

Many readers and critics have attempted to ignore Isabella's poten-tially discomforting question about "a kind of incest." Some call her words senseless and "hysterical" as though Shakespeare's words here had no meaning and hysterical words were not in some fashion sig-nificant.[17] Others, in much the same way, remain blind to the potential significance of the fact that Isabella pleads before Angelo both as a sister and as a Sister-in-training.[18] A few students of the play have noted in passing that Isabella's "kind of incest" might constitute some-how the central element in the structure of *Measure for Measure* as a whole.[19]

The question in itself, however, is not meant to be answered by the person to whom it is addressed, and indeed it is not answered. Clau-dio does not admit that taking life from his sister's shameful inter-course with Angelo would constitute "a kind of incest" any more or less than he says that it would not. (At this point in the play, in fact, Isabella will not let Claudio say anything at all [3.1.146–51], and the two say nothing more to each other for the duration of the play.) Yet Isabella's question, by virtue of the word "kind," or *genus*, virtually compels the reader or spectator to admit that such intercourse would be, if not literal incest exactly, then incest of some kind or another.[20] Exactly what kind of incest it would be, or is, is a key issue in the play.

Essentially, the ransom proposed to Isabella could be considered in-cest in four distinct ways:

1. The antonomasia, or conceptually epitomizing epithet, of all sex-ual acts is incest.

2. As Jonas of Orleans says, "all illicit sexual acts are incestuous,"[21] either because incest is the general telos of all fornication or bastardiz-ing or because when a condition of more or less universal illegitimacy has been realized (as it has been in Vienna; significantly, just after Isa-bella accuses Claudio of wanting her to commit "a kind of incest," she calls him a bastard), each and every sexual act risks incest.

3. A sexual act committed for the sake of someone is, to all intents, a sexual act committed with that person, so that for Isabella illicit sexual intercourse with Angelo amounts to incestuous sexual intercourse with her brother Claudio.

4. From Isabella's particular sexual intercourse with Angelo, Clau-dio would take life (that is, he would be born again) as though Claudio were Isabella's son as well as her brother.

Incest as the Antonomasia of Unchastity

Some readers of *Measure for Measure* note the problem of the connection between chastity and unchastity in the play but define that problem only in terms of the question whether the chastity to which Isabella appeals is a physical condition or a spiritual one—hence whether Isabella, in choosing chastity over unchastity, is blameworthy or praiseworthy.[22] Generally they do not consider that merely physical chastity, though perhaps blameworthy from a strictly Christian perspective, is essential to the political order, since the social telos of unchastity is universal bastardy, incest, and the destruction of the body politic. J. W. Lever, for example, has suggested that, in choosing not to sleep with Angelo, Isabella substitutes a pagan code of honor for a Christian one: "Chastity was essentially a condition of the spirit; to see it in merely physical terms was to reduce the concept to a mere pagan scruple."[23] Yet the "mere pagan scruple" of physical chastity is a necessary component of the political order in the states of Christendom. Isabella seems to be given the option of saving the individual body of her brother, but only at the expense of destroying, to all intents, the body politic.

The position that Isabella refuses to yield because she sees chastity "in merely physical terms" not only fails to give physical chastity its political due; it also fails to take into account what chastity as "a condition of the spirit" means within the logic of the plot of *Measure for Measure*. In that logic, incest is the antonomasia of unchastity.

One can arrive at this position either by noting that, since Isabella is a Sister to all mankind, for her any sexual relations would be incest or by pointing out the ambiguities of kinship, which can make it difficult or impossible to determine where to draw the line in calling a sexual act incest—that is, "intercourse between a man and a woman related by consanguinity or affinity."[24] What degree of blood kinship should constitute a diriment impediment to marriage?[25] Should sociological kinship? Intense spiritual affinity? The play amply hints at such ambiguities—for example, in the possible cousinship between Juliet and Claudio or in the overtones of a father confessor's intercourse with his penitent daughter in the Friar-Duke's manipulations of Isabella and Mariana. (The first was considered "legal incest" and the second "spiritual incest" by the Church Fathers.) But for any Christian, especially for any member of the monachal orders, such kinship concerns are arguably unimportant, since for the Christian all men are brothers— and hence all sex incest. This is not only because we are all, to some degree, physically consanguineous (children of Adam) but principally because the essentially Christian monachistic rejection of consanguinity as a criterion makes us all equally siblings, equally affined.

To this extreme conclusion—that all physical intercourse is incestuous—the Church itself is drawn. Aquinas argues that incest is an "antonomasia" for unchastity—that is, incest is not merely a determinate species of lust but lust in general. (See above, p. 45.) All sex acts happen, says Aquinas, because individual men and women are tempted by proximity or liking. In the family, one is more tempted than elsewhere because one is closer physically to those in one's own household and because it is natural (as Aquinas makes Aristotle say) that there be an excessive ardor between a man and a woman of the same kindred.[26] He therefore concludes: "Unlawful intercourse between persons related to one another would be most prejudicial to chastity, both on account of the opportunities it affords and because of the excessive ardor of love."[27] In Aquinas's view, sexual desire between people who are connected by the proximity that the consanguineous family affords does not differ in kind from sexual desire between people who are separated by the distance between families that the consanguineous family assumes. All sexual desire as such is essentially incestuous.

This argument for lust by proximity and ardor by kinship is extended to the position (as awesome in the medieval as in the modern, Freudian context) that incest is the ontogenetically original, hence the fundamental, or primal, form of sexuality. Fornication, adultery, and perhaps even marriage are, so to speak, moderate forms of incest. "Incest," writes Aquinas, "is not a species of lust, but is lust itself in general." It is but a step from this position to Freud's argument that civilization is born with the repression or sacrifice of sexuality, whose primal form is incest, a sacrifice for which no adequate compensation can be made. In the words of Stephen Reid, from a psychoanalytic discussion of *Measure for Measure*:

If the process of civilization has determined that sexuality must abandon the satisfaction of some of its component instincts and its original, incestuous object, society must compensate for this deprivation, or face the unjustified resentment of frustration. Hostility toward civilization, which Freud explores in *Civilization and Its Discontents*, is largely derived from this institutional deprivation.[28]

For this politically essential deprivation of physical incest, the Church might argue that spiritual incest would compensate. Others might hold that it is compensated in physical marriage. Whether marriage can ever be chaste—that is, essentially nonincestuous—will be discussed in chapter 6.

Incest and the Commensuration of Kinship Roles in Exchange

Wilt thou be made a man out of my vice?   (3.1.137)

We have seen that Isabella's appeal to chastity as the grounds for refusing to yield her maidenhead in exchange for Claudio's head—"More than our brother is our chastity" (2.4.184)—is linked with the notion that incest is the telos as well as the antonomasia of unchastity. Equally important for understanding both Isabella's charge that Claudio wants her to commit "a kind of incest" and the eventual salvation of Claudio precisely by "a kind of incest" is the sense in which for Isabella sexual intercourse with Angelo would constitute a mediated kind of brother-sister incest, father-daughter incest, or both.

The Exchange as Brother-Sister Incest.   One of the recognized analogues or sources for *Measure for Measure* is the story of a sexual ransom in Augustine's treatise *Concerning the Lord's Sermon on the Mount.*[29] This story glosses the New Testament passage "The wife hath not power of her own body, but the husband" (1 Cor. 7 : 4). In the story, an imprisoned man is condemned to die unless his wife sleeps with a rich man, who has promised to give her money to bribe a corrupt magistrate. The wife seeks and receives permission from her husband to sleep with the rich man. Then, as Augustine tells it, "the woman went to the mansion of the rich man, and did what the lecher wished; but she gave her body only to her husband, who was asking not, as at other times, to lie with her but to live."[30] Augustine passes no judgment on either the husband or the wife.[31] Shakespeare's version is more troubling, however, because (following Whetstone's *Historie* and Cinthio's *Heccatommithi*) the couple are brother and sister, so that the equation of the person for whom an act is done and the person with whom it is done results in sibling incest rather than marriage. Unlike a husband, a brother is never lawfully allowed the power to use his sister's body.

Yet a similar gift of a sister's body on behalf of her brother is the explicit crux of Thomas Heywood's *A Woman Killed with Kindness*, first produced in 1603, a year before *Measure for Measure.*[32] In this play Sir Charles asks his sister Susan to yield up her body to the rich Sir Francis Acton in return for Acton's having paid the brother's debts and hence having released him from prison. For the brother, repaying his benefactor with the only thing he "has"—his sister—is more important than civilized life, or life itself:

> *Sir Charles.* Call me not brother, but imagine me
>   Some barbarous outlaw or uncivil kern,

> For if thou shut'st thy eye and only hear'st
> The words that I shall utter, thou shalt judge me
> Some staring ruffin,* not thy brother Charles.
>
> .   .   .
>
> Dost love me, sister? Wouldst thou see me live
> A bankrupt beggar in the world's disgrace
> And die indebted to my enemies?
> *Susan.*   . . . knew I the means
> To buy you from the slavery of your debts,
> Especially from Acton, whom I hate,
> I would redeem it with my life or blood.
> *Sir Charles.* I challenge it, and kindred set apart
> Thus ruffian-like I lay siege to your heart.

The brother asks his sister to sleep with Acton ("Grant him your bed")
and thus repay Acton for saving him:

> With that rich jewel you my debts may pay.
> In speaking this my cold heart shakes with shame,
> Nor do I woo you in a brother's name,
> But in a stranger's.[33]

As a stranger, no longer a brother, Charles has no less right to use his
sister's body than any other man. Susan eventually consents to save his
honor and sleeps with Acton, then kills herself. She offers her life as
well as her chastity to her brother.

The following decades see a cluster of plays that involve sibling incest, often similarly mediated. In Webster's *The Devil's Law Case* (1623),
one of the most involuted, Romelio asks his sister Jolenta to pretend to
be pregnant with a child he has begotten upon the nun Sister Angiolella. The reason for his request, he says, is that he wants his illegitimate child, as the supposedly legitimate child of Jolenta and her suitor
Ercole, to inherit the property of two men, Contarino and Ercole,
which Jolenta claims under marriage agreements. (Contarino, her
previous suitor, apparently has died.) Romelio thus wishes to use his
sister's body (not to mention her husbands' goods) in a way that be-
longs, according to the Christian tradition, only to a husband.[34]

Jolenta responds to Romelio's suggestion with a deception, saying
that she cannot pretend to carry Romelio's child because she is already
pregnant with her own, by Contarino. At this point Romelio suggests
that Jolenta pretend to give birth to twins. She relents in deceiving

---

*"Ruffin," or "ruffian," means "pander" in Elizabethan idiom.

Romelio only when Romelio tells her that their mother, Leonora, was planning an affair with Jolenta's supposedly dead suitor, Contarino. To her brother Jolenta then says, "I will mother this child for you"; she is reported to say later that "the shame she goes withal was begot by her brother." [35]

Within the structure of the play, the phantom child Jolenta pretends to her brother that she carries in her womb and the actual child that Angiolella the Sister carries are not only twins but one and the same. Indeed, the sister and the Sister, the twins' mothers—or, if you wish, their mother—are further identified; they were "playfellows together, little children," [36] just as in *Measure for Measure* Juliet is Isabella's friendly "cousin." This limited interchangeability of Sister for sister motivates the plot of *The Devil's Law Case*. [37]

Even more than *Measure for Measure*, *The Devil's Law Case* ends in a series of marital couplings in which everyone is a sibling, a Sibling, or both, so that all the marriages smack of physical incest, spiritual incest, or both. Jolenta by now has joined a Sisterhood but marries Ercole, who as a Knight Hospitaler is bound like her by a vow of chastity; Romelio marries Angiolella; and Leonora, also become a Sister, marries Contarino, retrieved from the Brotherhood (that of a "Bathanite") in which he has all the time been secreted. (Romelio's and Contarino's "bloods embrace," like blood brothers, in the course of the play.) [38] Thus *The Devil's Law Case* concerns not only the coupling of brothers and sisters but also the marrying of Brothers and Sisters.

But the devil's law case in the play more profoundly echoes the themes of *Measure for Measure*—it concerns the unascertainability of consanguineous paternity. The case involves Leonora's comedically unsuccessful attempt to prove that Romelio (the only partner in the final couplings who has not become a Sibling) is not his father's son, so that she can avenge herself for his responsibility in Contarino's supposed death.

A more direct questioning of ideas about kinship appears in *A King and No King*, by Beaumont and Fletcher (1611). In its plot, the counterparts to *Measure for Measure*'s magistrate Angelo and brother Claudio (who, in terms of the sexual ransom, are for the novice Sister Isabella to all intents and purposes one and the same) are combined in a single person: the magistrate-brother Arbaces. He imprisons Panthea, whom he believes to be his sister, and then promises to release her from prison on the condition that she sleep with him:

> If thou dars't consent to this
> . . . thou mayst gain
> Thy liberty and yield me a content. [39]

As he tries to convince Panthea that their supposed kinship should not affect their sexual relationship, Arbaces puts the status of kinship terms, and in consequence kinship relations, into question. "Where / Have those words dwelling?" he asks. Proleptically echoing Freud, he argues that in forbidding incest the cost of civilized custom is too great:

> Accursed man,
> Thou bought'st thy reason at too dear a rate,
> For thou hast all thy actions bounded in
> With curious rules when every beast is free.
> What is there that acknowledges a kindred
> But wretched man? Whoever saw the bull
> Fearfully leave the heifer that he lik'd
> Because they had one dam?[40]

The play's comedic plot seems to bear Arbaces out: it finally reveals that the apparent siblings are not akin and thus transforms an apparently incestuous love into a chaste marriage.

The literal, or unmediated, wooing of actual siblings is unknown on the English stage before John Ford's *'Tis Pity She's a Whore* (1628). In lines reminiscent of Arbaces' complaint about civilized custom, Giovanni, sick with love of his sister, tells a Friar that his happiness—his very life—requires that he sleep with her:

> Shall a peevish sound,
> A customary form, from man to man,
> Of brother and sister, be a bar
> 'Twixt my perpetual happiness and me?[41]

Giovanni seeks an unmediated form of the bargain Claudio asks of Isabella: a brother's life in exchange for incest with that brother.* The mediated wooing in *Measure for Measure*—its mediation epitomized in Isabella's word "kind"—revolves around a similar commensuration of incest and dying.

The Exchange as Father-Daughter Incest. Isabella claims that Claudio wants "to take life / From thine own sister's shame" (3.1.138–39) just as a son takes life from his mother and is delivered from his mother's

---

*Marguerite of Navarre, in the *Heptameron* (3d day, tale 22), tells the story of a prior who tries to convince a nun to sleep with him (i.e., to commit "spiritual incest") so that he, her Brother, might not die. His argument weighs spiritual incest against fratricide: "I have a malady which all the physicians deem incurable, unless I delight myself with a woman I passionately love. I would not for my life commit a mortal sin; but even if it should come to that, I know that simple fornication is not to be compared to the sin of homicide. So, if you love my life, you will hinder me from dying, and save your own conscience."

womb. For Isabella to give birth to her brother, she must have had incestuous intercourse with his father, who is presumably her own as well. Sleeping with Angelo would thus amount to sleeping with her father. P. R. Vessie perceptively suggests of Isabella that "in an incestuous rebirth of her brother . . . she recognizes herself as playing an immoral role of her mother with Angelo."[42] As we have seen, though, Angelo in this context merely substitutes for Vincentio. "Be thou at full ourself," the Duke has said (1.1.43). He is the principal father figure in the play, who stands in for the natural father of Claudio and Isabella, the Pope of religious Brothers and Sisters, and the royal patriarch of all the Viennese.

Claudio's request that Isabella sleep with Angelo thus would involve her simultaneously in incest with both brother and father. Out of brother and father conflated in one sexual mate, figured in Angelo, Isabella would give (re)birth to her brother as to a son. As her brother is conflated with that son, so her father, conflated with her brother in the sexual act of the brother's conception, would also be conflated with her son, father and son thus becoming one in an outrageous imitation of the Christian union of Father and Son.[43] Libertine orders such as the Brethren of the Free Spirit emphasized the essential spiritual precondition for making such a union guiltlessly possible: "The spirit of the Free Spirit is attained when one is wholly transformed into God. . . . One can be, according to one's wish, Father or Son."[44]

Two English Monarchs Simultaneously Incestuous and Virginal

Isabella's fears of incest suggest how Shakespeare's treatment of the conflict between sovereign authority and liberty (*pater* and *liber*) may be interpreted in the specific context of Elizabethan political and religious history. Not only had virginity been made a topic of political importance, but slanderous accusations were rife about brother-sister and father-daughter incest in the families of the late Queen Elizabeth (who died childless in 1603) and the new King James.

Queen Elizabeth and Shakespeare's Isabella. "Isabella" is the translational equivalent of "Elizabeth" (both mean "consecrated to God") and Isabella's expressed fears about her family history echo those Queen Elizabeth must have had. One cannot make an airtight case for Isabella's being modeled on Queen Elizabeth; were that possible on the basis of what is said in *Measure for Measure*, Shakespeare might have been open to charges of treason.[45] (He might have been hung for slander, as Lucio is supposed to be.) But the "kind of incest" of which

Isabella accuses Claudio was not remote from people's minds in the Elizabethan era. Indeed, it was on Elizabeth's own mind at the sexually novice age of eleven and was reflected in her translation *The Glasse of the Synnefull Soule*, written in 1544.[46]

In 1544 the eleven-year-old Princess Elizabeth was under the care of her fourth stepmother, Catherine Parr. Her natural mother, Anne Boleyn, had been executed; her first stepmother, Jane Seymour, had died in giving birth to her half brother (later Edward VI); her second stepmother, Anne of Cleves, had died; and her third stepmother, Catherine Howard, had been beheaded. Anne Boleyn had risen to be queen after Henry VIII's first wife, Catherine of Aragon, was charged with incest (Catherine had been Henry's sister-in-law), and Anne had fallen when Henry accused her in turn of incest with her brother Lord Rochford.* (Others charged that Anne was herself Henry's illegitimate daughter, which would make her guilty of both the kinds of incest discussed in the previous section.)[47]

Just as Isabella in *Measure for Measure* may fear that her brother (and by extension she herself) is not legitimate, so Princess Elizabeth must have wondered about her legitimacy. (In fact, Henry VIII himself declared her illegitimate.)[48] First, the union between Catherine of Aragon and Henry VIII may not legally have been incestuous.[49] In Shakespeare's *Henry VIII*, which touches on this question, Henry is made to fear that the union was incestuous (H8 3.2.16–28), yet in the same play the common people are sympathetic to Catherine's argument that her marriage was legitimate, hence to the position that Elizabeth is a bastard (H8 4.1). Second, Elizabeth may have been conceived before marriage. Henry VIII and Anne Boleyn were married in January 1533, and Elizabeth was born in September of that year—a suggestive nine months later.[50] Moreover, the marriage was a secret one—much like Claudio's "fast" marriage to Juliet (or Romeo's to Juliet, for that matter)—and thus subject to challenge. (The analogy goes beyond *Romeo and Juliet* to Shakespeare's own marriage.) Finally, Thomas Cranmer, the Archbishop of Canterbury, declared Elizabeth illegitimate on yet other grounds. He argued that Henry's liaison with Anne was incestuous insofar as Henry had already had an affair with Anne's sister, Mary Carey, née Boleyn. (In England marriage to a former mistress's sister was defined as incest. In 1536 an Act of Parliament concerned with defining the degrees of consanguinity and af-

---

*Henry VIII's charge against Anne Boleyn was virtually reenacted when the aged Queen Elizabeth fell in love with the young Essex, whose maternal great-grandmother was Mary Boleyn, sister of Anne and onetime mistress of Henry (Duff, "Die Beziehung Elizabeth-Essex," p. 469).

finity that make for a diriment impediment to marriage ordered every man who had married his mistress's sister to separate from his wife and forbade all marriages with mistresses' sisters in the future.) Since Elizabeth was the product of an incestuous union, thought Cranmer, she must be illegitimate.[51]

In *Henry VIII* Shakespeare seems to go to great lengths to allay anxiety about the legitimacy of Elizabeth's birth (see esp. 2.4.165–233). Yet toward the end of the play the Porter suggests that Anne Bullen, who had been Henry's mistress (like her sister Mary before her), was a fornicatrix, so that the Princess Elizabeth may be a bastard (as she would be from a Catholic viewpoint). When the Porter cries out, "What a fry of fornication is at door!" (H8 5.3.34–35),[52] he refers in part to the crowd of common people, but the smallest "fry" in the play is, of course, Elizabeth herself. The last scene of *Henry VIII* shows the Duchess of Norfolk and the Marchioness Dorset, the baby princess's two godmothers, substituting for her biological mother, the absent Queen Anne Bullen, who is barely mentioned (H8 5.4.4); it also shows Henry VIII, presumably the princess's biological father, asking her godfather, Cranmer, "What is her name?" (H8 5.4.9). It is as though Elizabeth's verifiable gossipred had replaced her questionable consanguineous kindred.

The problem of incest in the play comes to infect even gossipred, however. The Porter explains that "this one christening will beget a thousand, here will be father, godfather, and all together" (H8 5.3.36–37). The question of Elizabeth's incestuous origin is replaced by a good-humored conflation of blood parentage with godparentage, or of consanguineous kin with godsibs—"all together." The Church forbids a father to play the role of a godfather,[53] however, so that the Porter's words again suggest the incestuous aspect of Elizabeth's birth, besides hinting, at her future role as virgin queen, a secular counterpart to that Virgin the Father of whose Son was not only his godfather but also God the Father.[54]

The real princess Elizabeth did not reject her purportedly incestuous mother, and she adopted as her own the badge of Anne Boleyn, with its significant inscription "Semper Eadem" (always the same). The interest in chastity of the queen-to-be-virgin—foreseen by Cranmer in *Henry VIII*, who predicts, at her birth, that she will die "yet a virgin, / A most unspotted lily" (H8 5.4.60–61)—is evident in her youthful writings. But also evident in Elizabeth's choice of a work to translate is an attraction to incest as the obverse of chastity.

In her introduction to her translation of Marguerite's *Miroir de l'ame pecheresse* (literally, *Mirror of the Sinful Soul*), Elizabeth hints that her

"Semper Eadem." The badge of Anne Boleyn, which Elizabeth adopted while a princess and retained after becoming queen. (Elizabeth, *Mirror*, ed. Ames, frontispiece.)

work concerns incest of a spiritual kind. She describes how the authoress, beholding and contemplating what she is, "doth perceyve how, of herselfe, and of her owne strength, she can do nothing that good is, or prevayleth for her salvacion; onles it be through the grace of god: whose mother, daughter, syster, and wife, by ye scriptures, she proveth herselfe to be."[55] Yet the adolescent Elizabeth's *Glasse* depicts a young woman in the throes of illicit passion trying to move that passion, like a nun or a spiritual libertine, from the physical to the spiritual level.[56] The woman is "bound by her concupiscence," having a body "redy and prompt to do all yvell" and subject to "my enemy, my sensuality (I beying in my beastely slepe)."[57] The tormented woman is drawn to seek, not physical incest like the mother-son incest depicted in the "Tale of Incest" in Margaret's *Heptameron* (in which an unwittingly incestuous couple is described as having "loved each other so much that never were there husband and wife more loving, nor yet more resembling each other; for she was his daughter, his sister, and his wife, while he was her father, her brother, and her husband") or like the brother-sister incest that Margaret spiritualizes in her greatest poetry,[58] but spiritual incest with God. The entire poem on the purification of the sinful soul revolves around the apparent riddle that both a spiritual libertine and a traditional nun, in imitation of the Virgin Mary, make of God a father, husband, brother, and son.[59]

John Bale, the influential Protestant reformer, possibly troubled that his purportedly illegitimate tutee Elizabeth should have chosen to translate an apparently libertine work of the French Spiritualists, translated the French title as *A Godley Medytacion of the Christen Sowle* and insisted, in his Epistle Dedicatory and Conclusion (which frame the *Meditation* as it was first published), that the standard of consanguinity as the measure of noble kinship is transcended properly only by the standard of "true," or spiritual, nobility. He claims it is by "plain" virtue—not by libertine celibacy or virginal incest—that one becomes God's "chylde of adopcyon."[60] Elizabeth, following out a hint in Bale's Epistle Dedicatory, later tried to quiet the slander that she was a bastard by appealing to this doctrine of adoption by God—a doctrine that transcends the distinction between legitimacy and illegitimacy, hence between chastity and unchastity—by making divine virtue, not consanguinity, the essential substance of kinship. Her interpretative translation of Boethius's *Consolation of Philosophy* confirms the doctrine, unusual coming from the pen of a hereditary monarch, that no people are bastards and all are essentially equal siblings.[61]

But it is at the level of incest both spiritualized and secularized that Elizabeth as monarch later established herself as the national virgin queen who was at once the mother and the wife of the English people. In a speech before the Commons she put it thus:

> I have long since made choice of a husband, the kingdom of England. And here is the pledge and emblem of my marriage contract, which I wonder you should so soon have forgot. [She showed them the ring worn at the accession.] I beseech you, gentlemen, charge me not with the want of children, forasmuch as every one of you, and every Englishman besides, are my children and relations.[62]

Elizabeth here secularizes the religious institution of incest; she adjusts a longstanding ideological commonplace (that the Virgin Mary is at once the parent and spouse of God) to the psychological requirements of her girlhood and the political requirements of her monarchal maturity.[63] Marriage for the secular ruler, like marriage for the clergy,[64] is out of the question. For Elizabeth, marriage—that "earthly paradise of happiness"[65]—is possible neither as an earthly wife nor as a paradisiacal nun but only as the royal mother/wife of England.*

In the context of religiously spiritualized incest (as in the *Glasse*) or secularly sublated incest (as in the institution of the virgin queen), Isabella in *Measure for Measure* appears to combine both Anne Boleyn the

---

*Elizabeth was so successful at establishing herself as the English spiritual Mama—in contradistinction to the Romish spiritual Papa—that Pope Sixtus "allowed his mind to dwell on the fantasy of a papal union with the English crown; what a wife she would make for him, he joked, what brilliant children they would have" (Johnson, *Elizabeth*, p. 109).

incestuous fornicatrix and Elizabeth the virgin. If the fear of incest, or of a desire for incest, can help spur a woman to contemplate being consecrated to God (becoming *elishabet*), that fear may have something to do with why Isabella and Elizabeth defy nature's injunction to reproduce.[66]

King James and Shakespeare's Vincentio. The same pattern—a fear of being or becoming wholly unchaste, hence a desire to be wholly chaste—informs the life of King James VI of Scotland, who succeeded Elizabeth as James I of England. The association of James with Vincentio in *Measure for Measure* has been a commonplace of criticism since at least 1799.[67] Scholars argue that the Duke is modeled on James insofar as some of James's actions and doctrines resemble aspects of *Measure for Measure*.[68] Beyond these, James's concern about the fornication and bastardizing of his ancestors and his wish to lay claim to virginity make him a counterpart not only to the monkish Duke Vincentio but also to the novice Isabella and to all persons in the play caught between incest and celibacy.

Just as Princess Elizabeth, the supposedly illegitimate daughter of the adulterous and incestuous Anne Boleyn, made a claim to chastity, so King James—the grandson of the notoriously libertine and bastardizing James V and the son of the purportedly adulterous Mary Queen of Scots—made a claim to chastity.[69] Like Elizabeth, James reacted against his family's past; despite a penchant for boys, he became as famous for (heterosexual) chastity as Elizabeth. Richard Baker writes of James that "of all the Morrall vertues, he was eminent for chastity" and claims that James challenged comparison with Queen Elizabeth in this regard.[70] Beginning in 1603 with his first address to the English Parliament, in his speeches James adopted Elizabeth's mode of reincarnating the Holy Family on earth, claiming that he was both the spouse of England ("I am the Husband, all the whole Isle is my lawfull Wife") and its "loving nourish-father."[71] Moreover, James was sensitive to the charge that he was the bastard son of Mary; appealing to a 1585 Act of Parliament that made slander of the king a treasonable offense, in 1596 James, like Vincentio sentencing the slanderous Lucio, ordered executed a man who called him "ane bastarde."[72]

The pattern of unchastity and (over)compensation in virginity that I have outlined may be summarized as follows: The novice Isabella reflects an internalized tension between the libertinism she fears in her mother and the celibacy she believes to inhere in her Mother Superior and aspires to attain as a Sister. Princess Elizabeth likewise reflects a tension between the libertinism for which her mother was condemned and the celibacy for which she would later become famous.

In the same way, Vincentio in *Measure for Measure* reflects a tension between libertinism (which Lucio's remarks about him and his entering a liberal [fraternal] order suggest) and chaste patriarchy. Finally, King James reflects the tension between the libertinism represented by James V, whose way of life he abhorred, and the mythic virginity to which he aspired.

The pattern echoes a schema in Shakespeare's second Henriade (*Henry IV*, Parts One and Two, and *Henry V*). There King Henry V combines the liberal as well as libertine Prince Hal and the patriarchal Henry IV. Despite the fact that he wishes to be of the people, to be a liberal, Hal comes to learn that as King Henry V he must also be above the people as a visible authority (cf. H5 4.1.85–102). Likewise, in *Measure for Measure* Henry's counterpart, Vincentio, combines in himself the sexual opposites chastity (as father-friar) and unchastity (as one who has refused to execute the law against fornication and perhaps also as the libertine that Lucio makes him out to be).

Atonement and Tragedy

> In *Measure for Measure*, the great scene between Isabella and Claudio so far transcends anything that English, anything that European, drama had had to show for nearly two thousand years, that in this special point of view it remains perhaps the most wonderful in Shakespeare.
>
> George Saintsbury[73]

What informs the scene in which Isabella raises the specter of incest is precisely what informs such great tragedies as *Oedipus the King* and *Antigone*—namely, the tension between political civilization and its natural discontents, between life (by incest) and death (by virginity). Isabella's reference to incest reflects that tension in several interrelated ways. First, her novitiate may be related to a fear that, even as a laywoman, for her any physical sexual union might be incestuous because of the potential for universal consanguinity in Vienna. Second, her decision to join a nunnery means that, as a Sister, for her any sexual union would be incestuous because of the universal affinity or Siblinghood monachism emphasizes. Moreover, not only is incest both the antonomasia of all sex and the telos of all fornication, but the incestuous aspect of Isabella's particular proposed fornication with Angelo is accentuated by the fact that fornication with Angelo is equivalent both to sleeping with her brother and to giving (re)birth to him.

For Isabella, then, the problem of how, if at all, she will enter the Sisterhood, choosing Universal Siblinghood over and above individual sisterhood, is the extended moment of *Measure for Measure*. That problem is further exacerbated when, fearing the kind of incest Claudio proposes, she tells the Friar-Duke that she "had rather my brother die by the law, than my son should be unlawfully born" (3.1.188–90). She regards filial illegitimacy (illegal birth) as commensurate with and better than fratricide (legal execution), concurring with Angelo that fornication is essentially murder. That her logic involves the assumption that a child will be born from sleeping but one time with Angelo should not surprise us, since birth is the telos of the act of sexual intercourse. That she assumes a son, as opposed to a daughter, will be born becomes explicable when we understand that she is thinking about the (re)birth of her brother; as we shall see, she does "kind of" give birth to a child who turns out to be Claudio himself. It is the irony of the play, moreover, that the commercial commensuration, hence interchangeability, of death with birth on which the logic of her decision not to sleep with Angelo relies is significantly akin to the incestuous conflation, hence interchangeability, of brother, son, and father that she would avoid.

5
Taliation, Part Two:
Likeness and Identity

Illustration of *Measure for Measure*, 3.1. (Lang, "'Measure for Measure,'" p. 76.)

Like doth quit like, and Measure still for Measure.
(5.1.409)

THE PLOT of *Measure for Measure* is informed by a series of exchanges, or proposed exchanges, in which things are taken for each other. These exchanges constitute a developmental series that motivates the play from beginning to end, a series that plays out the figurative basis of all transaction—commercial, sexual, and linguistic.

In this second examination of taliation, or "the return of like for like," we shall consider first the common measures of things that are traded (or that pass) for one another—both the commercial measures that can make life equal to death, for example, and the kinship measures that can make father equal to son. Then we shall describe the actual exchanges that take place in *Measure for Measure*, where Claudio is eventually "redeemed" as his own son.

Exchange and Use

Exchange Where the Given and the Taken are One and the Same. If person *A* takes object *X* from person *B*, then, according to the most literal interpretation of the lex talionis, he must return object *X* to person *B*. For example, if a man steals a certain cow, then that is the cow he must return. This is a barter transaction where what is taken (or purchased) is identical to what is given (or sold). Such a transaction is perfect in its symmetry and equation. Such perfection implies a simultaneity of purchase and sale, however, since otherwise the object(s) traded would differ in time, space, or use. Thus this perfect transaction is in some ways impossible. Yet it serves as the model for a second kind of exchange, a model the second kind cannot in any ordinary, literal sense attain.

Exchange Where the Given and the Taken are Two. In the first kind of exchange, there is no need to find a likeness or common measure between the object given and the object taken because they are identical. When what was taken away cannot be given back, however, some sort of commensuration is required. If a thief has taken a head or maidenhead by murder or fornification, for example, then, in the ordinary course of events—where resurrections do not occur and stolen heads or maidenheads cannot be returned—we must either reject the lex talionis or find an appropriate substitute for the lost head or maidenhead. In this case, person A takes object X from person B, but since object X cannot be returned, a substitute for object X is found, object Y, which can pass for it in some figural or fictional sense. The transaction now becomes: person A takes object X from person B, and person B gives object Y (which equals object X) to person B. (If what has been taken is the life of person B, however, then object Y must be given to person C, a person who substitutes for person B or represents person B's family or state.)*

We may think of this second kind of exchange as a monetary transaction because a moneylike intermediary, or measure, between X and Y is required. Much turns on the figurative measure that allows exchange, the likeness—"like doth quit like" (5.1.409)—of the items traded.

In *Measure for Measure*, as we shall see, the items exchanged—given and taken—for one another are generally human beings. They are, at least initially, two different human beings; and what has to be, or is, given in return for what was taken is figured in terms of two moneylike measures, or means of substitution. The first half of *Measure for Measure* (i.e., up to the prison scene between Claudio and Isabella) is informed by an interchangeability of persons based on the commensurability of life and death that we considered in the preceding chapter; the second half of the play is informed by a closely related interchangeability of persons by means of disguise.

In the first half of the play, things have been taken that cannot be given back, and suitable substitutes must be found, ones that will be commensurable with, or pass for, the thing taken. Barnardine, Claudio, and Angelo are all confronted with this situation. Barnardine the murderer, for example, cannot give back the head (life) that he took from another man according to the literal terms of the lex talionis, "life for life"; Claudio the fornicator has illegitimately taken a maidenhead, or, in the legal terms that Isabella and Angelo employ, he has

---

*Where A takes the life of B, not only is A unable to return that life to B, but whatever A does return, say his own life, he cannot return to B but merely to an appropriate representative of B, such as B's family or state. Just who that representative should be is always important in settling cases of taliation of the second kind.

stolen a life from nature;* and Angelo is the would-be thief both of a head (Claudio's) and of a maidenhead (Isabella's). According to the commensuration of life with death discussed in the preceding chapter, it makes sense for Barnardine to pay for the life of his victim with his own life, for Viennese law to substitute Claudio's forever-to-be lost head for Juliet's forever-lost maidenhead, and, in Angelo's proposed ransom, for Isabella's maidenhead to substitute for Claudio's head.

The central prison scene between the brother and the sister expresses the failure of such commensuration to solve the dilemmas at issue in the play. Commensuration fails not because it is absurd (some such commensuration informs most all exchanges) but because Isabella refuses to ransom Claudio's head by yielding her maidenhead to Angelo; more specifically, it fails because this particular commercial exchange, or taliation, of flesh would constitute a conflation of kinship roles that resembles incest. Thus the substitution that might redeem Claudio's life—Isabella's maidenhead as a substitute for Claudio's head, or Isabella's maidenhead as a substitute for the maidenhead Claudio took—will not take place. In the middle of the play it seems that Claudio, who is like most all of us, must die.

But Claudio will not be lost if a substitute can be found for one or another of the items in the trade "Isabella's maidenhead for Claudio's head"—that is, if a maidenhead that somehow measures up to the maidenhead of Isabella or a head that somehow measures up to the head of Claudio can be substituted. Instead of "Isabella's maidenhead for Claudio's head," the exchange might be "Mariana's maidenhead ([somehow passing] for Isabella's) for Claudio's head"—which is the Duke's first plan—or "Ragozine's head ([somehow passing]) for Claudio's head," which is his second.

In the latter part of the play, both these substitutions occur by means of disguise. Disguise, the essential motor of drama, not only provides commensurability but is the visible dramatization of the ultimately fictional or figurative basis of all commensuration informing transactions of the second type (where the given and the taken are two).

In the second kind of exchange, what is given is somehow rationalized as being commensurate with what was taken away. Such figural commensurations that make X the equal of Y, or somehow give X the guise of Y for purposes of the transaction, involve a fiction of identity—that is, involve a principle resembling disguise. The socially necessary fiction upon which these exchanges depend has a central place

---

*So why couldn't he just return it—the infant's life—to nature? To the problems of feticide and infanticide, to which this question leads, we shall return in chapter 6.

in social, legal, and religious thinking because, whether or not we accept a particular rationalization of commensuration, some figurative rationalization must underlie any or all exchange by taliation of the second type.* As the chief element in drama, disguise or its dramaturgy makes possible a sympathetic critique of the notion of identity on which exchange often relies.

The second half of *Measure for Measure* enacts the figural or fictional but necessary ground of the lex talionis—that one thing can be another—through a series of transactions in which one thing passes for another and hence, to all structural intents and purposes of the plot, becomes the other. In the first half of the play, one human being is traded for another by virtue of a conceptual commensurability of life with death; in the second half, this means of taliation is modified so that one human person passes for another by seeming to be the other. Beginning in the middle of the play, X equals Y by virtue of Y being disguised as X. This new equation is neither "an eye for an eye," where the two terms are ontologically identical (as if a man could be given back the eye, i.e., the eyesight, taken from him in the same way he can be given back a cow); nor is it "an eye for an eye" where the two terms are ontologically different but commensurate (as where a man is given the eye, i.e., the blindness, of the man who took his eye). It is rather "an eye for an eye" where one eye, ontologically different from another, counterfeits the other to the point where, to all intents and purposes, they are ontologically identical in the transaction and one passes for the other. In the course of *Measure for Measure*, maidenhead is substituted for maidenhead and head for head in such a way that, for the taliation proposed by Angelo and seconded by Claudio (Isabella's maidenhead for Claudio's head), there is substituted another taliation (Mariana's maidenhead for Claudio's head).

Exchanges by disguise recall the commonplace trickery found in most bed-trick plays. Yet in *Measure for Measure* the dilemma that necessitates this trickery (the *guilt* associated with the inevitable imperfection of, or *Geld* in, the law of taliation in cases of human reproduction and human killing) points toward an ultimate reidentification of the objects given and taken. This reidentification—would it were possible!—informs a third kind of exchange under the lex talionis. According to its terms, what was believed unreturnable turns out to be returnable. It reverts, at a transcendent level, to the first, or original, kind of exchange.

---

*Although taliation is not the only way to justify punishment as retribution, it may be the only way to know just how much punishment should be meted out.

Exchange Where the Given and the Taken Are One (Atoned). In the first way of satisfying the lex talionis, what was taken can be returned; in the second, what was taken cannot be returned, and a substitute must serve instead. The third way of carrying out the lex talionis incorporates and transcends the second way in such a fashion that the first is reached again at a higher level. In such a transaction, what was taken is unreturnable, or is believed to be unreturnable, but then is returned. Person *A* here takes object *X* from person *B*, and then object *X*, though forever lost or believed to be so, is somehow found and returned to person *B*. This reverts to a barter form of transaction, at a higher level.

In *Measure for Measure* such crimes as murder and fornication are made up, if at all, by a dramatic progression from substitution by commensuration (in which the punishment for stealing human lives and virginities is death) to substitution by disguise or likeness, and then from substitution by disguise to a reidentification of the object sold and the object purchased in such a way that they are not merely like each other but are identical to each other. "Both are two but each is one," as in the Platonic formula.[1] By this reidentification the fictional or figurative aspect of the lex talionis, on which our commercial and vital exchanges, and hence our societies, are based, is visibly dramatized or literalized. In other words, in *Measure for Measure* the law of taliation by substitution through commensuration and disguise is carried out, but at the same time it is both "razed" (or erased) and also "raised" up to a higher level where, as in Hegelian sublation and Christian resurrection (or re-membering), what was taken can be given again. This new rule of taliation, or new way of carrying out the old rule, treats unreturnable stolen human lives and virginities as though they were returnable and retreats from a money to a barter economy; it does not destroy but rather fulfills the old law.

That the way from the figural taliation of human lives to their resurrection should involve incest is not surprising. Disguise, dramatizing the legal and politically necessary fiction that typifies all commensuration, essentially allows all human beings to pass alike. One consequence of this is the power of disguise to allow commercial exchanges, as in Vincentio's plans to exchange Mariana's maidenhead for Isabella's and Barnadine's head for Claudio's. Another consequence is its power to allow—to all intents demand—incest, as in a grand carnival: "All masquerades are potentially incestuous."[2] Disguise not only allows Mariana to pass for Isabella and Ragozine to pass for Claudio; it also and essentially allows Claudio to pass for Angelo; that passing is one of the substitutions Isabella has in mind when, in the middle of the play, she suggests that sleeping with Angelo would be incest of a kind. In this sense, disguise informs not only the commercial but also the sexual and incestuous exchanges of *Measure for Measure*. And incest is what makes resurrection of a kind possible within the probable but impossible plot of *Measure for Measure* and so solves the otherwise ineradicable problems of commensuration.

By incest a man such as Claudio can be born again (resurrected) as his own son, so that two different human beings become one, or are (re)identified. In the play resurrection results from a dramatization both of the relation between (sexual) intent and (sexual) act and of the manner, given the incestuous telos of all sexuality, one can become the father of oneself: "Both are two but each is one." The close relationship between commercial taliation and incest—both involve commensuration and substitution—is thus a principal key to understanding the structure and meaning of the play. Without it much of the action in the second half must seem unnecessary, impossible, or ridiculous.[3] With it we can see why Friar Vincentio, faced in the prison with the dilemma that Claudio must die, does not reveal himself as Duke and confront directly either Angelo's commercial mentality (his proposal that Isabella give him her maidenhead for Claudio's head) or Claudio's incestuous mentality (the same proposal reinterpreted by Isabella as "a kind of incest") but instead tries to use those potentially subversive mentalities to his own ends by disguise.

Yet what Vincentio does by disguise is not qualitatively different from what has preceded. The new kind of substitution on which he relies (homogeneity through disguise) is in no absolute wise different from the kind of substitution that informs the proposal of Angelo (whereby Isabella and Claudio are commercially equated) and that of Claudio (whereby Claudio's sister is incestuously equated with his mother or wife and Claudio can be born again as his own son). The hint of this incestuous transcendence, the discomforting but only adequate solution to the essential dilemma of the play, is the intent, or *use* (supplement), of the plot of *Measure for Measure* taken as a whole.

Wergeld and Natural Usury. The monetary role of human beings in *Measure for Measure* as objects given and taken (they are commensurate, hence, interchangeable) should be distinguished from that in several of the play's recognized sources. In the sources the ransom is often money given for a body; in *Measure for Measure* it is a body given for another body. In Thomas Lupton's *Too Good to be True*, for example, the wicked magistrate demands money from the unfortunate woman as a partial ransom for the imprisoned husband, and in Augustine's story the magistrate demands money as the complete ransom.[4] In these sources, human beings are bought and sold for money, as in the institution of wergeld. Shakespeare depicts such buying and selling in the institutions of prostitution and, at least on one level, marriage. Thus Mistress Overdone, Kate Keepdown, and perhaps Mistress Elbow sell their bodies to men; Lucio and the Gentlemen rent women's bodies for money (1.2), and the enlightening Lucio accuses the Duke himself of having similarly connected human bodies with money: "His use was to put a ducat in her clack-dish" (3.2.123–24). (Compare the Duke's identifying animal with monetary use in 1.1.36–40.) In the institution of marriage as reflected in *Measure for Measure*, moreover, one person purchases another for money; the Duke, for example, offers Mariana money with which "to buy you a better husband" (5.1.423). And it is for lack of money that people refuse to buy and be bought in marriage; Angelo, for example, did not marry Mariana because he did not receive her dowry (3.1.215–23), and the sexual propagator Claudio did not marry Juliet because he was awaiting the "propagation of a dower" (1.2.139). The pimp Pompey, like a good structuralist, holds this human commerce to be the necessary state of human affairs: "You will needs buy and sell men and women like beasts" (3.2.1–2).

Thus *Measure for Measure* depicts the purchase and sale of human beings *for* money, which is Pompey's business and the business transacted in several of Shakespeare's sources. The essential aspect of flesh-mongery or the "trade" of lechery (3.1.148) in the play is, however, the use of human beings *as* money. *Measure for Measure* explores the significance not only of paying money for a body but also of using a body as money, for in this play heads and maidenheads are traded as if they were commensurate. Thus Angelo does not ask Isabella to pay money, or *Geld*, to ransom her brother; instead he asks her to yield "the treasures of your body" (2.4.96) for another body somehow commensurate with it. ("To yield" in English is cognate with the German *gelden*, "to pay with money." See 2.4.103, 163, 180; 3.1.97–98.)

The Use of Flesh. Like a "fleshmonger"—which is what Lucio calls him—Vincentio sees fit to make others "exchange flesh" (WT 4.4.281). By this he gains a kind of profitable advantage or use. In that sense *Measure for Measure* is about natural usury, or the "use of flesh," where one gets more than one gives. If one considers monetary usury to be unnatural, then the process of gaining that supplement—a process that is the only possible solution to the dilemma posed in the play—is in the same category as unnatural incest.

At the beginning of *Measure for Measure*, Duke Vincentio suggests that nature regards animal progenitors, including the human kind, as monetary principals and all animal progeny as monetary interest, or "use":

> Spirits are not finely touch'd (1.1.35)
> But to fine issues; nor nature never lends
> The smallest scruple of her excellence
> But, like a thrifty goddess, she determines
> Herself the glory of a creditor,
> Both thanks and use.

The Duke implies that sexual, moral, and monetary reproduction are of the same kind. Interest, the offspring of a monetary principal, is like a human child, the offspring of a human progenitor. Pompey, the pimp or sexual usurer,* makes a similar association of sexual reproduction with monetary usury: "T'was never merry world since, of two usuries, the merriest was put down, and the worser allowed by order of law" (3.2.6–8). Pompey's statement, which insists upon the similarity between sexual and monetary usuries, educates the listener to one or another discomforting position: either (1) to reject Pompey's (and the Duke's) analogy between human and monetary offspring, or (2) to accept the analogy and hence both to regard Angelo's new policy as inherently contradictory and to regard the Duke's age-old tolerance of both kinds of usuries as consistent.

Aristotle rejects the kind of association between sexual and monetary production that both Pompey and the Duke make, attacking the association as a merely philological connection between *tokos* as "natural offspring" and *tokos* as "interest": "Interest increases the amount of money itself (and this is the actual origin of the Greek word *tokos*: offspring resembles parent and interest is born of money); consequently this form of the business of getting wealth is of all forms the most contrary to nature."[5]

Aristotle influenced Church theorists, especially Aquinas, who called moneylending unnatural. During the Reformation in England and elsewhere, the question of whether interest was indeed "contrary to nature" became a major focus of the Protestant controversy about monetary use. Perhaps a contemporary questioning of the Aristotelian position influenced the fact that the Duke and Pompey, like Shylock and unlike Antonio in *The Merchant of Venice*, seem to accept the identification of the two usuries. But this identification leads to the second position stated above: that Angelo's new policy in regard to sexual and monetary usuries is contradictory (he allows one but not the other) and that the Duke's old policy was logically consistent, if

*One of the meanings of "usurer" is "pimp."

strictly speaking illegal (he allowed both). And for total consistency, the Duke's old policy should allow not only sexual and monetary usury but also incest, whose natural (animal) or nonnatural (either human or monstrous) status is as questionable as that of usury.

Moneylending and incest are indeed associated in the Western tradition. On the Greek side, Oedipus's unnatural sexual generation is matched by his tyrannical concern with monetary generation.* On the Judaeo-Christian side are laws that outlaw taking interest from brothers or, insofar as all men are brothers, from everyone. According to the laws of Deuteronomy and Leviticus, a Jew is allowed to lend money at interest not to brothers (Jews) but only to others (non-Jews); hence moneylending depends on knowing who is kin.[6] Knowing who is kin depends in turn on the enforcement of such laws against bastardizing as the one the Duke has overlooked and Angelo tries to execute. In Christianity, however, all people are brothers, so it is equally bad or good to lend at interest to anyone. Such a universalist response outlaws all monetary usury just as it endorses Universal Siblinghood, or incest of the kind that Isabella either flees (in Vienna) or seeks (in the nunnery).

In *Measure for Measure*, Vincentio acknowledges the usefulness of nature and himself becomes a usurer. As "fleshmonger," he uses Mariana's body in place of Isabella's in order to gain "advantage" (4.1.23, cf. 3.1.255), or "use";† he tells Escalus, justifying his presence in Vienna, that his "chance is now / To use it for my time" (3.2.211–12). The difference between him and Pompey as fleshmongers is only the difference between secrecy and openness: Pompey openly calls women "trouts" (1.2.83) and treats them as such; the Duke quite secretly uses them the same.[7]

Disguise as Agent of Commensurability: The Duke's Counterfeits

The lex talionis of "eye for eye," under whose interpretation by Angelo and Isabella as "legal execution for illegitimate procreation" Claudio the fornicator is condemned to die—and under whose ordinary interpretation as "legal execution for illegal killing" Barnadine the murderer is condemned to die—makes a man repay with his own life

---

*I argued in *The Economy of Literature*, chap. 3, that Oedipus the "tyrant" is allied with the rising class of merchants and moneylenders. The "unnatural" incest in his family is a counterpart to the "unnatural" usury practiced by that class.

†In Elizabethan English, "advantage," like "use," connotes "monetary interest." See the conversation between Antonio and Shylock: "Methoughts you said you neither lend nor borrow / Upon advantage." "I do never use it." (MV 1.2.65–66.)

the life he has taken. It demands a form of substitution for the original thing taken: a head for a head "from nature stolen" (2.4.43). For the taliation of "head for head" that the law demands of Claudio (his own head in return for the head he stole), Angelo proposes to Isabella the taliation of "maidenhead for head" (her maidenhead in return for Claudio's head). What makes the commercial, even incestuous, substitutions of human being for human being avoidable in *Measure for Measure* is another kind of substitution, namely, disguise: "So disguise shall by th' disguised / Pay with falsehood false exacting" (3.2.273–74).

Vincentio, merchantlike, tries to manage the exchanges of one person for another and to use them to advantage. His role recalls the merchant disguises of the historical and fictional rulers on whom Shakespeare may have modeled him; his actual guises as Friar and Duke are crucial to this vital commerce, or fleshmongery. As Friar he has the ability to confess Mariana, which allows him to know her contract with Angelo, and as Duke he can overrule Angelo's death sentence on Claudio and arrange for the exchange of Barnardine's head for Claudio's.

The ability to know the invisible heart, like a friar, and to interfere with visible action, like a duke, makes Vincentio a mighty merchant of men. But he is no Platonic philosopher-king or Christian man-god, not even an ideal Holy Roman Emperor. His knowledge of intent fails because he does not know that Angelo will break his bargain with Isabella, and his power to act fails when he cannot arrange a sinless death to save Claudio.

Maidenhead for Maidenhead. In *Measure for Measure* the exchange of maidenhead for maidenhead—like the exchange of head for head—involves the monetary kind of interchangeability. In the brothel that Lucio frequents and the vineyard that Angelo frequents, for example, one maidenhead passes for another just as, in monetary exchange, one coin is as good as another.[8]

What makes Mariana like enough Isabella to become, to all Angelo's intents, Isabella herself is her near-silence and the invisibility conferred by the cloth veil that covers her face and by the veil of night. The rules that Isabella learned in the nunnery were "You must not speak with men / But in the presence of the prioress; / Then, if you speak, you must not show your face" (1.4.10–12). In her conversation with Angelo, Isabella uses both her speech and her face—both her "reason and discourse" and her "speechless dialect," or body language (1.2.173–75). But Isabella seems to teach her convent ways to Mariana: Mariana uses the night to veil her face, and she speaks only a little. This disguise by silence and invisibility utilizes the means by which the hooded Clares would ensure that Sisters not attract men and by which all hooded maidens can pass for one another in much the same way that prostitutes ("nuns" in the Elizabethan idiom) can pass for one another as sexually interchangeable commodities; disguise as such is what allows for sexual substitution.

Head for Head. In *Measure for Measure* two substitutions disguising head for head are arranged: first Barnardine for Claudio, then Ragozine for Barnardine. In the end Ragozine's head passes for Claudio's, and it is a death and likeness unplanned by Vincentio that enables Claudio to live. In the retaliative structure of the play these two substitutions play a crucial role.

When Angelo breaks his promise and Vincentio's plan to substitute maidenhead for maidenhead inside the secret garden of the vineyard fails to free Claudio, Vincentio plans to substitute head for head (Barnardine for Claudio) inside the secret hold of the prison. But two problems present themselves. First, all individuals have unlike heads. Happily, "death's a great disguiser" (4.2.174), and trimming a dead man's beard can homogenize bodies in the same way as veiling a living woman's face.* In death one body passes for another body just as in monetary exchange one coin is as good as another coin of the same denomination. (Thus Aeschylus writes of Mars, the death-dealing god, that he is "the moneychanger of men.")[9] In his first appearance as Friar, the Duke already refers to death as a homogenizer: "Yet death we fear / That makes these odds all even" (3.1.40–41). Claudio is not brought to spiritual atonement by these last words of the Friar-Duke's speech about the art of dying, yet the way death unites men, or makes them one by an extreme version of the Clares' invisibility and silence, is the means that will save Claudio's physical being.[10]

But a second difficulty in arranging the exchange of Barnardine for Claudio, one with disturbing political implications, presents itself. Vincentio must convince the Provost to disobey Angelo, and he is almost forced to reveal himself as Duke when he shows the reluctant Provost the ducal seal ring. (Shakespeare makes the power of the invisible Duke appear through the visible Friar, a trick that Plato's tyrannical Gyges, who used his magic ring to become invisible and hence to act unseen, would have appreciated.)[11] The ducal seal ring helps prove

---

*The fact that in *Measure for Measure* taking hair off the dead Ragozine and putting on the veil serve the same purpose echoes other connections between hair and social death. In many Catholic orders the ceremony of becoming a nun includes shaving the head. First the novice dies to the world. While she lies as if dead, her hair is removed; only then is she ready to put on the veil and marry God as Christ. Compare Leach and Malinowski on the shaving of widows' heads as a sign of social death in the Trobriand Islands (Leach, "Magical Hair").

to the Provost that Angelo, as a mere substitute, is a counterfeit who bears ill the ducal figure (compare 4.2.183 and 1.1.16), so that his orders can be countermanded. (Seal rings were the original stamps for coins.)[12] In this way Friar Vincentio, like the liberal and libertine Lucio, brings into question the political authority of Angelo at a time when Angelo is the only visible secular authority. (And men, not being angels, need visible authority.) The ducal seal ring can "pluck all fears out" (4.2.190); it gives Vincentio the same kind of access to the prison that the "pick-lock" gives Pompey, prime agent of liberty, to the whorehouse (3.2.16) and Angelo's keys give Isabella to the vineyard and garden (4.1.30–33).

The Provost thus agrees to substitute Barnardine's head for Claudio's. On one level, this seems well and good. Vincentio's playing simultaneously the roles of religious Friar and secular Duke seems to give him the knowledge and ability to rule and act well. (Just such a combination of secular and religious power was the ideal solution to the problem of bad government offered by the ideology of the Holy Roman Empire, whose seat was Vienna.)[13] Yet the comic aspect of the play begins to falter as the illusion that a religious Friar can accomplish what needs to be done disappears,[14] to be replaced by a new questioning of secular authority.[15] Just as there is an authority above Angelo, might there not be an authority above the Duke? A king? Human sympathy of the kind the Provost feels for Claudio? And comedy distinctively does falter when Friar Vincentio contends that Barnardine, whose demise his new plan to save Claudio requires, is "unmeet for death" (4.3.66).

By this contention, Friar Vincentio extends his challenge of Angelo's particular secular authority to all secular authority, including his own as Duke Vincentio. This is not merely because Duke Vincentio is bad, that is, is like Angelo (which may or may not be so), although that would be problematic enough. It is because secular authority, which heeds only acts, must hold the position that there are both legal and illegal killings (the state's execution of Barnardine, say, versus Barnardine's murder of his victim), whereas religious authority may hold the position that some so-called legal killings (e.g., the planned execution of Barnardine) are damnable and may even imply that all legal killings are damnable, since God is the only one who can punish outlaws without himself committing a sin. What man can cast the first stone?[16] As usual in this play, the problem is put in its most extreme, not to say schizophrenic, form. Vincentio's political authority as Duke—symbolized by the seal ring he used to countermand Angelo's command—

now turns out to be useless, if not devilish. Without the seal ring or with it, both Friar and Duke are helpless to counter Angelo.

Nature, which eventually takes every man's life (1.1.36–40), redeems the situation. It provides for the death by "cruel fever" (4.3.69) of the pirate Ragozine, "a man of Claudio's years; his beard and head / Just of his colour" (4.3.71–72). Ragozine, who is "more like to Claudio" than Barnardine (4.3.75), provides the body that the Duke requires.

Friar Vincentio calls this death "an accident that heaven provides" (4.3.76), a *deus ex machina*. The end of dramatic art, however, is not chance pleasure.[17] It is fitting, even essential to the internal logic of the plot machinery that a pirate should provide the head, the *caput in machina*, that enables the series of bodily substitutions to proceed without political authority's abusing religious authority—that is, without killing Barnardine. It is fitting because a pirate is a thief, a suprapolitical thief who operates on the "high seas" beyond the boundaries of individual states; moreover, he is an extralegal thief because he falls under the jurisdiction of no single nation. (In this he is like the partly divine Jesus, who would be partly above the law he says he came to fulfill.)*

Ragozine's suprapolitical thieving is the common denominator between murder and bastardizing, the offenses of the two condemned prisoners for whose two heads he provides the one substitute. Just as Ragozine stole by water, so Barnardine stole a man already made and Claudio stole a man as yet unmade. (In *Measure for Measure* the conception of theft may include Angelo's and Isabella's celibacy as well as Barnardine's murder and Claudio's fornication, for celibates do not pay to nature the "use," or children, that they owe.) Yet *Measure for Measure* moves beyond the solution—universal duplicity in exchange—represented by the role of Ragozine's head and toward that expressed in Lucio's tale of the "sanctimonious pirate," who:

> went to sea with the Ten Commandments, but   (1.2.8)
> scrap'd one out of the table.
> *2 Gentleman.* "Thou shalt not steal"?
> *Lucio.* Ay, that he raz'd.

*The archetypal taker in Shakespeare's Vienna is a pirate but the real Vienna has no seacoast. Why? That Vienna has no seacoast might encourage us to wonder whether there really is such a place as the high seas—a place that, because we conceive it as being outside the law (either above the law or the grounds of the law), helps us to define and understand the law. Compare the similarly idealist seacoast of Shakespeare's Bohemia in *The Winter's Tale*—a coastline of a landlocked state that provides the utopean spot where the infant Perdita is both lost and found.

Measure for Measure razes the commandment against thieving (taking without giving) not by enjoining men to commit theft but by raising or transforming the commandment against theft into a call for pardon, for giving without taking or expecting to take.

The Pardon of Angelo

Angelo as judge, believing his discovered intentions to have been actions, passes the death sentence on himself (5.1.371–72, cf. 5.1.168–69 and 2.1.30–31), demanding, like the Duke, "an Angelo for Claudio" (5.1.407). In his version of the story, Martin Luther justifies such a sentence with the remark that the two items stolen—the head of the man and the maidenhead of the woman—cannot be returned.[18] *Measure for Measure* takes this Lutheran view into account through the Duke's sentence on Angelo, but the play supersedes it by a significant disassociation of intent and act. In *All's Well That Ends Well*, the chaste Diana says the purported crimes of Bertram—also fornication and breach of promise—are extralegal: "He's guilty, and he is not guilty" (AWW 5.3.289). *Measure for Measure* adapts this approach to Angelo's similar crimes.

The UnSisterly Separation of Intent from Act. The lustful Angelo intended to fornicate with Isabella. The substitution of Mariana for Isabella, however, kept his intended act at the level of intention. Isabella's show of mercy to Angelo as fornicator depends upon this distinction of lust from fornication, or intent from act:

> For Angelo, (5.1. 448)
> His act did not o'ertake his bad intent,
> And must be buried but as an intent
> That perish'd by the way. Thoughts are no subjects;
> Intents, but merely thoughts.

Isabella's explanation of her pardon of Angelo is usually either condemned as sophistic or praised as genuinely Christian,[19] but it is neither: it is a variation of Angelo's secular position that being tempted to do an act (here confused with attempting to do it) and actually doing it are absolutely distinct (2.1.17–18). Her rationale contradicts Jesus' principle that intent is act, or that lust is fornication. (Were Jesus to pardon Angelo, he would do so, not because Angelo failed to act out his intentions, but because no man—not even the partially human Jesus—can properly cast a stone against a sinner.) This secular rationale shows that the familiar sister is no longer a Christian Sister-in-training; she has become instead a spokeswoman for Protestant secular authority and its separation of act from intent.*

Yet at least one astute critic of *Measure for Measure,* Samuel Taylor Coleridge, is less concerned with enactment than with intention. Coleridge argues that the pardon "and marriage of Angelo . . . baffles the strong indignant claims of justice—(for cruelty with lust and damnable baseness, can not be forgiven, because we cannot conceive them as being morally repented of)."[20] Angelo, implies Coleridge, remains guilty of cruelty and lust (deadly sins associated with intention) whether or not he is innocent of actual murder and fornication. Angelo does not repent lovingly of his intents; fearful, he is merely ashamed of his actions as discovered by the patriarchal Duke. His unloving attitude indicates a general human weakness: Angelo cannot master himself and, in order to behave well, requires the presence of a masterful, external authority figure. So that such a secular authority figure can be restored, Vincentio willy-nilly removes his Friar's hood, or rather has it removed against his will. As an affirmation of secular authority, the Duke's becoming publicly visible in this scene of pardon thus matches Isabella's publication of the separation of intent from act.

"*Death for Death.*" For Isabella, forgiving Angelo's taking Claudio's head proves more difficult than pardoning his intended taking of her maidenhead. She knows that Angelo did not actually take the maidenhead, but she does not know that Angelo did not actually take the head. She has forgiven what she knows to be merely an attempted crime; will she now forgive what she believes to be the inexorably final act of killing?

The Duke, citing a significantly altered variation of the biblical lex talionis, warns against granting mercy to the supposed killer:

> The very mercy of the law cries out   (5.1.405)
> Most audible, even from his proper tongue:
> "An Angelo for Claudio; death for death."

What is the significance of the Duke's changing the Mosaic formulation "life for life" (Exod. 21:23) to "death for death"? For a murderer to give back the life he took to the man from whom he took it—"life

---

*Contrast Heloise's way of absolving herself from guilt for having intercourse with Abelard while she was a layperson, he a monk: "Though I have committed much wrong, I am, as you know, very innocent; for the crime lies not in the act but in the intention behind it, and the test of justice is not in what is done, but in the spirit in which it is done." (Letter from Heloise to Abelard, in Owen, *Noble Lovers,* p. 18.) Isabella claims that not the intention but only the physical act matters; Heloise claims the reverse.

for life"—would be better, say the Jewish rabbis, than for him to give up his own life.[21] Because, unfortunately, no one can give life back to a dead man (with the exception, for Christians, of God the Father, who forsook and then resurrected his Son), the law must settle for second best—in the Duke's phrase, "death for death."

But to whom should the killer give his life? To the state of the murdered man? To his family? This is the second major problem involved in executing the lex talionis when what was taken cannot be returned. (The first is commensuration.) Just as there can be no adequate substitution for a life, so there can be no adequate recipient: compensation cannot be made directly to a man whose life has been taken, but only to his family or his state. The problem is figured in terms of the right of the family versus the right of the state to the death, or life, of the murderer.

In *Measure for Measure*, the state, represented by the Duke of Vienna, demands Angelo's death, but the right of the family to vengeance intervenes. Family right, moreover, is split between Isabella and Mariana. The murdered man, Claudio, was Isabella's as much as the murderer husband, Angelo, is now Mariana's.[22] Mariana the wife of Angelo appeals for mercy from Isabella the sister of Claudio.

The Duke's representation of the mercy of the law crying out to Isabella for retaliation recalls the archetypal crying out of familial blood, particularly fraternal blood: "The voice of thy brother's blood," says God to Cain, "crieth unto me from the ground" (Gen. 4:10). Isabella, like Cain, has not been her brother's keeper (Gen. 4:9); her last words to him were, "I'll pray a thousand prayers for thy death; / No word to save thee" (3.1.145–46, cf. 3.1.188–90). Is she now to be the keeper of someone who not only is other than a brother but also killed her brother?* If Isabella will now be the merciful keeper of Angelo—as Mariana would have her do, and as the Duke, it seems, would not— she must be more generous to Angelo than she was to her brother. She must either deny that she is her brother's keeper more than she is the keeper of any other human being or else transcend the distinction

---

*The God of Genesis, in speaking to Cain not about Abel his fellow human being but about Abel his brother, might seem to argue for preferential treatment of kin. Yet the secular or political order, by means of a fiction that all those human beings who are kin are not kin, demands that all people be treated alike. Thus the Provost says that he would not pity Barnadine "though he were my brother" (4.2.56–57), and Angelo says of Claudio, "Were he my kinsman, brother, or my son, / It should be thus with him" (2.2.81–82). In the same way, the religious order, by means of a fiction that all those human beings who are not kin are kin (as in the Christian doctrine of Universal Sibling-hood, according to which everyone is related in much the same way that Cain and Abel were related), insists that everyone is essentially the same.

between brother and other—between a Claudio and an Angelo—that retaliation, as the Duke seems to interpret it, appears to presuppose.

If Isabella pardons Angelo's crime of taking a life—thus giving to Mariana or Angelo a free gift, one without expectation of an earthly counter-gift (the life that Angelo owes Isabella in return for Claudio's)[23]—then Barnardine's equal crime of taking a life and (by the commensuration of illegal killing with bastardizing) Claudio's equal crime of illegitimate procreation should also arguably be pardoned. Logically, at least, at the end of this chain Isabella's pardon should result in the redemption of Claudio in exchange for the redemption of Angelo. If resurrection were possible, her merciful pardon would result in the best kind of taliation—"life for life," Angelo for Claudio. But dead men do not ordinarily rise from the dead; their ghosts do not break their paved beds, as the Duke puts it (5.1.433). Thus Mariana asks Isabella to give more than she can ever expect to get in return. In fact, though, Isabella's pardon of Angelo will get—will beget—more than she thinks. By it, she will get measures for measure.

"Life for Life."   In *Measure for Measure* nature as creditor demands "use," or more than an equal exchange—not "life for life" but "lives for life." The plot of the play, like the nature whose teleology it imitates, outdoes the lex talionis by eventually exacting more than an equal transaction. Just as nature demands to get more than it gives, so the plot—and in its course such characters as Isabella—give more than they think they will get. They pardon.

When Isabella kneels before the Duke to beg mercy for Angelo, her action has the doubly profitable effect of giving life not only to Angelo but supplementally also to Claudio. Her pardon enables the intent of the plot to realize itself as the impossible act of rebirth. It is as though the Duke's prediction had been fulfilled:

> Should she kneel down in mercy of this fact,   (5.1.432)
> Her brother's ghost his paved bed would break.

Claudio's rebirth, the quintessential supplement to the series of commercial exchanges that have preceded it, occurs when the Provost unmuffles an anonymously hooded prisoner, of whom he says:

> This is another prisoner that I sav'd,   (5.1.485)
> Who should have died when Claudio lost his head;
> As like almost to Claudio as himself. (*Unmuffles Claudio.*)

The Duke pardons Claudio's look-alike (once purportedly Ragozine) for the sake of the purportedly dead Claudio, saying to Isabella: "If he be like your brother, for his sake / Is he pardon'd" (5.1.488–89).

Thanks to Isabella's pardon of Angelo, one like Claudio is pardoned and can be revealed, by unhooding, to be Claudio himself. In the general intent, or spirit, of the plot, like things (which are also unlike things) of the kind that must be traded in any taliation become identical: "Make not impossible / That which but seems unlike" (5.1.54–55). Claudio's life is thus redeemed, not by his sister's lying unchastely or incestuously with Angelo—"bending down" (3.1.143) to him—but rather by her kneeling before the Duke and begging for him the free gift of life. In this way a resurrectional "life for life" replaces the proposed repayment of death by death, and Claudio is finally remembered, or re-membered.[24]

The likeness of the hooded prisoner to Claudio is really complete identification; they resemble each other as much as Vincentio as Friar resembles Vincentio as Duke. As the Friar-Duke says to the Provost:

Duke. You will think you have made no offence if the Duke   (4.2.184)
   avouch the justice of your dealing?
Provost. But what likelihood is in that?
Duke. Not a resemblance, but a certainty.

The movement of *Measure for Measure* is from substitution and likeness to identification. It travels from the likelihood that the man with the ducal seal ring who appears to the Provost in the likeness or semblance of the hooded Friar is authorized to interfere in the secular affairs of Vienna, to the certainty that the Friar is, or will again become, the Duke.

6

Incest in
Pardon and Marriage

The Marriage of Saint Francis to Lady Poverty. (Fresco by a student of Giotto,
?1267–1337, in the lower basilica of San Francisco d'Assisi. Reproduced in
Formaggio, *Basiliche*, p. 111.)

Thou art myn and I am thyne.
Princess Elizabeth, *The Glasse
of the Synnefull Soule*

BY DISGUISE and pardon, the exchange of "death for death" (Angelo for Claudio), which otherwise would be the inevitable end of *Measure for Measure*, is transformed into "life for life" (Claudio for Angelo), thus ending a cycle of purchase and sale and solving the special dilemma of the play. The soul of the plot—what Aristotle calls its telos—is still not fully revealed, however. To seek that surprising soul, we must reinterpret at another level the process of Claudio's salvation and investigate the problems of marriage raised in the play.

Two essential exchanges of life for life in *Measure for Measure* supplement the exchanges already outlined. In the first, Claudio is saved, not only by the literal substitutions of disguise and by Isabella's pardon of Angelo, but also, and essentially, in a figurative resurrection through "a kind of incest" between him and Isabella, which is also his pardon by Isabella. This incest is necessary to the movement whereby Claudio is born again, both as a "child of adoption" and as his own newborn son. The first exchange is thus Claudio for Claudio's son. The second, and consequential, supplemental exchange of life for life is marriage (in particular the marriage ultimately proposed by Vincentio), both as a reciprocal giving and taking and also as "a kind of incest." Taken together these two interrelated exchanges—an incestuous pardon and an incestuous marriage—account for the incorporation and apparent transcendence of the lex talionis, or the rule of "measure for measure."

The hint of this incestuous transcendence is the intent or use (supplement) of the plot of *Measure for Measure*. Unless we understand these supplemental exchanges, two disturbing and far-reaching questions remain obscure: Does Isabella pardon Claudio? and, Does Isabella marry the Duke?

Incest and Isabella's Pardon of Claudio

> Sister Francesca said that one time . . . she saw, on the
> knees of Madame Clare, just in front of her breast, an in-
> comparable little child, whose beauty was ineffable; and at
> its sight alone she felt an inexpressible sweetness and dou-
> ceur. And she did not doubt that this child was the Son of
> God.   S. E. Garonne, *The Canonization of St. Clare*[1]

Claudio is the focal point of both the political need that gave rise to
Vincentio's placing in power such a severe governor as Angelo and the
equally political need to mitigate Angelo's proposed punishment,
which between them occasion most of the dramatic action in *Measure
for Measure*. Claudio is almost entirely unheard and unseen, however,
after Isabella accuses him of wanting her to commit "a kind of incest"—in fact, in the last scene he seems to obey the rules of her Sisterhood, "If you speak, you must not show your face; / Or if you show
your face, you must not speak" (1.4.12–13). After Isabella flees from
his prison cell, Claudio urgently petitions Friar Vincentio: "Let me ask
my sister pardon; I am so out of love with life that I will sue to be rid
of it" (3.1.170–71). Friar Vincentio replies, "Hold you there"
(3.1.172). What does this mean? Whether the Duke intends to bring
Isabella back or is encouraging Claudio to hold to a renewed reconciliation with death,* his words have the effect of transfixing Claudio
"there," in almost invisible and silent petition, until the last act. Yet
even in that scene of general pardon, Claudio is not explicitly pardoned by his sister. Why not?[2]

I would argue that an implicit mediating process of pardon (giving
without taking) informs the play in such a way that an explicit pardon
would be redundant and that the implicit, or "speechless" process of
this pardon is linked to the problem of whether or not Juliet should
appear pregnant at the end of the play. What is Juliet's significance in
the plot taken as a whole? What might her largely silent role (she
speaks only in 2.3, when Friar Vincentio confesses her and finds her
penitence to be sound) mean in a play in which silence is a critical aspect of many episodes (in the chaste nunnery and the unchaste vineyard) and Claudio himself is silent almost throughout the second
half?[3] The "speechless dialect" (cf. 1.2.173) of Juliet's extraordinarily
large and fruitful body (a major presence on stage in 1.2.108–84 and
perhaps 5.1.476–536, for example) exposes the confrontation be-

---

*Compare Angelo's statements "Sequent death / Is all the grace I beg" (5.1.371–72)
and "I crave death more willingly than mercy" (5.1.474). In his *ars moriendi* speech earlier, in scene 3.1, the Friar-Duke has tried to bring Claudio to a similar reconciliation.

tween nature and law that is the central dilemma in the play. Moreover, our anticipation of when, even whether, Juliet will deliver her child is connected with our anticipation of when, even whether, Claudio will die or be liberated from prison.

Soon after the Justice tells Escalus, who has earlier in the scene been protesting Claudio's execution, that it is literally the eleventh hour (2.1.274), the Provost tells Angelo that Juliet is "very near her hour" (2.2.16). Similarly, the Provost's question, "What shall be done, sir, with the groaning Juliet?" (2.2.15), reminds us that Juliet is ready to go into labor to deliver her child at nearly the same moment Isabella enters to begin laboring to deliver her brother from death (2.2.27). The literal text, however, keeps us in ignorance about whether Juliet ever does deliver her child. (Compare how Isabella and Angelo are kept in ignorance about Claudio's delivery from death.) As directors, if not as readers, we must figure it out for ourselves.

Insofar as the aesthetic teleology that informs the plot of *Measure for Measure* matches the biological teleology that provides its content, Juliet's pregnancy, or the birth of her child and Claudio's, is *the* issue of *Measure for Measure*. That issue is double, however. Claudio waits throughout the play for the deliverance, or birth, not only of the child of Juliet but also of the child of Isabella (himself), conceived in the "kind of incest" that his sister had accused him of wanting. The children for whose deliverance Claudio waits are alike, more than alike. The typical dramaturgical emphasis on the likeness of fathers and sons (a likeness Isabella plays upon in the prison scene) assures that Juliet's child will be like Claudio, perhaps "as like almost to Claudio as himself" (5.1.487), in the way the hooded man turns out to be Claudio himself, "not a resemblance, but a certainty" (4.2.187). With the unhooding we see that Claudio's hoped-for child by Isabella, Claudio himself, is already there on stage. In the most profound and unusual trope of the drama, Juliet's literal child is figured on stage in the person of Claudio.[4]

The logical consequence of the plot is thus not to present Juliet's child on stage because that child is already figured in Claudio. There is no need to present Claudio's child by Juliet on stage because Claudio's child by Isabella is already there.[5] Yet in the absence of the child and the presence of the now unpregnant Juliet, a spectator might conceivably ask whether Juliet has committed feticide or infanticide— a question that, given the play's concern with the political end of illegitimacy in liberty and universal genocide, is especially pointed.[6] Killing either the fetus in Juliet's womb or the infant delivered from her womb would help both to control the spread of bastardy (and hence incest) in Vienna and to cancel out the offense of bastardizing. For in *Measure for Measure* the law of Vienna must seek to abort illegitimately conceived fetuses before they are "hatch'd and born" (2.2.98), that is, before they achieve, by "successive degrees" (2.2.99), infancy and eventually that adulthood in which they will become willy-nilly incestuous sexual partners.

In the context of *Measure for Measure*, to answer the question of whether feticide would be better than bastardy and incest involves, not the problem of whether a fetus is a human being, but the problem of whether interference with the natural telos of sexuality is worse than incest. Saint Bernardine of Siena (whose name echoes, intentionally or not, the murderer Barnardine) argues that "it would be better for a woman to permit herself to have relations with her own father than it would be for her to engage in 'unnatural' relations with her husband."[7] Before we reject as outside the Shakespearean pale this apparent preference of incest to acts, such as sodomy, that interfere with the natural process of conception, we might recall that in *The Winter's Tale* Leontes orders Antigonus (whose name, like Antigone's, means "against generation") to kill Perdita because Leontes presumably believes that she is a bastard—that is, because he rates the unnatural act of infanticide as preferable to the natural conclusion of bastardy.*

One might argue that no audience could see so much in the presence or absence of a newborn babe. But this is precisely a play about pregnancy: Escalus is pregnant with knowledge (1.1.11), Angelo with unvirtuous intentions (4.4.18), and Juliet with a human fetus. And it is a play about delivery: Angelo gives birth to unvirtuous actions that reflect his actual intentions, and Claudio is delivered—liberated— from the prison of death. In discussing Juliet's offspring, I hope to get at the one literal offspring, the son (*liber*), of the play. That son, the "thanks and use" (1.1.40) offered to nature for our lives, demonstrates or represents in nuce all the issues of *Measure for Measure*. In *The Comedy of Errors*, the Abbess notes that "Thirty-three years have I but gone in travail / Of you, my sons, and till this present hour / My heavy burden ne'er delivered" (ERR 5.1.401–3). Such a delivery, one that outnatures nature, is a telos of *Measure for Measure*.

The identification of Claudio reborn with Claudio's son born, or of rebirth with birth, involves the various interchangeabilities of Claudio

* *The Winter's Tale*, like *Measure for Measure*, explores desired homicide (the intended infanticide of Perdita [cf. WT 2.3.5, 2.3.134–40]) and desired incest (the attraction between Mamillius and Hermione [WT 2.1.21–33], and the attraction between Leontes and Perdita when he meets her grown up [WT 5.1.222–25]).

with Angelo (insofar as Isabella's unchaste sleeping with Angelo would be "a kind of incest," insofar as the planned death of Claudio is repaid by the planned death of Angelo, and insofar as the actual or resurrected life of Claudio is paid for by the life of Angelo) and also the interchangeabilities of Isabella both with Mariana (apart from the bed-trick substitution, "Sweet Isabel, take my part," says Mariana [5.1.428], hoping Isabella will bend down on her husband's behalf, as she has on Claudio's) and with Juliet (Isabella's "cousin" by nominal adoption [2.4.45−47]). With the help of Mariana, who played Isabella's role with Angelo (a role that, for Isabella, would have implied incestuous intercourse with Claudio), and with the help of Juliet, who gives birth to a child we can assume will be like Claudio, Isabella has— by substitution, adoption, and likeness—both slept with Claudio-Angelo and given birth to Claudio-Angelo. All the while she has remained a virgin, like Mary the mother and daughter of God, and Claudio has become one who begets himself, like the Christian God. If Isabella does not commit incest, Isabella-Juliet-Mariana does. Thus Isabella does not pardon her brother's petition that she commit "a kind of incest" because that incest, with its consequent birth, has been the business of the whole plot.

As we have seen, Isabella's plea that Angelo's life be spared has the complementary effect of resurrecting Claudio. This effect is ironic: in virtually her last words to Claudio Isabella had said, "Might but my bending down / Reprieve thee from thy fate, it should proceed" (3.1.143−44). Isabella, who refused to bend down to Angelo on Claudio's behalf, takes Mariana's part and kneels to the Duke on Angelo's (5.1.441)—an act, says the Duke, that should cause her brother to rise from the grave in "horror" (5.1.434). From this act Claudio is born or reborn the son of a "whore," an "Abhorson."

The complement to the view that Isabella-Mariana is in some fashion a whore who has given birth to her brother as a son is the view that Isabella as novice "nun" (an Elizabethan euphemism for "whore") has given virgin birth. In his essay "Virgin Birth," the anthropologist Edmund Leach asks, "Can we offer any general explanation as to why people should maintain a dogma which seems to reject the facts of physiological paternity?"[8] In discussing *Measure for Measure*, we can say that Isabella might reject these facts because she fears the tendency toward universal incest that she observes throughout her world and that her church regards as the antonomasia of all sexual relations. She would choose Universal Siblinghood over a particular sibling incest. Her church's dogma, which seems to reject the facts of physiological paternity in its thesis of the Son Who Fathered Himself on a virgin, has its counterpart in the telos of *Measure for Measure*, which tentatively rejects the facts of physiological generation as part of its movement toward rebirth. The awesome problem that the lex talionis poses in cases of murder and fornication—that a life taken from a living person or from nature cannot be returned except by means of resurrection—has for its solution this incest of the apparently virginal kind.

That the act of sexual intercourse between Angelo and Mariana constitutes, in some kind, an act of sibling incest between Isabella and Claudio or, in the loftiest sense of the play, an act of divine incest, is suggested by the place where the bed trick occurs, the "garden circummur'd with brick" (4.1.28) inside a vineyard. "A garden inclosed is my sister, my spouse," says the Song of Songs (4:12). What is enclosed in that garden, according to Saint Jerome, "is a type of the Mother of the Lord, a mother and a virgin."[9] The Virgin Mary, the daughter of Anne (compare "Mariana"), is an archetype of the "garden circummur'd" in *Measure for Measure*, a garden that makes possible the virginal and incestuous rebirth of Claudio, who is father not only of his own son (by Juliet, his spouse) but of himself (by Isabella, his sister).

The play's incorporation and transcendance of incest by substitution, adoption, and likeness brings with it an appearance of atonement. Perhaps, as Battenhouse suggests, *Measure for Measure* is a play of Christian atonement;[10] but the unmediated expression of that atonement is not Mariana's actual intercourse with Angelo but the incestuous intercourse between sister and brother that Isabella fears. Shakespeare would have found the suggestion of atonement by such intercourse in *Promos and Cassandra*, where the philosophical sister, unlike Shakespeare's novice Isabella, sleeps with the magistrate in some awareness of the relationship between atonement and incest: "Lyue, and make much of this kisse, which breatheth my honour into thy bowels, and draweth the infamie of thy first trespasse into my bosome."[11] In *Measure for Measure*, this incestuous intercourse is dramatically mediated by substitution and disguise, but the atonement is still incestuous.

The play thus moves from "a kind of incest" in the figural sense of an unchaste act that is like, or that resembles, incest, toward "a kind of incest" in the literal, if mediated, sense of a certainly incestuous act with one's own kin. The plot of *Measure for Measure* acts out this certain incest through resemblance (e.g., the similarity between Ragozine and Claudio), yet it is "not a resemblance but a certainty" that saves Claudio. That a certain incest has been incorporated and transcended accounts for the feeling of hope accompanying the reunion of brother and sister near the end of the play.[12] The pregnancy, birth, and delivery of Isabella-Juliet-Mariana's son accurately mirrors not only the hoped-for rebirth of Claudio but also the needful rebirth of Vienna itself.

Bed Trick and Trick Birth

In *Measure for Measure*, the bed trick seems to allow Mariana, with whom Angelo enacted sexual intercourse, to be substituted for Isabella, with whom he intended to enact it; the trick seems to allow the spiritual incest with a quasi-Sister that Angelo intended ("Shall we desire to raze the sanctuary / And pitch our evils there?" [2.2.171−72]) to be transformed into the consummation of a chaste marriage with a quasi-wife. This comforting view is the basis of Isabella's public, if un-Christian, rationale for pardoning Angelo. Jesus said that the intention to fornicate and fornication are one and the same; however, in the last words she speaks in the play, Isabella says, "Thoughts are no subjects; / Intents, but merely thoughts" (5.1.451−52).

Depending on how one looks at it, the dramatic technique of the bed trick either simply foils an individual's conscious intentions (apparently Isabella's view) or both incorporates and transcends his conscious intentions in such a way that a more basic intention is revealed— the individual's "unconscious" intention, the generic intention, or the aesthetic intention (whether social or asocial, comedic or tragic) of the series of happenings in which his act is a part. In the two principal sexual unions of the play—that of Juliet with Claudio and that of Mariana with Angelo—individual intents are tricked into revealing such generic intentions.

The tricking of Claudio's and Juliet's individual intentions is the motivating dilemma of the play: as individual actors, the pair may have consciously intended merely to satisfy sexual desire, yet, since pregnancy and birth are the natural ends of sexual intercourse and since the plot of *Measure for Measure* is both motivated by and demonstrates (i.e., is both informed by and has as its content) the natural and political teleology of sexual desire, Juliet willy-nilly becomes pregnant. The very presence on stage of her fruitful body is the necessary sign, or *tekmērion*, of birth (the telos of sexual reproduction from the viewpoint of nature) and of bastardy (the telos of sexual reproduction from the viewpoint of politics).

The tricking of Angelo's individual intentions by what seem at first to be only the individual intentions of other people (e.g., Vincentio, Isabella, and Mariana, by the bed trick they stage) provides the solution to the dilemma that the first sexual union posed. Yet Angelo is, to all intents, Claudio (he has stood for Claudio and Claudio has stood for him), and Mariana is, to all intents, both Isabella and Juliet (Mariana and Isabella take each other's part, which is also Juliet's part because Juliet and Isabella are akin). Thus the bed trick fulfills intentions beyond any one individual's dreams by allowing Isabella to consummate a kind of incest with Claudio. The aesthetic telos of the sexual unions conjunct in this bed trick is an extraordinary, superlegal trick birth at once incestuous and resurrectional: nothing more or less than the delivery of Claudio as Claudio's son, the telos of the plot.

The effect of the bed trick in *Measure for Measure*, and in bed-trick plays generally, depends upon our holding, for a while at least, the ordinary opinion that there is a significant difference between one person and another. (Not everyone holds this opinion: for a religious celibate in the Catholic tradition, it should make no difference whether he slept with one person or another because for him any act of sexual intercourse would amount to incest of a kind.) In particular, the effect of the bed trick in plays involving incest depends upon our holding the ordinary opinions that there is such a thing as real, absolute knowledge of who one is (i.e., of where one stands in the ordinary kinship structure), or that there is such a thing as real knowledge of what one wants (i.e., of which person one desires sexually).

The ordinary opinion that it makes sense to assume that one can really know where one stands in the kinship structure can contribute to tragedy, as it does for Sophocles' Oedipus. Or it can contribute to comedy, as when a man who intends to sleep with his sister does not, either because in the course of the plot he finds that the woman is not his sister, or because another woman has been substituted. In either case, his intent of incest has been transformed into an act of chastity.

The ordinary opinion that it makes sense to assume a difference between ignorance and knowledge of which person one desires sexually can pave the way to some seemingly grand teleological revelation. Just as some narratives start with a man such as Angelo, who thinks that he is in love with someone kind of akin to him (his Sister), though he is not, so others start with a man who thinks he is not in love with someone who is akin to him, though he is. A comic plot might reveal that the man is really not in love with the kinswoman with whom he wrongly thinks he is in love, and a tragic plot might reveal that the man really is in love with the kinsperson with whom he wrongly thinks he is not in love.[13] To conceive *Measure for Measure* as having an unambiguously comfortable ending, one might argue that, although Angelo thought he was in love with a quasi-Sister, he was, without consciously knowing it, all along really in love with, and seeking, a quasi-wife; the bed trick and the ensuing events would then reveal to him the real direction of his desires. The same reversal and revelation can be argued for an incest plot: Oedipus, one might say, thinks his wedded love is chaste, but the plot tricks him into acting out his real desires. Similarly, Vincentio in *Measure for Measure* is at first only vaguely aware of his spiritually incestuous desire for Isabella.

In plots where people are in love with persons about whose kinship with themselves they are mistaken or where people are in love unknowingly, it is as though, if one is lucky enough to live in a comedic world, one can have one's cake and eat it too. That is, one can both intend to commit incest and not commit incest, or both raze the sanctuarial taboo against incest and rise above it. In the Hegelian sense, one can both incorporate and transcend—one can sublate—incest and its taboo. All's well here if it ends well and because it ends well.

The possibility of postulating transcendentally teleological intention in any such plots depends, however, on granting that there are essential moral and aesthetic differences between: (1) ignorance and knowledge of one's sexual desire and its target, (2) intent and act, or what is private or invisible and what is public or visible, and (3) ignorance and knowledge of who are one's blood kin. Granted these differences, even in the unhappy case of an Oedipus the notion that knowledge of kinship is at least possible means that there can be a happy ending elsewhere. (Indeed, from one point of view a social purpose of the myth of Oedipus is to convince us that absolute knowledge of kinship is possible: when all is said and done, we do not doubt that Jocasta is Oedipus's mother, do we?) On these differences depends our belief in the possibility of marriage (as the union of a man and woman whose relative unrelatedness is ascertainable) and of ordinary politics.

But do these various differences make sense? Are they meant to make sense within *Measure for Measure*, which pushes to their extreme limits the implications of personal substitutions and playacted intentions. And, within the context of the simultaneous sisterhood and Sisterhood of the novice Isabella, do they make moral sense according to the Christian orders and the essential teaching of Christianity?

The bed trick in *Measure for Measure* provides one apparently successful case in practice of the disassociation of individual intent from act, which, from a moral viewpoint, Jesus denied. Without the bed trick and its apparently clear-cut separation of intent and act, Angelo would not be pardoned and Claudio would not be reborn. To a certain extent Isabella's insistence upon the separation of individual intent and act attempts to get over not only their Christian conflation but also the play's aesthetic teleology, which ultimately treats every act in terms of its generic end, whether natural or political. (That is, her separation of individual intent from act might apply not only to Angelo's intended fornication but to Claudio's enacted, but not intended, bastardizing.)

But what if we hold the Sisterly and, within the context of *Measure for Measure*, aesthetic view that an intent is, to all intents and purposes, an act? Then to desire, at any level of consciousness—whether thinking, say, or dreaming—sexual intercourse with anyone forbidden (i.e., with anyone except a spouse) constitutes in itself the forbidden act. Then, given the economy of possible sexual substitutions, even to desire sexual intercourse with someone like someone forbidden constitutes the forbidden act. If so, the bed trick and the rationale that Isabella consequently employs to convince the Duke to take no head from Angelo because Angelo actually took no maidenhead from her is untenable, a merely secularist deus ex machina.

Understood literally, as the simple foiling of an individual's intention rather than as the realization of a greater intention, the bed trick encourages the secular rationale that separates intent from act. But the bed trick also emphasizes the difficulties in knowing who are one's blood kin. Thus it returns us by a different route to the position that all sexual intercourse is incest. Angelo's ignorance during the bed trick reminds us that no one—not we, not our ancestors—can know for sure who slept with whom the night we were conceived. By this logic, we are, at least to all religious and psychological intents and purposes, bastards or changelings, so that either no men are our kin (the final position of Shakespeare's universally misanthropic Timon of Athens) or all men are our kin before the only Parent, if any, that we might know (the position of such a would-be universally philanthropic Sister as the novice Isabella originally aspired to become).[14]

For the bed trick to work and the end of *Measure for Measure* to come off, one must maintain two positions in apparent polar opposition. (Or, like a novice, one must vacillate between them.) There is first the secular, sisterly position that an intent is not essentially an act—which allows for the pardon of Angelo. And there is second the religious, Sisterly position that all men are essentially akin or alike—which allows for the trick birth that rescues Claudio as his own son. That trick birth mirrors the hoped-for and needed political rebirth of Vienna itself.

Life for Life: The Proposed Marriage of the Duke and Isabella

Our expectation of the political rebirth of Vienna is disappointed, at least at first, by the counterfeit Brother's unsettling marriage proposal to the novice Sister. This proposal figures both commerce and incest back into the play and suggests that if Vienna is to be delivered truly it will first have to be liberated, one way or another, from all external restraints on human sexual activity.

Equal marriage, in which neither the husband's nor the wife's right to the mutual and exclusive use of the other spouse's genitals can rightly be traded away, would seem to solve the conflict between nature's requirement that we generate offspring and law's requirement that we keep track of parentage so that incest will not destroy the political order as we know it. But *Measure for Measure* shows that the kind of equality presupposed by genuinely reciprocal marriage is uncomfortably close to both the commensurability underlying commercial exchange and the interchangeability of kinship roles in incest. That is, the play shows marriage to be an exchange of persons similar to the exchanges of persons that, in the course of the play, we learn to distrust.

The series of exchanges motivating the plot of *Measure for Measure* is made possible by some common measure that makes two things the same for the purposes of a transaction. Commercial exchange suggests one such measure; sexual exchange suggests another. Money turns all human beings into wares, and incest similarly levels the distinctions kinship roles create among them. If marriage, the loftiest type of "life for life" in *Measure for Measure*, is to solve the dilemma in the play, it must somehow arrest the kinds of human exchange typified by sales of human beings and by incest; it must incorporate and transcend such exchanges. The principal step in this process of transcendence, the play has led us to believe, ought to be an act of pardon, or free gift, that breaks through the cycles of exchange and rises above them.

Isabella's pardon of Angelo in the fifth act appears to be such a gift. Her pardon smacks of the kind of economic and sexual commerce that has plagued Vienna from the beginning of the play, however, for when she lends Mariana her knees, she is not so much granting a free pardon of Angelo as repaying a debt to Mariana. Or, like a usurer, she is striking a profitable bargain—she gets a whole life in exchange for part of a body. "Lend me your knees, and all my life to come," pronounces Mariana, "I'll lend you all my life to do you service" (5.1.429–30). Thus her kneeling is yet another transaction in the cycle of exchanges begun when Angelo proposed the bargain of head for maidenhead. For Mariana to take Isabella's part in the bed trick was not enough to redeem a life; to accomplish that, Isabella must now take Mariana's "part" (5.1.428) in turn. Isabella's kneeling—whether she intends to express or to win gratitude—focuses the relationship between the lex talionis and mercy in the play.

Delineating the essential connectedness between taliation and mercy—even their essential unity—has been, on one level, the business of the whole plot of *Measure for Measure*.[15] How is retaliation "merciful," as the Duke at one point calls it? ("The very mercy of the law cries out . . . 'death for death'" [5.1.405–7].) One might interpret this to mean that to punish an individual criminal is merciful to society insofar as it deters further crime. Besought by Isabella to show pity, Angelo answers, "I show it most of all when I show justice" (2.2.101). Another version of this position is that mercy to an individual punishes society insofar as it encourages further crime. Isabella tells Claudio, "Mercy to thee would prove itself a bawd; / 'Tis best that thou diest quickly" (3.1.149–50). She must mean best for Vienna, since Claudio's death would probably not be best for Claudio, Juliet, or their unborn child. (Indeed, a quick death would not even be best for Claudio's spiritual welfare; despite the Duke's sermon on the art of dying, Claudio, who sues to live at the price of "a kind of incest," is not much better prepared to die than is Barnardine.) In the Duke's statement, however, the phrase "the very mercy of the law" does not imply a benefit to society by discouraging crime, nor does it imply an opposition between mercy and legal justice—a concept in terms of which readers since Schlegel have interpreted *Measure for Measure*.[16] Instead, a complementary mediation between mercy and retaliation defines the measured movement of the plot.

The title of the play is significant: *Measure for Measure* tries to turn the lex talionis (or "measure for measure," as retribution is termed in *Henry VI* [3H6 2.6.55]), which the play treats as a species of merchantry, into mercy. The plot comes to reveal that revenge and mercy are not opposed (the usual interpretation of the Sermon on the Mount), but that mercy is itself a kind of lawful mercantile taliation. Isabella's eventual pardon of Angelo, for example, belies her first notions about the relationship between legal taliation and mercy:

> Ignomy in ransom and free pardon   (2.4.111)
> Are of two houses: lawful mercy
> Is nothing kin to foul redemption.

"Only a devil's logic," writes Battenhouse, concurring with what Isabella says, "would confound Christian charity with mortal sin."[17] Yet the position that ransom and pardon are of one house would not have surprised members of the orders of Ransom, organized to free prisoners from Muslim captivity. Usually such freedom was bought for money, but members were bound by vow to offer themselves (even ignominiously) in exchange for those they would ransom.[18] (The history of ransom thus provides part of *Measure for Measure*'s international context.) In the play, retributive ransom and merciful pardon are as closely connected as incest and free, lawful marriage, and the essential link between retaliation, or the lex talionis, and mercy resides in a kind of incestuous kinship.[19]

The First Marriage Proposal

> Have you any merchandise to sell us? . . .
> Upon my word, yours is excellent merchandise!
> We shall buy it.
> Marriage formula among the Christians of Mosul[20]

Just as Isabella's pardon of Angelo is related to Mariana's promise of service, so Vincentio's proposal to pardon Claudio is linked to his hope, even insistence, that Isabella will promise to become his wife.

> If he be like your brother, for his sake   (5.1.488)
> Is he pardon'd; and for your lovely sake
> Give me your hand and say you will be mine.

Some critics have seen in this a happy offer of genuine marriage, but it is actually a commercial proposition with overtones of wergeld and prostitution. Earlier in the scene the Duke said that Isabella should pardon Angelo "for Mariana's sake" (5.1.401). Isabella does pardon Angelo, but, significantly, not "for Mariana's sake"; her rationale is that Angelo's intentions and his actions are separable. The same retributive, even retaliative, notion of exchange informs Vincentio's proposed—or conditional—pardon of Claudio. His ducal "sake," or *sacu* (meaning "affair of law" in Old English),[21] casts a commercial gloom on the proceedings. Does the Duke's giving Claudio to Isabella depend on Isabella's first giving herself to the Duke? Does it depend on the Duke's hope that she will give herself out of gratitude? Is it still "head for maidenhead," Claudio for Isabella?[22] Significantly, the Duke does not offer *himself* to Isabella, as we might expect in a proposal for reciprocal marriage; he says only that Isabella is to be his. The univocal "say you will be mine" he requests is a formula for a prostitute or a slave.

In this first marriage proposal, then, Vincentio essentially acts just like Angelo. Indeed, from the first time he speaks (as a friar) to Isabella, Vincentio has in a sense been requesting that she give up her "leisure," or monachal *otium,* and give him "satisfaction," or sexual gratification. In his very first words, he echoes Claudio in making requests of her:

Claudio. O hear me, Isabella.   (3.1.150)
Duke. (*Advancing.*) Vouchsafe a word, young sister, but one word.
Isabella. What is your will?
Duke. Might you dispense with your leisure, I would by and by have some
    speech with you: the satisfaction I would require is likewise your own
    benefit.

(Compare "if for this night he entreat you to his bed, give him promise of satisfaction" [3.1.263–64].) The Friar-Duke's request, spoken just as Isabella leaves her brother, marks the turning point of the play, when the Duke advances into the brother-sister plot at the moment when it seems inevitable either that the sister will lose her chastity or that the brother will lose his life, or both. The Duke's interference is not mere manipulation;[23] he takes over from Angelo (hence also from Claudio) the wooing of Isabella. The first marriage proposal makes explicit the sexual meaning hidden in the Duke's earlier words: he is, in a sense, asking Isabella to yield him a satisfying reward for saving her brother. Trading him that reward means giving away her monachal *otium,* or "leisure"—in the Duke's rather commercial formulation of the lex talionis, "Haste still pays haste, and leisure answers leisure; / Like doth quit like, and Measure still for Measure" (5.1.408–9).

Exit Lucio: Putting Out the Light

> O Clara luce clarior
> Lucis aeternae filiae.[24]

It is in his old role of merchant, familiar from Shakespeare's sources, that Vincentio proposes marriage of this univocal sort—a discomforting, apparently conditional, commercial deal. The positive aspect of this merchantry is that it allowed Friar Vincentio to arrange the exchange of maidenheads and enabled Duke Vincentio to try to arrange the exchanges of heads and interchanges of heads and maidenheads. In one way or another, these changes benefited Claudio, Juliet, Isabella, Angelo, and Mariana. They also led to this first proposal of marriage. The negative, discomforting aspect of Vincentio's merchantry is that, since it tends to use human beings as money (as in the institution of wergeld) and to trade them for money (as in the institution of prostitution), it is antithetical to the genuine reciprocity in marriage that it seeks. Now that Vincentio has used the commercial part of himself to its fullest positive potential, when he receives from Isabella no spoken response to his first proposal (her last words in the play are her rationale for pardoning Angelo), Vincentio tries to, has to, separate himself from, or transcend, the negative aspect of the "trade of flesh." [25]

Vincentio's negative aspect, his hidden intents, is personified on stage in the figure of Lucio. Until the Duke rids himself of that negative aspect—or at least seems to—by dismissing Lucio, he cannot propose marriage in a fully respectable, or reciprocal, way. Thus Lucio by his eradication, like Ragozine by his death, is a scapegoat of the piece.

In *Measure for Measure* Lucio is a gadfly or motive spring, much like Mephistopheles in Goethe's *Faust*. Just as Faust both depends on and dislikes the force that Mephistopheles represents, so Vincentio both depends on and dislikes what Lucio represents. During the course of the play, for example, Vincentio uses to advantage the "trade of flesh" that, to all intents, militates against his own ducal patriarchy. Similarly, he slanders the only visible ruler in Vienna when he convinces the Provost to disobey Angelo, and he even casts doubt upon his own ducal authority. These two crimes, slander and illegitimate procreation, are the ones for which Lucio, the shadow that clings to Vincentio ("I am a kind of burr, I shall stick" [4.3.177]), is sentenced at the end of the play.

Slander. In *Measure for Measure* slander is confused with battery in the same way that intent is confused with act. Consider the exchange in which Constable Elbow protests Pompey's imagined slur on Elbow's "respected" (2.1.161) wife:

> *Elbow.* Prove this, thou wicked Hannibal, or I'll have mine (2.1.175)
> action of battery on thee.
> *Escalus.* If he took you a box o' th' ear, you might have your action of slander too.

The action of slander is battery. Just as a punning malapropism conflates a "respected" woman with a "suspected" prostitute, so the conflation of "slander" with "battery" elides talk with act. If it is the hidden intent of respectable people (like Isabella and Angelo) to behave like suspected prostitutes and their clients, so it is the intent of slander to be battery. It is willy-nilly the telos of such talk as Lucio's slander, for example, to enact the destruction of the figure of the Duke as political leader; the telos of his talk is therefore a kind of treason. In this sense Lucio the soldier has battered the legal authority of his home, attacking laws that, as Heraclitus knew, are the real walls of a town.[26]

This is not to say that Lucio, in slandering the Duke, has said anything essentially incorrect. The text of the play gives us good reason to suppose that what Lucio says is partly true (the more so if we conflate intent and act), good reason to conclude that Vincentio himself is, as Escalus's accusation "Slander to th' state!" (5.1.320) suggests, the greatest slanderer of the state in *Measure for Measure*. We may say, then, that Lucio (from *lux*, which means "light") sheds as much light on the world of *Measure for Measure* as Clare (from *claritas*, which also means "light") was supposed to shed on the world.[27]

Lucio's role as gadfly is to remind both the human Duke and ourselves of the Duke's questionable intentions, if not questionable acts. (Compare the Duke's outbreak: "Twice treble shame on Angelo, / To weed my vice, and let his grow!" [3.2.262–63].) By the time the Friar-Duke asks in the final act, "And was the Duke a fleshmonger?" (5.1.331), the constant buzzing of Lucio's aspersions (e.g., "his use was to put a ducat in her clack-dish" and "the Duke yet would have dark deeds darkly answered" [3.2.123, 170–71]) has made us aware that this question is not easy to answer.[28]

That Lucio's slander is substantially true helps to locate within the logic of the play one of his most important, if ignored, aspects. As Coghill and Lawrence suggest, Lucio is in the know.[29] Although in his first words Lucio, conversing with the Gentlemen, implies that the Duke is absent from Vienna on some international political mission (1.2.1–3), he soon afterwards claims that the Duke is "very strangely gone from hence" (1.4.50) and that "His giving out were of an infinite distance / From his true-meant design" (1.4.54–55). Lucio means either that the public is not aware of what the Duke intended or that the Duke himself is not aware, or both. Friar Thomas hints at the possibility that the Duke himself is unaware of his intentions by suggesting that the Duke's actual design is some kind of love affair (1.3.1–3). Similarly, the scene in which Lucio accurately criticizes Angelo as a would-be "motion ungenerative" (3.2.108) includes an equally suggestive series of passages between Lucio and the Duke as Friar that comes remarkably close to unmasking as a usurping, libertine beggar the Duke for whom Angelo substitutes:

Lucio. What news, friar, of the Duke? (3.2.83)
Duke. I know none: can you tell me of any?
Lucio. Some say he is with the Emperor of Russia; other some, he is in Rome: but where is he, think you?
Duke. I know not where: but wheresoever, I wish him well.
Lucio. It was a mad, fantastical trick of him to steal from the state and usurp the beggary he was never born to.

Does Lucio know that the Duke is dressed as a mendicant? How could he know? Lucio says "I know what I know" (3.2.148), whatever that means. When Lucio tells the Friar-Duke, "Thou art deceived in me, friar" (3.2.162–63), does he mean that the Friar-Duke is wrong to suppose that he does not recognize the Duke under the hood that he himself will eventually remove?

It is what Lucio knows or can make known about the Duke—that Vincentio has strong liberal or fraternal feelings, both as Brother and as libertine—that makes Vincentio unwilling to remove his Brother's hood. Part of Vincentio does not wish to reestablish the institution of patriarchy (and strictly exogamous marriage) that militates against the institution of Universal Siblinghood. This unwillingness of the Duke to remove himself from the order of universal brotherhood—his unwillingness to be "behooded"—perhaps best explains the timing of the unhooding in the fifth act.[30]

For Vincentio the moment of unhooding is unhappy because he has liberal, or antipatriarchal, tendencies. But, willy-nilly, Vincentio must come out of the Brother's hood and leave the fraternal Brotherhood, or "covent," for which it stands. Against his will, or against the liberal part of it, Vincentio resumes his role as patriarchal Duke, not so much by Lucio's apparently whimsical act of unhooding as by the ineluctable movement—the aesthetic teleology—of the play.

For revealing to Friar Vincentio in Act 3 the thoughts and methods of Duke Vincentio, which Vincentio is reluctant to see, and, similarly, for revealing to the public in Act 5 that the Duke is the man under the Friar's hood, Lucio is recompensed with a sentence of whipping and hanging (5.1.511–14). (Under King James the punishment for slander of the ruler was death.) By sentencing Lucio, Vincentio would divest himself of his own bad intentions, for which Lucio stands. In passing this sentence, moreover, Vincentio is separating acts from intents—his acts (which, for the sake of argument, I shall say are "chaste") from his intents (the "unchaste" ones that Lucio both describes and represents). From this viewpoint, the Duke's earlier acceptance of Isabella's justification for pardoning Angelo—her separation of intent from act—prepared the way for separating his own acts as patriarch from his own intended acts as liberal libertine, which Lucio represents.[31]

Vincentio eventually seems to forgive Lucio's slander (5.1.517, cf. 522). He does not act on the sentence, or intention, of whipping and hanging. Why not? Is it because he has no choice but to retain, in some fashion, the libertine aspect of himself—in order, say, to have something to get exercised or aroused about? Or is it because Lucio has repented? Yet Lucio does not even apologize for slander. "I spoke

it but according to the trick" (5.1.502–3) is all he says by way of defense. (This "trick" recalls the "mad fantastical trick" of the usurping
Duke himself.)[32] Perhaps the Duke pardons Lucio's slander because he
finally recognizes Lucio in himself (cf. 5.1.334), just as Lucio may have
recognized the Duke in the Friar.

By virtue of such recognition, Lucio is the Duke's illuminating "glass
of the sinful soul." The greatest slanderer of the Duke in *Measure for
Measure* is not Lucio: Lucio's outrageous statements are generally reserved for the private audience of the Duke as Friar. The Duke himself, whom Lucio reflects, is ultimately his own greatest slanderer.
"The Duke's unjust" (5.1.298) he says before the only public assembly
in the play—an assembly he has called for the very purpose of exposing injustice. The Duke himself commits "slander to th' state"
(5.1.320). And in not enacting the corporal punishment of Lucio, Vincentio is, so to speak, forgiving himself for the slander he has done
himself.

Bastardizing. The principal political telos of marriage in Elizabethan England (and perhaps whenever and wherever it is practiced)
is to avoid illegitimacy.[33] Gilbert Burnet writes that "the end of Marriage [is] the ascertaining of the Issue."[34] Ascertaining the issue is important to prevent incest, which is a fundamental challenge to the political order. That is why Vincentio as liberal can forgo punishing
Lucio for the offense of slander, but as parentarchal Duke he cannot
leave uncorrected Lucio's offense of bastardizing.

Illegitimate procreation, or the conflict between illegitimate procreation and the need to establish paternity, gave rise to the action of
Measure for Measure in the first place. Even before the action began the
Duke had sought unsuccessfully to establish legally the paternity of a
typical bastard, the son of the prostitute Kate Keepdown (4.3.167–72;
cf. 3.2.192–94). At the end of the play, the Duke forces Lucio to become the legitimate father of this child, whose natural paternity the
play has revealed.[35] In this way Vincentio seems, by establishing a paternity, to transcend the problematic part of himself figured on stage
in the person of Lucio; and in one representative case (that of Lucio's
natural son), at least, he begins to weaken the stranglehold that illegitimacy, and hence incest, have on the political order of Vienna.

We may ask, Can Lucio's illegitimate child be made legitimate? The
significance of the question itself is more important than any answer.
On the one hand, Thomas Aquinas suggests that it can be done;[36] and
since at least the medieval Council of Merton, in England the Church
had urged "that children born before the marriage of their parents
should be counted as legitimate at English law."[37] On the other hand,

the secular authority in England allowed no such thing. (English law made no changes in practice until a 1920 Act of Parliament.) This rule of the secular authority against legitimating bastards was seen by legal theorists as more than merely one law among many; it was understood as the foundation of all law. Thus the highest English court ruled in 1830 that illegitimate children cannot be made legitimate. The rule against legitimation, claimed the court, "is sown in the land, springs out of it, and cannot according to the law of England, be abrogated or destroyed by any foreign [i.e., essentially extrinsic] rule of law whatsoever."[38] This statement, which uses the language of natural propagation, recalls how in *Measure for Measure* the rule against fornication, hence against bastardy, cannot be changed insofar as it goes to the basis of laws.

It is, of course, the possibly unavoidable illegitimacy of the child of Claudio and Juliet, not that of Lucio and Kate Keepdown, that constitutes the more essential threat to the political order and to a happy ending. There are two ways, at least, to make a happy ending plausible. One is for Claudio to marry Juliet some time after his delivery from prison and before his child's delivery from the womb. The best reason for Juliet to appear still pregnant at the end of the play is to make conceivable this way of providing a happy ending. As we have seen, however, it is essential to the logic of the plot that Juliet appear already delivered of her child, since Claudio's delivery from death is itself the delivery of his child from the womb.

A second way to make a happy ending seem plausible is to imply that Juliet and Claudio were married all along.[39] There is some textual basis for this view, since Claudio says that he and Juliet were associated by a "true contract" and that he intended to marry her (1.2.134). The best reason to argue that intent is conflated with act throughout *Measure for Measure* is to make conceivable this second way of providing a happy ending. In the logic of the play, however, the argument by which Isabella saves the life of Angelo, and hence of Claudio himself, is that an intent does not make for an act. A corollary of this argument is that Claudio's presumed intent to have chaste sex in wedlock does not make for a chaste act, or that his desire to have a legitimate child (the telos of his intent to marry) does not turn his bastard into a legitimate child. As we have already seen, moreover, the plot of *Measure for Measure* is informed by a conflation of aesthetic with biological teleology. Were Claudio and Juliet already married, the movement of that plot would not have been necessary, and its real motor would be not the inevitable confrontation between nature and law but rather an accidental event—Angelo's mistakenly choosing the wrong person to prosecute. I do not wish to argue that Claudio and Juliet either are or are not married, however. Rather, I would suggest that the position that they are not married raises at the end the specter of fornication, hence of illegitimacy and incest, whereas the position that they are married is a necessary condition for a happy ending.

Claudio's intention to marry Juliet must be considered in the context of the overall relationship between intent and act in the plot. In the teleology of the play, individuals' private purpose of marriage matters no more to the political or secular order—whose purpose is to use marriage to ensure public acknowledgment of parentage—than individuals' intention to fornicate but not to reproduce matters to nature, whose purpose is reproduction no matter what. The secular law can and must make its rulings about legitimacy only on the basis of such visible acts and signs as public marriage banns and pregnancy. (Neither illicit sexual liaison nor unintended pregnancy is in itself a direct threat to the social order, but the future illegitimacy they signify is.) Thus the secret, or invisible, aspect of the marital contract between Juliet and Claudio, a contract lacking "outward order" and public "denunciation" (1.2.138, 137), necessitates that their child be illegitimate from the point of view of the secular law. What concerns the law is essentially the public establishment of paternity. William Harrington thus writes that if there is something wrong with any marriage, "such as . . . the banns not lawfully asked," then "the children born to the couple are bastards." [40] Whether or not Juliet and Claudio are privately married, their child is thus, to all political intents, a bastard. [41]

The confusion about the marital contract between Juliet and Claudio echoes similar ambiguities throughout the play involving intentions to enter into a contract or estate with someone, or Someone, else. One example is the contract between Mariana and Angelo. Another is Isabella's novitiate, her intention to become the spouse of God; that novitiate is left hanging just as is the spousal of Juliet and Claudio.

Either for Juliet to be still pregnant or for Claudio and Juliet to be actually married would easily result in a happy, unproblematic ending. For the authority in Vienna finally to become both secular and religious—as in the Viennese Holy Roman Empire, where the laws set down in heaven and on earth were one and the same (as they are not in Isabella's pleas before Angelo [2.4.50])—would provide a third way to escape the problem of bastardy. By the end of the play, however, Vincentio as Friar has slandered the secular state, claiming not only that he himself as Duke is unjust but implying that no temporal ruler has the right to enforce the law by beheading people. (The public recognition of the conjunction of Church [Friar] and State [Duke] is accomplished, ironically, only by a forceful "behooding.") Vincentio hardly represents an easy conjunction of Church and State.

These three positions—that Juliet's child is yet unborn, that Juliet is actually married, and that the political figure is now also a religious figure who will rule against such regulations as those set out in the council of Merton [42]—would provide a happy solution to the dilemma of the play. Yet the actual solution rises above them. In the telos of the plot, Claudio's wonderful son (Claudio himself) is superlegal, or nonnatural, rather than (but not in absolute opposition to) illegitimate. This is not so much in accord or conflict with secular or religious law as it is above the law. (Consider the similar problem of whether Jesus is illegitimate or above the law.) From this perspective, we may hope that Claudio, who has been delivered from death, can marry Juliet and thus similarly deliver their child from nature into legitimacy. Shakespeare himself made a legitimate child of his first-born, who came into the world "soon after marriage." [43]

The Second Marriage Proposal

> Marriage promises to turn strangers into friendly
> relatives—a nation of siblings.
> Maxine Hong Kingston [44]

Only after Vincentio has both pardoned Angelo and put down Lucio, thus rising above the elements of himself that Angelo and Lucio have represented, does he make Isabella a proposal of mutually reciprocal marriage. Instead of "You will be mine" (5.1.490), a univocal statement from master to servant, he now says, "What's mine is yours, and what is yours is mine" (5.1.534). (Princess Elizabeth, translating in her *Glasse of the Synnefull Soule* passages from both Marguerite's *Miroir* and the *Song of Songs*, speaks just such words to the quadrifold kinsperson she would engage in mystical union: "Thou art myn and I am thyne.") [45] This reciprocal exchange of lives—"life for life," and vice versa—would wholly transcend the sexual and commercial aspect of human affairs. It would raise up the apparently inherently contradictory condition of free dependency, which until now has been the loftiest relation formulated in *Measure for Measure*. ("I am your free dependant" [4.3.90], says the Provost to the Friar with the ducal ring.) It would raise the condition of free univocal dependence up to a condition of free interdependence where, as in Plato's dialectic, "both are two but each is one,"[46] or, as in Genesis, "they shall be one flesh" (Gen. 2:24).[47]

Carnal Contagion and Marriage. The sexual and political implications of such at-one-ment as marriage presupposes are important to understanding both how kinship is passed intragenerationally from person to person in the West and how the estate of marriage is presented in *Measure for Measure*. It is a central tenet of Pauline Christianity that a man shall "leave his father and mother, and shall be joined unto his wife, and they two shall be one flesh"; this conjunction of two into one is "a great mystery" (Eph. 5:31–32). Thus Shakespeare's Hamlet says bitterly that his uncle-father Claudius and aunt-mother Gertrude are one and the same: "Father and mother is man and wife, man and wife is one flesh" (HAM 4.3.50–51). The same eucharistic union informs Pompey's first words in prison, which not only respond to the Provost's question, "Can you cut off a man's head?" (4.2.1), but also echo Saint Paul's belief that in the corporate union of the marriage estate the man is the head (Eph. 5:23). Pompey answers, "If the man be a bachelor, sir, I can; but if he be a married man, he's his wife's head; and I can never cut off a woman's head" (4.2.2–4). In making the professional transition from the pimp's "mystery" of taking women's maidenheads to the executioner's "mystery" of taking men's heads (4.2.26–39), Pompey suggests the mystery of marriage itself.

The Church Fathers extend the corporate union of two into one in marriage to the conjunction of fornicator and fornicatrix as well. (They take marriage to be the essential telos of all sexual intercourse.) Here they follow Paul, who wrote, "Know ye not that he which is joined to an harlot is one body? for two, saith he, shall be one flesh" (1 Cor. 6:16, cf. Gen. 2:24). Outside marriage, as inside it, sexual intercourse makes two people essentially one, which is to say that sexual intercourse spreads kinship, bringing the relatives of each party into the kindred of the other.[48]

This Christian extension of the corporate union in marriage to all sexual relationships casts into doubt the old, or the Old Testament, distinction between legal and illegal sexual relations, or between marital and extramarital relations; it holds that one is no more or less closely related to the kin of one with whom one has marital sexual relations than to the kin of one with whom one has extramarital sexual relations. Treating all sexual intercourse as essentially marital puts into question the crucial distinctions between incest and endogamy (whether one marries or not is now essentially immaterial) and between endogamy and exogamy, a distinction by which most societies are informed.[49] (In this sense Christianity casts off the distinction between nature and culture.)

Moreover, the Fathers' position makes clear how promiscuity gives rise to incest. One becomes kin to the kin of anyone with whom one sleeps, whether within marriage (in which case these new kin are "in-laws") or without. Thus *Jacob's Well* states that "whan a man hath medlyd wyth a womman, or a womman wyth a man, neyther may be wedded to otheres kyn, into the fyfte degre, ne medle wyth hem; for if thei don, it is incest."[50] As J. H. Fowler summarizes the medieval theologian Rabanus Maurus: "There is something like a communicable disease metaphor involved in early medieval notions of sexuality. If one sleeps with a woman who sleeps with another man who sleeps with another woman who sleeps with me, then whether I will it or not my flesh is inextricably bound up with the flesh of that first man's. A term which continually shows up in these canons and letters to describe fornication is *contagio carnalis*—carnal contagion."[51] Thus fornication not only leads to venereal disease and to incest through illegitimacy, it also leads to incest through the secret spread of kinship by contagion of the flesh. Accordingly, Isabella is the "cousin" of Juliet (who is Claudio's lover) in ways other than the one she tells Lucio.

In the trial that allowed Henry VIII to marry Anne Boleyn, the doctrine of carnal contagion was used against that of the Jewish levirate, according to which a man must marry the childless widow of a deceased brother (Deut. 25 : 5–6), in order to claim that Henry's marriage to his sister-in-law Catherine was incestuous. If the king's brother had slept with a woman, it was argued, then she was the king's kin and his marriage to her was null and void. Had this argument not been judged successful, the Princess Elizabeth, later the Queen, would have had to be judged a bastard.

Something like the idea of carnal contagion underlies most notions of kinship and incest in the West, allowing marital sexual relations to create kinship, or "in-laws." But by conflating extramarital with marital sexual intercourse, the Christian doctrine of carnal contagion undermines and transcends the ordinary notion of kinship, which cannot hypothesize a principle of incest without an absolutely opposite principle of chaste marriage. Catholic celibates hold the transcendent position that there can be an incest (literally "non-chastity") beyond the distinction between chastity and its opposite. In the last analysis, *Measure for Measure*, if it can be said to be "about" anything at all, is about a similarly transcendent position: the perfect reciprocal exchange, or end of exchange, where marriage is at once both wholly chaste and wholly unchaste. Just such a marriage is figured in the second proposal that the Duke makes to Isabella: "What's mine is yours, and what is yours is mine" (5.1.534).

But does Isabella accept? To judge from her verbal response, or rather lack of it, Isabella no more accepts or rejects the second proposal of the Duke than she pardons or does not pardon Claudio. (Isabella's silence does not, in itself, mean refusal in either case; compare the apparent refusal of marriage at the end of *Love's Labor's Lost*.) Yet we should not dismiss the question of whether the Duke and Isabella eventually marry, calling it as irrelevant as the question How many children had Lady MacBeth?[52] The question of marriage in *Measure for Measure* concerns not only what Isabella says but also the gist of the plot. Is it the telos of the plot for Isabella and the Duke to marry? To put it another way, would such a marriage solve the confrontation between the natural requirement to reproduce and the political necessity to prohibit incest, the essential human problem that gave rise to *Measure for Measure* in the first place?[53]

An answer to the question of whether Isabella marries the Duke depends upon answers to two other questions: What are her options? and What is marriage? One purpose of *Measure for Measure* is to bring us to ask the latter question in a new way. To see how the play raises questions about marriage, let us take the question Does Isabella marry the Duke? to mean, Is it consistent with the plot or hypothesis of *Measure for Measure* that Isabella marry the Duke? An answer involves a number of related issues connected with the general problem of incest.

Blood Siblings and Siblings-in-Law. The first issue concerns whether anyone in Vienna (or in the world, for that matter) can know with certainty who his father is, and thus whether his spouse is not his blood kin. The secular, political need for public marriage to establish paternity is as intense at the end of the play (when the question of whether a marriage will take place involves Isabella and the Duke) as it was at the beginning of the play (when the question of whether a marriage has taken place involved Juliet and Claudio). The threat to the political order represented by Juliet's pregnancy has by no means been resolved. Making Lucio the husband of Kate Keepdown and thus establishing one (albeit representative) paternity does not so much transcend (or master through loving moderation) as repress, or keep down through fear of punishment, the problem of natural lust within the individual and within the city. The punishment of Lucio is a failure of genuine moderation or temperance (as opposed to mere restraint or continence); moreover, the drawn-out final dialogue between Lucio and the Duke reminds us of the motivating dilemma of bastardy and of incest. (The libertine Lucio had warned Friar Vincentio, "Nay, friar, I am a kind of burr, I shall stick" [4.3.177], and stick he does.)

Even after Lucio is married off, in a small step toward establishing the natural paternity of everyone in Vienna, the situation at the play's beginning—the almost universal potential for illegitimacy and incest that motivates some people to try to make a spouse of God—still exists. From this near-universality of potential kin relations it follows that Vincentio, who proposes marriage to Isabella, may be her father, her brother, or both.[54] In fact, Vincentio is called "father" and "father friar" ("friar," from *frater*, means "brother"), and he calls Isabella both "daughter" and "young sister" (3.1.238, 3.2.11, 4.3.111, 3.1.150). That any of these terms correctly names a blood relationship between Vincentio and Isabella is, of course, an unlikely possibility (compare "Make not impossible / That which but seems unlike" [5.1.54–55]), but it is scarcely less likely than that Angelo enacted the fornication he intended.

The possibility of consanguineous as well as political or religious kinship between Isabella and the Duke is figured when the Duke, who has already called her both a "daughter" and a "sister," claims near the end of the play that her brother, whom he has already called "son" (3.1.159), is "my brother" (5.1.491). It follows from this that Isabella, whom Vincentio has asked to become his wife, is already his sister. Vincentio, we suppose, means to say merely that Claudio will become his brother-in-law when (and if) Isabella marries him. Yet only the significantly unspoken phrase "in-law" distinguishes the Duke as Isabella's proposed husband from the Duke as her brother. The critical distinction of husband from brother, which resides in law, recalls again the motivating conflict between nature and law—the requirement to reproduce and the political necessity to limit the kinship relationships between reproducers.[55] The same two words, "in law," play a crucial role in *All's Well That Ends Well*, which concerns a potentially incestuous marriage like the one in *Measure for Measure*.

All's Well That Ends Well (1602–4), written about the same time as *Measure for Measure* (1604), contains the closest parallel in Shakespeare to the bed trick. As in *Measure for Measure*, incest of a kind drives its action. *All's Well That Ends Well* begins: "In delivering my son from me I bury a second husband" (AWW 1.1.1, cf. 5.3.70). The widowed Countess of Rousillion here reminds her son Bertram that, having replaced his late father as Count of Rousillion, he has been a second husband to her. Bertram now wants to leave home, however,

so the Countess must deliver to the world at large him whom she long
ago delivered from the womb. In this sense, Bertram is both his mother's son and her husband. From this hint of mother-son incest develops the suggestion, central to this play as to *Measure for Measure*, of
sibling incest—between Bertram and Helena, the Countess's daughter
by adoption.

Thus *All's Well*, like *Measure for Measure*, concerns the question of
adoption. Helena in *All's Well* is the daughter by adoption of the
·Countess and loves the Countess's son; Juliet in *Measure for Measure* is
the cousin by adoption of Isabella and loves Isabella's brother. Helena
takes great care to determine that she is eligible to marry her legal
brother, insisting that she is not the natural daughter of the Countess:

> *Helena.* Mine honorable mistress.   (AWW 1.3.141)
> *Countess.*   Nay, a mother.
>   Why not a mother? When I said "a mother,"
>   Methought you saw a serpent. What's in "mother,"
>   That you start at it? I say I am your mother,
>   And put you in the catalogue of those
>   That were enwombed mine. Tis often seen
>   Adoption strives with nature.
>
>   .   .   .
>
> *Helena.*   Pardon Madam.
>   The Count Rossillion cannot be my brother.
>
>   .   .   .
>
> *Countess.*   Nor I your mother?
> *Helena.* You are my mother, madam; would you were—
>   So that my lord, your son, were not my brother—
>   Indeed my mother! Or were you both our mothers
>   I care no more for than I do for heaven,
>   So I were not his sister. Can't no other
>   But, I your daughter, he must be my brother?
> *Countess.* Yes, Helen, you might be my daughter-in-law.

The Countess loves Helena as if she were a natural daughter. "If she
had partaken of my flesh and cost me the dearest groans of a mother,"
says the Countess, "I could not have owed her a more rooted love
(AWW 4.5.10–11). Because of that love, the Countess would transform
Helena from a daughter by legal adoption into a daughter by nature.
But if Helena is to be united with Bertram in chaste marriage, either

she must not be the Countess's daughter or Bertram must not be the Countess's son. Helena insists on the first, that she can be the daughter-in-law, but not the daughter, of the Countess.[56] The plot suggests the alternative condition for a chaste marriage, namely, the figurative disestablishment of Bertram as the Countess's son. "He was my son," says the Countess to Helena when she learns of Bertram's flight, "But I do wash his name out of my blood / And thou art all my child" (AWW 3.2.68–70). The Countess's daughter (as the Countess would make Helena) would be able to marry the Countess's ex-son.

"My sister, my spouse" (Song of Sol. 4 : 12). The distinction in law between spouse and sibling on which Helena relies recalls the conflict between nature and law in *Measure for Measure*. There is a crucial difference between the two plays, however. In *All's Well*, it is clear enough that Helena is not actually Bertram's blood sister, and the question of whether one can legally marry one's legally adopted sibling is not raised. (As Shakespeare knew, the Roman Church is equivocal in treating the question of whether siblings by legal adoption can marry.) In *Measure for Measure*, on the other hand, it is unclear who is the blood relative of whom, hence who can marry whom. And *Measure for Measure* raises a question kept in abeyance in *All's Well*: whether our status as equal children (*liberi*) of God the Father (*pater*)—as His born-again adopted children—does not, on account of the universality of our Siblinghood, either bar us from all sexual relations (as in celibacy) or require us to commit incest of a kind (as in libertinage). *Measure for Measure* thus confronts directly the tension between nature and law.

Children of Adoption.   Vincentio is, politically speaking, the father of the patriarchal, secular community in which Isabella is a citizen (a child); religiously speaking, he is both her "ghostly father" (5.1.128)—insofar as he is her confessor and the purported representative of the Pope[57]—and her brother, insofar as he has played at being a Brother by virtue of his disguise and she has played at being a Sister in her novitiate. (Vincentio is also both a father and a brother to Mariana: like a father, he offers to give her a dowry [the sentenced Angelo's possessions] with which to buy a husband [5.1.423]; in giving this new dowry, he restores what her brother lost at sea [3.1.215–18].) But what is the precise significance of a layman disguised as a friar or of a novice nun within the context of this play?

Let us first take up the question of Isabella's novitiate. There is a remarkable confusion in *Measure for Measure* about whether the novice Isabella is a nun or a laywoman. The Provost introduces her to Angelo as "a very virtuous maid; / And to be shortly of a sisterhood, / If not already" (2.2.20–22). Thereafter Claudio's sister is introduced simply as a "sister" (2.4.18), as though her "re*nounc*ement" (1.4.35; emphasis mine), as Lucio calls it, had already made her to all intents a *nun*.

To the novice who may become a nun in the sense of Sister, Angelo gives the opportunity to become a "nun" in the sense of prostitute:

> Be that you are,   (2.4.133–37)
> That is, a woman; if you be more, you're none.
> If you be one—as you are well express'd
> By all external warrants—show it now,
> By putting on the destin'd livery.

What is Isabella's livery at the end of the Play? Is it the heavenly Sister's hood or the earthly sister's bridal veil?[58] The question of what Isabella finally wears—the outfit of a novice, nun, laywoman, bride, or some combination of these—is as crucial to the play's resolution as are Claudio's delivery and Barnardine's liberty.

Let us assume for a moment that in the last scene Isabella is still a novice. Is she, as novice, free according to canon law or traditional morality to give up her novitiate and marry the Duke?[59] A novitiate is an engagement to God, and the same problems that affect earthly engagements affect heavenly ones. The earthly engagements between Claudio and Juliet and between Angelo and Mariana suggest that engagements cannot be broken off easily: Claudio says that he and Juliet are "fast" married ("Save that we do the denunciation lack / Of outward order" [1.2.137–38]), and the Duke says that Angelo and Mariana are virtually married. In this context, Isabella's breaking off her promise to become the bride of Christ must be treated as a serious breach. Even as a novice, Isabella might as well be thought of and treated as a nun; to all intents and purposes, she *is* a nun, the telos of a Catholic novitiate.

Let us assume, then, that Isabella has already taken vows. How can she marry the Duke? Marriage between a nun and a layman would be an outrage in a Catholic context; it would be spiritual incest of the kind that occurs when a Sister marries most any man. The one eligible bachelor for Isabella as nun is the man-god Jesus. But for her as nun, marrying the Duke would be a blessing—even an allegorical enactment of the meaning of celibate monachism—if and only if the Duke were, or represented, Jesus, so that Isabella, as the Duke's bride, would also be Christ's bride.

To the topos of the nun as the spouse of God the Son several critics have pointed,[60] but no one has discussed the equally pervasive topos of the nun as the daughter of God the Father. *Hali Meidenhad*, a meditation on female virginity that popularized in England the concept of "spiritual marriage" (especially in regard to the marriage between Joseph and the Virgin Mary),[61] describes a woman who has renounced an earthly husband as being "God's bride and his noble daughter, for she is both together."[62] Taken together, the topoi of nun as wife and daughter of God allow a satisfactory conclusion to the play. But does the play treat the player-friar Vincentio unambiguously as God?

The all-too-human vices of Vincentio suggest that, despite the fact that he may be conceived as divine by subjects who require an authority outside themselves, he is a man merely made in the image of God, not His only Son. Isabella's marrying such a man—any Adam's son rather than God's only Son—would be the mortal sin of "spiritual incest."

And what if Vincentio as player-friar is, to all intents, a friar? (Theologically speaking, this places him somewhere between Jesus and a layman.) He is able, after all, to "satisfy," or confess, Mariana (who lives under the order's jurisdiction in a Grange at Saint Luke's [3.1.265, 4.1.8–9]),[63] and he sends Angelo "letters of strange tenour, perchance of the Duke's death, perchance entering into some monastery" (4.2. 199–201). (The Duke is lying, of course, but why should he choose this lie, just as he chose this disguise?) That the Duke does not wear his hood when he proposes marriage, moreover, does not mean that he is not a monk. For just as wearing a hood does not transform a man into a monk, as Lucio knowingly says (5.1.261), so removing a hood does not unmonk a man. Schlegel aptly remarks that in *Measure for Measure*, "contrary to the well known proverb [the hood does not make the monk], the cowl seems really to make a monk of the Duke."[64]

The Chaste, Incestuous Marriage.   The question of whether the Duke and Isabella are actually Brother and Sister, as the play sometimes seems to suggest, is not as important as the fact that, to all their intents and for the penultimate purposes of the plot, they are. Unlike things are not impossible (Angelo could have done what Isabella publicly accuses him of), and likeness or resemblance can become identity or certainty (the hooded man can become Claudio, a novice become a nun, a player-friar become a friar). In this sense, at least, the proposed marriage between the Duke and Isabella is one between a Brother and a Sister.

Such a marriage is a special, indeed, a revolutionary "kind of incest." From the point of view of the Roman church, it is the sin of libertinism; from the point of view of Protestant reformers, it is the sign of liberation. The proposed marriage between Isabella and the Duke is recognizably a symbol of the Reformation and of the dissolution of the monasteries. In his Hegelian reading of *Measure for Measure*, D. J. Snider catches this Protestant quality in the proposed marriage between the Duke and Isabella, a marriage which Snider assumes will take place: "Luther the monk, like the Duke, took a wife."[65]

There are other precedents besides the 1525 marriage of Luther and his Cistercian wife Catherine von Bora for Sisters and Brothers becoming husbands and wives. Among these are two married monks who directly influenced the education of Princess Elizabeth. One is Bernardino Ochino, whose works the religious instructor of the Princess apparently had read; he was driven from England during Mary's accession to the throne (1553).[66] The other is John Bale, who wrote the Epistle Dedicatory and Conclusion to Elizabeth's translation of *The Mirror of the Sinful Soul*. Bale argued for the impossibility of absolute temperance and embraced marriage for the clergy. He forsook his monastic habit and got married.[67] In Bale's play, *The Three Laws of Nature* (1538, 1562), Sodomy appears dressed as a monk.[68] There are other precedents for Sibling marriage—for example, Leo Judae, a disciple of Zwingli, married a Beguine in 1523.[69]

None of these examples is as important as Luther, of course, whose doctrine of justification by faith instead of by acts and corresponding view of the relationship between intent and act sparked the Reformation.[70] An Augustinian eremite who thought that his unfulfilled desires made him prey for the devil, Luther argued that few if any men were perfect enough to be celibate.[71] (He would have argued that Brother Thomas and Sister Francesca in *Measure for Measure* could be not as we credit them.) Thus he denounced both monastic vows and distinctive dress for the clergy; like Lucio in *Measure for Measure*, he would tear hoods (cowls) from Brothers and hoods (maidenheads) from Sisters. Luther's marriage in 1525 to a nun was a decisive act in the history of Western sexuality and its comprehension of incest.[72]

Incest is central to English discussions of Luther's marriage. Sir Thomas More, for example, argued that clerical marriage "defileth the priest more than double or trebel whoredom";[73] and in his *Confutaycon with Tindale* (1537) he accused Luther and his wife, "the frere and the nunne," of incest:

Let not therfore Tyndall (good reder) wyth his gay gloryouse wordes carye you so fast & so far away, but that ye remembre to pull hym bakke by the sleue a lytle, and aske hym whyther his owne hyghe spyrytuall doctour mayster Martyne Luther hym selfe, beynge specyally borne agayne & new created of the spyryte, whom god in many places of holy scrypture hath commaunded to kepe his vowe made of chastyte when he then so far contrarye there vnto toke out of relygyon a spouse of Cryste, wedded her hym selfe in reproche of wedloke, called her his wyfe, and made her his harlot, and in doble despyte of maryage and relygyon both, lyueth wyth her openly and lyeth wyth her nyghtly, in shamefull inceste and abominable lycherye.[74]

Incest of a kind thus became the charge not only against such secular notables as Anne Boleyn, Queen Elizabeth's earthly mother, but also against such religious notables as Bernardino Ochino and John Bale, Elizabeth's spiritual fathers. "A kind of incest" at once both physiological and spiritual is suggested by the absence of an answer to the player-Brother Vincentio's proposal of marriage to the player-Sister Isabella.

The Fiction of Chaste Marriage. In *The Elementary Structures of Kinship*, Lévi-Strauss writes, "Marriage is an arbitration between two loves, parental and conjugal. [The two] are both forms of love, and the instant the marriage takes place, considered in isolation, the two meet and merge; 'love has filled the ocean.' Their meeting is doubtless merely a prelude to their substitution for one another, the performance of a sort of *chassé-croisé*. But to intercross they must at least momentarily be joined, and it is this which in all social thought makes marriage a sacred mystery. At this moment, all marriage verges on incest."[75]

In *Measure for Measure* the "kind of incest" that Isabella is asked to perform, first by Angelo and then by Claudio, is made more or less acceptable by way of a series of commercial exchanges in which, for the original barter exchange of maidenhead for head, are substituted the monetary exchanges of maidenhead for maidenhead (Mariana for Isabella) and of heads for head (Barnardine and Ragozine for Claudio). Isabella kind of gives birth to her own brother, and the kind of incest that Claudio (Angelo) proposes she commit is incorporated and transcended by the kind of marriage that the Duke proposes. Marriage as such appears to dissolve the dilemmas involving both commercial taliation and sexual commensuration that inform the play. In the essential moment of *Measure for Measure*, however, "all marriage verges on incest."

Marriage appears to solve the fundamental issue of taliation by creating or hypothesizing a condition of identity in difference where "both are two but each is one," and it appears to solve the fundamental issue of sexual exchange by creating or hypothesizing an essentially chaste relationship. This appearance is both its major ideological role (marriage as estate or contract orders most all societies) and its major dramaturgical role (marriage ends most all comedies). Thus marriage of the traditional kind that the Duke first proposes may appear to be a welcome political and aesthetic closure, the desperately needed solution to the dilemmas of law and nature that the play has delineated. To liberals it may well be disconcerting that marriage of this kind seems to require both the oppression of women (it keeps kissing Kate down) and, more essentially, the repression of all human beings who live in the sexual and propertal discontent of civilization. (Marriage as such is essentially parentarchal, although it appears patriarchal in one setting and matriarchal in another.)[76] However, we most all of us come to accept such marriage, gratefully even, as the only dramatic and political solution, and we structure our plots and societies accordingly. We believe that, by certain aesthetic and societal marital establishments, we can avoid the supposed horror of universal communism and incest as represented in such asocial institutions as the Catholic orders and tragedy.

Measure for Measure suggests, however, that marriage is itself incestuous. At the crux of this play in which all siblinghood verges on Universal Siblinghood and intent verges on act, husband and wife are also brother/Brother and sister/Sister. In that vertiginous moment, marriage of the ordinary political kind is exhibited as an ideological figure whose bias toward property and exogamy is at once socially necessary and fictional, if not downright hypocritical. *Measure for Measure* reveals that universal ownership (communism) and Universal Siblinghood (incest) are, on the one hand, the teloi and antonomasias of marriage and, on the other hand, the very anarchic "institutions" against which marriage militates for the sake of civilization as we ordinarily conceive it. Just as monachism promises to turn everyone into siblings under God, so marriage promises to turn all strangers into friendly relatives—"a nation of siblings."[77] Any essential liberation can be got only at the cost of general copulation.

In this disconcerting, not to say absurd, context, a purely parentarchal (chaste) marriage—that is, one without an underlying, subversive propertal and sexual component—is both essentially impossible and also a repressive (if socially necessary) myth or figure of speech. With the proposed marriages of the chastized bastardizers (Claudio and Juliet, Lucio and Kate Keepdown) and of the player-Brother and player-Sister (Vincentio and Isabella), we may, of course, be tempted to hope that the "liberty" (1.2.117) infecting all Vienna will be extirpated from the city. Such an extirpation of unchastity is a precondition for the establishment of social order as it is traditionally conceived, since liberty threatens the political authority whose public acknowlegment most all of us (the ilk of Angelo) require in order to behave continently, like good children of the state. "It is impossible to extirp it quite" (3.2.98), however, not only because "the vice is of a great kindred," pervading the life of Vienna as much as "eating and drinking" (3.2.97, 99) (as Lucio says), but because liberty, illegitimacy, and incest are spiritual conditions within (or antonomasias of) the marriage relationship that Vincentio, torn between wanting to be an ordinary man and needing to be a figurehead, seeks. It is the final irony of *Measure for Measure* that marriage, to which we look as the only solution to the dilemma of incest, or of the confrontation between nature and politics, exhibits incest as its telos and antonomasia.

Marriage does not transcend the dilemmas inherent in the liberal incest and commerce of flesh that, in the plot of *Measure for Measure*, constitute the way towards marriage. As in incest the places of "father" (*pater*), "brother" (*frater*), and "free son" (*liber*) are conflated, so in marriage "husband" and "wife" become, as Paul suggests (Eph. 5:23, 1 Cor. 7:4), one another's property. The fusion of husband and wife into one body or fictive corporation is remarked by Pompey as he moves from being pimp to being head-chopping executioner: "If the man be a bachelor, sir, I can; but if he be a married man, he's his wife's head; and I can never cut off a woman's head" (4.2.2−4). The marriage formula in *Measure for Measure*, "What's mine is yours, and what is yours is mine" (5.1.534), implies that the unsettling commercial exchangeability and interchangeability of male head with female maidenhead might be transcended if a man and a woman might become together one artificial person—a couple like "sister and brother" or "wife and husband." The figure of marriage thus defined, in terms that transcend the incestuous conflation of kinship roles and the monetary commensuration of life with death, is the contractual estate that organizes the play. Like the figure of the father of the city, however, chaste marriage so defined is no more attained within the context of *Measure for Measure* than it is more than a legal fiction in the Elizabethan political economy, or perhaps in any.

Conclusion

Hieronymous Bosch, *The Garden of Earthly Delights.* (About 1500; Prado.)

Sisters and brothers,
Brothers and sisters,
Ain't we every one?

Stephen Lawrence and Bruce Hart,
on *Free to Be . . . You and Me*

THE TELOS of *Measure for Measure* and the informing element of its plot is the ideal taliation of a chaste, incestuous marriage. The play integrates a study of incest in the ordinary sense (we risk committing incest in any act of intercourse because no one can be certain who his father is) with a study of incest in an extraordinary sense (we are all children of the same Father, so all sex is antonomastically incest). Isabella flees from promiscuous Vienna, where any man might be her blood kin, to the convent, where all men are certainly her spiritual kin. The religious (or extraordinary) aspect of *Measure for Measure*—figured by the Catholic orders—is thus the logical telos (the place where *we* are driven) of the secular, or ordinary, life of the play. The religious aspect of the play is thus not in any sense foreign to it, but is rather its formal or teleological essence. The plot goes to and from a nunnery.

The Form of Marriage

To understand how the form (*eidos*) of marriage is the telos of *Measure for Measure*, we must examine the connections between teleology and plot in Western drama as a whole. From Aristotle to Kant, at least, a discussion of the precise relationship between teleology in nature and in art was crucial to considerations of art. "The plot," writes Aristotle, "is the end [*telos*] of a tragedy; and the end is the chief thing of all."[1] In the plot, he implies, an intention that informs the play is realized[2]—the likely is made necessary. Telos, so understood, is not merely an end; it is also the term of a process of generation like the natural one. In Aristotle, entelechy concerns that process of development (whether artistic or natural) from potential existence to form (*eidos*) or perfect actuality (*entelechia*)—from pregnancy, say, to birth. The first part of Kant's *Critique of Judgment* similarly presents art as purposive (it considers structural organization and the tendency to ending); the second part concerns the heuristic purposiveness which Kant argues that we must conceive for the organism.

Such an analogy between nature and art informs my understanding of the plot of *Measure for Measure* as "giving birth to a birth," which I mean both in a figurative and a literal sense. I see *Measure for Measure* as a play whose plot has both a kind of biological telos (for Aristotle all plays do) and a biological content. The greatness of the play lies partly in its critical, even self-critical, combination of form (telos) and content. This artful drama, with its aesthetic teleology analogical to the natural teleology we must assume, has as its content the confrontation of natural teleology with the artful requirements of human civilization. By the fiction of plotting (the Greek *hupothesis*) it depicts one of the grandest fictions of the political order: perfect taliation, or marriage.

In many plays of Shakespeare, especially the comedies, marriage or reunion is the end of the plot. Not only is it the last event, it is also the logical consequence of the preceding action.[3] Yet in *Measure for Measure*, remarkably, marriage and reunion, whether we want them or not, are not agreed to within the context of the drama. To assume that they do take place distorts and simplifies the play as a whole, just as the argument that marriage in the actual world could in any but a fictional sense solve the problems inherent in the actual political economy is mere ideology.

One position on the topic (I would call it the "Protestant" one) might be stated as follows. Sublimation or suppression of the natural sexual urge (e.g., the sublimation that Angelo, Isabella, and the Duke seek, each in his or her own way) is impossible. A modern Augustinian Sister (a member of Luther's order) says of sexual desire: "You can't sublimate it. You can't suppress it. You simply have to damn well sacrifice it."[4] Sacrifice of sexuality, however, can entail (some would say must entail) a kind of internal mutilation—a castration of the heart—that makes not so much for transcendentally temperate, whole men (which is the monachist goal) as for merely continent, hence damnable, eunuchs for God. Surely it is better to marry than to burn in a damnable castration of the heart. Moreover, marriage redeems (or makes chastely possible) the generation on which depends, God knows, our present world order—which order, being neither virginal (like Eden) nor supervirginal (like the world of the Second Coming), requires that some of us, at least, procreate. "Long live chaste marriage!" That, some say, is realism.

The Protestant position recognizes the falseness of mere continence, whether internal (as in the case of Angelo) or external (as in the case of physically castrated and imprisoned men). *Measure for Measure* certainly takes this tack—that it is better to marry than to burn—a certain distance. *Measure for Measure* takes an opposing tack, however, when it suggests that to marry is also to burn, since marriage is essentially incestuous.[5] Does a marriage take place, then, within or without the play? Maybe the spectator must take things as they are; the Brothers (Luther, say) are already—essentially and historically—married to the Sisters. The greater question, however, is: What does the play reveal about the meaning of marriage?, or, What does marriage mean for our culture? Does marriage really solve the confrontation between nature and culture, or the civilized human being's discontented desire for, and fear of, incest?

The Protestant charge against Catholic monachism—that celibacy is worse than marriage—is not allowed to stand in *Measure for Measure*. Whatever the validity of the view that celibacy is perverse, the play shows that psychological repression of a similar or worse kind obtains in the institution of marriage. Marriage, which enacts incest, is worse than celibacy, which merely intends incest, insofar as a bad act is essentially worse than a bad intent. *Measure for Measure* suggests the fictional, or dreamlike, quality of marriage as a chaste solution to the confrontation between nature and culture. Marriage is fictional because what marriage purports to accomplish—a chaste solution to the confrontation between civilization (the rule against incest) and nature (the rule to reproduce no matter how)—it accomplishes only by violation of the incest taboo.

The violation of the incest taboo informing, or motivating, marriage involves the doctrine, essential to Christianity, that we are all siblings. In many societies, what is most important is not to know one's biological kin but rather to know the group of people that constitute one's sociological kin and to which, willy-nilly, one's biological kin belong or should belong. If we take the side of sociology against that of biology—that is, if we universalize our civilized, or social, aspect—then the children's song has a point: "Sisters and brothers, / Brothers and sisters, / Ain't we everyone?"[6] Sisters and brothers all. Marriage, which in this version *must* be to a sibling, is as much a profane violation of the taboo on endogamy/incest as it is a sacred attempt not to violate the taboo. The figural line separating my biological daughter, with whom my son may have sexual intercourse under no circumstances, from my sociological daughter-in-law, with whom my son may in certain circumstances have intercourse, suggests the precarious position here of law itself.

The formal idea, or *eidos*, of marriage in *Measure for Measure* thus combines in one vision both incestuous and chaste, both tragic and comic, teloi. For incest, though abhorrent to the political order as we know it, is, from a Christian spiritual perspective, an essential requirement of the Holy Family as of Universal Siblinghood generally, and, from a Christian physical perspective, the antonomasia for and telos of all sexual activity, including that in wedlock. Ordinary marriage is the typical, even perfect, end of comedy, which is only political; incest is the typical end of tragedy, which is only natural. The plot of *Measure for Measure*, however, brings together marriage and incest, comedy and tragedy, in an extraordinary union. This union is at once impossible and aesthetically necessary. It is what Aristotle calls a "likely impossibility," like any atonement of two different things. Thus necessity (as opposed to chance) and aesthetic probability (as opposed to realistic possibility) play a key role in the narrative teleology of the drama—for example, in the death of Ragozine, which is at once accidental and necessary. Through the remarkable union of incest (by virtue of which "all are one") and marriage (by virtue of which "both are two but each is one")[7] the great problems of dialectic, if not of all knowledge, are solved. In this sense the plot—maybe literary plotting in general—"is a source of knowledge which we absolutely require, and which we have no other way of acquiring."[8]

The humanist and literary disciplines may be especially well suited to explore the claim that a fiction of adequate commensuration in exchange, or of chastity in marriage, underlies most all human societies. Literary fiction—and above all its most social expression, dramatic plotting—is closely tied to the societal need for fictions of atonement or commensuration in commercial and sexual transactions. Do such social fictions as commercial identity and incest give rise somehow to such literary fictions as disguise and the interchangeability of meaning? Do we do well, or as well as we might, to approach the social and political problems of taliation and incest by analyzing a work of literature—albeit a brilliant one—rather than by statistical surveys, anthropological fieldwork, or psychological investigation?

Great drama is a response to, and in some measure is born with, the conflict between nature and culture that informs the Western tradition of understanding incest and its taboo. To glimpse the repression inherent in one's tradition from within that tradition requires the indirection of aesthetic form. Drama is peculiarly able to delineate the problem of sociobiological telos since dramatic form imitates that telos, treating the general as though it were the particular, transforming the like or likely into the necessary, and conflating intent (or desire) with act. Dramatic art is what best explains the more or less artful combination of two different things—two siblings or two spouses—into one. Such oneness and atonement are formally definitive in incest, which may help explain why Racine, who incorporated Aristotelian and other unities into his works, generally chose incest as the informing content of his plots.[9] In incest one closes the circle of time,[10] moving forward from birth to death and backward from death to birth: "On this day," says Sophocles' Tiresias to Oedipus, "you will be born and die at the same time."[11]

"Make not impossible / That which but seems unlike" (5.1.54–55). The principle of economy in *Measure for Measure* is the unlikely collapse of intent with act and of every act with its telos. This collapse allows the exploration of problems otherwise inaccessible. It also allows the exploration of how the process of the play—a series of hypothetical, taliational exchanges—conjoins the natural demand for incest (the only solution apparent in the middle of the play) with the political demand for chaste marriage (the only solution apparent at the end). These exchanges lead up to the unlikely exchange of Claudio for Claudio's own son, as the precondition for the concluding chaste, if incestuous, marriage.

My claims for the meaning of the plot are not necessary to enjoyment of the play, but they help one understand its telos. Chapman writes: "If the Body (being the letter, or history), seems fictive, and beyond possibility to bring into Act: the scene, then, the Allegory (which is the soul) is to be sought."[12] As we have seen, the intrigue of *Measure for Measure* moves from "a kind of incest" in the figural sense "an unchaste act that is like, or that resembles incest" toward "a kind of incest" in the sense "a certainly incestuous act with one's own kin." The plot of *Measure for Measure* acts out this certain incest through resemblance, although it is "not a resemblance, but a certainty" (4.2.187) that saves Claudio. This concentration on resemblance gives literature its power to pose the problem of incest and perhaps ultimately to dispose of it.

Incest and Repression

What is't I dream on? 2.2.179

Taken as a whole, *Measure for Measure* offers a glimpse of a liberty that, were it understood and realized, would mean the essential transformation, if not the probably impossible end, of politics. In such moments as the beginning of the play, when Isabella seems to vacillate between remaining in the Sisterhood and pleading as a sister, or the end of the play, when she seems to vacillate between being a Sister to all men and being a wife to Vincentio, *Measure for Measure* seeks out the "glassy essence," or social archeology, of the "angry ape" that is Man (2.2.121). To recognize this exposure of the role of incest and its taboo in society is to challenge—if only for a moment—the basis of all political union as we know it.

The radical nature of such a challenge may explain why more critics and readers have not discussed the centrality of incest to the play. By ignoring it, critics willy-nilly serve the politically conservative purpose of suppressing discontent so that marriage and politics can go on essentially unquestioned. Their frequent claim that *Measure for Measure* is motivated by the desire to uphold an ideal of chastity[13] echoes a desire to uphold that ideal themselves—for it is still upon chastity that such ideologically and politically important institutions as property and kinship are conceptually grounded. Their treatment of incest—or obliviousness to it—has been in effect a kind of repression.

Literary Criticism. Contemporary criticism has treated incest in terms of solipsism, narcissism, exclusivity, rebellion, difference versus repetition, sexist oppression, and individuation.[14] Psychoanalysis treats incest in literature as an oneirological fulfillment of individual oedipal fantasy, and anthropology treats it as an allegorical expression of social structure.[15] There are a few anthologies of literary works about incest and only one work that attempts to provide a bibliographical survey of major works about incest as it is ordinarily understood in the Western tradition.[16] In these treatments, incest has been regarded as but one possible erotic theme among many, albeit a theme with an especially "pornographic" component.[17] Those writing more generally about art have tended to treat incest in an equally limited way—as a literary issue at once moral and aesthetic. T. S. Eliot argues that a play about consciously committed incest can be a "good" play only insofar as calling the hero and heroine brother and sister does not make the spectator feel that their love for each other is essentially incestuous.[18] He was preceded in this argument by Thomas Rymer, who objected to the sibling love in Speroni's *Canace* (1546) and in *A King and No King*, by Beaumont and Fletcher, on the quasi-Aristotelian ground that a knowingly incestuous hero cannot be tragic because he is too unlike us to elicit pity or fear.[19]

I believe that, as drama is peculiarly suited to the working out of cultural concerns expressed by the idea of incest and the incest taboo, so literary interpretation and commentary are especially suited for discussing incest. The distinction between biology and sociology (or nature and culture) can be brought into question in terms of the intellectual and linguistic place of kinship words or names and in terms of a poetics, or metaphorics, or the classification of kin and kind—"a little more than kin, and less than kind." Insight into the figural aspect of language can enable literary scholars to deal anew with the figure of incest in literature. In doing so, they can reconsider the predominantly Western view that consanguinity is the primary, or literal, kind of kinship, and that other kinds—friendship, gossipred, even friendship and politics—are merely secondary, or figural kinship.

Anthropology and Psychoanalysis. Anthropology and psychoanalysis, both born in the wake of revolutionary romanticism and in reaction to it, are often limited in their regular approach to the hypothesis of Universal Siblinghood, and hence to universal incest and the possibility of the withering of the incest taboo. The structuralist view of Lévi-Strauss and the psychoanalytic view of most Freudians—that a society without incest is an impossibility and that nuns and monks are essentially parasitic (or subsocietal) neurotics—does not permit the open question of whether there can be, or could have been, incestuous societies or freely celibate individuals.

Anthropology (versed, like Angelo, in the study of the state [2.4.71]) has attempted, sometimes as a central purpose, to elucidate politics and the incest taboo. But anthropology has usually not concerned itself with the incest taboo in the Christian society at its own origins. A good example of a myth passed over is the Virgin Birth, or the fiction of the father as the son of himself (as Claudio is born as his own son from Isabella/Mariana/Juliet).[20] I have tried to direct attention to a similar question, or "mystery," in the Christian tradition by focusing not on parthenogenesis but on celibacy and incest in the Holy Family.

Another sign that anthropologists and sociologists have passed over their own Christian institutions is the relative scarcity of studies about the Catholic orders.[21] Perhaps this silence may be explained, not just by blindness to one's own culture, but by the fact that the orders threaten the very idea of society as most social science conceives it. The sexual and economic structures proposed by the orders—celibacy and communism—deny reproduction and property, essential to our society, if not to all societies. In a fundamental sense the orders thus challenge the very tenet of most anthropology as well as much sociology: the tenet that the incest taboo and the "principle of legitimacy" order the human world.[22] The orders sublimate, or sublate, or damn well sacrifice the complex structure of any and all human societies as social scientists perceive it; they focus exclusively on one spiritual parenthood rather than on either sociological or biological parenthoods; and, to a certain extent, they admit incest as an inevitable part of human life. In changing siblings to Universal Siblings, the orders are absolutely radical.

Lévi-Strauss, for example, may seem to begin from a fundamental observation that the incest taboo, or society itself, as he sees it, might never have been;[23] but he treats all histories or stories of a society where there is no incest taboo—all discussions of "a haven where women will no longer be exchanged" and where "one might keep to oneself"—as purely ideological ideas unattainable in "this" life.[24] He does not consider those people who do live at once in supramarital endogamy (incest) and celibacy. (In the same way anthropologists routinely except from anthropological study the abstract principle of universal love.)[25] Structuralist anthropology's later literary developments are no better. The semiotic view of Roland Barthes is that incest is a "nominative" crime, merely "a surprise of vocabulary": "The crime consists in transgressing the semantic rule, in creating homonymy: the act *contra naturam* is exhausted in an utterance of counter-language, the family is no more than a lexical area."[26] This view of incest as pun might be apt in analyzing individual incest, where one man is, for example, the father of himself as son, but when the same man plays all roles—father, son, brother, and husband—the pun becomes universalized and a new theory of punning is required. Julia Kristeva similarly responds to Lévi-Strauss's structuralist view that a linguistic system of exchange is analogous to a kinship system of exchange by arguing that the counterpart to incest is poetic language: "If it is true that the prohibition of incest constitutes, at the same time, language as communicative code and women as exchange objects in order for a society to be established, poetic language would be for its questionable subject-in-progress the equivalent of incest."[27] But insofar as incest marks the end of all ordinary exchange, the better counterpart to incest might be silence, or the end of verbal exchange—silence of the type practiced by the Sisters of the Order of Saint Clare or implied by Benedictine sign language.[28]

Psychoanalysis, like anthropology, comes to the rescue of the political order as we know it when it denies the possibility of the lifting up (sublation) or cleansing (purgation) of the human soul postulated by, for example, the Catholic orders or the libertine Brethren of the Free Spirit. Freud joins the Victorian attack on the early romantic doctrine of universal fraternity when, while admitting a grudging admiration for Saint Francis, he expresses his doubt that the Christian ideal of civilized society—"Love thy neighbor"—can be realized. He argues from common sense that "a love that does not discriminate forfeits a part of its value by doing an injustice to its object" and, moreover, that "not all men are worthy of love."[29] Like Aristotle, and like James Fitz-james Stephen in *Liberty, Equality, and Fraternity*, Freud criticizes the ideology of fraternity as a hypocritical substitution of the abstract general for the particular.

An attack on the Catholic orders and their ideology is critical even to the origins of psychoanalysis.[30] Freud's central notion of repression, for example, had to do in the first place with novices and nuns, and ever afterwards traditional Victorian psychoanalysis has passed off universal love (the Franciscan ideal) as simple continence—namely, repression.[31] (There are some noteworthy post-Victorian exceptions.)[32] Moreover, Freud's early ideological understanding of the relationship between the cloister and mental illness has been allowed to stand unquestioned. Freud had argued that "for the asylum of the cloister of an earlier time individual neurotics substitute the isolation of illness."[33] This view of the cloister may be helpful in the clinical treatment of patients—even monachal patients;[34] however, the fundamental Freudian position, that religion is a universal compulsive neurosis,[35] leaves little room for studying the historical and theological genesis of religious celibacy and the significance of the idea of Universal Siblinghood.

From a Freudian viewpoint, sibling incest in a family or horde where the parent rules supreme (or in a state where a monarch rules supreme) might be, instead of an instrument of equality, an instrument of tyranny. In the Freudian "primal horde," as in the "Cyclopean family" hypothesized by Atkinson in Victorian England, the will of the patriarch is supposed to be unrestricted. Rules of sexual conduct affect first the freedom of the younger generation (i.e., incest between brothers and sisters and between sons and mothers) and only later the freedom of the older generation (i.e., incest between fathers and daughters).[36] Freud himself wonders, however, whether his "horde" is an unhistorical, or hypothetical, phenomenon,[37] and he suggests that perhaps all father figures are essentially figural representations, "ghostly" internalizations, of social forces—representations that can be overcome, if at all, only by overcoming the social forces that led to, or made inevitable, the tyrant-making trope of the father. But his fiction of tyranny-linked, original incest does not bear on Universal Siblinghood because it fails to observe both the qualitative difference between universal incest and ordinary incest and also the hypothesis of a place where all human beings are equal Siblings. Such a place is the province not only of Christian brotherhood but also of the romantic and revolutionary fraternity to which traditional anthropology and psychoanalysis constitute a conservative and imperialist response.

The Idea of Universal Siblinghood:
Just Friends and Kissin' Cousins

Is she your cousin?   1.4.46

The same and different.   Plato, *Parmenides*

And what's the point of a revolution without
general copulation?   Weiss, *Marat/Sade*

To the extent that one puts the whole law of the land into question, one stands at land's end. Maybe that is why the principal words that characterize the journey we have made are somehow outlandish. "Universal Siblinghood" is a case in point. It suggests an association of men and women that recognizes essentially only one tribe of human beings with no essential intergenerational or intragenerational differences and no essential gender differences, an association that is universalist, equalitarian, and gender neutral. But in ordinary language, and in most all realizable politics, "siblinghood" indicates an association that does recognize some such difference.

Many alternative kinship structures in the history of the West have aimed at the radical sameness Siblinghood presupposes, but each step taken in the direction of homogeneity has most always been matched by a step taken in the direction of heterogeneity. These apparently universalist, equalitarian, or gender-neutral kinship structures have striven for, but never attained, the Universal Siblinghood, or ideal association, that marks the fulfillment and end of kinship as we know it. They are worth examining both for the light that they can shed on our ability to realize the hypothesis of Universal Siblinghood and for the light that the hypothesis of Universal Siblinghood can shed on the traditional understanding of kinship in the West.

Beyond Christian Siblinghood.   The kinship structure posited by the Catholic orders exemplifies Universal Siblinghood, yet its universalism, equalitarianism, and gender neutrality are generally unrealized or utopian in practice. To test whether such a structure is possible, let us consider a few apparently nonuniversalist and nonequalitarian tendencies in Christian doctrine and practice and a few universalist and equalitarian tendencies in Judaism, a religion against which Christianity often defines itself.

Early Church thinkers promulgated the view that all human beings are essentially members of one siblinghood, or tribe, insofar as anyone could be converted to Christianity.* Jesus is reported to have said, "All ye are brethren" (Matt. 23:8). And Paul writes: "For ye are all the children of God by faith in Christ Jesus. For as many of you as have been baptized into Christ have put on Christ. There is neither Jew nor Greek . . . for ye are all one in Christ Jesus." (Gal. 3:26–28.) Some Christian thinkers, following out the gist of Jesus' saying, urged their followers to call all human beings "brethren."[38] Yet most Christian doctrine supports hierarchies that militate against tribal oneness or universalism. Thus some authorities—eventually the dominant ones—claimed that, although the old distinction between Jew and Greek to which Paul refers may no longer obtain, a new distinction, that between Christians and non-Christians, does obtain.

But who, or what, are "Christians" according to a Christian? (Another way of putting this question might be: Who, or what, are "human beings" according to a Christian?) Paul implies that faith and baptism are the distinguishing characteristics of the tribe of Christians; mere human being and sonship to God are not enough. Many Church Fathers argued that only those who have already become baptized or become active members of religious orders are "brothers" (i.e., sons of the same Father). Origen writes: "Learn then what gift you have received from my Father. You have received, by your new birth in me, the spirit of adoption, in a manner to be called sons of God and brothers."[39] Similarly, some authorities claim that only members of one's own holy order are brothers.[40] When Jerome says, "Te universa salutat," he means that only his own community of Eremites are brothers to him.[41] Optatus says that it is impossible for a Christian not to be a brother to other Christians;[42] he thus implies that there are human beings in the world who are, to Christians, other than brothers.

Just as Christianity involves these nonuniversalist or intertribal differences, so it involves nonequalitarian or intratribal differences within the group of Christians. Jesus is reported to have erased or risen above intergenerational differentiation within the tribe, saying, "Call no man your father upon the earth: for one is your Father, which is in heaven" (Matt. 23:9). This rule would seem to collapse all

---

*The view that the human world is, or ought to be made, one is, in this context, the imperialist legacy of Alexander the Great and Greek and Jewish Hellenist philanthropic and metropolitan thinking in general (Torrey, *Second Isaiah*, p. 126, and Finkelstein, *Pharisees*, 2:566). The post-exilic community of Israel had already established the "new and Revolutionary principle" that one day the Temple would "be called a house of prayer for all peoples" (Is. 56:7; cf. Bickermann, *Ezra to Maccabees*, p. 19). Although all peoples entering the Temple is not necessarily the same as all people becoming one people, yet every individual could become a Jew (Zech. 8:23; cf. Bickermann, *Ezra to Maccabees*, p. 20).

human generations into one generation, but it can be disturbing in at least two ways. First, a group of human beings that becomes a brotherhood by positing a common Father merely replaces one hierarchy (son versus father) with another hierarchy (sons versus Father). The sons are unequal to the Father in the second hierarchy just as the sons are unequal to their fathers in the first hierarchy, even though one of the sons in the second hierarchy is the equal of, even is, the Father, being at once the vaguely illegitimate son of no one earthly and also the Son who, as Father of himself and of all of us, is the theological and structural lynchpin of Christianity. If we call ourselves equal siblings only by virtue of sharing in common a divine Father who is above us all, then Christianity is in no absolute wise a universal siblinghood.

Second, Christian sects soon began to call the priest "father."[43] They thus violated the letter both of Jesus' rule ("Call no man your father") and of most Jews' rule ("Call your father your father" by way of respecting him according to the Ten Commandments),[44] adopting instead the practice of the pre-Christian mystery cults, in which the priest was routinely called "father."[45] Indeed, the Christian authorities apparently violated more than the rule of Jesus against calling any man father; they became more hierarchized in intragenerational terms than the pagan cults. Some authorities argued that within the Christian tribe only confessors were to be called "brothers";[46] others said that bishops were to call one another "brothers" and to call their abbots and priests "sons."[47] (A single man could thus be father and brother to one person; as in *Measure for Measure* the Duke as friar is a "father friar" [3.2.11].)

I mean to suggest not that Christian authorities were unduly lax but that there is a historical tendency for most any Christian church to differentiate between tribes and within the tribe. I would characterize this tendency as more inevitable than hypocritical. After all, the full implications of universal and equalitarian Siblinghood are utopian and idealist, even unbearable, for most all of us. If Christendom were really equalitarian it would lack any kind of parental authority. Not only do most all people need a visible authority in order to behave well, much as the people in Shakespeare's Vienna need the Duke, but Jesus' rule "All ye are brethren" is, for all practical biological and political purposes, impossible to obey insofar as the hypothesis of Universal Siblinghood requires either celibacy or incest, both of which lead to the ending of the body politic as we know it or as we need to know it. If Christian doctrine were realized, Christendom would become the spiritually and physically libertine society envisioned by the

186

Brethren of the Free Spirit, which official Christendom is compelled to condemn.

The Christian claim that we are all brothers, when taken together with the Christian promise of liberty, must present itself either as a call for universal incest (the call of the Brethren of the Free Spirit) or as a Pauline call for absolute celibacy. Paul, seeming to retreat from the Christian ideal of a free association of *liberi*, writes: "For, brethren, ye have been called unto liberty; only use not liberty for an occasion to the flesh, but by love serve one another. For all the law is fulfilled in one word, even in this: Thou shalt love thy neighbour as thyself." (Gal. 5 : 13 – 14.) We are enjoined to love all people equally (as free sons, or *liberi*, of the Father), while we are enjoined not to disobey the old rule against loving all people equally. (The old rule enjoined a different kind of love for siblings and kinsmen than for others and a different kind of love for spouses—who were others before marriage—than for siblings, kinsmen, or others.) Paul refuses to transcend the old rule. (He ejects the incestuous Corinthians from the Christian community and perhaps also executes them.) It is as though the politics of Christianity were that political liberty is possible only by the death, in celibacy universalized, of the body politic.

The most disturbing aspect of the Christian idea of Universal Siblinghood is not the inevitability of a retreat from it but the inevitably inhuman or inhumane practical consequence of making a retreat that is not openly acknowledged. The Christian ideology of universal human brotherhood tends to conflate intraspecies difference with interspecies difference, or, put otherwise, it can encourage us to call or treat as "animals" all living beings outside the "universal" group of siblings. The question Who, or what, are "Christians" according to a Christian? is too often posed, or re-posed, as Who, or what, are "human beings" to a Christian? Even if we agree to love all human beings equally, as Jesus enjoins us, we still have to determine which beings are human, hence to be loved, and which are not.

According to the doctrine of Universal Siblinghood, all human beings are brothers and all brothers are human beings; it follows that all beings who are not brothers but others must be other than human, namely, animal. In this respect the universalist ideology of Christianity resembles the ideology of primitive societies in which "human being" and "fellow tribesman" are indicated by the same word or are thought of as being the same[48] and the ideology of modern nationalist states that think of, and treat, non-nationals as though they were animals. The universalist doctrine that "all men are my brothers" can turn out easily enough to mean "only my brothers are men; all others are animals." This formulation tends to transform any being whom we would ordinarily call human but who cannot or will not become a member of our brotherhood into an animal or to lead us to treat him as an animal (the fate of the "dog" Shylock), just as it can tend to transform beings that we would ordinarily call animal into members of a human family (the fate of household pets).[49]

If the human family and the human species are one and the same, as the idea of Universal Siblinghood holds them to be, then inter-familial crossover (marriage) and interspecies crossover (dehumanization and anthropomorphism) are also one and the same. When Paul says, "Love thy neighbour as thyself" (Gal. 5:14), implying that we humans are all brotherly neighbors, whom does he leave us to love in a sexual manner without committing sibling incest? Only those outside the neighborhood, or the brotherhood. But if all human beings are brothers (i.e., if the species and the family are one and the same), then we humans can love only animals in a sexual way. Then bestiality would be the only way, besides celibacy, to avoid incest, as would be figured in such folk tales as Beauty and the Beast, in which a beast is transformed into a human being at the instant it is kissed.

For would-be universalist Christian philanthropists, then, there can develop an ideologically overwhelming need to dehumanize certain beings that we might ordinarily call human (*anthropoi*)—that is, to treat beings from outside their own neighborhood as extra-species, not merely as extra-tribal. Among such philanthropists the quintessential other has been the Jew, against whose religion in general and whose doctrine of love in particular Christendom for millennia has sought to define itself. A disapproving Matthew thus claims that the Jews teach limited misanthropy, not philanthropy (Matt 5:43); and anti-Semites for centuries have argued that it is impossible for a Jew to understand universal love.[50] Yet the idea of universal brotherhood is no stranger to Judaism. It is a dominant Jewish view that Abraham, by his piety and philanthropy, "made brothers" of the whole world.[51] The Old Testament asks, "Have we not all one father? hath not one God created us?" (Mal. 2:10). This transcendence of kinship by consanguinity moves the injunction to be one's brother's keeper in the direction of loving neighbors (Lev. 19:18), strangers who dwell within the community (Lev. 19:34), strangers who dwell in strange lands, and finally everyone. Rabbis Hillel and Meir enjoin that one should love all mankind, or all "creatures," and Aaron ibn Hayyim writes, in a book whose publication in cosmopolitan Venice he oversaw in 1609, that the law of "Love thy neighbour," which he endorses, includes in its purview non-Israelites as well as Israelites.[52]

In the Judaeo-Christian tradition as a whole, then, there appears to be a radical and ineradicable tension between the demands of tribal heterogeneity and the demands of Universal Siblinghood. Toward universal kinship Judaism, which began as a practical, particularist tribal religion and has long existed as an other in the diaspora, seems bound to strive; and away from Universal Siblinghood Christianity, which began in an idealist rejection of particularist kinship, seems bound to stray.

Greek Phratry, French Revolution, and Hurrian Fratriarchy. Within the Western tradition, a few non-Christian, noncelibate groups have, like the celibate Catholic orders, striven for but never attained the universal or ideal association that marks the fulfillment and end of kinship as we know it. They have accommodated tribal differences while tending toward tribal homogeneity. Among these kinship systems are the ancient Greek phratry, which emphasized intertribal difference together with intratribal homogeneity, the French Revolution, which emphasized intratribal difference along intergenerational lines together with intertribal homogeneity; and the Hurrian fratriarchy, which emphasized intratribal difference along intragenerational (primogenitural) lines, together with intratribal homogeneity along familial lines.

The Greek phratry—a religious and political association from which, it is said, politics as we now know it developed—involved an absolute erasing of, or rising above, differences between living generations in the same tribe. In its festival of initiation, or Apatouria ("feast of men of the same fathers"), all *phrateres* became at once brothers and sons of the same fathers.[53] For all its radical equalitarianism, however, the phratry remained bound to tribal consanguinity (not all men had the same fathers, only fellow tribesmen); it was not universalist in vision.

The French Revolution may be a similarly imperfect example of Universal Siblinghood. Its very goal, universal fraternity, undoes itself because fraternity implies a common (in Christian terms, a divine) father.[54] We can call ourselves all one brotherhood only by assuming a common father in heaven; in the words of one Elizabethan poet, only "Our Father, which in heaven art, / . . . mak'st us all one brotherhood."[55] Similarly, "Alle Menschen werden Brüder!" (All men will be brothers!), writes Schiller in the great romantic "Ode to Joy" that Beethoven set to music in the Ninth Symphony. But men will become brothers, according to Schiller's "Ode," only because "above the stormy canopy / There must dwell a loving Father."[56] The very term "brothers," which implies a common parent, is thus an obstacle—semantic and ideological—to comprehending or effecting the collapse of intergenerational difference that Universal Siblinghood presupposes.

By contrast, according to historical hypothesis, the pre-Abramic Hurrian fratriarchy—the "rule of the brothers" from which Judaism may have developed—emphasized intragenerational differences because of its rule of primogeniture. In the fratriarchy, "authority is exercised by the eldest brother and is handed on from brother to brother as something inherited, the inheritance passing to the oldest son of the first brother on the death of the last brother."[57] At the same time, the fratriarchy denied interfamilial differences by officially adopting spouses into the family as "sister," either at the time of marriage or earlier.[58] Such adoption provides one explanation for the motif of the sister-wife in the Old Testament, notably in the vaguely incestuous nominative relationship between Abraham and Sarah and between Isaac and Rebecca.[59] Despite its emphasis on intertribal equality—even, arguably, on intertribal incestuous homogeneity—the pre-Abramic fratriarchy involved a strict hierarchical division of power among the brothers.

The Hurrians did not allow for intragenerational equality, just as French revolutionary fraternity did not allow for intergenerational equality and as the Greek phratry did not allow for intertribal equality. Before considering two more kinds of intratribal differences of particular interest in the contemporary West—those that divide the tribe along gender lines and along social, or economic, class lines—we might pause to wonder whether there is not an appropriate illustration of universal, equalitarian Siblinghood that overcomes the differences we have considered so far. Is there a more appropriate terminology to express the idea of inter- and intratribal equality, the idea of the ending of tribalism?

Just Friends and Kissin' Cousins. A term that would express the idea of Universal Siblinghood, of a Siblinghood where both inter- and intragenerational differences were overcome and all human beings were equally affined, would have to imply both universal kinship and either celibacy or incest. It might therefore be an outlaw term relegated to the linguistic peripheries of archaism, obscenity, slang, or humor, where it could least forcefully put into question ordinary social and linguistic interaction. "Blood brotherhood" is such a term; the practice that it denotes was actually outlawed.[60] Two other such terms are the archaic "just friends" and the humorous "kissin' cousins."

English "friend," to which we usually attach only the general meaning "intimate associate," has the alternate meanings "kinsman" and
"sexual lover."[61] "Kinsman" is its basic meaning in Old Scandinavian
and High German dialects,[62] and its unequivocal meaning in several
Elizabethan genealogical discussions of "all the sons and daughters
of Adam and Eve the which were our first friends"[63] and in such
Shakespearean plays as *Two Gentlemen of Verona*:

> But she I mean is promis'd by her friends   (TGV, 3.1.106)
> Unto a youthful gentleman of worth,
> And kept severely from resort of men,
> That no man hath access by day to her.

"Sexual lover" is the meaning of "friend" in such Shakespearean plays
as *Love's Labor's Lost* (5.2.404–5) and in our contemporary phrases
"boyfriend" and "lady friend."

If a friend as "kinsman" and a friend as "sexual lover" were to be
combined in one person, the result would be incest. Such combination
occurs in *Measure for Measure*. Lucio uses the word "friend" to convey
"kindly" (1.4.24) greetings to Isabella from her brother, and he reports that Claudio "hath got his friend with child" (1.4.28). But the
friendship between Claudio and Juliet involves kinship as well as sexual love because of the cousinship between Isabella and Juliet, and
hence between Claudio (Isabella's brother) and Juliet, whether this
kinship be consanguineous or somehow adoptive. Thus friendship in
Measure for Measure combines elements of kinship and sexual love; it
indicates a potentially universal relationship that is at once chaste and
unchaste, or incestuous.

Among the ancient Greeks such friendship—whether in idea or in
practice—was the basis of a remarkable new politics, if not of politics
itself. The history and theory of Greek political association reveal a
motivating tension between ordinary kinship structures, which insist
on essential family differences, and such friendship societies as the
Pythagorean "union of friends" (*haetery*), which, in contrast to the ancient phratry, "provided bonds that transcended consanguinity and
thereby enabled members of different kin groups to associate in a
polis."[64] Similarly, Plato discounts "ordinary" family kinship in favor
of friendship, which he calls the only truly "natural" kinship.[65]

The Pythagorean doctrine, in particular, went beyond seeing
friendship as an association mediating family and state to conceive
of friendship as an association transcending family and state taken together. The Pythagoreans argued that friends were obliged to share
in the perfect communion of the spirit, to share everything (or to have

all things in common), to be equal to each other, and to be second selves to one another;[66] they insisted, moreover, that admittance to the Pythagorean Order was, potentially, open to all men. Friendship in this universalist sense later influenced Plato's republican emphasis on equality and justice and the Stoics' doctrine of the universal love of mankind (*philanthropia*).[67] The Stoics took the Pythagorean doctrine of universal friendship to its logical conclusion that, insofar as equalitarian friendship transcends all hierarchical kinship, such prohibitions as the incest taboo are null.[68]

Shmuel Eisenstadt has argued that friendship always involves an aspect of submerged kinship,[69] but in the republic hypothesized by certain ancient thinkers—and perhaps practiced in the Pythagorean colonies—one is no longer a kinsman to some men and not to others but a friend to all men. In this universalizing of kinship, "friend" means, to all intents, a kinsman with whom one legitimately could have sexual intercourse, the definition of "friendship" that is also suggested in *Measure for Measure*.

The second term that may simultaneously imply both chastity and incest is American "kissin' cousin."[70] "Cousin" already implies a certain indifference to tribal as well as generational distinctions: "All cousins are equal" in the language of the kin-cousin monarchs of Europe, "none share parents, which leaves each cousin free in relation to every other."[71] By virtue of a good-natured ambiguity, "kissin' cousin" (unlike, say, "motherfucker") suggests an incestuous relationship without downright disapproval.

The Dictionary of American Slang says that "kissin' cousin" refers to: (1) a "Platonic" friend who is granted the same intimacy accorded to close blood relations and (2) a member of the opposite sex with whom one is sexually familiar when the parties involved believe mistakenly that their intimacy is unknown.[72] Neither "official" definition says that a kissin' cousin is a consanguineous relative. According to the dictionary, in the hillbilly dialect where "kissin' cousin" originated, however, the term does denote a consanguineous relative; in the hills, "kissin' cousins" are cousins who kiss. If we accept this commonsense view, then "kissin' cousinship," which by the "official" definitions denotes both a chaste, "Platonic" relationship and an unchaste sexual one, really denotes both a chaste and an incestuous family relationship.

To be tongue-in-cheek about it, the difference here between chastity and incest depends both on the kiss and on the degree of cousinship. Kisses may be of the familial, chaste kind or of the extrafamilial, sexual kind, and cousinship may be of so close a degree as to allow legitimately only for chaste kisses (in the family way) or of so distant a degree as to allow for sexual kisses (in the romantic way).

The distinction between chaste familial kisses and unchaste extrafamilial kisses involves the ordinary distinction between incestuous and nonincestuous associations, the by now familiar rules about whom one can kiss and how. There is an extraordinary view, however, that all kisses are essentially at once both chaste and unchaste, a totalitarian or potentially universalist doctrine that holds all kisses to be essentially the same. This doctrine looks to such osculatory models as St. Peter's "kiss of charity" or St. Paul's "holy kiss"[73]—a kiss "promiscuously given without any restriction as to sexes or ranks, among those who [are] all one in Christ."[74] Such a kiss is typically mouthed by everyone during such holidays as Christmas, when many Christians celebrate the birth of Christ with a public and universal liberty, a Saturnalian festival that gives every man the license of kissing any woman found under the mistletoe.[75] If we accept the Christian doctrine of Universal Siblinghood, or Cousinship, then unrestricted kisses of this kind are the only kisses there can be.

The danger inherent in such a universalist doctrine of kissing is that it leads to ordinary incest between ordinary cousins or siblings. This danger encouraged the Church Fathers to outlaw the "new" totalitarian practice of the promiscuous kiss among lay people and reestablish the "old," strict rules about who can kiss whom and how.[76] At the same time, however, the Church Fathers held fast to the totalitarian ideal of Universal Siblinghood. They maintained, for example, that all kissing—both marital and extramarital—is the first step in the consummation of marriage, or, teleologically speaking, that kissing is sexual intercourse. In this way the Fathers came to look upon all kissing between unmarried nonkin as either spousal or adulterous (not merely as fornicatory) and upon all kissing between kin as incestuous.[77] All "mouthing" was thus understood to be either a sacred or a perverse violation of social bonds, with the one delicate exception of a kiss between a husband and his wife, that is, a kiss between a "brother" in the universalist sense and the particular woman whom kissing was once illegitimate (by virtue of an incest taboo that outlaws kissing any woman because she is a "sister" in the universalist sense) but who has become legitimately kissable by virtue of a sacred marriage. When one's sibling is also one's sacred spouse—"My sister, my spouse"—all kisses are not only incestuous, but also chaste.

The bipolar tension between chastity and incest that "kissin' cousin" expresses can be resolved, if at all, only in a chaste, incestuous union where the ordinary boundary between kin and nonkin seems to disappear, as in a miraculous comedy. (What brings a smile to our lips when we hear the term "kissin' cousin" in Elvis Presley movies and Al Capp's *'Lil Abner* cartoon strips[78] is the term's referring simultaneously to both kinds of kisses and to both kinds of cousinships.) "Kissin' cousin" suggests cousinship at that ideal point where kin can kiss legitimately in both the familiar and the romantic way, or at the point—and this is the same thing—where they can kiss legitimately in neither way. Such cousinship exists on the borderline of legitimacy or transcends law altogether. At such a point we toe the line of civilization; we are cousins who kiss—"a little more than kin, and less than kind."*

Class Difference. The stoic philosopher Epictetus implied that a universal siblinghood rules out intratribal differences along the lines of social or economic class when he cried to a master beating a slave: "Slave, do you not want to help your sibling [*adelphos*], who has Zeus for father, who is born of the same germs as you and is of the same heavenly descent?"[79] In imagining a homogenization of class difference by rejecting the bonds of ordinary consubstantiality, Epictetus agrees with the gist of Christian monachism as promulgated by such mendicant orders as the Franciscans, who adopted a universalist theory of kinship and a communal theory of property (or antiproperty). For them, beggars and those who sustain beggars should become one "for the Lord's sake," as the beggars put it in *Measure for Measure* (4.3.19–20), and dukes everywhere should come into composition with the king (1.2.1–2).[80] The Gospel's counterpart to the collapse of essential difference between classes imagined by Epictetus and Francis is the class homogeneity imagined by Paul. "There is neither bond nor free," says Paul, "for ye are all one in Christ" (Gal. 3 : 28).

Homogenization of two or more social classes can be realized, in familial or superfamilial terms, only when either (1) members of different classes recognize their common descent (the way of Epictetus) or (2) members of those classes intermarry. Recognition of common descent and marriage ordinarily exclude each other, however, because the common descent two people share can rule out the possibility of nonincestuous marriage between them. In literature, marriage across class boundaries has often been represented as incestuous, by the same means used to present sexual liaisons with members of the Catholic orders as incestuous: the offending fictional pair turn out unwittingly to be blood relatives. In some works of early American literature, for example, masters who marry slaves or bourgeois who

---

*HAM 1.2.65. These words, Hamlet's first in the play, respond to his incestuous uncle-father Claudius's calling him "cousin" as well as "son."

marry workers discover too late that their spouses are also their siblings.[81] In such works, the penalty for marrying outside one's class was to discover that one had married inside one's family. Thus the conservative injunction to maintain existing social class structure, or the endorsement of class exogamy, was bolstered by the taboo against familial endogamy.

Sophocles' *Oedipus the King* is the classic example of a literary work in which the penalty for class exogamy, or apparent class exogamy, is familial endogamy. In Sophocles' drama, which is partly about class upheaval during the period of equalitarian democratization under the Greek tyrants,[82] Oedipus ascribes Jocasta's outbreak at learning he is not the biological son of Polybus and Merope to her fear that he may have been born from the lower classes. It is in an egalitarian and democratic spirit that Oedipus says, "I at least shall be willing to see my ancestry, though humble. Perhaps she is ashamed of my low birth."[83] Where Oedipus sees class exogamy, Jocasta sees familial endogamy.

Gender Difference. A universal siblinghood, even when it transcends intertribal difference and the kinds of intratribal differences we have discussed so far, does not always entail gender neutrality. Indeed, the patriarchal aspect of the traditional Catholic orders already suggests how gender hierarchy can still exist.[84] Robert Paul, writing of Tibetan monasteries, even blames misogyny for the rise of the monastic brotherhoods, quoting the French song, "Without these damn women we'd all be brothers / Without these damn women we'd all be happy."[85]

But is not the "pure" relationship of brother to sister the human association that most nearly approaches absolute gender neutrality? (That is the romantic thesis of Hegel.)[86] Nowhere are the dual themes of Universal Siblinghood (by autochthony) and gender neutrality, taken together, better expressed than in the meeting of siblings in *Cymbeline*. Imogen, disguised as "Fidele," meets Arviragus, her brother, who has been kidnapped in infancy and brought up in Wales as "Cadwal." Sibling extends friendship to sibling:

> *Arviragus.* Are we not brothers? (CYM 4.2.3)
> *Imogen.*　　　　　So man and man should be,
> 　　But clay and clay differ in dignity,
> 　　Whose dust is both alike.

Soon after the Welsh meeting scene—in which man and woman recognize each other as absolutely equal siblings in the universal sense but not as brother and sister in the familial sense or as man and woman in the sexual sense—Imogen takes one beheaded man for another (much as does Angelo in *Measure for Measure*); she takes Cloten her half-brother for her husband Posthumus, with whom she was raised as with a brother.

Although the Catholic orders affirm a patriarchal God, significant factors mitigate gender hierarchy within the orders. As Christian theology conceives marriage—for example, the marriage union of a man and woman into one body—the corporeal union, the new body, must be androgynous or hermaphroditic.[87] Thus marriage to Christ must erase or rise above gender differences. The ideology of many orders thus tends towards gender neutrality, at least ideally. This tendency has sources in the New Testament ("There is neither male nor female," says Paul, "for ye are all one in Christ Jesus" [Gal. 3:26–28]),[88] as well as in apocryphal works.[89] The "kiss of charity" or "holy kiss"—a kiss given without any restriction as to gender or kinship—suggests the effect in general practice of the doctrinal tendency towards gender neutrality. In some English devotional works, moreover, Jesus is female, or is both a male lover and a female parent taken together.[90] And gender neutrality was a tenet of such physically or spiritually incestuous sects as the Shakers and Perfectionists.[91]

For some Franciscan Brothers and Sisters, finally, there was not only an incestuous conflation of kinship roles (in which spouse, child, parent, and sibling become one) but also an androgynous conflation of gender roles (in which Franciscan friars alternately took on the roles of Mother and Son in relation to each other).[92] As the first conflation involves "spiritual incest," so the second involves "spiritual androgyny." The realization of both spiritual incest and spiritual androgyny, taken together, was the heretical project of the Brethren of the Free Spirit.

The equal marriage between siblings or Siblings idealized, but not realized, in *Measure for Measure* suggests not only the end of intertribal hierarchy (the foreign wars) and intratribal hierarchy (the civil strife)—the dukes come to composition with the king and Vincentio is at once Brother and Father—but also the end of inequality between the sexes. In the gender union of marriage, where two become one, the domestic conflict about which gender constitutes the "head" ("he's his wife's head" [4.2.3]) appears or disappears together with the international wars and the civil strife.

Plato's Retreat: The Lie of the West

Foucault has called the seventeenth century, at the beginning of which Shakespeare wrote *Measure for Measure*, an age of great sexual liberation.[93] Whatever conceptual breakthroughs may have been made in that century, our present ability safely and cheaply to cut off the human reproductive process has made for widespread and permissible extramarital intercourse. That is why, despite renewed fears of venereal disease, *we* say we live in an age of sexual liberation.

At the same time as old rules against fornication and adultery seem to be disappearing, however, we stress ever more the rules against incest. The many tracts against incest published in the last few years represent, I take it, an ancient problem keeping us from genuinely liberal freedom even in "the era of the pill."[94] Of course there are a few proponents of the view that incest can have "positive" effects, and some Western democracies even have lobbyists for "pro-incest" laws.[95] But discussion of whether the taboo can be overcome—as opposed to discussion of whether incest should be practiced or legalized in violation of the taboo—is still considered heretical (like the Brethren of the Free Spirit), or bestial (like Beauty and the Beast), or utopianly anarchic (like theorists who call for a willful ignoring of the taboo),[96] or—most powerfully—abusive of children.

The popular contemporary argument that incest is basically child molestation focuses on the unhappy fact of father-daughter seduction or rape in our vestigially patriarchal society. Exposing and preventing intergenerational molestation is, I think, an admirable goal; it is one with which, I trust, the argument of my book does not interfere.[97] An exclusive focus on incest as molestation and rape can be intellectually harmful, however, since it can serve to prop up the taboo with yet another rhetorical defense ("There is an incest taboo because it protects children from disaster") rather than help us understand the taboo.[98] Our contemporaries' attacks on incest have focused on such beleaguered figures as Saint Dymphna, who refused to marry her father and consequently was killed by him,[99] but I have focused on such figures as the saintly founders of the Catholic orders, men and women who refused to marry their beloved siblings and so entered a state of Universal Siblinghood.[100] This focus on universal incest is not much immediate help to women "kept down," like Kate Keepdown, in a vestigially patriarchal society; but it may be of use to male and female students of the incest taboo and what may become of it. That is why I have dared to entertain for a while the heretical, not to say beastly, view that incest of a kind is an essential precondition to liberty, or that incest is essential to, and is the measure of, any truly equalitarian society.

"What is't I dream on?" (2.2.179) Angelo asks as he attempts to "raze the sanctuary" and as the player-Brother Vincentio and novice-

Sister Isabella try to raise themselves above the sanctified taboo. Without some such external agency as genetic surgery, which, as in science fiction, might remove the incest taboo from individuals (with what consequences to our political institutions we are now almost in a position to understand), or some such social transformation as liberal, or libertine, revolution presupposes—without some almost inconceivable or outlandish transformation of human families and political organizations—we shall remain but half-awake to the possibilities of another kind of humankind.

Is Universal Siblinghood, then, finally a pipe dream? Consider the birth of classical political theory with the ideal political state Plato's Socrates proposes to explain the fears and desires of the individual human soul. This republic, says Socrates, must rest fundamentally upon the "noble," or "well-bred," lie of universal kinship,[101] a lie that Socrates likens to such poetic fictions as autochthony in Thebes (the birthplace of Sophocles' Oedipus) and other mythic expressions of common origins.[102] Such fictions play a role in social ideology like that of the bed tricks in *Measure for Measure* and *All's Well That Ends Well*; they cozen cousins for the cousins' general good. "To cozen," said Randle Cotgrave in 1611, means "to clayme kindred for aduantage,"[103] and the Universal Siblinghood Socrates would pretend to claim might benefit universally humankind.

Myths of common origin do have their political use. (We treat brothers better than others, don't we?) But it is almost impossible to persuade the first ("original") generation of people who must be convinced they are all kin—that is, to persuade our generation—that we are kin. We are predisposed, after all, to saturate with reason whatever ideology has lived long—the nuclear family, say, or the emphasis on consanguinity.[104] In the *Republic*, Socrates expresses his hope to overcome such predisposition by means of persuasive reeducation:

> I'll attempt to persuade first the rulers, then the rest of the city, that the rearing and education we gave them were like dreams; they only thought they were undergoing all that was happening to them, while, in truth, at that time they were under the earth within, being fashioned and reared themselves, and their arms and other tools being crafted. When the job had been completely finished, then the earth, which is their mother, sent them up. And now . . . they must think of other citizens as brothers born of the earth.[105]

It is especially hard to convince people that they are all essentially autochthonous siblings—or, in the ideology of the French Revolution, children of the earth—when, and if, they come to understand that such kinship requires a kind of incest.[106] This requirement surfaces for a moment in the *Republic*, when Plato says of the guardian of the City: "With everyone he happens to meet, he will hold that he's meeting a brother, or a sister, or a father, or a mother, or a son, or a daughter, or their descendants or ancestors."[107] Whether or not Plato himself regarded sexual unions between consanguinous brothers and sisters as illegitimate,[108] the noble lie of Universal Siblinghood and incest that underlies the *Republic*—together with the practical dependence of most all political orders on the incest taboo—was so disturbing that, in a moment of prudence, Plato retreated from his extremist view, or rather submerged it, cozening his interlocuters back into believing that some of them are cousins and some are not.[109] One interlocuter attributes to Socrates' prudential "shame" Socrates' hesitancy to reveal fully the noble lie of the republic.[110] And shame is what keeps Plato from pursuing very far the connection of universal kinship with friendship and politics. He goes no farther than quoting Aristophanes' comedic *Assembly of Women*: "The law will grant that brothers and sisters lie together if the lot falls out that way and the Pythia [at Delphi] concurs."[111] However, we all know that "the lord whose oracle is at Delphi neither speaks nor conceals, he only gives signs."[112] We can hardly say whether the end of kinship is the ending of the taboo that informs kinship.

Reference Matter

Notes

FOR COMPLETE bibliographical information and for abbreviations used in the notes and footnotes, see the Bibliography, pp. 249–81 below.

Introduction

1. For folktales, see Brewster, *Incest Theme*; for psychologists and political theorists, see Fox, *Kinship*, pp. 57–58. In a related argument, both Augustine (*City of God*, 15.16.1) and Margaret Mead's Arapesh informants (*Sex and Temperament*, pp. 93–94) hold that incest would inhibit the formation of the interfamilial relationships that bind society together. For the view that inbreeding is biologically harmful to the human species, see Adams and Neal, "Children"; Seemanov, "Study of Children"; and Livingstone, "Genetics."

2. Westermarck, *Human Marriage*, presents the second thesis.

3. For this position, see Slater, "Ecological Factors."

4. See here Bischof, "Comparative Etiology."

5. Whether the taboo is, in any case, universal among human beings in society or a unique species characteristic has been the subject of intense debate for millennia. Cf. Sidler, *Inzesttabu*, and Fox, *Red Lamp*, pp. 83–107.

6. The extension of kinship by the extension of kinship terms is discussed in: Murdock, *Social Structure*, pp. 31–84; Radcliffe-Brown, introduction to *African Systems*, pp. 1–86; Evans-Pritchard, "Kinship in Primitive Societies" and "Kinship Extensions."

7. See, e.g., Pitt-Rivers, "Pseudo-Kinship," and Eisenstadt, "Ritualized Personal Relations."

8. See Claude Lévi-Strauss's summary position (*Elementary Structures*, p. 30) that "it is the social relationship more than the biological tie implied by the terms 'father,' 'mother,' 'son,' 'daughter,' 'brother,' and 'sister,' that acts as the determinant."

9. On the relatively recent establishment, in the late seventeenth century, of the facts of sexual reproduction as we now know them, see Cole, *Early Theories*, and Bowler, "Preformation."

10. Burnet, *Exposition*, p. 288; Alfonso el Sabio, *Siete partidas*, pt. 4, title 13. Alfonso goes so far as to commend a man for keeping only one concubine, so that her children can more certainly be recognized as his (Karras, "Tragedy and Illicit Love").

11. For Freud on religion as a social neurosis, see his "Obsessive Acts."

12. *Ulysses*, p. 207.

13. *Eumenides*, line 736. In an Orphic hymn (31.10) Athena is called both

male and female, and in a Homeric hymn (9.3) she is called a virgin divinity (W. Smith, *Roman Mythology*, s.v. "Athena").

14. *Generation*, 1.2.729a. See also Plato's similar view of the male Eros of begetting (*Timaeus*, 73, 90–91) and related evidence collected by Onians, *European Thought*, pp. 108–9. In Anaxagoras the mother is merely the "breeding ground" and the father is "the seed"; in Diogenes of Apollonia the father, not the mother, provides the offspring (Freeman, *Pre-Socratic Philosophers*, pp. 272, 282).

15. Dewey, "Legal Personality," pp. 566–67. Jesus, like Melchizedek in Saint Paul's interpretation, is "without father or mother or genealogy" (Heb. 7:3, 6:20, and John 2:3–4, 3:3; cf. N. Frye, *Fearful Symmetry*, p. 388).

16. Fuller, *Legal Fictions*, p. 300.

17. In Thayer, *Preliminary Treatise*, pp. 346–47.

18. For the societal need for a "principle of illegitimacy," see Malinowski, "Parenthood," pp. 137–38: "The most important moral and legal rule concerning the physiological state of kinship is that no child should be brought into this world without a man—and one man at that—assuming the role of sociological father, that is, guardian and protector, the male link between the child and the rest of the community. I think that this generalization amounts to a universal sociological law."

19. Cf. Engels's thesis that in group marriage, or the "Panuluan family" (*Origin*, p. 106), "it is uncertain who is the father of a child; but it is certain who its mother is" and Bachofen's similarly reassuring thesis of "mother right" (see *Mutterrecht*).

20. For the changeling motif and its widespread influence, see Briggs, *Fairies*, s.v. "Changeling"; S. Thompson, *Folk Literature*, esp. "Substituted Children" (K1920), "Deception by Substitution of Children" (K1847), and "Substitution of Children to Gain Inheritance" (K1847.1); and Grimm, *Wörterbuch*, s.v. "Wechselkind" and "Wechselbalg." In such tales devious nurses, midwives, mothers, and fairies abound; see Mark Twain's *Pudd'nhead Wilson*.

21. In Judaism an entire body of law has grown up around the *asufi*, or foundling about whom one cannot know whether he or she is a bastard or not. By some accounts such a child, if a male, "can marry neither a legitimate Jewess (because he may be a *mamzer* [bastard]) nor a female *mamzer* (because he may in fact be legitimate)" (Schereschewsky, "Mamzer"). The *asufi* thus conjoins anxiety about changelings with anxiety about bastards.

22. *O.E.D.*, s.v. "Changeling," sb. 2. With the term "changeling" compare "supposititious": "One set up to displace the real heir or successor; sometimes used for 'illegitimate'" (*O.E.D.*, s.v. "Supposititious," sb. 1b.).

23. *O.E.D.*, s.v. "Changeling," sb. 3.

24. On the exposure motif in mythology, see Rank, "Birth of the Hero."

25. I refer to the love between Imogen and Arviragus. See esp. CYM 4.1.

26. The exception is Siamese twins. For them blood (*sang*), the usual figure for the bond in kinship, is more than figural: the same blood literally flows through their veins, assuring their consanguinity. See Mark Twain's *Pudd'nhead Wilson*, which, although it concerns changelings, originated in Twain's thoughts about two Siamese twins.

27. Pitt-Rivers, "Kith and the Kin," p. 92.

28. *Politics*, 2.1.

29. On the taboo against marriage between milk siblings—people who re-

ceived the "milk of human kindness" from the same nurse—see Crawley, *Mystic Rose*, 2 : 230; and *Koran*, chap. 4, "Women," p. 75. On the many kinds of nominal incest, see Crawley, *loc. cit.* For a discussion of the purchase of family names in relation to incest, see B. Thomas, "Writer's Procreative Urge in *Pierre*," esp. p. 419. On the Ba'ale ha-Rikkub, which explains how Abraham's wife is his sister insofar as he calls her sister, see chapter 6, below. For kinship by adoption, see chapter 2, below. Racine's *Phèdre* presents a stepmother's love for her stepson. On kinship "in law," see chapter 6, below. One might also include in this list of kinds of pseudo-kinship or kinship by extension that can make for a diriment impediment to marriage the relationship between trading partners, between feudal lords and their servants, between brothers-in-arms, and so on. On kinship by spiritual alliance, an elaborate form of elective friendship in sixteenth-century France, see Telle, esp. pp. 299–312. Jourda, in his edition of Rabelais, suggests that the social structure of Rabelais's Island of Ennasin (bk. 4, chap. 9) parodies such spiritual alliances as that between Marot and Anne d'Alençons.

30. On gossipred and kinship, see: Gratian, *Decretum*, 30, q. 1–4; Rolandus, *Summa*, 144–45; Stephanus Tornacensis, *Summa*, p. 241; Feije, *De impedimentis*, chap. 16; Council of Trullo (A.D. 692), in *Colección de canones*; and C. E. Smith, *Papal Enforcement*, pp. 48–51. For the anthropological view of gossipred, see: Pitt-Rivers, "Spiritual Kinship," p. 55, and "Pseudo-Kinship," p. 408; Gudeman, "Compadrazago"; Mintz and Wolf, "Ritual Co-Godparentage"; and Anderson, "Comparaggio." In English literature, Chaucer links incest and gossipred: "For right so as he that engendreth a child is his flesshly fader, right so is his godfader his fader espiritueel. For which a womman may in no lasse synne assemblen with hire godsib than with hire owene flesshly brother" (*Parson's Tale*, 908, in *Works*, p. 258).

31. D'Anglure, *Esquimaux*.

32. General studies of blood brotherhood include Tegnaeus, *Blood-Brothers*, and Brain, *Friends and Lovers*, chap. 3. Relevant literary works in English include D. H. Lawrence's *David* and *Women in Love*, and the Old English version of the *Gesta Romanorum*: "I pray the let me drinke thi blood and thou shalt drink myne in tokening that neither of us shall foresake other in wele ne in woo."

33. On Pythagoras, see the Conclusion, below.

34. Much Christian doctrine holds that female religious celibates stand, like the Virgin Mary, in four kinship relationships to God: they are children and spouses of God the Parent and sisters and mothers of God the Son. For the relevant ecclesiastical and literary evidence concerning the *sponsa Christi*, see chapter 2, below. For an anthropological view of the institution of women marrying gods in Christianity and in other cultures, see: Westermarck, *Human Marriage*, 1 : 403–6; and M. E. Harding, *Woman's Mysteries*.

35. Cf. the principle in Judaism that "'a proselyte is as a new born babe' who stands in absolutely no relationship to any pre-conversion relation. Consequently, his brothers and sisters, father, mother, etc. from before his conversion lose his relationship on his conversion. Should they too subsequently become converted, they are regarded as strangers to him, and he might marry, e.g., his mother or sister. This is the Biblical law" (Freedman, note to Sanhedrin 58a, in I. Epstein, ed., *Talmud*). Of course, the rabbis found a way to forbid marriages between such "new born babes."

36. See, e.g., Council of Rome (A.D. 402), can. 1, 2, in Hefele, *Conciliengeschichte*, 2:87; Pope Gelasius I (A.D. 494), letter to the bishops of Lucania, c. 20, in Gratian, *Decretum*, causa 27, q. 1, c. 14; Council of Macon (A.D. 585), can. 12, in Hefele, *Conciliengeschichte*, 3:37; Gratian *Decretum*, 30, q. 3, c. 1, 5.10; and G. Oesterlé, "Inceste," in Viller et al., *Spiritualité*. In, e.g., [Lacy], *Ten Commandments*, it is written that "Incestus is he þat dlith with nonne, with kosyn, or with amaydon, þe wich is called defloracio"; and Lydgate writes (*Fall of Princes*, 2.4068–71) that "Incestus is trespassyng with kyn or with blood, / Or froward medlyng with hir that is a nunne." See also More, *Complete Works*, 1:48–49.

The Roman Catholic doctrine that insofar as we are all brothers and sisters all marriage is incestuous was one focus of debate during the Reformation. Luther, for one, acknowledges the doctrine but tries to short-circuit it. He claims, in his argument against the diriment impediment to marriage posed by gossipred relations, that the siblinghood promulgated by Christianity, at least insofar as it pertains to all baptized souls, should not be taken literally. Of the Roman Catholics who follow out the doctrine to the letter, Luther says that they have "concocted new degrees of relationship, namely, the god-parents, godchildren, and their children and brothers or sisters. It was really the devil who taught them that, for if the sacrament of baptism is supposed to create an impediment, then no Christian man could take a Christian wife, since all baptized women are in a spiritual sense the sisters of all baptized men." (Luther, "Persons . . . Forbidden to Marry," *LW*, 45:8.) See also Luther's rhetorical question: "Then must I be forbidden to marry any Christian woman, since all baptized women are the spiritual sisters of all baptized men by virtue of their common baptism?" (Luther, "Estate of Marriage," *LW*, 45:24).

37. For Aristotle's comments on recognition (*anagnorisis*), see *Poetics*, 11.2–3. Else (*Poetics*, pp. 349–50) has argued that the bond of "love" (*philia*) thus recognized refers specifically to blood ties.

38. Examples of tragedies of fate (*Schicksaltragödie*) include Müllner's *Schuld* and Grillparzer's *Ahnfrau*.

39. In Goethe's *Wilhelm Meister*, "Old Harper" (Augustine) has sexual intercourse with his sister (Esperata). In Walpole's *Mysterious Mother*, the hero learns that the young woman he has married is both his sister and his daughter.

40. In *Nathan the Wise* the sexual act is desired but not enacted. See Daemmrich, "Incest Motif."

41. Perhaps detective fiction like *Oedipus the King* has become so popular because we who watch such dogged detective work as Oedipus carries out easily come to believe in the logically absurd but psychologically and socially reassuring doctrine that men and women can know for sure who their parents are. Porter, *Pursuit of Crime*, p. 223, suggests that detective stories "are experienced as reassuring because they project the image of a cosmos subject to the operations of familiar laws." Cf. Nicolson, "Professor and the Detective."

42. Sophocles, *Oedipus the King*, line 780.

43. For Marguerite of Navarre, the Franciscan writers, and others, see also chapters 2 and 4, below. On the incestuous relationship between Jesus and Mary, see Heuscher, *Psychiatric Study*, p. 207. For the related Athanasian doctrine that Father and Son are not merely similar (*homoiousios*) but literally the same (*homosusios*) in such a way that the Son is the Father of Himself—a doctrine first officially debated at the Council of Nicea in 325 A.D.—see Hamlin's

note in *Faust*, p. 316. Incest in the divine family is a widespread but generally unrecognized topos in Christian art. Even Steinberg, who discusses the physical sexuality of the baby Jesus in the visual arts—including paintings where Mary touches Jesus' genitals, Jesus suckles at Mary's breast, and the magi come to inspect the newborn Jesus' penis to determine that he is "complete in all the parts of a man" (Steinberg, *Sexuality*, pp. 65–71)—ignores almost entirely the specifically incestuous relationship that obtains among members of the Holy Family. Mary is not only the mother of God and his wife—Steinberg quotes Augustine's *Sermons* to this effect (pp. 3–4; Augustine, *Sermons*, 109)—but also his sister and daughter. Yet Irwin (*Doubling*, pp. 129–30) focuses on Christian mother-son incest in the writings of William Faulkner: "The fecundation of Mary by God is a supplanting of Joseph . . . , and since Jesus, the son, is himself that God, then it is, in a sense, the son who has impregnated his own mother, and Jesus' birth, as befits the birth of a god, is incestuous."

44. For Tamar, see Matt. 1:3 and Gen. 38:6–30. Rahab, a harlot, and Bathsheba, an adulteress, are also included among the human ancestors of Jesus, whose mother, it has been argued, was a kind of harlot or adulteress insofar as his conception was extramarital. On the genealogy of Jesus, see: Santiago, *Children of Oedipus*, p. 50; and Layard, "Incest Taboo," pp. 301–2. For the magi, see Catullus, poem 90, cited in H. D. Ranken, "Catullus," p. 119. For incest among the Persians, see: Antisthenes of Athens, *Fragmenta*, cited in Ranken, "Catullus," p. 120; and Sidler, *Inzesttabu*. On the particularly magian practice of incest, see Moutlon, *Early Zoroastrianism*, esp. pp. 204, 249–50, and Nietzsche's remark that "an ancient belief, especially strong in Persia, holds that a wise *magus* must be incestuously begotten" (*Geburt*, sect. 9, pp. 56–57; trans. Golffing, *Birth*, pp. 60–61). During the Sassanian period of Persian history, there was a Christian martyr by the name of Mirhamgushap who had married his sister before conversion; the Church did not request that they divorce but instead excepted the siblings' "chaste incest" from common law (see Gray, "Next-of-Kin Marriages in Iran"). Incest was practiced, apparently without guilt, in ancient Egypt (Middleton, "Brother-Sister and Father-Daughter Marriage") and Hellenistic and Roman Egypt (Thierfelder, *Geschwisterehe*). In Roman Egypt, claims Hopkins ("Brother-Sister Marriage"), incest involved not only the royal family but one-third of the entire population.

45. Dante, *Paradiso*, canto 33. The love with which the *Paradiso* ends is a transcendent form of the Assyrian Semiramis's physical incest, on which see *Inferno*, canto 5. For Dante the process of making the transcendental counterpart to incest is like the process of squaring a circle (*Paradiso*, 33:124ff.). On Saint Bernard and incest, see chapter 2, below.

46. For Saint Albanus, see Rank, *Inzest-Motiv*. For Saint Julian, see Bart and Cook, *Flaubert's Saint Julian*, and Berg et al., *Saint Oedipus*. For the story of Gregory, see Hartmann von Aue, *Gregorius*.

47. Stendhal, *Cenci*, esp. pp. 181–82.

48. Prat, "Freudian Character"; Lope de Vega, *Outrageous Saint* (*La fianza satisfecha*, lit. "The Fair Bond," or "Redemption," act 3, p. 91). Like his protagonists, in his early years Lope was licentious, and in his later years he mortified himself in remembrance of Christ's passion. It may be interesting that both his sister and his wife were named Isabella.

49. Schiller, *Bride*, 1.86–87, 720–22.

50. Both Mackay, "Fate and Hybris," and Weigand, "*Oedipus Tyrannus* and

Die Braut von Messina," in discussing *The Bride of Messina,* designate incest committed by an ancestral "Ahnherr" as the crime that gives rise to the sibling incest. Cf. Prader, *Schiller und Sophokles,* pp. 70ff.

51. My conjunction of Sibling and sibling incest suggests that Thorslev ("Romantic Symbol," p. 43) is mistaken to dismiss the incest theme in Matthew Lewis's *The Monk* as mere sensationalism calculated to arouse a "gothic appetite jaded with murders and tortures and uncomplicated rapes."

52. Martin du Gard, *Sorellina,* 1 : 1134–250.

53. Lope de Vega, *El vaquero de morana.*

54. See Brewster, *Incest Theme,* p. 14.

55. On Chateaubriand's devotion of Lucile, see Lucile's own writings and Aubrée, *Lucile et René;* on his entering the orders, see Chateaubriand, *Mémoires,* 1 : 78, and *Oeuvres romanesques,* pp. 121–22; and on his libertinism, see Barberis, "*René,*" pp. 51, 249–50.

56. Chateaubriand, *René,* in *Oeuvres romanesques,* pp. 134–38.

57. Thus Saint Clare marries Christ, and, since it might appear perverse for a man to marry a male God, Saint Francis marries the divine Lady Poverty. Of the service for the dead, Chateaubriand says in *René,* "Nothing can be more tragic than assisting at such a spectacle" (*Oeuvres romanesques,* p. 139).

58. *Ibid.,* p. 139.

59. *Ibid.,* p. 160. "The Awful Truth" is the title of Leo Carey's film (1937) about a couple's marriage and ultimate remarriage. In their first marriage the relations between the man and woman are like those of a brother and sister; in the second they are like those of a husband and wife. See Cavell's remarkable study *Pursuits of Happiness.*

60. Chateaubriand, *René,* in *Oeuvres romanesques,* p. 142. The novella may have autobiographical resonances: Chateaubriand was deeply devoted to his sister Lucille, and he declared early in his life that he would join a Catholic order, as does the hero of *René.* He became a religious libertine during the fraternalistic and antimonachist French Revolution, but he had returned to the Church by about the time he wrote the story.

61. Longchamps, *Mémoires d'une religieuse;* Bourges, *Crépuscule des dieux;* Rodenbach, *Le Carilloneur;* Pfeil, *Der Wilde.* For the first three references, I am indebted to Ponton, *La Religieuse,* p. 26.

62. Abelard, *Historia* (for their subsequent history, see Owen, *Noble Lovers,* p. 18); Marguerite of Navarre, *Heptameron,* 2d day, tale 19.

63. To leave the West for a moment, we might also consider in this group the Tibetan drama *Snang-sa,* where the only cure for a father's and son's incestuous rivalry for the same woman is that they both become celibate monks (Paul, *Tibetan Symbolic World*). In the Chinese *Dream of the Red Chamber,* one of the characters makes love to a nun on the evening of his sister's funeral. (The sister supposedly had had incestuous relations with her father-in-law.) According to Lucien Miller (*Masks of Fiction,* p. 229), this "is indicative of the sexual significance of both [the character] himself and his sister."

64. I take the phrase "cult of fraternity" from Sandell, "'A very poetic circumstance,'" chap. 2. Durbach, "Geschwister-Komplex," pp. 61–63, also focuses on sibling love in the romantic era. Rank, *Inzest-Motiv* anticipates Durbach's category "sibling complex" and gives several of Durbach's examples. All three works list nineteenth-century writers who were concerned with the love of one sibling for another or who loved their own siblings. Other

examples are not hard to find. Benjamin Disraeli writes, "Had I found . . . a sister, all might have been changed. . . . But this blessing, which I have ever considered the choicest boon of nature, was denied me" (*Contarini Fleming,* pt. 1, chap. 1; cf. pt. 1, chap. 7). And Thomas De Quincey thanks providence "that my infant feelings were moulded by the gentlest of sisters" (*Autobiographical Sketches,* chap. 1, quoted by Murray in his explanatory notes to *Pierre,* pp. 433–34). In *Origin* (p. 102), Engels reports a letter from Marx that says, arguing against what Marx took to be Wagner's views, "In primitive times, the sister was the wife, and that was moral."

65. In *Sorrows of Young Werther* and *Elective Affinities,* Goethe expresses "a strong belief in the existence of some law of male and female friendship and kinship higher than our actual marriage would in every case now imply" (Dixon, *Spiritual Wives,* p. 361). Thus Goethe's Lotte says that "it seems to me that these things are related to each other not in the blood, so to speak, so much as in the spirit" (Goethe, *Elective Affinities;* translated in Dixon, *Spiritual Wives,* p. 365).

66. This is Mrs. Alving's remark in Ibsen, *Ghosts,* Act 2. She is considering whether to allow a legal marriage between Osvald Alving, her son, and his beloved Regina Engstrond. Unbeknownst to the couple, Regina is the illegitimate daughter of Osvald's dead father.

67. Smith and Lindeman, *Democratic Way of Life,* p. 33.

68. McWilliams, *Fraternity,* p. 1.

69. For Plato's view, see *Republic,* 414c–15d.

70. "Français, encore un effort si vous voulez être républicains," in *Philosophie dans le boudoir,* pp. 179–245.

71. For Augustine, see *City of God,* 15.16.1.

72. Sade, *Philosophie dans le boudoir,* pp. 221–22. On incest and the revolutionary ideals of Mirabeau and Shelley, see Jones, *Hamlet,* pp. 89–102.

73. For discussions of incest in the eighteenth century, see Benrekassa, "Loi naturelle," and Aldridge, "Meaning of Incest." For Montesquieu, see his "Histoire d'Aphéridon et d'Astarte" in Letter 68 of *Lettres persanes.* The argument that incest is politically necessary to a truly fraternal government runs counter to the moralistic impulse to base republican governments on the historical model of Rome; incest has, since at least Gibbon's *Decline and Fall,* been singled out as a cause of republican decline. For a modern-day version of the argument, see Fowler, "Incest Regulations," esp. chap. 3.

74. See Diderot's *La Religieuse* and other texts discussed in Ponton, *La Religieuse.*

75. The central scene of the *Dialogues* involves a sister's decision to become a Sister against the will of her brother; the last scene depicts a series of triumphantly sacrificial decapitations of the Carmelite Sisters, with the last to lose her head being the sister. On monachism and the revolution more generally, see Estève, "Théâtre."

76. Coleridge, letters of September 20 and October 14; in Robert Southey, *Life and Correspondence,* 1:219–27.

77. Coleridge, *Notebooks,* no. 1637 (November 1803). In his remarks about William Paley's chapter on incest (Paley, *Principles,* bk. 3, chap. 5), Coleridge writes: "Brotherly & Sisterly Love . . . The Existence of strong Affection to one of the other sex, greatly modified by the difference of Sex, made more tender, graceful, soothing, consolatory, yet still remaining perfectly pure,

would be a glorious fact *for* human Nature, if the Instances were only here and there; but being, as it is, only not universal, it is a glorious fact *of* human Nature—the object therefore of religious Veneration to all that love their fellow men or honor themselves" (*Notebooks*, no. 1637). Coleridge adapted this argument in his interpretation of Shakespeare's *Romeo and Juliet* (*Lectures and Notes*, ed. Ashe, pp. 110–13).

78. In much the same restrictive vein, Lord Byron wrote to his beloved sister Augusta: "I have never ceased nor can cease to feel that perfect and boundless attachment which bounds and binds me to you—which renders me utterly incapable of *real* love for any other human being—for what could they be to me after you?" (*Selected Works*, p. 35).

79. Shelley's *Revolt of Islam* is, in part, an attempt to revive these ideas in the sphere of poetry.

80. Coleridge, *Notebooks*, no. 1637.

81. John Dryden, *Don Sebastian*, Act V, pp. 128–29.

82. Coleridge, *The Friend*, no. 16, and *Biographia Literaria*. Cf. Coleridge's question, "Is there not a sex in souls?" (letter of 1811 to Crabb Robinson; quoted in *Lectures and Notes*, ed. Ashe, p. 114n).

83. Coleridge, Letter to Francis Wrangham, September 26, 1794, in *Letters*.

84. P. 238.

85. *Politics*, 2.1.12–13.

86. Just as in some tribes "the contrast between man and not-man provides an analogy for the contrast between society and the outsider" (Douglas, *Implicit Meanings*, p. 289; cf. Needham, *Primordial Characters*, p. 5), so in some universalist groups or subgroups, such as the sixteenth-century English Family of Love, "whosoever is not of their sect they account him as a beast that hath no soul" (Rogers, *Horrible Secte*, sig. I.vii^v). On the Family of Love, see Milward, *Religious Controversies*. On universalism and dehumanization, see below, pp. 184–89.

87. In focusing here on the "family" and the "species," I overlook the "tribe" as a mediating classification. As marriage within the family is prohibited, so marriage within the tribe—for the Jews, say, marriage within one of the twelve tribes of Israel—is enjoined.

88. Westermarck's "law of similarity" has it that we animals tend to mate with those like ourselves; we shy away from sexual intercourse outside the species, or from bestiality. His "law of dissimilarity," however, has it that we tend to mate with those unlike ourselves; we shy away from sexual intercourse inside the family, or from incest. See his *Human Marriage* (1894), chap. 13, and (1922), 2:37–47.

89. Quoted in Teppe, *Chamfort*, p. 53. This 1793 remark about Jacobin ethics led to Chamfort's arrest.

90. Chamfort said: "The fraternity of such people is the fraternity of Cain and Abel" (quoted in *ibid.*, *loc. cit.*). Connolly (*Unquiet Grave*, p. 78) suggests that "the complexity of Chamfort's character would seem to be due to his temperament as a love-child; he transmuted his passionate love for his mother into a general desire for affection."

91. Paine, *The Rights of Man*, in *Writings*, 2:304–5.

92. Smith and Lindeman, *Democratic Way*, p. 19.

93. See Noyes's letter of January 15, 1837, to David Harrison; quoted in Dixon, *Spiritual Wives*, 2:55–56.

94. *Bible Communism*, p. 53. Cf. Noyes's monograph on eugenics, "An Essay on Scientific Propagation."

95. *Bible Communism*, p. 27. Noyes also says: "The sons and daughters of God, must have even a stronger sense of blood-relationship than ordinary brothers and sisters. They live as children with their Father forever, and the paramount affection of the household is . . . *brotherly* love. . . . A brother may love ten sisters, or a sister ten brothers, according to the customs of the world. The exclusiveness of marriage does not enter the family circle. But heaven is a family circle; and . . . brotherly love . . . takes the place of supremacy which the matrimonial affection occupies in this world." (*Bible Communism*; quoted in Dalke, "Incest in Nineteenth Century American Fiction," p. 88.)

96. Ellis, *Free Love*, pp. 187–88. For other relevant references to Noyes's own writings, see Kern, *Ordered Love*.

97. For the community, see Lippard, preface to *Quaker City*, p. 2. On the Brotherhood of Union, see Fiedler, introduction to *Quaker City*, p. viii. Fiedler notes that the ménage in Lippard's book "seems all siblings and no parents" (introduction to *Quaker City*, p. xxx).

98. For the romantic topos, see Dryden, "American Novelists"; See, "Kinship of Metaphor"; and Thomas, "Writers' Procreative Urge in *Pierre*." Damon, "Pierre the Ambiguous," puts *Pierre* squarely in the group of literary works about incest; Mogan, "*Pierre* and *Manfred*," p. 231, discusses the incestuous crime of Byron's magian hero in relationship to *Pierre*.

99. Melville, *Pierre*, p. 33. References to Pierre are from the edition by Murray with an afterword by Thompson.

100. Watkins, "Melville's Plotinus Plinlimmon," pp. 46–47, focuses on the religious aspect of the incestuous relationship between Pierre and Mary.

101. Melville, *Pierre*, pp. 37, 58.

102. *Ibid.*, pp. 232, 141.

103. Melville's Billy Budd is "a foundling" who, when asked, "Who was your father?," has to answer, "God knows, Sir" (*Billy Budd*, p. 298). Budd's "entire family was practically invested in himself" (p. 297). For the reference to Ishmael, by which name the narrator of *Moby Dick* calls himself, see Melville, *Pierre*, p. 116.

104. *Pierre*, p. 310.

105. *Pierre*, pp. 178, 171.

106. *Ibid.*, p. 171.

107. *Ibid.*, p. 304.

108. *Ibid.*, pp. 304–5. Cf the reference to a utopian "new Canaan" or "Circassia" in *Pierre*, pp. 55–56.

109. *Pierre*, pp. 56–57, 318–19.

110. For this etymology of "Isabella" and its cognate "Elizabeth," see Gesenius, *Hebrew and English Lexicon*, p. 45.

111. For his "gospelizing," see *Pierre*, pp. 304–5, 56–57, 318, 333.

112. *Ibid.*, p. 388.

113. *Ibid.*, p. 342.

114. The same theme appears in Pierre's relationship to Lucy, who, before Pierre met Isabel, was to have become his wife. Lucy becomes convinced that she has been called "to do a wonderful office" toward Pierre. Thinking him to be the complete incarnation of *all* her family—her "brother and mother . . .

and all the universe"—Lucy comes to the Church of the Apostles to serve Pierre as a nunlike cousin (*Pierre*, pp. 350, 351, 353, 364). She is both Cousin and cousin to him, just as Isabel is both sibling and Sibling.

115. Murray, explanatory notes to *Pierre*, p. 491, remarks that Bayle, in his *Dictionary*, reports that Mohammed, though he forbad incest to his followers, allowed it to himself by a special privilege.

116. *Pierre*, p. 186.

117. *Ibid.*, p. 403.

118. *Ibid.*, p. 341.

119. Heraclitus, frag. 60, my translation.

120. For Nero's incest with his mother, see Tacitus, *Annales*, 14.1, p. 199. Since the publication of Wilson's *What Happens in Hamlet?*, it has been critical custom to say that "nunnery" in *Hamlet* must mean "brothel." The opposing view—that "nunnery" means "nunnery"—is presented in a long note by Harold Jenkins in his edition of *Hamlet*, pp. 493–96.

121. The topos of the love affair between a nun and a friar that begins inside a convent informs the central scene of *Measure for Measure* (where a player-friar is attracted to a novice nun). It should be distinguished both from the topos of the love affair that begins before the lover enters the convent (Chateaubriand's *René*) and from that of the love affair that begins after the lover leaves the convent (Schiller's *Bride of Messina*). For more examples, see Ponton, *La Religeuse*, pp. 28–33.

Chapter One

1. Lever, in the Introduction to *MM*, p. lxxxiv, says Reformation thinkers regarded it as "the first of the divine commandments."

2. For Plato, see *Republic*, 507; for Aristotle, see *Politics*, trans. Rackham, 1258. On the identification of natural and economic offspring in *The Merchant of Venice*, see Shell, *Money*, chap. 3, and in *Oedipus the Tyrant*, see Shell, *Economy*, chap. 3.

3. Compare 2H4 3.2.229–30: "We owe God a death." "Death" was pronounced like "debt."

4. See, e.g., Nicholas of Cusa, *De ludo globi*.

5. See Exod. 20:14; Lev. 18:6–18, 20:10; Deut. 27:20. In Genesis, incest as defined in Leviticus and Exodus is practiced by the patriarchs: e.g., Abraham marries his paternal halfsister (Gen. 20:12) and Jacob marries two sisters (Gen. 29:21–30). Some rabbinic theory explains such quasi-incestuous marriages by saying that the patriarchs were subject only to the Noachite law (Sanhedrin 58a–b, in I. Epstein, ed., *Talmud*; Maimonides, *Mishna Torah*, Melkaim 9.5, in Maimonides, *Werke*. Cf. M. Greenberg, "Incest"). For the extraordinary view that, before the Flood, "those hideous instances of incest had not yet happened," see Luther's commentary on Gen. 6.1, 2 (Luther, *Lectures on Genesis*, in *LW* 2:10–11). For a historical and anthropological explanation of the patriarchs' incest, see the discussion of the Hurrian fratriarchy in the Conclusion, below.

6. See Edmund's speech in LR 1.2.1–22 and the remark in John Webster's *The Devil's Law Case* (4.2.246–52) that "though our civil law makes difference / 'Tween the base, and the legitimate, / Compassionate Nature makes them equal; / Nay, she many times prefers them."

7. Fox, *Red Lamp*, p. 3.

8. Cf. the connection between cannibalism and incest or fornication in PER 1.1.65–66 and the speech containing Elbow's malapropism "Hannibal" for "cannibal" (2.1.171–76).

9. Augustine, *Against Julian*, 3.21.42; quoted in Goergen, *Sexual Celibate*, p. 37.

10. See Vest, "Syphilographer," p. 130. For the date of the play's action, see Empson, *Structure of Complex Words*, p. 287, and n. 52 below.

11. Empson, *Structure of Complex Words*, p. 287. Critics who say that Isabella or Angelo is a Puritan range from Birch, *Inquiry* (1848), pp. 353, 370, to Sypher, *Ethic of Time* (1976), pp. 58–62.

12. The Nuer call incest "syphilis" because they see in one the punishment of the other (Evans-Pritchard, "Exogamous Rules," p. 11). Incest was once considered to be a cure for syphilis (Masters, *Patterns of Incest*, p. 31).

13. Vest, "Syphilographer."

14. Aristotle, *Poetics*, 6.10–11.

15. That the intent of sexual intercourse (reproduction) is conflated with the act helps to explain why the Duke insists that Angelo marry Mariana, with whom he has had sexual intercourse on only one occasion (3.1.188–90, 5.1.375). In enforcing this marriage the Duke seeks not so much to make an honest, or chaste, woman out of Mariana as to ensure public recognition of the paternity of the child she has conceived. In any case, the biblical penalty for such intercourse as that between Angelo and Mariana is marriage (Deut. 22:29).

16. Thomas Aquinas, *Summa contra gentiles*, bk. 3, chap. 2, "That Every Agent Acts for an End," in *Introduction to St. Thomas Aquinas*, p. 429.

17. Thomas Aquinas, *Summa*, q. 154, art. 2 (p. 1817).

18. There is some question as to whether Claudio and Juliet are not in one way or another already married. The question itself, if not the answer, is important, since it bears upon our understanding of the relationship between intent and act (Claudio says they intended to marry) and upon the overall problem of kept and broken contracts and estates.

19. Some editors (e.g., Bald) believe lines are missing.

20. For Aristotle on the necessary sign (*tekmērion*), see his *Rhetoric*, 1.2. 16–17.

21. For Aristotle on chance and necessity, as well as on particular and universal, see Butcher's critical notes to the *Poetics*, pp. 178–85.

22. For comparable remarkably high illegitimacy ratios in Shakespeare's England, see Wrightson, "English Illegitimacy," and Quaife, *Wanton Wenches*.

23. Pater, *Appreciations*, p. 182.

24. Cf. WT 1.2.208, in which Mamillius says, "I am like you, they say," to which Leontes responds, "Why, that's some comfort." See, too, Paulina's comment to Leontes in WT 2.2.95–97: the child "is yours; / And might we lay th' old proverb to your charge, / So like you, 'tis the worse."

25. The voice from the father's grave brings to mind the ghostly father in *Hamlet*, along with Hamlet's questions about whether his promptings are good or ill (e.g., HAM 1.4.40–44, 2.2.584–89). Moreover, the particular counsel that Isabella figures her dead father has uttered from the ground—that Isabella should not be the keeper of her brother so far as to save his life through an unchaste act—recalls Genesis 4:9–10: "And the Lord said unto Cain,

Where is Abel thy brother? And he said, I know not: Am I my brother's keeper? And he said, What hast thou done? the voice of thy brother's blood crieth unto me from the ground." Is Isabella to all intents a fratricide? Giraldi Cinthio's *Hecatommithi* (1565) already appeals to the brother's paternity. Vico (the counterpart to Claudio) speaks thus to Epitia (the counterpart to Isabella): "Do you wish, Epitia, to see me with the axe upon my neck, and with my head cut off, I who was born of the same womb as you and begotten of the same father?" (quoted by Lever, ed., *Measure for Measure*, p. 159).

26. Erasmus, *Ryght frutefull Epistle*, sig. Aiii.

27. Whetstone, *Promos and Cassandra*, pt. 1, act 2, scene 1, and pt. 1, act 3, scene 4.

28. For *antigonē*—literally, "generated in place of another" (Wilamowitz-Moellendorf, *Aischylos*, p. 92, n. 3)—as meaning essentially "anti-generation," see Benardete, "*Antigone*," no. 1, p. 156.

29. Martz (*Place of 'Measure for Measure,'* p. 64) assumes that Isabella's mother *was* an adulteress: "Given Isabella's intelligence and sensitivity, we can only assume that her mother was indeed unfaithful to her father." Whether or no, Isabella cannot be *sure* either that Claudio is or that he is not her paternal brother.

30. Sypher, "Casuist," p. 278.

31. See M. Jackson, "Ambivalence and the Last-born," and contrast the Forest of Arden, where people of different generations and different birth orders can be, or pretend to be, "co-mates and brothers in exile" (AYL 2.1.1; see Montrose, "'Place of a Brother'"). For laws concerning lineal descent and primogeniture in Shakespeare, see also Clarkson and Warren, *Law of Property*, pp. 207–14, and the argument about inheritance between Robert Faulconbridge and his bastard brother Philip in KJ 1.1.57–83.

32. Helmholz, "Bastardy Litigation," p. 361. Dr. Johnson remarks that the chastity of women is "of the utmost importance, as all property depends on it" (quoted in Hill, *Puritanism*, p. 384).

33. Sophocles, *Oedipus*, l. 415. During the Middle Ages the Oedipus legend was known through such works as Statius, *Thebaid*, and the twelfth-century *Roman de Thebes*. See Edwin H. Zeydel's introduction to Hartman von Aue, *Gregorius*, p. 4.

34. Baring-Gould, ed., *Mother Goose*, no. 158, p. 118.

35. Jonas of Orleans, *De institutione laicailli*, PL, 106:183–84: *Cum omnis illicitus concubitus incestus sit.*

36. Montaigne discusses in his *Essaies*, which were translated into English in 1603, societies supposed not to have ordinary incest taboos (*Essays*, 1:115–17). Charron, whose *De la sagesse* was translated into English in 1606, argues that the incest taboo is a "mere custom" that "mastereth our souls, our beliefs, our judgements, with a most unjust and tyrannical authority" (*Of Wisdome*, pp. 310–11). Cf. Aquinas's suggestion that incest is natural (*Summa*, q. 154, art. 9 [p. 1824]).

37. See Aquinas's gloss on Aristotle, *Politics*, 2.2: "It is natural that a man should have a liking for a woman of his kindred" (*Summa*, q. 154, art. 9 [p. 1824]).

38. Ford, *'Tis Pity*, 2.5.29–34.

39. Luther's position is discussed in Durkheim, *Incest*, p. 61, and Huth, *Marriage of Near Kin*.

40. Cooper, "Incest Prohibitions," p. 2. Cooper suggests the same view was held by John Chrysostom, Plutarch, and Philo Judaeus.

41. Cf. Mead's report of her Arapesh informants (who are, admittedly, atypical among primitive societies): "What would the old men say to a young man who wished to take his sister to wife? . . . The answers . . . came to this: 'What! you would like to marry your sister! What is the matter with you anyway? Don't you want a brother-in-law? Don't you realize that if you marry another man's sister and another man marries your sister, you will have at least two brothers-in-law, while if you marry your own sister you will have none? With whom will you hunt, with whom garden, whom will you visit?'" (Mead, *Sex and Temperament*, pp. 93–94.)

42. Burton, *Anatomy*, discussed in Durkheim, *Incest*, p. 61. For Gregory the Great's theory, see Muller, "Physiological Explanation," pp. 294–95. Cf. 1 Cor. 6:18–19.

43. See Cooper, "Incest Prohibitions," p. 2. Benardete summarizes ("*Antigone*," no. 2, p. 39) a comparable argument from Thomas Aquinas, *Summa contra gentiles*, 3.124: "To endow parents with the authority of wisdom, it is first of all necessary to look upon them as nonsexual beings, i.e., as not possible objects of sexual desire. The prohibition against incest embodies this reverence."

44. Sophocles, *Oedipus*, ll. 424–25.

45. Concerning the variant theory that there can be societies where the practice of incest strengthens the patriarchy, see the Conclusion, below.

46. Pope, "Renaissance Background," in Geckle, ed., *Interpretations*, p. 58. See also Aristotle, *Politics*, 1.2–5.

47. Nashe, introduction to *Menaphon*, 3.315.

48. James I, *Trew Law* (1598), esp. pp. 64–66.

49. Locke, *Two Treatises on Civil Government*, p. 6.

50. Brown, *Love's Body*, p. 4.

51. From this viewpoint, the army figured by the soldier gentlemen (1.2) and the religious orders have the same democratizing tendency to homogenize individual differences of kinship. Freud makes a similar parallel in "Two Artificial Groups: The Church and the Army." See Brown's argument that "military society, like the church, tends towards equality" (Brown, *Love's Body*, pp. 12–13).

52. R. G. White (*Shakespeare's Scholar*, pp. 126–32) allies the Duke with Frederick III, Duke of Austria and Holy Roman Emperor, and associates the King of Hungary with Corvinus, King of Hungary, who conquered Vienna in 1485. Battenhouse ("*MM* and Christian Doctrine," p. 1058n) errs in saying that *Ferdinand* III was Duke of Austria in 1485. For the reference to the Turks, see J. Dover Wilson's introduction to Quiller-Couch's edition of the play, pp. 104–5. Albrecht (*Neue Untersuchungen*, pp. 216–53) allies the Duke with James I, the King of Hungary with the real King of Spain, and the other dukes with the United Netherlands. See, too, Lever's introduction to his edition, pp. 31–32.

53. Cook, "Metaphysical Poetry," p. 124.

54. Schlegel remarks of the Duke that "as he ultimately extends a free pardon to all the guilty, we do not see how his original purpose, in committing the execution of the laws to other hands, of restoring their strictness, has in any wise been accomplished" (*Lectures on Dramatic Art*, p. 388). I would take

issue with Schlegel's position that the pardons are free but would agree that the official purpose of the Duke is not accomplished. Tennenhouse writes ("Representing Power," p. 146) that "the duke does not and cannot change the law that equates the crime of Mistress Overdone with that of Claudio, nor can he alter the law that condemns Claudio to death."

55. Lévi-Strauss, *Elementary Structures*, p. 124.

56. Traversi (*Approach*, p. 112), e.g., writes that the central issue of the play is "to find for the law a necessary sanction in experience without depriving it of the firmness and impartiality upon which its maintenance depends." But why should Shakespeare choose this particular law? The law against fornication not only represents the others as part to whole but is also the foundation of all law.

57. Lévi-Strauss, *Elementary Structures*, p. 490. Cf. Malinowski, "Parenthood," pp. 137–38.

58. Aquinas, *Summa*, q. 154, art. 9 (p. 1823). For "antonomasia," see *idem*, p. 1824.

59. The discrepancy between the two numbers (see 1.3.21 and 1.2.157) lends a mythic vagueness to the action.

60. John Gower's *Confessio Amantis* (8.67–74), a source for Shakespeare's *Pericles of Tyre*, considers the fratricide Cain's incestuous relations with his sister Calmana. On the pair, see also Sanhedrin 58b, in I. Epstein, ed., *Talmud*.

61. We should not take Pompey's remark too lightly. In eighteenth-century Russia, the Skoptsy sect's distrust of the body extended to the logical extreme of castration. "After an orgiastic farewell to the genitals the Skoptsy castrated themselves" (Peterkiewicz, *Third Adam*, p. 123). The Church Father Origen castrated himself, though he later regretted having done so (Eusebius, *History of the Church*, VI, 8, p. 247). Some people interpret castration to be the significance of circumcision, or fear castration the result of circumcision (Reik, *Fragments*, p. 336; Cavell, *Claim of Reason*, p. 480); for them, Saint Paul's argument that people should substitute for the old Jewish commandment to circumcize the penis the new Christian injunction to circumcize the soul—"circumcision is that of the heart, in the spirit, and not in the letter" (Rom. 2:29)—would amount to an injunction to become religious celibates.

62. Dumm, *Theological Basis*, p. 21; and Jerome, *Adversus Jovinianum*, 1.16, in PL, 23:246.

Chapter Two

1. Bale, Epistle Dedicatory to Elizabeth's *Godly Medytacion*.

2. See Battenhouse, "MM and the Atonement," pp. 1029–59, esp. p. 1031; Reimer, *Begriff der Gnade*; Chambers, *Jacobean Shakespeare and MM*; and Knight, *Wheel of Fire*. Even Sister Maura (*Shakespeare's Catholicism*) and Father Milward (*Shakespeare's Religious Background*) fail to recognize in what ways the play is about religious celibacy.

3. Miles, *Problem of MM*, p. 174, writes, "It can't be claimed that the friar disguise is essential to the plot of *Measure for Measure* as a whole"; she discusses Elizabethan dismissal of the friar disguise on pp. 171–72. For the rarity of the device, see Freeburg, *Disguise Plots*. As for possible sources, writing in 1541, Elyot (*Image of Governaunce*, sig. M3r–v) describes the Roman Emperor Alexander Severus as disguising himself "sometyme in the habite of a scholer of philosophie . . . oftentimes like a marchaunt," and in 1592 Riche (*Adven-*

tures of Brusanus, chap. 7) describes King Leonarchus in the disguise of a merchant. Similarly, King James disguised himself as a merchant in order to pay secret visits to the London Exchange (Dugdale, *Time Triumphant*, sig. B2).

4. See Miles, *Problem of MM*, pp. 216–18. Isabella's counterparts include Cassandra in Whetstone's *Historie*, Epitia in Cinthio's *Heccatommithi*, and the Gentlewoman in Lupton's *Too Good to Be True*.

5. For examples of the satires to which *MM* has been compared, see those by Henry Bullinger, George Buchanan, and Erasmus. The extensive pre-Reformation tradition of anti-monachal satire can be amply documented from such familiar works as *The Romance of the Rose* or the writings of Chaucer and Boccaccio. See also Gless, *MM, the Law, and the Convent*, pp. 67–70. For Buchanan's satirical assault on the Franciscan friars, see especially his poems "Somnium," "Palinodia," and "Franciscanus & Fratres." Both Milward, S.J., *Shakespeare's Catholicism*, and Sister Maura, *Shakespeare's Religious Background*, do not recognize that *Measure for Measure* is largely about religious celibacy.

6. For a recent summary of the arguments for Shakespeare's Catholicism, see Honigmann, *Shakespeare*, chap. 10. Honigmann notes, as I do, that *Measure for Measure* views Catholicism from the inside.

7. For this thesis, see Mutschmann and Wentersdorf, *Shakespeare and Catholicism*, p. 92; for the thesis that Shakespeare engaged in "antenuptial fornication," see Schoenbaum, *Shakespeare*, pp. 88–91.

8. Chambrun, *Shakespeare*, p. 374, argues that this Joan Shakespeare—to be distinguished from William's sister Joan (*b.* 1558)—was his aunt; that position is criticized by Groot, *Shakespeares and the Old Faith*, pp. 103–4. For Isabella Shakespeare, see Albrecht, *Neue Untersuchungen*, appendix 1, p. 294; Elze, *Shakespeare*, p. 12; and Milward, *Shakespeare's Religious Background*. Mutschmann and Wentersdorf, *Shakespeare and Catholicism*, p. 291, suggest that Isabella Shakespeare may have been "a relative of the poet's grandfather." Her religious community, the Guild of St. Anne, was Benedictine; Saint Clare served with the Benedictines before founding the Franciscan Clares.

9. Freud, *Totem*, p. 6.

10. *Ibid.*, p. 7.

11. *Ibid.*, p. 35. For Freud on religion as a social neurosis, see also his "Obsessive Acts and Religious Practices."

12. With the double meaning of "taboo" as both "unclean" and "holy," compare Latin *sacer*. For other such terms, see Freud, *Totem*, p. 18.

13. "Elizabeth," from the name of Elisheba, the wife of Aaron the priest (Exod. 6:23; a later Elizabeth appears in Luke 1:5), has been interpreted as "God is fullness," "God of the oath," "God's oath," "God is an oath [by which one swears]," and "consecrated to God." In his Epistle Dedicatory to Elizabeth's *Godly Medytacion* (fol. 8B), John Bale puts forward "consecrated to God" as the definitive translation of "Elizabeth." Cf. Gesenius, *Hebrew and English Lexicon*, p. 45.

14. See Freud, "Taboo on Virginity."

15. Freud, *Totem*, p. 22.

16. See Leclerq, *Monks and Love*, p. 14, on nuns' and monks' knowledge of love acquired before entering the orders.

17. Birje-Patil, "Marriage Contracts in MM," p. 110, even suggests that 1.4.45 indicates Isabella's foreknowledge of Claudio's fornication.

18. For adoption as an impediment to marriage, see Justinian, *Digest*, 1.23, tit. 2, lex 17; Gratian, *Decretum*, caus. 30, q. 3, c. 6; and Ivo Carnotensis, *Decretum*, PL, 161:657. See also G. Oesterlé, "Inceste," in Naz, ed., *Dictionnaire*, 5:1297–314. C. E. Smith, *Papal Enforcement*, p. 6, shows that "adoption has the same effect in precluding marriage as does kinship by blood." Fowler, *Incest Regulations*, p. 40, suggests, however, that this view has been contested frequently since the fall of Rome. On adoption as an impediment to marriage in Shakespeare, see Bertram's reluctance to marry Helena in *All's Well That Ends Well*.

19. See Saxo Grammaticus, *Historiae*, in Gollancz, ed., *Sources*, pp. 108–9.

20. In the *Phaedrus* Plato explores the similar doctrine that "the lover forgets mothers and brothers . . . all alike" (*Phaedrus*, 239e–240a, cf. 252a). To leave the West for a moment: "In one of the Chinese secret societies in Singapore the oath was, 'I swear that I shall know neither father nor mother, nor brother nor sister, nor wife nor child, but the brotherhood alone'" (Heckethorn, *Secret Societies*, 2:132; cf. Brown, *Love's Body*, pp. 32–33).

21. Transcripts and letters from the trial for canonization, which took place in 1253–54, are included in Garonne, *Sainte Claire*, p. 23. Isabella is about to join Saint Clare's order.

22. For Antigone in this context, see Benardete, "Reading," pt. 2, p. 11, and Hegel, *Phänomenologie*, *Werke*, vol. 6, chap. 6.

23. See, e.g., Council of Rome (A.D. 402), can. 1 and 2, in Hefele, *Conciliengeschichte*, 2:87; Pope Gelasius I (A.D. 494), letter to the bishops of Lucania, c. 20, in *Decretum Gratiani*, causa 27, q. 1, c. 14; and Council of Macon (A.D. 585), can. 12, in Hefele, *Conciliengeschichte*, 3:37. In England the legal and literary tradition that for religious celibates all sexual intercourse constituted incest was widespread. In [Lacy], *Treatise on the Ten Commandments*, for example, it is written that "incestus is he þat dlith with nonne, with kosyn, or with amaydon, þe wich is called defloracio"; and in Lydgate, *Fall of Princes* (?a1493; Hrl. 1766, 2.4068), it is written that "incestus is trespassing with kyn or with blood, Or froward medlyng with hir that is a nunne."

24. Courtly love may be a similar way to love one's sibling *in extremis* without violating the taboo against physical incest. Indeed, "in the middle ages a sister was not infrequently the object of courtly love, partly, it appears, because the presence of the incest barrier served to re-inforce the knight errant's resolution to adhere to the ideal of chastity" (Murray, introduction to Melville, *Pierre*, p. 55).

25. Bollandists, *Acta sanctorum*. See Harney, *Brother and Sister Saints*, for a useful discussion of sibling saints mentioned in that work.

26. *Encyclopaedia Britannica*, 11th ed., s.v. "Monasticism." See also Athanasius (?), *Vita Antonii*.

27. *Encyclopaedia Britannica*, 11th ed., s.v. "Monasticism."

28. St. Gregory the Great, *Vita S. Benedicti*.

29. Hartmann von Aue, *Gregorius*. For a modern version of the medieval Gregory legend, see Thomas Mann's *Der Erwählte* (lit., The Chosen One), translated as *The Holy Sinner*, with its monkish narrator.

30. St. Leander, *Regula, sive liber de institutione virginum et contemptu mundi, ad Florentinam sororem* (late seventh century), quoted from Montalembert, *Monks*, 2:188.

31. *Ibid.*, 5:331–32.

32. St. Damasus, *Epigrammata*, trans. Joseph F. M. Marique (Holy Cross College, Worcester, Mass.); quoted by Harney, *Brother and Sister Saints*, p. 20.

33. Harney, *Brother and Sister Saints*, p. 93. See also Willibald of Mainz, *Vita S. Bonifacii*. Saint Boniface asked that at her death Saint Lioba be buried in his grave, but the monks of Fulda did not carry out his request.

34. Lincoln, *Teresa*, p. 10, p. xxv. Cf. Egido, "Historical Setting."

35. Teresa, *Life*, 4.

36. Teresa, *Way of Perfection*, IV, in her *Complete Works*, trans. Peers, 2:17; cf. VIII, 2:39.

37. Teresa, *Exclamations of Soul to God*, XIV, in her *Complete Works*, trans. Peers, 2:415.

38. Teresa, *Way of Perfection*, XXXVII, in her *Complete Works*, trans. Peers, 2:161.

39. John of the Cross, *Precautions*, V, in his *Collected Works*, trans. Kavanaugh and Rodriguez, p. 656.

40. Lincoln, *Teresa*, p. 24; cf. Teresa, *Life*, 2.6.

41. See Santiago, *Children*, p. 65.

42. Knowles and Hadcock, *Medieval Religious Houses*, esp. pp. 104–5, 194–95, 202.

43. See Marguerite of Navarre, *Heptameron*, 3d day, tale 30, 3:202. Robert d'Arbissel, the founder of the abbey of Fontevrault, was himself accused of sleeping in the same bed with nuns; see Bayle, *Dictionnaire*, ed. Desoer, 6:508–19, art. "Fontevraud."

44. *Encyclopaedia Britannica*, 11th ed., s.v. "Monasticism." To the list of saintly siblings mentioned in this chapter might be added Heloise and Abelard. They lived together, first in spiritual incest of a physical kind (he a Brother, she a laywoman), then as secret husband and wife. After Abelard was castrated at the command of Heloise's uncle, she became a Sister and they lived as "brother and sister" (to quote the letters between them). See Leclerq, *Monks and Love*, esp. p. 119.

45. Muir, *Shakespeare's Sources*, p. 108, esp. no. 3.

46. Gless, *MM, the Law, and the Convent*, p. 259.

47. For Bernard of Vienne (France), see his Letter to Ludovico. For Bernardine of Siena on incest with one's father as a less offensive act than "unnatural" acts with one's husband, see Noonan, *Contraception*, pp. 260ff. Bernardino Ochino was an instructor of Princess Elizabeth.

48. Quoted in Harney, *Brother and Sister Saints*, p. 114.

49. St. Bernard, *Sermones in Cantica Canticones* (twelfth century). The theme of *soror mea sponsa* appears in the Song of Songs at 4:9, 4:10, 4:12, 5:1, 5:2. Bernard's sermons on the Songs demonstrate "la dernière libération de l'âme"—the ultimate liberation of the soul—of which Paul preaches (Viller, ed., *Dictionnaire de spiritualité*, "Bernard [Saint]," col. 1470). See Bugge, *Virginitas*, p. 90.

50. See, e.g., Gless, *MM, the Law, and the Convent*, pp. 262–63.

51. See G. K. Hunter, "Six Notes," pp. 167–69. For the rule itself, see Sbaralea, ed., *Bullarium Franciscanum*, esp. 2:477–86.

52. Lempp, "Anfänge des Klarissenordens."

53. MacKay, "MM," p. 110.

54. See Thomas of Celano, *Sainte Claire*, esp. pp. 125–27, cited in Dhont,

Claire, p. 91. On Saint Clare and the privilege of poverty, see Fiege, *Princess of Poverty*, pp. 80–89; Lazzeri, "Il 'Privilegium Pauperitatis'"; Sabatier, "Privilège de la pauvreté"; and Garonne, *Claire*, p. 161.

55. O.E.D., s.v. "Privilege."

56. Dhont, *Claire*, p. 163.

57. On Isabella and the Order of Ransom, see Desplandres, *L'Ordre des Trinitaires*.

58. Harney, *Brother and Sister Saints*, p. 119.

59. On this rumor, see Jacquemet, ed., *Catholicisme*, and Schmitt, "Isabelle."

60. Thus Little, *Religious Poverty*, p. 204, writes of Margaret, daughter of Raymond Berenger, count of Provence, that "Louis's wife founded a convent of Poor Clares outside of Paris." Cf. *Récueil des historiens*, 23 : 426.

61. Cf. Friar Francis in *Much Ado About Nothing*, the name of Sister Francesca in the trial for the canonization of Saint Clare (Garonne, *Claire*, p. 80), and the bungling Friar Francis in *Romeo and Juliet*.

62. *Encyclopaedia Britannica*, 11th ed., s.v. "Clara, Saint."

63. Freud, *Civilization*, pp. 48–49.

64. In this poem, variants of the name "Clare" signify both Sister Clare and divine radiance: "Laudato si', mi Signore, per sora luna e le stelle / il celu l'ai formate clarite et pretiose et belle" (All praise be yours, my Lord, through Sister Moon and Stars; / In the heavens you have made them, bright / And precious and fair; "Il Cantico di Frate Sole," in St. Francis, *Scritti*, p. 168; trans. as "The Canticle of Brother Sun," in St. Francis, *Omnibus of Sources*, ed. Habig, 130–31).

65. For some of the genealogies, see Garonne, *Claire*, p. 151. See also Abate, "Casa paterna," esp. pp. 78–81, 151–60.

66. Cousins, *Bonaventure*, p. 20. For this and the following reference I am indebted to Susan M. Glaeser.

67. Bonaventure, *Itinerarium mentis in Deum* (thirteenth century), p. 93. Franciscans generally regarded Bonaventure, the "Seraphic [or Franciscan] Doctor," as the principal theological and philosophical spokesperson for their order.

68. Pater, *Appreciations*, p. 184.

69. Quoted in Telle, *Marguerite*, p. 297.

70. Quoted in McDonnell, *Beguines and Beghards*, p. 497. For an account of the Brethren, see Cohn, "Cult of the Free Spirit."

71. Carey, Foreword, in Nigel Smith, ed., *Ranter Writings*, p. 7. On Coppe as an adept of the Brethren, see Cohn, *Millennium*, p. 68; for Coppe's writings, see Nigel Smith, ed., *Ranter Writings*, pp. 39–158; for a bibliographic consideration of the influence in England of the Brethren's principal text, Marguerite Porete's work, see S. M. Doirion, "Middle English Translation."

72. Quoted in Cohn, "Cult of the Free Spirit," p. 68.

73. *Ibid.*, p. 59.

74. *Ibid.*, p. 56.

75. "Fay ce que voudras" (*Gargantua*, chap. 57). The liberty of Rabelais's abbey is often interpreted as mere Epicurean intemperance or desire for a heaven on earth (see, e.g., Kennard, *Friar in Fiction*, p. 58), but it also has a serious libertine aspect. Bakhtin, *Rabelais*, p. 412, compares Thélème to the medieval parody "The Rules of Blessed Libertine."

76. "Amye, amez et faites ce que tu vouldrez." Porete, *Le Mirouer des simples ames* (ca. 1300), f. 20r–v or p. 20. Porete's work is unique; other reports about the Brethren are for the most part transcripts of trials in which they were found guilty of various antinomian heresies.

77. Leff, *Heresy*, 1 : 310.

78. Nigg, *Heretics*, p. 235.

79. Leff, *Heresy*, 1 : 325, summarizing Trithemius, *Annales Hirsaugiensis*, 2 : 140.

80. See Hartmann's interrogation at Erfurt by Walter Kerling, recounted in von Döllinger, *Sektengeschichte*, pt. 2, p. 386.

81. Leff, *Heresy*, 1 : 378–79.

82. Conrad Kannler's testimony is found in Haupt, "Ein Beghardenprozess," pp. 487–98, and Leff, *Heresy*, 1 : 380. For Joris, see Fränger, *Millennium*, p. 42. Fränger, *Bosch*, p. 42, discusses the influence on Hieronymus Bosch of the doctrine of the Brethren of the Free Spirit.

83. Collins, "'Excommunication,'" p. 253.

84. For this position, see Allo, *Saint Paul*, p. 121; and Conzelmann, *1 Corinthians*, p. 97.

85. Pomerius, *De origene monasterii Viridisvallis*, p. 286. On the Men and Women, for whom the virtue of chastity was replaced by the Freedom of the Spirit, see McDonnell, *Beguines and Beghards*, p. 502. The *Homines Intelligentiae* of Brussels were a local sect that shared their principal doctrines with the Brethren of the Free Spirit; their leaders Giles Cantor and William Hilderniss were condemned by Pierre Ailly, bishop of Cambrai, in 1411. Bloemardinne (or Hadewich) was a great poetess of Brussels.

86. On the Adamites and Bohemia (the native home of Barnadine in *Measure for Measure*), see Heymann, *George of Bohemia, John Zizka*, and "Hussite and Utraquist Church." A nineteenth- and twentieth-century counterpart to the Brethren can be found among the Mariavites of Poland, in whose cloisters Sisters and Brothers enjoyed sexual intercourse in "mystical marriages" and raised their offspring as children without original sin. On the Mariavites, see Peterkiewicz, *Third Adam*.

87. Quoted as the epigraph to Nigg, *Heretics*.

88. Von Döllinger, *Sektengeschichte*, pt. 2, p. 664. See also G. Schneider, *Libertin*, p. 60.

89. Thomas More, for example, said that the monk Martin Luther—who married a nun—not only promulgated an incestuous doctrine but also practiced incest itself (More, *Confutaycon*, pp. 48–49). Luther, of course, had held that many Romish priests practiced incest.

90. In his *Articles of Visitation* Melanchthon claims, for example, that Luther's doctrine of the "freedom of a Christian" was interpreted by some Protestant reformers as a charter for moral laxity; Melanchthon argues for the preaching of the Ten Commandments as a guide to the good works that are to follow true faith (Franklin Sherman, introduction to Luther, "Against the Antinomians"). Luther resented the canonical imposition of celibacy laws, which, given the conflation of intent and act that characterizes his notion of faith, were impossible for almost all human beings—including such monks and priests as himself—to fulfill. For a historical study of the relationship between the Brethren of the Free Spirit and one branch of French Protestantism, see

Frederichs, "Luthérien français"; and for a general discussion of the role of the doctrines of the free spirit in the Reformation, see Guarnieri's discussion in "Libero spirito," pp. 464–500 passim, and Appendix, pp. 685–708.

91. Wilkinson, *Supplication*, p. 34.

92. *Ibid.*, p. 19.

93. Rogers, *Displaying*, sig. I5r.

94. See Shepherd's introduction to his edition of *Family of Love*, p. iii; and Cherry, *Most Unvaluedst Purchase*. On the Family of Love generally, see Halley, "English Family of Love."

95. Millin, *Antiquités nationales*, 3.28.6; my translation. On this and similar riddles conflating kin roles—including some dating back to the Spanish writer Julian Medrano, born in Navarre about 1540—see Rank, *Inzest-Motiv*, pp. 334–35.

96. Millin, *Antiquités nationales*, 3.28.6.

97. Luther *Tischreden*. For Luther and others, see Montaiglon's note to the thirtieth tale in his edition of the *Heptameron*, by Marguerite of Navarre, 4:281–83, and Saintsbury's note in his edition, 3:214–16. The same topos influenced such writers as William Blake (perhaps by way of the English Ranters). Consider, for example, this passage from Blake's "The Gates of Paradise": "Thou'rt my Mother from the Womb, / Wife, Sister, Daughter, to the Tomb."

98. Taylor, *Shakespeare's Darker Purpose*, p. 69, compares the riddle in *Pericles* with similar riddles in two of Shakespeare's sources, Gower's *Confessio Amantis* and Twine's 1594 translation of Apollonius of Tyre, *The Patterne of Painefull Adventures*; however, *Confessio Amantis* and *The Patterne of Painefull Adventures* do not play up the spiritual—the nunnish or monkish—quality of simultaneous parenthood, spousehood, and childhood in the same way as *Pericles* does.

99. Dagens, "'Miroir.'"

100. *Contre la secte phantastique et furieuse des Libertins qui se nomment spirituels* (1545). For the antinomian beliefs of the Libertins, see Walker, *Calvin*, pp. 293–94. Calvin's attack on the Libertins offended Marguerite, and he wrote an ambiguously apologetic letter to her on April 28, 1545 (*Opera*, 12:65). On Marguerite and the Libertins, see G. Schneider, *Libertin*, esp. pp. 81–84, and Dagens, "'Miroir.'"

101. See Perrens, *Libertins*.

102. Champneis, *Harvest*.

103. See esp. Lefranc, *Découverte* and *Masque*, and the endorsement of Lefranc's position in David's introduction to LLL, p. 39.

104. *Le Miroir de l'ame pecheresse* (1531). A good recent edition is that of Allaire. The *Heptameron* was published in 1558 under the title *Les Amants fortunés* (The Fortunate Lovers).

105. The tale is entitled "A Tale of Incest" in Valency, *Palace*.

106. Marguerite, *Heptameron*, trans. Saintsbury, 3:192.

107. *Ibid.*, 3:200.

108. *Ibid.*, 3:201.

109. *Ibid.*, 3:195.

110. Saintsbury, introduction to *Heptameron*, p. 56.

111. Marguerite, *Miroir*, ll. 267–68.

112. Elizabeth, *Glasse*, folios 49, 50.

113. The charge of adultery and incest with her brother, Lord Rochford, was made on May 2, 1536. Lord Rochford's wife was a principal witness for the prosecution. Anne was beheaded on May 19.

114. Elizabeth, *Glasse* (1544), folios 13 and 19.

115. "Spouse of Christ" (*sponsa Christi*) is a technical term used as early as Tertullian; it eventually became a byword of the Catholic tradition. See Jerome's relevant theory of the virgin as the bride of Christ and of "spiritual matrimony": (Jerome, Letter 107, in CSEL, 55:298; cf. Dumm, *Virginity*, pp. 74–100. For a modern version of the theory, see Pius XII, "Sponsa Christi."

116. Cf. Norman O. Brown's argument that "sonship, or brotherhood, freed from its secret bondage to the father principle . . . would be free from the principle of private property" (*Love's Body*, p. 7).

117. *Epistolae ad virgines*. Bugge, *Virginitatis*, p. 72, discussing Pseudo-Clement; *Ad virgines*, PG, l. 379–452.

118. Bugge, *Virginitatis*, p. 73. See Matt. 23:19; "Call no man father"; and pp. 185–86, below.

119. Dumm, *Virginity*, pp. 119 and 121, citing Jerome, *Epistulae*, Letter 130, 14, in CSEL, 56:119; and Gregory, *Vita S. Macrinae*, PG, 46:969.

120. Dumm, *Virginity*, p. 121, citing John Chrysostom, *De virginitate*, 73, PG, 48:586.

121. See Dumm, *Virginity*, p. 4, discussing John Chrysostom, *De virginitate*, 21, PG 48:548.

122. For the Elizabethan conjunction of "unrestrained violence and sexual licentiousness," see Saffady, "Fears of Sexual License."

123. *Letters*, p. 279.

124. Mutschmann and Wentersdorf, *Shakespeare and Catholicism*, pp. 43, 15.

125. On the Archpriest Controversy in relation to *Measure for Measure* in particular, see Kaula, *Shakespeare and the Archpriest Controversy*, esp. p. 71.

126. Kelly, *Thorns*, p. 3.

127. See Leff, *Heresy*, 1:64–68.

128. Relevant sixteenth- and early-seventeenth-century works on the begging orders in England include Awdelay's *Fraternity of Vacabondes* (1561); various works mentioned by John Bale in his Epistle Dedicatory to Princess Elizabeth's *Godly Medytacion*; and a printing of Wycliffe's *Two Treatises Against the Orders of the Begging Friars* (1608).

129. O.E.D., s.v. "Beg."

130. Erbstösser and Werner, *Ideologische Probleme*.

131. N. O. Brown, *Love's Body*, p. 4, quoting Locke, *Civil Government*, p. 6.

132. Stone contends, in *Crisis of the Aristocracy* (quoted in Staves, *Players' Scepters*, p. 114), that in the sixteenth and seventeenth centuries "the most remarkable change inside the family was the shift away from paternal authority" and that "it was slowly recognized that limits should be set not merely to the powers of kings . . . , but also those of parents and husbands."

133. See Perrens, *Libertins*.

134. Quoted in Morison, *History of the American People*, p. 205. We may also note the role of the "Sons of Liberty" in the American Revolution (Morison, pp. 192–98).

135. *Encyclopaedia Britannica*, 11th ed., s.v. "Cathars."

136. See Melcher, *Shaker Adventure*, and Schroeder, "Shaker Celibacy."

137. Murry's anti-Catholic analysis of *Measure for Measure* is entitled "Shakespeare: The Redemption of Generation."

Chapter Three

1. Swinburne, *Spousals*, sigs. M2v–M3r.

2. *Basilicon Doron*, 2:61, quoted in Schanzer, *Problem Plays*, p. 122, with reference to 1.1.29–36.

3. Some interpreters argue that in this passage, which is said to be a late addition to the Gospel, Jesus writes down the sins of those who have accused the adulteress. Others claim that he distinguishes between judging (*krinein*) and sentencing (*katakrinein*), or between verdict and punishment. (For these views, see R. E. Brown, *John*, commentary on John 8:6.) If Jesus were merely distinguishing between judging and sentencing, he could not be charged with making sin more palatable insofar as, according to his doctrine, a guilty person might go unpunished. However, it seems to me that the distinction between judging and sentencing relies on the distinction between intent or thought and act, which Jesus casts into doubt in the Sermon on the Mount.

4. Schlegel, *Lectures on Dramatic Art*, p. 386. Even psychoanalytical and anthropological critics of *Measure for Measure*, who might be expected to notice the informing significance of incest in the play, have been misled by Schlegel to consider only the theme of justice versus mercy. The psychoanalyst Ernest Jones, for example, unquestioningly accepts Masson's Schlegelian thesis that *Measure for Measure* is mainly about "mutual forgiveness and mercy" (Masson, *Shakespeare Personally*, p. 133); he discusses incest in *Hamlet* and *Julius Caesar* but fails even to mark the incest theme in *Measure for Measure*, although he notes that the plays were probably written in sequence (Jones, *Hamlet and Oedipus*, p. 121).

5. About the time *Measure for Measure* was being written, the name of Shakespeare's troupe was changed to "The King's Players."

6. Does it makes a difference that Angelo's teacher and initiator is a woman rather than a man, say, Escalus? Dom Gregoire Lemercier, Prior of the Monastery of Sainte-Marie-de-la-Resurrection, thinks that a woman doctor can make a special contribution to the psychoanalysis of celibate males: "Freud's central vision traces all life and love back to their sexual origins, rediscovering the great Biblical intuitions from Genesis through the Prophets to the Song of Songs. This made it imperative for us not to be influenced by considerations of prudery in sexual matters. This was a particularly difficult endeavor for monks, whose religious commitment takes the precise form of a rejection of the biological realities of sex. For this reason, we chose a woman analyst for the initial period of analysis of new recruits, thus putting them, from the outset, face to face with their unknown." (Lemercier, "Freud in the Cloister," p. 34.)

7. *Ibid.* Cf. Luther's interpretation of those who are eunuchs for God (Matt. 19:12) in his "Estate of Marriage," LW, 45:18–20.

8. M. Evdokimov, a Russian Orthodox author, writes, "The asceticism of the desert Fathers was an immense psychoanalysis, followed by a psychosynthesis of the universal human spirit" (quoted in Lemercier, "Freud in the Cloister," p. 34).

9. See, e.g., Durham, "What art thou, Angelo?" or Lever, introduction to *MM*, p. 94.

10. Plato, *Republic*, 359b–360b and 612b; discussed in Shell, *Economy*, chap. 1.

11. "Magistratus virum indicat" (Erasmus; from Tilley, *Dictionary of Proverbs*, A402).

12. For Aristotle on temperance or moderation, see Aristotle, *Nicomachean Ethics*, 3. For James I on temperance, see his *Basilicon Doron*, quoted in Pope, "Renaissance Background," in Geckle, ed., *Interpretations*, p. 62.

13. Cf. Milward, *Religious Background*, p. 34.

14. Adequation of desire with act can lead to perfect libertinism as well as to perfect temperance. *The Revelation of AntiChriste*—"a staple on lists of forbidden books" during the Reformation (Saffady, "Fears of Sexual License," p. 63)—claims that "the people of Christ doth nothing because it is commanded but because it is pleasant and acceptable to them" (in Wilkins, ed., *Concilia Magnae*, 3 : 729). Such an adequation of desire and act can lead to either libertinism or temperance.

15. James I, *Basilicon Doron*, quoted in Pope, "Renaissance Background," in Geckle, ed., *Interpretations*, p. 62.

16. James I, *Political Works*, p. 5; cf. Goldberg, "James I and the Theater of Conscience."

17. See Schanzer, "Marriage Contracts," in *MM*, ed. Soellner and Bertsche, p. 112.

18. Cf. Skura, *Psychoanalytic Process* (p. 252), on "the curious resemblance between his behavior and that of his subjects."

19. Pope, "Renaissance Background," in Geckle, ed., *Interpretations*, p. 62.

20. In the *Apology*, Plato's Socrates explains the Delphic oracle's claim that Socrates is the wisest man in the world by remarking that he is aware of his own ignorance: "I do not think that I know what I do not know" (Plato, *Apology*, 21d).

21. Mackay, however, argues that the Duke falls in love with Isabella gradually—step by step—beginning in Act 4 ("*MM*," pp. 109–13).

22. Battenhouse, "*MM* and Atonement," p. 1052.

23. For these two definitions of satisfaction, see the O.E.D.

24. Cf. Cook, "Metaphysical Poetry," pp. 124–25.

25. "Covent" and "convent" meant not only "monachal institution" but also "brothel." (Cf. the name "Covent Garden" and similar ambiguities in "nunnery.")

26. Schanzer, "Marriage Contracts" (in *MM*, ed. Soellner and Bertsche, p. 246), points out that Shakespeare has made the Duke both "the ideal ruler" and, in his failure to enforce the law, "the exemplar of one kind of misrule." In seeing this as a matter of mere "dramatic economy," however, Schanzer fails to consider how the play enlightens us about the reasons the Duke neglected the law, reasons that should influence our opinion of his omniscience and benevolence.

27. Pope ("Renaissance Background," in Geckle, ed., *Interpretations*, p. 66) says that Vincentio here "frankly describes his laxity as a 'vice,'" but the lines also indicate one possible reason for that laxity—his own vice of lust.

Chapter Four

1. One might compare Angelo with Philip Stubbes, who in his *Anatomie of Abuses* (1583) urged the death penalty for prostitution, fornication, adultery, and incest. It is easy to deride such urgings and to call for "more lenity to lechery," as did Thomas Nashe in his *Anatomie of Absurditie* (1590). *Measure for Measure* does encourage us to hope that there could be lenity without the destruction of society through lechery, but it forces us to confront the problems inherent in lenity. Cf. Lever, introduction to his edition of *MM*, p. xlvi.

2. Cf. CYM 2.5.6–7: "Some coiner with his tools / Made me a counterfeit." See, too, Kaufmann, "Bond Slaves," p. 91.

3. Fleetwood, *Sermon Against Clipping*.

4. Locke, *Civil Government*, p. 6.

5. Skulsky, "Pain, Law, and Conscience," p. 148, points out that the equivalence of fornication and murder is set down in Viennese law, which makes both fornication and murder capital offenses, but he does not discuss Isabella's odd claim.

6. E. J. White, *Law in Shakespeare*, p. 53; see also *MM*, ed. Rolfe, p. 174n. We do not learn in *Measure for Measure* why, according to the Friar, the religious law considers Juliet's sin "of heavier kind" than Claudio's (2.3.28) or why the secular law punishes male fornication more harshly than female. (Is it because the man is the head of the woman?) In Marguerite of Navarre's *Heptameron* (4th day, tale 33), the capital punishment of a friar and his consanguineous sister for incest is delayed until after the birth of their child.

7. McGinn, "Precise Angelo," p. 133, tries to explain Isabella's statement by referring to "the repeated demands by Puritan leaders that the laws against adultery in the Old Testament be revived," but he fails to note that the Old Testament does not enjoin execution for fornication and that Claudio is not an adulterer. Gless, *MM, the Law, and the Convent*, p. 125, says Isabella is in error and that the New Testament would not enjoin such cruelty. Roscelli, "Isabella, Sin, and Civil Law," p. 216, and Harding, "Elizabethan Brothels," p. 157, argue that the reason Isabella draws the distinction between divine and human law is that in the eyes of the civil law Claudio and Juliet's betrothal would constitute a binding contract.

8. Aquinas, *Summa*, a. 154, art. 2 (p. 1816).

9. *Ibid.*, art. 4 (p. 1818). A similar claim that fornication, hence bastardizing, amounts to murder is put forward by the Christian pastor in Melville's *Pierre*: "Is not the man who has sinned like that Ned worse than a murderer?" (Signet ed., p. 127).

10. Gregory (in *Moralium*, xxi) places lust among the capital vices. See Aquinas, *Summa*, a. 153, art. 4 (p. 1812). On lust's being a "deadly" sin (3.1.110) in Christian popular thinking, see Bloomfield, *Seven Deadly Sins*.

11. Gratian, *Decretum*, 22, q. 1, an. Praedicandum. Quoted by Aquinas, *Summa*, a. 154, art. 2 (p. 1816). Cf. Adriana's remark in ERR 2.2.140–43.

12. Josephus refers explicitly to the "unmarried Essenes" and to the "marrying Essenes" (*Bellum Judaicum*, 2.160 and 2.161). On the Essenes' desire to preserve the *genus* ("mankind" or "race"), see Hippolytus, *Philosophumena*, II, 28; and Vermes, "Essenes," p. 101. Cf. Ford, *Wisdom and Celibacy*, pp. 28–29. For the influence of this dogma of the Essenes on major Christian move-

ments, including Jansenism, see Racine's interpretive translation of Josephus's *De Bello Judaico*, 2.2, in his *Oeuvres complètes*, p. 602. To the Christian conflation of the creation and destruction of life, cf. the Talmudists' view that in some circumstances "the man who does not marry is like one who sheds blood" (Yebamoth, 63b, in Epstein, ed., *Babylonian Talmud*); the Jewish writer Caro writes similarly that "every man is obliged to marry in order to fulfill the duty of procreation, and whoever is not engaged in propagating the race is as if he shed blood" (*Shulchen aruch*, EH 1 : 1).

13. See Collins, "'Excommunication' in Paul."

14. Cf. ROM 1.1.27–28, 2H6 4.7.119–25. Pompey alludes, of course, to such biblical passages as Eph. 5 : 23. See also Frey, "Shakespearean Interpretation," and Skura, *Psychoanalytic Process*, p. 261.

15. G. K. Hunter, "Six Notes," p. 168, says that "Abhorson" is a portmanteau version of "abhorred whoreson."

16. Some critics argue that the play is flawed because Isabella's outburst about bastardy and incest is inconsistent with the drama of which it is the turning point; others claim that the two halves of the play are unified, but they do not demonstrate the mode of that union. (For a representation of these views, see Tillyard, *Problem Plays*, in Stead, ed., *Casebook*, p. 223.) I think that the two halves are of one consistent piece, and shall show that the union involves incest, the lex talionis, and the conflation of intent with act.

17. For example, both Gless, *MM, the Law, and the Convent*, p. 145, and Lever, introduction to his edition of *MM*, pp. lix, lxxx, use the term "hysterical" to describe Isabella's question; they intend thereby to discuss the possibility that Isabella's words may mean more than is apparent at first blush. With the hysterical refusal to consider incest in the play as anything other than hysterical, compare Howard, *Spirit of the Plays*, which even deletes Isabella's lines about incest from the caption to a sketch illustrating 3.1, and the productions of Joseph Younger (1770) and John Philip Kemble (1803), which excised all "bawdy" language from the play. For Freud and Breuer, "hysterical deliria often turn out to be the very circle of ideas which the patient in his normal state has rejected, inhibited, and suppressed with all his might" (Freud, "Hysterical Phenomena: A Lecture," *SE*, 3 : 38). Freud's theory presumes to explain why "the hysterical deliria of nuns revel in blasphemies and erotic pictures" (Freud, "Footnotes to Charcot," *SE*, 1 : 138: cf. "Treatment by Hypnotism," *SE*, 1 : 126; and Freud and Breuer, "Hysterical Phenomena," *SE*, 2 : 10–11). According to Freud, "the asylum of the cloister" is nothing more than a social counterpart to the insulation of illness that he found in individual neurotics (comment of Freud quoted in Hitschmann's "Uber Nerven- und Geisteskrankheiten," p. 271).

18. Lascelles (*Shakespeare's MM*), for example, writes of Isabella that "many times, in her most moving passages, it would be possible to substitute 'neighbour' for 'brother,' and hardly wake a ripple." Earlier, however, Walter Pater (*Appreciations*, p. 184), opposing *Measure for Measure* to *Promos and Cassandra*, pointed to the importance of Isabella's being a Sister. Samuel Johnson (*Johnson on Shakespeare*, in Stead, ed., *Casebook*, p. 41) pointed to the importance of Isabella's chastity being that of a nun, as opposed to a mere virgin. In his edition of Shakespeare's *Dramatic Works*, 2 : 167, Harness calls Claudio "an object of disgust" for Isabella, showing an awareness of how her brother focuses her

hidden emotions. Stone, *Family, Sex, and Marriage*, p. 115, presents evidence that the brother-sister relationship was the closest one in the typical Elizabethan family.

19. See, for example, Vessie, "Psychiatry Catches Up"; Kott, "Austauschdienststruktur in *MM*"; Sypher, "Casuist"; and Bache, *MM as Dialectical Art*. In commenting on Isabella's question, Bache notes (p. 39) that "the incest will be controlled and the shame will be conditioned by the brotherly acts of Claudio, of Angelo, and of the Duke."

20. "Kind," in the phrase "a kind of incest," recalls Latin *genus*, which, like "kind," retains a connection with the idea of kinship. See the Church Fathers' discussion of the three genres of affinity in Hefele, *Histoire des conciles*, vol. 5, pt. 2, p. 1372; and Bernard of Pavia, *Summa*, pp. 168−69.

21. Jonas of Orleans, *De institutione laicailli*, PL, 106 : 183−84.

22. Nineteenth-century critics who praise Isabella's chastity include Singer, in his edition *Dramatic Works of Shakespeare*, 2 : 3; Jameson, *Characteristics of Women*, 1 : 43; Dowden, *Shakespeare*, p. 125; and Bowdler, in his edition *Family Shakespeare*. More recently, Stevenson, *Achievement of MM*, pp. 88−89, and Jaffa, "Chastity as a Political Principle," have invoked this aspect of her character.

23. Lever, introduction to his edition of *MM*, p. lxxviii.

24. Gratian, *Decretum*, 36, q. 1; quoted by Aquinas, *Summa*, q. 154, art. 9 (p. 1823).

25. Various Church decrees and controversies reflect the universalizing tendency that threatens to undo all attempts to limit the degree of blood kinship defining incest. In A.D. 868 a Church council ruled that "we will not define the number of generations within which the faithful may be joined. No Christian may accept a wife . . . if any blood relationship is recorded, known, or held in memory." (Worms, can. 32; in MANSI, 15 : 875.) Julius I, in *Decreta Julii papae* (no. 5, PL, 8 : 969) specified the seventh remove as the limit of diriment impediment to marriage. But there were enormous practical problems of record keeping, and even where the numerical degree was both agreed upon and ascertainable, there were controversies about the correct method of counting. Thus Stephanus Tornacensis notes that "the counting begins with the brothers according to some and with the sons of the brothers according to others" (*Summa*, p. 255). Cf. C. E. Smith, *Papal Enforcement*, chap. 2.

26. Aquinas refers to Aristotle's argument in *Summa*, q. 154, art. 9 (p. 1824). Cf. Aristotle, *Politics*, 2.1.2−4.

27. Aquinas, *Summa*, q. 154, art. 9 (p. 1824). For Aquinas on incest, see *idem*, p. 1823.

28. Reid, "Psychoanalytic Reading," p. 280. Reid ascribes this opinion both to Shakespeare (p. 273) and to the Duke (p. 280).

29. Augustine, *De Sermone Dei in Monte*. Bullough, *Narrative and Dramatic Sources*, pp. 399−400, regards Augustine's story as an important analogue to *Measure for Measure*.

30. Augustine, *Lord's Sermon*, p. 60. Battenhouse, *Shakespearean Tragedy*, and "MM and Atonement," pp. 1029−59, overlooks the story.

31. Some theologians have been upset by this refusal to judge the man and woman. It has been argued, for example, that Augustine overlooked the fact that "in the marriage contract the parties are not free to give up or transfer their rights, because these rights have been fixed by God *ab initio*" (Jepson, note in Augustine, *Lord's Sermon*, p. 189, n. 129).

32. See Halliwell-Phillipps, *Memoranda on MM*, p. 6, and P. E. Smith, "Incest Motif."

33. Heywood, *Woman Killed*, scene 14, ll. 4–8, 11–13, 31–36, 46, and 48–51.

34. Bradbrook, *Webster*, p. 157, notes of Romelio's conduct that "acting as bawd to one's kin might be considered 'a kind of incest,'" without further developing the comparison to *Measure for Measure*. Brennan, "Relationship Between Brother and Sister," p. 489, discusses the idea of a brother's obsession with his sister's body (cf. Leech, *Webster*, pp. 49, 101–4) and remarks the likeness between the incestuously obsessed brother in *The Dutchess of Malfi* and his brother the Cardinal. She fails to recognize the brother/Brother incest thematic, however, or to link it to *The Devil's Law Case*.

35. Webster, *Case*, 3.3.159, 5.2.34–35.

36. *Ibid.*, 5.1.3.

37. Pearson, *Tragedy and Tragicomedy*, p. 105.

38. For Ercole and the Brotherhood of the Knights of Malta, see *Case*, 1.2.29, and Pearson, *Tragedy and Tragicomedy*, p. 105; for Contarino as a Bathanite, see stage directions at *Case*, 5.2.17; for the "blood embrace," see *Case*, 4.2.575.

39. Beaumont and Fletcher, *King*, 4.4.74–76.

40. *Ibid.*, 4.4.118–19, 131–38.

41. John Ford, *'Tis Pity*, 1.1.24–27; 1.2.185–86.

42. Vessie, "Psychiatry Catches Up," p. 144.

43. Compare Shakespeare's *Pericles of Tyre*, which begins by presenting an incestuous father-daughter couple and which eventually transcends the fear of such incest when, in a manner of speaking, it shows a daughter giving birth to her father. Thus Pericles calls Marina, his daughter, "thou that beget'st him that did thee beget" (PER 5.1.195).

44. Quoted by Cohn, "Cult of the Free Spirit," p. 56. For Lucrezia Borgia, the union that Isabella as sister fears and Isabella as Sister desires was an outrageous reality, since Lucrezia "descended in 'un-history' as 'the pope's daughter, wife, and daughter-in-law.'" Accused of father-daughter incest, Lucrezia retreated to a nunnery (Santiago, *Children of Oedipus*, pp. 59, 69).

45. Shakespeare apparently was not a great admirer of Elizabeth. Unlike most English poets of the age, for example, he did not write a word of direct mourning on her death. (On Shakespeare's silence, see esp. Chettle, *Englandes Mourning Garment* [1603], in Munro, *Shakespeare Allusion-Book*, p. 123, cf. pp. 124 and 140; and Albrecht, *Neue Untersuchungen*, pp. 235–36.) Shakespeare's dislike for Elizabeth may have had something to do with his connection to the Earl of Essex (Robert Devereux). Shakespeare's *Richard II* played a part in Essex's ill-fated 1601 rebellion, and in a conversation of August 4, 1601, Elizabeth herself drew the production's moral: "I am Richard II. Know ye not that?" (Quoted in Nichols, *Progress*, 3:552–53; see also Greenblatt, Introduction to *Forms of Power*.) Essex's conspiracy may have been linked to pro-Catholic groups; one of the conspirators was the Earl of Southampton (Henry Wriothesley, or W. H.), possibly Shakespeare's patron.

46. Elizabeth made her translation of Marguerite of Navarre's *Le Miroir de l'âme pecheresse* from a copy of the 1535 edition in the book collection of Anne Boleyn (Ames, introduction to his edition of Elizabeth's *Mirror*, p. 31). She entitled it *The Glasse of the Synnefull Soule* and sent the manuscript—"bound in an

elaborate needlework cover worked by herself" (Neale, *Elizabeth*, p. 12)—to her stepmother, Catherine Parr, as a New Year's gift for 1545. Catherine sent the manuscript to John Bale, Elizabeth's tutor. Bale "mended" some of the words, added a long Epistle Dedicatory and a Conclusion, retitled the work *A Godley Medytacion of the Christen Sowle*, and arranged to have it published by Dirik van der Straten in 1548. That edition was reprinted, with a few minor changes, in 1590 in London by R. Wood. A copy of the 1590 edition is in the possession of the Houghton Library. Another edition, by James Cancellar, was produced in 1568 (?1570) and reprinted in 1582 in *Bentley's Monument of Matrones*, vol. 1, sigs. F2v–H4v. The original manuscript, now at the Bodley Library (described in Madan, *Western Manuscripts*, no. 9810), was reproduced in facsimile by the Royal Society of Literature of the United Kingdom in 1897. The letter with which Elizabeth gave it to Catherine Parr, December 31, 1544, is included in Harrison, ed., *Letters of Elizabeth*, pp. 5–7. For further bibliographical information, see Steele, "English Books Printed Abroad, 1525–48"; Hughey, "A Note on Queen Elizabeth's 'Godly Meditation'"; and Craster, "An Unknown Translation by Queen Elizabeth."

47. On the indictments of Anne for sibling incest and for an account of the trial, see Friedmann, *Boleyn*, 2:262–63, 278–81.

48. See *Ibid.*, 2:287, 351.

49. As Jones points out (*Hamlet and Oedipus*, p. 68), "Had the relationship [between Claudius and Gertrude] not counted as incestuous, then Queen Elizabeth would have no right to the throne; she would have been a bastard, Katherine of Aragon being alive at her birth." On Hamlet and the relationship between Henry VIII and Catherine of Aragon, see Rosenblatt, "Aspects of Incest Problems." Blackmore, "Hamlet's Right to the Crown," says that "the diriment impediment to marriage with a deceased brother's wife was part of English church doctrine since earliest times and was retained by the English secular authorities until the nineteenth century." For the polar opposite view, that one must marry a deceased brother's wife, see the biblical law of the levirate (Deut. 25:5–6).

50. According to Johnson, *Elizabeth*, p. 9, Elizabeth was conceived in early December 1532, and Anne and Henry were married secretly on January 25, 1533. See too Friedmann, *Boleyn*, 2:338–39. For the date of the marriage between Henry and Anne, see Cranmer's letter to Dr. Hawkyns of June 17, 1533, and Stow's *Chronicles* (1605).

51. For Cranmer's views on the matter, see Lingard, *History of England*, 5:74, 5:540–42, and Friedmann, *Boleyn*, 1:43, 2:323–27, 2:351–55. Contrast Cranmer's prophetic praise of Elizabeth in H8 5.5.14–62.

52. Cf. "I knew the young Count to be a dangerous and lascivious boy, who is a whale to virginity, and devours up all the fry it finds" (AWW 4.3.231–34).

53. In *The Devil's Law Case* (4.2.222–24), Webster jokes about the fact that a father cannot be godfather to his own child: "thus are many serv'd / That take care to get gossips for those children, / To which they might be godfathers themselves." As Webster suggests in the next line, the Puritans did allow fathers to be godfathers.

54. Whether or not John Fletcher, rather than Shakespeare, wrote the last scene of *Henry VIII*, as some critics aver (for the controversy see Foakes, introduction to H8, pp. xv–xxviii), an ambiguous attitude toward Elizabeth is characteristic of the entire play.

55. Bale, Epistle Dedicatory to Elizabeth, *Mirror.*

56. In 1546, at the age of thirteen (two years after making her translation, Elizabeth allegedly either was sexually molested by Thomas Seymour or had an affair with him. Seymour was the brother of Jane Seymour, who had married Henry VIII the day after Anne Boleyn's execution, and he was to become Elizabeth's stepfather when he married the queen dowager, Catherine Parr, in 1547—the very year of Henry's death. After Catherine's death the following year, he tried to marry Elizabeth, who was both his step-niece and his step-daughter. For a review of the evidence concerning the Elizabeth-Seymour liaison, see Seymour, *Ordeal by Ambition,* pp. 215–19, 225–26.

57. Elizabeth, *Glasse,* folios 7, 8, 23. Marguerite gives the last lines as "Ma voisine, ma sensualité / En mon dormir de bestialité" (*Miroir,* ed. Allaire, ll. 429–30).

58. Margaret of Navarre, *Heptameron,* 3d day, 30th tale, 3 : 200. Saintsbury's claim, generally accepted nowadays, is that Margaret and her brother did not have physically incestuous relations (introduction to *Heptameron,* p. 56). Even before Marguerite's great poems expressing her sisterly love were published, however, rumors that they did have such relations were circulated widely.

59. For the poetess lover in this quadrifold kinship role, see such passages as: "O my father, brother, child, and spowse" (fol. 21); "O what a switte reste it is, of the mother, and the sonne togyther" (fol. 26); "I am syster unto thee, but so naughty a syster, that better it is for me to hyd suche a name" (fol. 26); and "Nowe than that we are brother and syster together, I care but lytell for all other men" (fol. 29).

60. Bale, Epistle Dedicatory, p. 10; in Elizabeth, *Mirror.*

61. "Al humain kind on erthe / From like begininge Comes; / One father is of all, / One Only al doth gide. . . . What Crake you of your stock / Or for-fathers Old? / If your first spring and Auther / God you view, / No man bastard be, / Vnless with vice the worst he fede / And Leueth so his birthe" (*Queen Elizabeth's Englishings,* ed. Pemberton, p. 54).

62. Elizabeth, Speech to Commons, 1558/59; in Rice, *Public Speaking of Queen Elizabeth,* p. 117. Elizabeth became the godmother—the spiritual mother—of more than a hundred English subjects (Williams, *Elizabeth,* p. 218). John Harington writes of her as "oure deare Queene, my royale god-mother, and this state's natural mother" (Harington, *Letters,* p. 96). With Elizabeth's statement that her subjects should never have "a more natural mother than I meant to be unto all" (Neale, *Elizabeth I and Her Parliament,* p. 109), cf. the curse that Shakespeare's Margaret (the widow of Henry VI), in *Richard III,* speaks to Queen Elizabeth (the wife of Edward VI): "Die neither mother, wife, nor England's Queen" (R3 1.3.208).

63. On the cult of Elizabeth as the virgin queen, see Montrose, "'Shaping Fantasies,'" and Schleiner, *"Divina Virago."* On visual representations and icons of Elizabeth as the Virgin Mary, see Strong, *Cult of Elizabeth,* esp. p. 66, on the "Sieve Portrait" of Elizabeth. Consider the aged Elizabeth's public identification with Saint Elizabeth (Chamberlain, *Sayings of Queen Elizabeth,* no. 301); Saint Elizabeth was the niece of Saint Anne (of the Immaculate Conception) and the cousin of Saint Mary (of the Virgin Birth)—nominally, therefore, a close relation to Shakespeare's Mariana in *Measure for Measure.*

64. Elizabeth strongly disapproved of clerical marriage but did not make a legal issue of it. See Johnson, *Elizabeth,* pp. 94–95.

65. Crosse, *Lover*, sec. 11.

66. Often Elizabeth tried to transform the injunction of nature in general (that one should reproduce) into a command of a more or less individual nature of her own (that she should not marry). Thus Salignac reports that Elizabeth said to the French ambassador, "When I think of marriage it is as though my heart were being dragged out of my vitals, so much am I opposed to marriage by nature" (Chamberlain, *Sayings of Queen Elizabeth*, pp. 61, 68).

67. Chalmers, *Apology*, pp. 404–5.

68. For overviews of similarities between Vincentio and James I considered by the critics, see Goldberg, *James I*, pp. 231–39, and Levin, *New Readings*, esp. pp. 187–88. Levin claims that there is no real evidence that *Basilicon Doron* was an actual source of *Measure for Measure*; see his similar questioning of previous critics' views on connections between Queen Elizabeth and *Measure for Measure* (Levin, *New Readings*, p. 192).

69. Bennet, *MM as Royal Entertainment*, p. 98.

70. Baker, *Chronicle*, p. 155. As Bennet (*MM as Royal Entertainment*, p. 180, n. 39) points out, "James's fondness for young men is sufficiently notorious."

71. James, *Political Works*, pp. 272, 24; cited by Goldberg, *James I*, pp. 141, 142; cf. Tennenhouse, "Representing Power," p. 153.

72. Craigie, in note to his edition of *Basilicon Doron*, 2 : 208.

73. Saintsbury, *Short History*, p. 323.

Chapter Five

1. For the Platonic formula "Both are two but each is one," see Plato, *Theaetetus*, 185; *idem, Hippias Major*, 300; and Shell, *Money*, chap. 3.

2. Peterkiewicz, *Third Adam*, p. 209. "In the world of the carnival," writes Bakhtin, "all hierarchies are cancelled. All castes and ages are equal. During the fire festival a young boy blows out his father's candle, crying out . . . 'Death to your father, sir!'" (Bakhtin, *Rabelais*, p. 251). During such festivals or masked balls every person can pass for any other. Not only can a son pass for his father or a father for his son—resulting in liberty of the kind that Goethe witnessed in the celebration of the Saturnalia at Rome (Goethe, "Roman Carnival," p. 446)—but one's sister can pass for a woman who is not one's kin, resulting in incest.

3. As Empson suggests in "Sense in *MM*."

4. Lupton's work was published in 1581; for Augustine's version, see chapter 4, above. Lascelles, *Shakespeare's MM*, p. 6, points out that John Donne refers to Augustine's version in his *Bithanatos* (1648), p. 127.

5. Aristotle, *Politics*, 1258b. See Shell, *Economy*, esp. pp. 94–95. Cf. *sitos* and *faenus*, which have the same financial and biological meanings as *tokos*. On the same analogy in *The Merchant of Venice*, see Shell, *Money*, chap. 3; and in *Measure for Measure*, G. K. Hunter, "Six Notes," p. 168, and Pearlman, "Shakespeare, Freud, and the Two Usuries."

6. For this and the Protestant controversy, mentioned above, about whether interest is contrary to nature, see Nelson, *Idea of Usury*, and Shell, *Money*, chap. 3.

7. Members of religious orders often learn a secret sign language. In fact, certain orders share Pompey's conflation of "woman" with "trout" (Barakat, *Cistercian Sign Language*, p. 26).

8. "The money and the maidenhead is the subject of our meditation," writes Daniel Defoe in *Marriage Bed*, p. 33. In *Measure for Measure* maidenheads are not traded for money; they are traded as though they were money.

9. Aeschylus, *Agamemnon*, line 437. On the significance of the phrase "moneychanger of dead bodies," see Thomson's commentary on *Agamemnon*, ll. 438–44, in his edition of the *Oresteia*.

10. Cf. Seneca, *Epistulae morales*, 91.16: *pares morimur* (we die equal).

11. On Herodotus' and Plato's story of Gyges as a political and economic allegory, see Shell, *Economy*, chap. 1.

12. See *ibid.*, chap. 2.

13. Cf. Lever's introduction to his edition of *MM*, p. xlv.

14. Cf. the similar illusion in *Romeo and Juliet*.

15. Pope, "Renaissance Background" (in Geckle, ed., *Interpretations*, p. 59), notes that the Duke's measures in substituting one head for another might "savour dangerously of conspiracy against a lawful magistrate if Shakespeare did not slip neatly away from the whole difficulty by making the chief conspirator the highest officer of the State himself." I would argue, however, that this is no solution. Vincentio's essential conspiracy lies not so much in the attempt to exchange one head for another (on which Pope focuses) as in the position, which he takes later, that it can be illegal for the state ever to take a head. Thus Vincentio as Friar, in his eventual argument that no secular authority has the right to take the life of any man, tends to subvert not merely the secular rule of a bad officer like Angelo but secular rule itself. From this difficulty Shakespeare does not slip neatly away. Toward the end of the play, Escalus not unwisely holds the Friar guilty of treason against the Duke.

16. It was sometimes argued in the Reformation that the sovereign had no right to execute a man since "neither Christ nor his apostles had put any creature to death." This is the position of Anne Askew, the English Protestant reformer martyred in 1546; see Bale, *Select Works*, p. 202.

17. Aristotle, *Poetics*, 14.2. Cf. *Politics*, 5.8.5 (1339b32).

18. Luther, *Secular Authority*, esp. pp. 400–402.

19. See Quiller-Couch's and Dover Wilson's introduction to their edition of *MM*.

20. Coleridge, *Lectures and Notes*, p. 21.

21. For an elaboration of this point, see Daube, "Lex Talionis," esp. p. 103.

22. Cf. 1 Cor. 7:4: "The husband hath not power of his own body, but the wife."

23. On the hypothesis of the "free gift," see my *Money, Language, and Thought*, chap. 2.

24. On the theme of re-membering in *Measure for Measure*, see Bache, *"Measure for Measure" as Dialectical Art*.

Chapter Six

1. Garonne, *Sainte Claire*, p. 80. Translation mine.

2. This question disturbed Samuel Johnson, who remarked that "it is strange Isabella should not express either gratitude, joy, or wonder, at the sight of her brother" (Pye, *Comments*, p. 34). Some critics, to redeem the situation, have argued that stage directions permit a "mimed reconciliation" between the

brother and sister (see Lever's introduction to his edition of *MM*, pp. xxvi and lxxxii). A reconciliation is hardly possible at so early a stage in the plot; moreover, Isabella subsequently tells the Duke, "I had rather my brother die by the law, than my son should be unlawfully born" (3.1.188–90). In the edition of the play he edited with John Dover Wilson and others, Quiller-Couch suggests that there is a lacuna in the text of Act 5 where Isabella's words of pardon were once to be found; similarly, Coghill's 1955 production introduced a verbal reconciliation between Claudio and Isabella in Act 5 (see Lever's introduction, p. lvii, n. 6). My own interpretation is closer to the view of P. E. Smith ("Incest Motif," p. 12), who claims that "eventually through the Duke's maneuvers both Claudio and Isabella come to know themselves to conquer their fears, becoming ready to both face death and exercise love, lovingly respecting each other as brother and sister," although Smith does not inquire into the incestuous quality of that sibling love.

3. Reacting to the fact that Juliet's role is largely speechless, Lascelles, *Shakespeare's MM*, p. 71, regards her part as insignificant; Quiller-Couch, in the edition he edited with Dover Wilson and others (pp. 155–56) argues that her speaking parts must have been lost from an original manuscript.

4. In two analogues, the Roman play *Canace parturiens* (on which see Suetonius, *Nero*, 21:3; and Dio, *History*, 62:9) and Speroni's *Canace* (1546), the dramatic issue is the delivery from the womb, on stage, of the child of twin siblings. These formally remarkable plays take place in a single day—both the birthday of the incestuous twin brother and sister, Macereus and Canace, and the day of the birth of their child. Canace's labor, like Juliet's in *Measure for Measure*, strikingly counters the movement of the plot. On the Canace story in the English tradition, which takes Ovid's version, *Heroides*, 11, as its *locus classicus*, see Lydgate, *Falls of Princes*; Gower, *Confessio Amantis*, 3.142; Chaucer, *Squire's Tale*, ll. 667–69; and Spenser, *Fairy Queen*, 4.3. Cf. Nohrnberg, *Analogy of the Faere Queene*, pp. 622–23; Goldberg, *Endlesse Worke*, pp. 114–16.

5. It is possible, of course, to have Juliet appear onstage with a baby, perhaps a baby boy like the one whose conception Isabella foresaw as the result of intercourse with Angelo, or like the figure of Claudio writ small. This is the tack of Cedric Messina's BBC production. The appearance of the child has the effect, however, of obscuring the play's conflation of Isabella's brother with her son.

6. For a demographic consideration of abortions and infanticides of illegitimate children in England, see Laslett, "Comparing Illegitimacy."

7. Noonan, *Contraception*, pp. 26off.

8. Leach, "Virgin Birth," pp. 95–96.

9. Jerome, *Adversus Jovinianum*, PL, 23:265. Cf. Bugge, *Virginitas*; and Dumm, *Theological Basis*, p. 33.

10. Battenhouse, "MM and Atonement," esp. p. 1032.

11. Whetsone, *Promos and Cassandra*, 3.4 (in the edition of *MM* by Soellner and Bertsche, p. 83).

12. A production must decide whether the brother and sister should manifest their reunion in the finale by refusing to look at each other (as Pericles at first violently, if unknowingly, rejects his long-lost daughter Marina [PER 5.1.83]) or by a warm embrace (as Viola/Cesario promises to embrace Sebastian when, and if, the Captain who has her maiden weeds in safekeeping is liberated from durance at Malvolio's suit [TN 5.2.247–55, 270–71]). In the

most recent BBC production, Isabella and Claudio say nothing, but embrace (as they had in 3.1); in Cedric Messina's production, Isabella otherwise avoids physical contact with men.

13. Examples of plots involving the revelation of an unwitting love for one's sibling are Chateaubriand's *René*, where the brother is unaware of his physically incestuous attraction to his sister until the moment when she becomes a Sister, and Boccaccio's *Decameron* (fifth Story, fifth Day), where both brother and sister are drawn together "as by some occult instinct." In Fletcher's *Woman Pleased*, where the brother and sister are named Claudio and Isabella, as in *Measure for Measure*, the brother appears to woo his sister in disguise (she does not quite recognize who he is), but he does so in such manner that the audience concludes he earnestly intends to bed his sister and she actually agrees to bed him. Cf. Tourneur's *Revenger's Tragedy*, in which a disguised brother tests the chastity of his sister by play-acting the pandar.

14. See Shakespeare's *Coriolanus*, in which divorce of all earthly kin leads not to Christian philanthropy (all men are brothers) but to Timonic misanthropy (all men are others).

15. Discussing Elizabethan commentators on the Sermon on the Mount, Pope ("Renaissance Background," in Geckle, ed., *Interpretations*, p. 55) notes that Elizabethan writers approved of both retaliation and mercy, but she wrongly (to my mind) sees the two notions as essentially contradictory.

16. Schlegel, *Lectures*, p. 386.

17. Battenhouse, "MM and Atonement," p. 1044.

18. *Encyclopaedia Britannica*, s.v. "Monasticism"; see also s.v. "Trinitarians." The Blessed Isabella similarly ransomed her brother Saint Louis from the Muslims.

19. Isabella's original view that ignominy in ransom and free pardon are of "two houses" or are "nothing kin" admits the possibility of their union by an exogamous and nonincestuous marriage. This conceptual marriage of two kinds of exchange might take place sometime between Act 2, when the sisterly novice says that they are not akin, and Act 5, when she pardons Angelo and considers the Duke's proposal of familial marriage. If such a "marriage" took place, it would be the point of intersection between "foul redemption" and "lawful mercy," between retaliation (punishment) and mercy, between incest and chaste marriage. (Cf. Thirlby, Manuscript Notes, 2.4.110–13).

20. Kyriakos, "Fiançailles et marriages à Moussoul," p. 775.

21. For the connection between "sake" and "sacu," see O.E.D., s.v. "sake."

22. Cf. Goldberg's claim that the Provost's phrase "as like almost to Claudio as himself" (5.1.487) involves the Duke's wooing Isabella and "presenting— representing—Claudio as a double of himself" (Goldberg, *James I*, p. 237).

23. For the accusation that his interference is manipulation, see Tillyard, *Problem Plays*.

24. Quoted by Dhont, *Claire*, p. 7. The synonymy of *lux* and *claritas* is typical of the literature about Saint Clare.

25. For Elizabeth's use of the phrase "trade of flesh," see *Godley Medytacion*; for the French, see Marguerite of Navarre, *Miroir*, l. 384.

26. "The people should fight for their laws as for their city wall" (Heraclitus, frag. 44; for the original, see Diels, ed., *Fragmente*).

27. The Bull of Canonization of Saint Clare contains many verbal plays on the name "Clare" ("light," from *claritas*); see Garonne, *Claire*, p. 123. Saint

Francis also played on the meaning of "Clare" in his "Il Cantico di frate sole" [The Canticle of Brother Sun]; see chapter 2, above. Even though Shakespeare's Lucio may be modeled after such figures as Gloriosus in Barnabe Riche's *Adventures of Brusanus* (1592), the literal meaning of his name ("light") should also be taken into account.

28. Siegel, "MM," p. 320, writes Lucio off as a plain liar.

29. Coghill, "Comic Form," and W. W. Lawrence, "MM and Lucio."

30. Act 5 seemed flawed to Henry James Pye, who writes (*Comments*, p. 33): "How much stronger would the interest be if the friar was not known to be the Duke till he suddenly broke forth, which should have been while Angelo was treating the remonstrance of Isabella (which might be made to Escalus) with insult, and just as he was saying, 'Away to prison with her.'" And unless Lucio is an agent of enlightenment about the Duke, the Duke's fuss about Lucio at the end will seem unnecessary or inexplicable. William Empson, for example, claims ("Sense in *MM*," in Stead, *Casebook*, p. 204): "What makes the Duke ridiculous on the stage is the fuss he makes about the backbiting Lucio."

31. Nancy Leonard argues ("Substitution," pp. 300–301) that the Duke takes "another Angelo—Lucio by name—to scapegoat his own flaws."

32. The association of fornication with the "tricke of youth" was common in popular tracts of the time. See the homily "Against Whoredom and Uncleanness," in Griffiths, ed., *Homilies*, p. 118; see also Wrightson, "English Illegitimacy."

33. For other postulated purposes of Elizabethan marriage—companionship, satisfaction of desire, production of an heir, and increase of property—see Stone, *Crisis*, pp. 612–19.

34. Burnet, *Exposition*, p. 288.

35. Not all critics ignore Kate Keepdown's son; Bache (*MM as Dialectical Art*, p. 31) speculates that he is the boy who sings to Mariana at the beginning of Act 4.

36. Thomas Aquinas, *Summa*, esp. suppl. q. 68, art. 3 (p. 2825). It is worth remarking that Brother "Rabelais's children were granted the unusual privilege of an official legitimization by the Pope Himself" (Screech, *Rabelaisian Marriage*, pp. 19–20; see also Lesellier, "Deux Enfants naturels").

37. Helmholz, "Bastardy Litigation," p. 360. For the various ways to legitimate a bastard under Roman law, hence under English law, see W. A. Hunter, *Roman Law*, pp. 201–3. But see also Swinburne, *Testaments*, 162: "For of adoption, arrogation, or any other meanes to make children lawfull, except marriage, we have no use here in England."

38. Cited by Helmholz, "Bastardy Litigation," p. 383.

39. Schanzer, "Marriage Contracts," wonders whether the precontract between Juliet and Claudio was *verbis de futuro* or *de praesenti* and thus whether sexual union between the young lovers was an act of fornication or lawful intercourse. Either kind of precontract, together with consummation ("an old contracting" [3.2.275]), would constitute legal marriage, however, provided that the precontract was witnessed (visible), or public. On the subject of courtship fornications, see also Downame, *Four Treatises*, esp. p. 177.

40. Harrington, *Comendacions of Matrymony*, sigs. A4–A6. For the opposing view, that such marriages are legitimate, see Clerke, *Triall of Bastardie*, pp. 39, 47.

41. *Romeo and Juliet*, in contrast, seems to allow a private or unpublished

marriage. But *Measure for Measure* differs from *Romeo and Juliet* in that its essential issue involves pregnancy, whereas *Romeo and Juliet* focuses merely on marriage. Shakespeare himself, who may have been married without posting public banns, is another analogue to Claudio.

42. At the Council of Merton, the medieval barons refused absolutely to count as legitimate children born before the marriage of their parents. "Nolumus mutare leges Angliae," they shouted in unison. Only in 1920 did the English Commons classify as legitimate children born before their parents' wedlock. (See Helmholz, "Bastardy Litigation.")

43. Empson, "Sense in MM," in Stead, ed., *Casebook*, p. 204.

44. Kingston, *Woman Warrior*, p. 14.

45. Elizabeth, *Glasse*, fol. 20.

46. Plato, *Republic*, 524; *Theaetetus*, 185; *Hippias Major*, 300. On the relevant dialectical connection between the sexes in Shakespeare, see Shell, *Money*, chap. 3, esp. pp. 63–64.

47. The notion that a man and his wife are one person is part of the so-called catenary theory (in Hebrew, *rikkub*, literally "compounding" principle) in the logical system of a group of Jewish Karaites, the Ba'ale ha-Rikkub. Their position is summarized by the *Aderet Elijahu* at the beginning of *'Arayot*, 5, p. 148c–d; see Epstein, *Marriage Laws*, 266–67. Perhaps the greatest single book on incest, the Karaite scholar Jeshua ben Judah's *Sefer ha-Yashar*, written in Arabic in the eleventh century and subsequently translated into Hebrew, argues against the catenary and associated theories of kinship. For an English translation of extracts from *Sefer ha-Yashar*, see Nemoy's *Karaite Anthology*, pp. 127–32.

48. On the relationship engendered by sexual intercourse, see Gratian, *Decretum*, 35, q. 5, 10; Rolandus, *Summa*, 203; Stephanus Tornacensis, *Summa*, 250; Bernard of Pavia, *Summa*, 168; and Feije, *De impedimentis*, chap. 14. During the sixteenth century, the universalizing contagion of kindred through marriage came to include marriage as a spiritual as well as a corporate estate. Just as in physical marriage man and woman become, according to the New Testament, "one in flesh" (*et erunt in carna una* [Matt. 19]), so in sixteenth-century Christian spiritual marriage God and human become one in spirit (*Qui autem adhaeret Domino, unus spiritus est* [1 Cor. 6:17]). On spiritual marriage so defined, see Peers, *Spanish Mystics*, esp. pp. 213–25.

49. Anthropologists make much of the distinction between the incest taboo (which prohibits sexual relations within one's kinship) and exogamy (which prohibits marriage within one's kinship group). Since marriage is always public and sexual relations are generally private (often secret), this distinction has its pragmatic advantage: public and licit liaisons are easier to study than secret, possibly illicit ones. We need a thoroughgoing anthropological investigation of the relationships of incest to chastity and of endogamy to exogamy as these two relationships bear on each other.

50. Brandeis, ed., *Jacob's Well*, 162/15. For the humorous side of the doctrine of carnal contagion in Shakespeare's works, see AWW 1.3.46–55: "He that comforts my wife is the cherisher of my flesh and blood."

51. Fowler, "Incest Regulations," pp. 112–13. For the Latin term, see Rabanus Maurus, *Concilium moguntium*.

52. See, e.g., Knights, "How Many Children?"

53. Most readers and most critics apparently want to demonstrate that Is-

abella wants to marry the Duke. Gless, *'MM,' the Law, and the Convent*, p. 211, for example, says that Isabella must marry the Duke because the play is a comedy and comedies end happily. Mackay, *"MM,"* addressing the large dramaturgical problem, says that she acts as though she will marry the Duke, that she either takes his hand at 5.1.490 or joins him in a processional exit at 5.1.536. (We may imagine the play ending with a procession of several united couples: Juliet and Claudio, Angelo and Mariana, Lucio and Kate Keepdown, perhaps Mistress Elbow and Elbow, possibly Abhorson and Pompey. Yet if we imagine the Duke and Isabella in monachal garb, their presence in, or even overseeing, such a procession would be disquieting.) Finally, Nathan, "Marriage," pp. 43–45, says that Isabella will marry the Duke because she is, according to King James's *Basilicon Doron*, the "kind of woman a prince *should* marry." This consensus shows how much we ordinarily depend on and even require marriage, as we conventionally conceive it, to solve the human problems brought to show in *Measure for Measure*; it also suggests the important role that marriage plays in our own contemporary ideology. Just as the assertion that Isabella and the Duke marry has the effect of closing off discussion of the way marriage is defined by the action of the plot as a whole, so the conventional conception of marriage has the ideologically useful role of closing inquiry into the connection between marriage and incest.

54. Bache, *MM as Dialectic Art*, p. 39, remarks that "the principal symbolic movement of the play is towards the established enlarged family. The Duke will end as brother, father, and husband."

55. To speak of an apparently casual phrase like "in-law" in this way may seem to stretch the point. Yet the Church Fathers speak the same way. Thus Jerome congratulates a woman for having become the "mother-in-law of God" when her novice daughter becomes the spouse of God: "Grande tibi benefactum praestitit: socrus Dei esse coepisti" (Saint Jerome, Letter 22.20, in CSEL, 54:170). Precisely the distinction between a legal brother and an extra-legal Brother drives the Catholic tradition of celibate monachism. See Dumm, *Theological Basis of Virginity*, p. 75.

56. The incest/in-law theme is repeated at AWW 3.2.21 and 4.5.4.

57. "Ghostly father" (5.1.129) means "spiritual father," a friar or priest. For this use of the term, see 3H6 3.2.107; ROM 2.2.189 and 2.3.45; Chaucer, *Canterbury Tales, Parson's Tale*, I.392; Black, ed., *Life of Thos. Beket*, l. 757; and Bale's Epistle Dedicatory to Elizabeth, *Godley Medytacion*.

58. On the question of Isabella's dress, see Mackay, "MM," p. 111.

59. Lascelles, *Shakespeare's MM*, p. 57, assumes she can give up her novitiate with no difficulty. In contrast, Aphra Behn's seventeenth-century novel *The History of the Nun; or the Fair Vow Breaker* makes much of the difficulty of leaving the convent and, predictably, links that departure to eloping with a lover.

60. See especially Coghill, "Comic Form."

61. Spiritual marriage was a special interest of Hugh of St. Victor; see his *De beatae Mariae*.

62. Cockayne, ed., *Hali Meidenhad*, p. 7; trans. in Bugge, *Virginitas*, p. 103.

63. A grange was "a demesne farm, directed by lay brethren and worked by a dependent peasantry"; it was "sited, for reasons of control, as much practical as moral, within easy reach of the abbey, to which it would return its produce" (Platt, *Monastic Grange*, pp. 94, 12).

64. Schlegel, *Lectures on Dramatic Art*, p. 387. Schlegel adds (*loc. cit.*) that

"the Duke acts the part of the Monk naturally, even to deception." "L'habit ne faict le moyne," is how Rabelais puts the proverb (quoted by Kennard, *Friar in Fiction*, p. 45). "Cucullus non facit monachum" (the cowl does not make the monk), Feste the Fool says to Olivia, whom he calls "Madonna," in *Twelfth Night* (TN 1.5.53–55). See Fineman, "Fratricide and Cuckoldry," pp. 105–6.

65. Snider, "Shakespeare's MM," p. 425.

66. On Ochino and his stay in England from 1547 to 1553, see Benrath, *Ochino*, pp. 172–99. On Elizabeth's 1547 translation of Ochino's *Sermo de Christo*, see Craster, "Unknown Translation," p. 723. Ochino also influenced Milton.

67. For Bale's defense of his marriage, see *Scriptorum illustrium maioris Brytanniae*, p. 702; for Rome's condemnation, see Pits, *Relationum Historicum*, pp. 53–59. Cf. Harris, *Bale*, pp. 22–23.

68. In *Image of Both Churches*, chap. 18, p. 537, Bale criticizes Catholic restrictions on marriage, saying: "No more shall that free state of living be bound under the yoke of thy damnable dreams, neither for vows unadvised, nor for popish orders, nor yet for any gossipry, but be at full liberty."

69. Telle, *Marguerite d'Angoulême*, p. 326.

70. A literary counterpart might be Rabelais's Panurge. Rabelais, a contemporary of Luther, was a Franciscan, then a Benedictine, before he put off the orders' garb for that of a secular priest. Panurge's question about whether he should marry motivates a large part of *Gargantua*; Rabelais, like Panurge, died a bachelor.

71. For Luther's critique of religious celibacy, see his "Exhortation to All Clergy," esp. pp. 40–52, and "Exhortation to the Knights."

72. "Love needs no laws," said Luther, sweeping away "those stupid barriers due to spiritual fatherhood, motherhood, brotherhood, sisterhood, and childhood"—or so Brain, *Friends and Lovers*, p. 94, has it. (Cf. Luther, "Persons . . . Forbidden to Marry," LW, 45:8, and "Estate of Marriage," LW, 45:24.) Luther did not sweep away *all* barriers to marriage, however. He stressed the distinction between figure and letter, or spirit and body, and thus redefined the incest taboo in terms of a literal, or corporeal, principle.

73. *Encyclopaedia Britannica*, 11th ed., s.v. "celibacy."

74. More, *Tindale*, pp. 48–49. (Cf. Luther's reference to the incestuous celibacy of the papists: "pro agnitione coniugii, praesertim cum confero illud cum incesto coelibatu papistarum et abominationibus impiis et nuptiis Italicis" [talk no. 1575, in Luther, *Tischreden* 2:138–39].) Certain regulations of the Benedictine orders have been linked with the idealist policies that More promulgates elsewhere, e.g., in *Utopia* (Chambers, *More*, p. 136; see More, *Utopia*, pp. 281–82). Although More generally admired the Catholic orders and their doctrines (Hexter, *More's Utopia*, pp. 85–90), he was not a monk or friar but a husband and legitimate father.

75. Lévi-Strauss, *Elementary Structures*, p. 489. By *chassé-croisé*, Lévi-Strauss suggests a chiasmatic situation of reciprocal and simultaneous exchanges having for their end no result.

76. At first blush, *Measure for Measure* seems to end with the reimposition of a patriarchal order. Neither patriarchy nor matriarchy is imposed on Vienna, however, and the basic problem in the play, the ascertainability of parenthood, affects both genders equally. Isabella responds neither to the defrocked ducal patriarch's offer of univocal marriage nor to his offer of reciprocal mar-

riage. The end of the play thus vacillates between the polar opposites of marriage and Sisterhood—or between parentarchy and liberty. The most discomforting aspect of *Measure for Measure* for liberal ideologies ought to be, not its depiction of the oppression of one sex by another (which would appear to be remediable), but its expression of the irremediable oppression of all political beings. *Measure for Measure* delineates how any doctrine of liberation must first erase belief both in an essential distinction between chastity and unchastity (or between marriage and incest) and in an essential difference between the genders. The transcendence that some liberals seek can be figured in the play only by the unfruitful Franciscan Sisters of Saint Clare.

77. Kingston, *Woman Warrior*, p. 14.

Conclusion

1. Aristotle, *Poetics*, 50a.22–23.

2. Butcher's notes to Aristotle, *Poetics*, p. 347.

3. Some critics believe that *Measure for Measure* ends with the marriage of Isabella and Vincentio and the reunion of Isabella and Claudio; they believe that this marriage and reunion present a definite solution to the problems that the play shows. Thus Murry claims that the Duke and Isabella marry and that this is a case of "generation redeemed"—which he sees as a wholly comfortable and chaste state of affairs ("Redemption of Generation").

4. Bernstein, *Nuns*, p. 109.

5. In an essay entitled "Il n'y a d'amour qu'incestueux donc impossible" (There is only incestuous love, hence love is impossible), Remond similarly argues that, according to the systems of kinship relations set out in Chateaubriand's *René*, "Il n'y a d'amour qu'incestueux et l'inceste est présent, mis en scène par l'auteur comme pour expliquer définitivement une total impossibilité de communication entre les deux sexes."

6. Stephen Lawrence and Bruce Hart, "Sisters and Brothers," on the record album for children entitled *Free to Be . . . You and Me*, by Marlo Thomas and Friends.

7. Plato, *Republic*, 524; *Theaetetus*, 185; *Hippias Major*, 300.

8. Redfield, *Nature and Culture in the Iliad*, p. 61.

9. Giraudoux writes (*Racine*, pp. 44–45) that "all Racine's theatre is a theatre of incest." See also Hesse-Fink, *Thème de l'inceste*, chap. 1. Many of Racine's protagonists have been in love since birth, or even since conception; examples include the rivalry in the womb between the brothers in *Thebaide* (4.1), the brother-sister love in *Bajazet* (their love is "formed from infancy" [5.5; ch. 1.4, 5.6]), and the brother-sister love in *Mithridate* (they have loved "since almost forever" [1.1, 1.2, 3.5]). In *Britannicus* (1.2), Agrippina calls herself "the daughter, wife, sister, and mother of your masters." The result is a dramatic claustration in which all men who count are kin to one another. "In Racine," says Giraudoux (*Racine*, pp. 42–43), "the stage is nothing other than *the sanctuary of the family*, or the *central cage*." The dramatic content of incest in Racine thus verges on formal unity, or atonement.

10. Poulet, *Temps humain*.

11. Sophocles, *Oedipus the King*, l. 438.

12. Chapman, "To the Earl of Somerset," in *Odyssey and Lesser Homerica*, p. 5.

13. See, for an extreme example, Jaffa, "Chastity as a Political Principle."

14. Narcissism and solipsism are the themes of James D. Wilson, "Incest and American Romantic Fiction." For exclusivity, see the discussion of the myth of "inbreeding Jews," in Erlich, "Race and Incest in Mann's 'Blood of the Walsungs.'" Thomas ("Writer's Procreative Urge in *Pierre*," p. 422) argues that "artistic procreation is incestuous. The metaphor of incest accounts for both the difference necessary for the creative act and the continual reduplication of personality (repetition) that no artist can avoid, for in incest we make love to someone of the opposite sex in whom we see ourselves mirrored." Cirlot (*Symbols*, p. 150) claims that incest symbolizes the longing for union with the essence of one's own self, or for "individuation." For Jung on incest and individuation, see his "Psychology of the Transference," esp. pp. 217–30.

15. For psychoanalysis, the standard work is Rank's *Inzest-Motiv*. Rubin and Byerly (*Incest*, sec. 7) provide a short annotated bibliography of selected literary articles about incest. For anthropology, see, e.g., Ehrmann's allegorical analyses in "Structures of Exchange in *Cinna*."

16. The anthologies include Masters and Webster, *Violation of Taboo*, and parts of Masters, *Patterns of Incest*.

17. One treatment of incest in erotic literature is H. Miles, *Forbidden Fruit*.

18. Eliot, *Drama*, pp. 129, 139; cf. Kaufmann, "Ford's Tragic Perspective."

19. For Aristotle's formulation, see *Rhetoric*, 1386–87, and *Ethics*, 1155. For Rymer's criticism, see *Works*, pp. 48, 49. Cf. Roper, introduction to Ford, *'Tis Pity*, p. 33; and Sherman, introduction to *'Tis Pity*, pp. 45–53.

20. Leach, "Virgin Birth," looks into the question of Virgin Birth in the Christian tradition; but see the critique in Spiro, "Virgin and Birth" and "Virgin Birth, Parthenogenesis, and Physiological Paternity."

21. Even such exceptional studies as Séguy, "Sociologie," and Campbell-Jones, *In Habit*, pass over the orders' concern with incest transcendent. There is a group of works written by ex-nuns, constituting a virtual subgenre, that attempts to explain female monastic life, for example: Ebaugh, *Out of the Cloister*; Griffin, *Courage to Choose*; Baldwin, *I Leap over the Wall*; and the movie *Out of Order* (1982), which Diane Christian made with Bruce Jackson.

22. For the statement of this principle, see Malinowski, "Parenthood," pp. 137–38.

23. Lévi-Strauss, *Elementary Structures*, p. 490.

24. Lévi-Strauss, on the last page of his monumental *Elementary Structures*, uses these phrases to describe the Andaman myth of the future life. On Lévi-Strauss's own conceptual hankering after a state both without exchange and with incest, see Simonis, *Lévi-Strauss*.

25. Pitt-Rivers ("Kith and the Kin," p. 100) remarks that "such abstract generosity finds little place in the simple bounded societies studied by most anthropologists." Cf. Freud's and Stephen's dismissive critique of universal love. (For Freud, see the Introduction and chapter 2, above; for Stephen, see his *Liberty, Equality, and Fraternity*, esp. p. 238.)

26. Barthes, *Sade*, pp. 137–38. On the incest taboo and language, or on kinship systems and grammar, see also Steiner, *After Babel*, p. 39; and Ceccarelli, *Tabu dell' incesto*. For the view that merely being called "sister" makes one a sister, see also the *rikkub* principle of the Jewish Karaites (Epstein, *Marriage Laws*, pp. 266–67). On the *rikkub* principle in general, see also

241

Jeshua ben Judah, *Sefer ha-Yashar*; and Nemoy, ed., *Karaite Anthology*, esp. pp. 127–32.

27. Kristeva, *Desire in Language*, pp. 136–37. Lévi-Strauss (*Elementary Structures*, p. 396) writes that "the emergence of symbolic thought must have required that women, like words, should be things that were exchanged." The analogy between language and persons (here, women) suggests that literary analysis, the study of the metaphorical exchanges of meaning, is able to discover the "secret" of incest. Cf. Jacques Lacan's discussion of how "it is essentially on sexual relations—by ordering them according to the law of preferential marriage alliances and forbidden relations—that the first combinatory for the exchanges of women between nominal lineages is based, in order to develop in an exchange of gifts and in exchange of *master-words* the fundamental commerce and concrete discourse on which human societies are based" (quoted in Kellman, *Self-Begetting Novel*, p. 6). For Lévi-Strauss on his own analysis of women as speaking objects, see his "Language and the Analysis of Social Laws," esp. p. 61. On the political implications of Lévi-Strauss's claim that women are exchanged by men, not vice versa, see Sacks, *Sisters and Wives*, pp. 55–57, and Delaney, *Jewel-Hinged Jaw*, pp. 64–69.

28. Cf. Norman O. Brown's view that "the way of silence is not only death but incest" (*Love's Body*, p. 264).

29. Freud, *Civilization and Its Discontents*, pp. 49, 56, cf. p. 59. Cf. Freud's argument that "a democratic strain runs through the Church, for the very reason that before Christ everyone is equal. It is not without a deep reason . . . that believers call themselves brothers in Christ" (Freud, "Two Artificial Groups," pp. 93–94).

30. See Hitschmann's discussion in "Uber Nerven- und Geisteskrankheiten" and Freud's "Obsessive Acts and Religious Practices."

31. For Freud on repression and religious celibacy, see chapter 4, above. For later psychoanalytical articles on religious celibacy, see Steffen, "Das Zölibat"; Levi-Bianchini, "La neurosi antifallica"; Hitschmann, "Uber Nerven- und Geisteskrankheiten"; Pilcz, "Uber Nerven- und Geisteskrankheiten"; and Gilberg, "Ecumenical Movement."

32. See, e.g., Cohn, "Cult of the Free Spirit."

33. From a conversation with Freud quoted in Hitschmann, "Uber Nerven- und Geisteskrankheiten," p. 271.

34. On the psychoanalytic treatment of neurotic priests, see Lemercier, "Freud in the Cloister," and Layard, "Incest Taboo."

35. Freud, "Obsessive Acts and Religious Practices."

36. Freud, *Totem and Taboo*, esp. pp. 121–22, and Atkinson, *Primal Law*.

37. Freud, *Totem and Taboo*, p. 142.

38. Among the Church Fathers, for example, see: Ignatius of Antioch, "To the Ephesians," 10, 3, in PG, 5:653; Clement of Alexandria, *Stromata*, 7.14.5, in GCS, 3:61; Justinian, *Dialogue with Tryphon*, 96, in PG, 6:704; Tertullian, *Apologeticus*, 39.8–9, in CC.

39. Origen, *De oratione*, 15.4.

40. See, e.g.,: Basil, *Regulae brevius tractatae*, PG, 31:1153; Gregory of Nazianzus, *Epistolae*, 238; and Macarius, *Homiliae*, 3.1, in PG, 34:468.

41. Jerome, *Epistolae*, 134.2.1162.

42. Optatus, *Against Parmenian*, 1, 3, in CSEL, 56 (1893), p. 5.

43. See, e.g., Cyprian, *Epistolae*, 53, in *Opera omnia* and CSEL, 3 (1871), p. 620.

44. Exod. 20:12, "Honor thy father and thy mother."

45. See Preisendanz, ed. and trans., *Papyri graecae magicae*, 4:1135ff. Cf. CIL, vol. 6, nn. 406, 727, 2233. For additional evidence, see Henzen et al., eds., *Inscriptiones*, nos. 406, 727, 2233.

46. Cyprian, *Epistolae*, 53, in *Opera omnia* and CSEL, 3 (1871), p. 620.

47. Dolger, "Brüderlichkeit," col. 641–42.

48. Douglas, *Implicit Meanings*, p. 289.

49. In the same way, the injunction to love all equally as brothers can turn into an injunction to treat all equally as others. Consider how Saint John of the Cross makes the transition from brother to other: "You should have an equal love for or an equal forgetfulness of all persons, whether relatives or not, and withdraw your heart from relatives as much as from others." "Regard all as strangers." (John of the Cross, *Collected Works*, pp. 656–57.)

50. See, e.g., Stade, *Geschichte des Volkes Israel*, 1:510.

51. *Genesis Rabba*, 39.

52. Hillel, in *Avot* 1.12 (cf. Hillel, Shabbath, 31a); Meir, in *Avot* 6.1; Aaron ibn Hayyim, *Korban Aharon*. (Aaron, of Morocco, was a member of the *bet din*, or court of justice, at Fez.) The *Encyclopedia Judaica* (s.v. "Mercy") points out that in accordance with the tradition of the imitation of God—"as he is merciful so be you merciful" (Shabbath, 133b)—mercy transcends familial bonds to encompass the entire range of human relationships. (See Eccles. 18:13; *Genesis Rabba*, 33.1.) For the doctrine of universal human love in more modern Judaism, see Hirsch, *Horeb*; Cohen, *Religion der Vernunft*; Buber, *I and Thou*; Borowitz, "Love"; and the ruling of the synod at Leipzig held in 1869 and the German-Israelitsche Union of Congregations in 1885. On the injunction to love even outlaws and criminals, see Sanhedrin 45a. For Shabbath and Sanhedrin, see I. Epstein, ed., *Talmud*.

53. Thus *phrater*, which yields our "brother" (*frater*), denoted not a brother in the usual sense but a fellow member of the religio-political phratry to which a boy was admitted at the Apatouria, where the *phrateres* were at once "brothers and sons of the same fathers." On the ancient Greek phratries and the Apatouria, see Jeanmaire, *Couroi et Courètes*, pp. 133–44, 379–83; Thomson, *Aeschylus and Athens*, p. 28; and Kretschmer, "Benennung des Brüders," in his *Einleitung*, 2:210.

54. McWilliams, *Fraternity*, p. 4.

55. D. Cox, "The Lord's Prayer," in Farr, ed., *Selected Poetry*, 2:503. Cf. Schiller's "Ode to Joy."

56. Beethoven's music for Schiller's ode was first conceived in 1812, when Percy Bysshe Shelley was also making "the earth one brotherhood" (*"Prometheus Unbound,"* 2.2.95).

57. De Vaux, *Israel*, p. 197. I am indebted to Mark Koch for this reference. See also Koschaker, "Fratriarchat," and Gordan, "Fratriarchy."

58. The former is Speiser's view ("Wife-Sister Motif," pp. 15–18); the latter is Seters's (*Abraham*, pp. 72–75). Hurrian marriage may have resembled the Chinese practice of "minor marriage," in which a daughter-in-law is adopted into the family at an early age and raised by her mother-in-law as a sibling to her spouse on the grounds that this will preserve exogamy yet minimize the threat to the extended family posed by a disruptive spouse brought in from

the outside. See Wolf, "Adopt a Daughter-in-Law." On the husband as brother, see Raglan, *Jocasta's Crime*, esp. chap. 24.

59. For Abraham, see Gen. 20:2, 5, 12, 13. For Isaac, see Gen. 26:6. The *rikkub* principle in the logical system of a group of Karaites, the Ba'ale ha-Rikkub, includes the rule of "nominalism," whereby a stepsister, for example, has the status of a sister if she is called a sister by the Bible. (See Epstein, *Marriage Laws*, pp. 266–67.) For a consideration of the wife-sister motif in the Bible, see also Sanhedrin 58a–b, in I. Epstein, ed., *Talmud*.

60. Blood brotherhood implies an equality not obtainable within ordinary kinship structure. Brain (*Friends and Lovers*, p. 85) writes, "Blood brothers are friends and not kin because their relationship is one of absolute equality; between kinsmen there is always superordination and subordination." In the medieval ceremony of blood brotherhood, the Catholic priest "witnessed the declaration of a solemn oath between the two friends, who kissed and then scratched each other's arms, mixing a few drops with the wine, which they drank" (*ibid.*, p. 91). Insofar as blood brotherhood tends to replace natal consanguinity, it constitutes the same kind of threat to "normal" family relations as the eucharistic *sang real*—the "real blood"—of Jesus, who tells his followers to leave their families and become children of adoption to God. The institution of blood brotherhood was outlawed by the Church at about the time that the institution of gossipred became widespread.

61. O.E.D., s.v. "friend," nos. 3 and 4.

62. Old Norse *fraénde*, Swedish *frände*, Danish *fraende*, and, in some dialects, High German *freund* mean only kinsperson.

63. *Ordinarye of Crysten Men*, 2.8.4.

64. Hutter, *Politics as Friendship*, p. 34; cf. pp. 49–51, 126, 455.

65. *Lysis*, 221e6; see Bolotin, *Plato's Dialogue on Friendship*, esp. chap. 8, "Kindred as Friends." Friendship (or hospitality) as mediator between family and politics has played a part in the development of modern, as well as ancient, political theory.

66. Cf. Aristotle, *Ethics*, 1155a, 1168b; and Diogenes Laertius, *Lives*, 8, 10.

67. See Cicero, *Laelius de amicitia*.

68. Cf. Barth and Goedeckemeyer, *Stoa*, pp. 25–27. The view of the Stoic philosopher Epictetus is that man is essentially neither Athenian nor Corinthian but *kosmos* and *huios theou* (*Conversations*, 1.9.1–6; cf. 1.13.3, 3.22.83; and Zeller, *Philosophie der Griechen*, vol. 3, pt. 1, pp. 299–303).

69. In Eisendstadt, "Ritualized Personal Relations."

70. Cf. the British "kissing kind," which the O.E.D. defines as "kind enough to kiss," or "on affectionate terms."

71. Dölger, "Brüderlichkeit," col. 641; cf. O.E.D., s.v. "Cousin," no. 5a.

72. The term, like others that indicate the different kinds of incestuous lovers, is omitted from most other dictionaries, and even from such standard American kinship studies as Schneider, *American Kinship*.

73. For Peter, see 1 Pet. 5:14; for Paul, see Rom. 16:16, 1 Cor. 16:20, and 1 Thess. 5:26. See also Crawley, *Mystic Rose*, 1:344ff, and Perella, *Kiss*, esp. pp. 12–50, 229–30.

74. Venable, "Kiss," p. 902.

75. Frazer (*Golden Bough*, 11:291n) refers to various historical and literary counterparts to this kiss (including Washington Irving's "Christmas Eve") in his discussion of Christmastime Saturnalian license. In his essay on the Ro-

man Carnival, or Saturnalia, Goethe claims that "though it postponed the festival of the Saturnalia with its liberties for a few weeks, the birth of Christ (Christmas) did not succeed in abolishing it" ("Roman Carnival," p. 446).

76. Tertullian, *Ad uxorem*, 2 : 4.

77. Du Cange, *Glossarium*, s.v. "Osculum"; quoted by Crawley, *Mystic Rose*, 1 : 349. Kissing, say the Fathers, is *initium consummationsi nuptiarum*.

78. In *Kissin' Cousins*, a movie starring Elvis Presley, when the U.S. Air Force wants to build a missile base on Smokey Mountain, the "public relations" man (Presley) discovers that one of the hillbillies (also Presley) is his double.

79. Epictetus, *Discourses*, 1.3.3; cf. Zeller, *Philosophie der Griechen*, pp. 299–303.

80. For a brief sociological treatment of interclass equality within the orders, see Campbell-Jones, *In Habit*, esp. pp. 196–99, and Séguy, "Sociologie," p. 347.

81. "The earliest American fictionalists," speculates Dalke ("'Had I known,'" p. 88), "unconsciously used the incest theme to express their deepest anxieties about class upheavals." (Cf. Wagenknecht's remark, *American Novel*, p. 2, that, "judged by their fiction, the Founding Fathers might appear primarily devoted to incest.") For a Marxist condemnation of incest in literature as "a neurotic practice of the decadent upper class," see Zelnick, "Incest Theme." For the American passion for literature about incest in the late eighteenth century, see Wagenknecht, *American Novel*, p. 2.

82. Shell, *Economy of Literature*, chap. 3.

83. Sophocles, *Oedipus the King*, ll. 1077–79.

84. See Thompson, "Double Monasteries."

85. Paul, *Tibetan Symbolic World*.

86. For Coleridge on the theory that "there is a sex in our souls" and that he who "never truly loved a sister . . . is not capable even of loving a Wife as she deserves to be loved," see Coleridge, *Friend*, no. 16, in *Satyrane's Letters*, December 7, 1809. For Hegel, see *Phänomenologie des Geistes*, *Werke* 6 : 327–42.

87. For relevant Renaissance texts, see Nohrnberg, *Analogy*, chap. 4, esp. pp. 599–604.

88. Paul uses *heis* for "one," despite the fact that *heis* is masculine. Elsewhere in the New Testament the neuter pronoun is used in similar contexts.

89. In the Gospel according to the Egyptians, for example, it is written: "When Salome inquired when the things concerning which she asked should be known, the Lord said: 'When ye have trampled on the garment of shame, and when the two become one and the male with the female neither male nor female.'" Another version of the Egyptian Gospel goes: "For the Lord himself being asked by someone when his kingdom should come said: 'When the two should be one, and the outside (that which is without) as the inside (that which is within) and the male with the female neither male nor female'" (James, ed., *Apocryphal New Testament*, p. 11; cf. Knight, *Christian Renaissance*, p. 11, and Heilbrun, *Androgyny*, pp. 20, 179). On Rabelais's Island of Ennasin gender roles are thus confused in much the same way as kinship roles. He writes of those who live on the island that "they were so related and intermarried with one another that we found none of them who was a mother, or a father, an uncle, or an aunt, a cousin or a nephew, a son-in-law or a daughter-in-law, a god-father or a god-mother, to any other; except indeed for one tall *noseless* man whom I heard calling a little girl of three or four, Father, while the little

girl called him Daughter" (Rabelais, *Gargantua and Pantagruel*, book 4, chap. 9; italics mine). (Rabelais's French term "Ennasin" suggests "Essene" and is sometimes taken to mean "noseless.")

90. See, e.g., the Middle English translation of Aelred of Rievaulx's *De vita eremitica*, 329; Julian of Norwich, *Revelations*, 58–60; and Thompson, ed., "*Ureisun of Ure Louerde*," p. 2. Cf. St. Francis's marriage to Lady Poverty, and Bugge, *Virginitas*, p. 100. For the marriage of Francis with Christ as Lady Poverty, see J. M. Erikson, *Saint Francis*.

91. Noyes's Perfectionists, for example, held that the godhead was both male and female; Eldress Anna, a Shaker, says that her community "is the only society in the world, so far as we know, where women have absolutely the same freedom and power as men in every respect" (Evans, *Shaker*, p. 268). Ann Lee, founder of the Shaker sect, regarded herself as "the female element that supplemented Jesus and thus completed the revelation to the world of a father-and-mother God" (Andrews, *Shakers*, pp. 96–97; cf. Young, *Testimony*). On incest and androgyny, and on incest as androgyny, in literature, see Furness, "Androgynous Ideal."

92. Cousins, *Bonaventure*, p. 20.

93. See his *Sexualité*.

94. Recently published anti-incest books include: Renvoize, *Incest*, which attacks the "pro-incest" lobby in Sweden, England, and elsewhere; Armstrong, *Kiss Daddy Goodnight*, which focuses on the fact of "the object's [i.e., the daughter's] continuing fear, shame, and powerlessness" before the father (p. 242); and Herman, with Hirschman, *Father-Daughter Incest*, which presents the viewpoints of a psychiatrist and a social worker. See also Justice, *Broken Taboo*, and Forward, *Betrayal of Innocence*.

95. For the argument for the positive effects of incest and for examples of propaganda published by the pro-incest political lobbies, see Sawyer, "Lifting the Veil"; Leo, "'Cradle-to-Grave'"; Cohen, "Disappearance"; J. Greenberg, "Incest"; "Attacking the Last Taboo"; Ramey, "Dealing with the Last Taboo." Against the proincest lobby and the argument for the positive effects of incest, see Yudkin, "Breaking the Incest Taboo."

96. Hall (*Breaking the Tabu*, p. 39) writes that "if the incest tabu is authority's lynchpin, once this tabu is ignored we may look forward to truly self-directing communities made up of free families and ultimately to a larger society without bosses." Cf. doctrines of the London-based Guyon Society as expressed in Guyon, *Sex Life*. The turn toward incest as other than a taboo act finds a comedic and idealist expression in Vladimir Nabokov's *Ada*, in which Nabokov would appear to reject "the Freudian myth": "Let the credulous and the vulgar continue to believe that all mortal woes can be cured by the daily application of old Greek myths to their private parts. I really do not care." (Nabokov, *Strong Opinions*, p. 66.)

97. Certain legal scholars argue that intergenerational sex in the family would be punished more effectively and beneficially if it were treated not as the crime of incest but as that of the sexual abuse of authority. Slovenko ("Incest," pp. 4–5), for example, suggests that "incest laws be replaced by a law of 'sexual abuse of authority.' This law would include teachers and others who regulate children."

98. Just as focusing myopically on the aspect of incest that involves rape,

molestation, and child abuse can blind us to possibly more fundamental aspects of what incest is, so too can focusing myopically on homosexual incest or on homosexuality and incest. For that reason I have touched directly on the theme of homosexuality only once (in Chapter 1). There are interesting arguments that homosexuality and incest are always linked, however. What better way is there to avoid sexual intercourse with one's parent of the opposite sex or with the figure of that parent? (See Hamilton, "Homosexuality"; Silverman et al., "Male Homosexuality"; Raybin, "Homosexual Incest"; Kaslow et al., "Homosexual Incest"; and Awad, "Single Case Study." Any discussion of androgyny can be turned into a discussion of a unisexuality transcending both female and male sexuality. Are not hermaphrodites in this sense asexual, or transcendentally homosexual?

99. Herman, *Father-Daughter Incest*, pp. 1–2, takes Dymphna as the typological figure of incest. For other contemporary works that concentrate on the bad effects of father-daughter incest for the daughters, see Rofsky, "Father-Daughter Incest."

100. Fiedler (*Love and Death*, p. 112) writes: "The threat of the father to the daughter . . . [came] to stand for the tyranny of the past, the blighting restraint exercised by authority, while the joining of brother and sister . . . against the corrupt parent became the very symbol of justified revolution." Sibling incest does not oppose the generations, however; rather, it breaks down the distinction between parents and children and thus erases, or incorporates and transcends, the simple opposition of parental tyranny to liberal revolution, making us all Siblings of a kind.

101. Plato, *Republic*, 414c–415d. The Greek term for "noble" (*gennaion*) means "nobly born."

102. For autochthony and the Theban tale, see Plato, *Laws*, 663e. Other tales include Odysseus' stories among the Phaeacians. (See Bloom's remarks in his edition of the *Republic*, p. 455.) Plato's *Lysis* proposes to unify the state by guaranteeing a person's right to the land on which he dwells, thus turning autochthony into ideology: "Born of the earth herself, they possessed the same land as motherland and fatherland" (*Lysis* 2.17). "Ma mère, c'est la République," says a character in Victor Hugo's *Les Misérables* (quoted in N. O. Brown, *Love's Body*, p. 34).

103. Cotgrave, *Dictionarie*. See AWW 4.4.21–25.

104. Cf. Fox, *Red Lamp*, epigraph.

105. Plato, *Republic*, 414d–e; cf. *Menexenus*, 239a. Tyrrel, *Amazons*, p. 117, says that Plato's *Menexenus* (esp. 235b–c) involves a rejection of maternity. However, the Platonic theory of autochthony eventually rejects all human parenthood, both male and female.

106. Plato, *Republic*, 461a. See also Bloom's edition of the *Republic*, p. 141, n. 21. In "La Marseillaise," the anthem of the French Revolution, fighters for liberty are called "children of the fatherland" [*enfants de la patrie*]. When these fighters fall in battle "the earth produces new ones" [*la terre en produit ne nouveau*]. For the age-old hypothesis of abiogenesis (the hypothesis that living things sometimes arise without parents from such "lifeless" matter as earth), see Nigrelli, ed., "Modern Ideas on Spontaneous Generation."

107. Plato, *Republic*, 463c.

108. Cornford, in a series of interesting notes to his translation of the *Re-*

public (pp. 161–63), suggests that "Plato did not regard the . . . connections of brothers and sisters as incestuous."

109. Plato, *Republic*, 414d.
110. *Ibid.*, 460c–d.
111. *Ibid.*, 461e. Plato quotes Aristophanes' *Assembly of Women*, ll. 634–38.
112. Heraclitus, frag. 93, ed. Diels.

Bibliography

THROUGHOUT the bibliography, editions are located under the author's name if that is known, under the individual editor if it is not. The following abbreviations have been used:

CC   *Corpus Christianorum* (Series Latina). Turnhout, Belgium, 1953–.
CIL   *Corpus inscriptorum latinorum.* Ed. Koenigliche Akademie der Wissenschaften (afterwards Preussische Akademie der Wissenschaften, then Deutsche Akademie der Wissenschaften). Berlin, 1863–.
CP   Sigmund Freud. *Collected Papers of Sigmund Freud.* Ed. J. Riviere and J. Strachey. 5 vols. London, 1949–50.
CSEL *Corpus scriptorium ecclesiasticorum latinorum.* Vienna, 1866–.
EEB   *Early English Books (1475–1640).* University Microfilms. Ann Arbor, Michigan.
EETS Early English Text Society.
GCS   *Die griechischen christlichen Schriftsteller der ersten drei Jahrhunderte.* Leipzig, 1897–.
LW   *Luther's Works.* Ed. Jaroslav Pelikan and Helmut T. Lehmann. 55 vols. Philadelphia, 1960–62.
MANSI *Sacrorum conciliorum nova et amplissima collectio.* Ed. J. D. Mansi. 31 vols. Florence, 1759–98.
PG   *Patrologiae cursus completus (Series Graeca).* Ed. J. P. Migne. 161 vols. Paris, 1857–99.
PL   *Patrologiae cursus completus (Series Latina).* Ed. J. P. Migne. 221 vols. Paris, 1844–64.
SE   Sigmund Freud. *The Standard Edition of the Complete Psychological Works.* Ed. J. Strachey with Anna Freud. 23 vols. London, 1953–66.
STC   *Short Title Catalogue of Books Printed in England, Scotland, and Ireland and of English Books Printed Abroad, 1475–1640.* Comp. A. W. Pollard and G. R. Redgrave. London, 1926.

Aaron [ben Abraham ben Samuel] ibn Hayyim. *Korban Aharon* (Aaron's offering). Venice, 1609. 2d ed., Dessau, 1742.
Abate, Giuseppe. "La case paterna di S. Chiara e falsificazioni storiche dei secoli XVI e XVII intorno alla medesima Santa ed a S. Francesco d'Assisi." *Bolletino della Regia Deputazione di Storia Patria per l'Umbria* (Perugia), 41 (1944):60–160.

Bibliography

Abelard, Peter. *Historia calamitatum Abaelardi.* In *Petri Abelardi opera hactenus.* 2 vols. Paris, 1849–50.

———. *The Letters of Abelard and Heloise.* Trans. Betty Radice. Hammondsworth, Middlesex, 1974.

d'Acosta, José. *Acosta's Naturall and Morall Historie of the East and West Indies.* Trans. Edward Grimstone. London, 1604. Hakluyt Soc., London, 1880.

Acta Sanctorum. Editio novissima. Ed. and pub. Society of the Bollandists. 67 vols. Brussels, 1863.

Adams, Morton S., and James V. Neel. "Children of Incest." *Pediatrics,* 40 (1967):55–62.

Aelred of Rievaulx. *De vita eremitica.* Ed. C. Horstmann. *Englische Studien,* 7 (1884):304–44.

Aeschylus. *Agamemnon.* In *Aeschylus I,* trans. Richmond Lattimore. Chicago, 1953.

———. *Oresteia.* Trans. Richmond Lattimore. Chicago, 1969.

———. *The Oresteia of Aeschylus.* Ed. with intro. and commentary by Walter Headlam and George Thomson. New edition rev. and enlarged. Amsterdam, 1966.

Albrecht, Louis. *Neue Untersuchungen zu Shakespeares Mass für Mass.* Berlin, 1914.

Aldridge, Alfred Owen. "The Meaning of Incest from Hutcheson to Owen." *Ethics: An International Journal of Social, Political, and Legal Philosophy,* 61 (1950–51):309–13.

Alfonso el Sabio. *Las siete partidas.* Trans. Samuel Parsons Scott. Intro. Charles Sumner Lobringier. New York, 1931.

Allo, E.-B. *Saint Paul: Première épitre aux Corinthiens.* Paris, 1956.

Analecta Bollandiana. Paris-Brussels, 1882–.

Anderson, Gallatin. "Il Comparaggio: The Italian Godparenthood Complex." *Southwestern Journal of Anthropology,* 13 (1957):32–53.

Andrews, Edward D. *The People Called Shakers.* New York, 1953.

d'Anglure, B. Saladin. *L'Organisation sociale traditionelle des Esquimaux de Kangirsujuaaq (Nouveau Québec).* Centre d'Études Nordiques, Laval Univ., no. 17. Laval, Quebec, 1967.

Antisthenes of Athens. *Fragmenta.* Ed. Fernanda Decleva Caizzi. Milan, [1966].

Apollonius of Tyre, *The Patterne of Painefull Adventures.* Trans. Laurence Twyne. In vol. 1 of John Payne Collier, ed., *Shakespeare's Library.* London, 1850.

Ariosto, Lodovico. *Orlando Furioso.* Trans. John Harrington. London, 1591.

Aristophanes. *Assembly of Women.* Ed. and trans. Robert Glenn Ussher. Oxford, 1973.

Aristotle. *Nichomachean Ethics.* Trans. H. Rackham. Cambridge, Mass., 1934.

———. *On the Generation of Animals.* Trans. A. L. Peck. Cambridge, Mass., 1943.

———. *Poetics.* In *Aristotle's Theory of Poetry and Fine Art.* Trans. S. H. Butcher. Intro. J. Gassnero. 4th ed. New York, 1951.

———. *Politics.* Ed. and trans. Ernest Barker. Oxford, 1962.

———. *Politics.* Trans. H. Rackham. Cambridge, Mass., 1967.

———. *Rhetoric.* Trans. John Henry Freese. Cambridge, Mass., 1967.

Armstrong, Louise. *Kiss Daddy Goodnight: A Speak-Out on Incest.* New York, 1978.

Bibliography

Athanasius, Saint(?). *Vita Antonii*. In *Vitae Patrum*, ed. H. Rosweyd. PL, 73: 117–91.

Atkinson, J. J. *Primal Law*. In A. Lang, *Social Origins*. London, 1903.

"Attacking the Last Taboo." *Time*, April 14, 1980, p. 72.

Aubrée, E. *Lucile et René de Chateaubriand chez les soeurs à Fougères*. Paris, 1929.

Augustine, Saint. *Contra Julianum*. PL, 45: 1049–508.

———. *De civitate Dei*. CC, 47–48.

———. *The Lord's Sermon on the Mount*. Trans. John J. Jepson. Westminster, Md., 1956.

———. *Sermons for Christmas and Epiphany*. Trans. Thomas Comerford Lawler. *Ancient Cistercian Writers*, 15. Westminster, Md., 1952.

Avot. Tractate in Mishna, Order Nezikin. In C. Taylor, *Sayings of the Jewish Fathers, Comprising Pirque Aboth in Hebrew and English, with Notes and Excursuses*. 2d ed. Cambridge, 1897.

Awad, George A. "Single Case Study: Father-Son Incest—A Case Report." *Journal of Nervous and Mental Disease*, 162 (February 1975): 135–39.

Awdelay, John. *The Fraternity of Vacabondes*. EETS, extra series no. 5. London, 1869.

Bache, William B. *"Measure for Measure" as Dialectical Art*. Lafayette, Ind., 1969.

Bachofen, Johann Jakob. *Das Mutterrecht*. Ed. Karl Meuli. 2 vols. Basel, 1948.

Baker, Richard. *Chronicle of the Kings of England*. London, 1643.

Bakhtin, Mikhail. *Rabelais and His World*. Trans. Helene Iswolsky. Cambridge, Mass., 1968.

Baldwin, Monica. *I Leap over the Wall*. New York, 1950.

Bale, John. *The Image of Both Churches*. Ed. Henry Christmas. In Bale, *Select Works*. Cambridge, 1849; repr. New York, 1968.

———. *Selected Works*. Ed. Henry Christmas. London, 1849.

———. *The Three Laws of Nature*. London, 1908.

Balzac, Honoré de. *Le Vicaire des Ardennes*. Paris, 1822.

Barakat, Robert A. *The Cistercian Sign Language: A Study in Non-Verbal Communication*. Cistercian Studies series, no. 11. Kalamazoo, Mich., 1975.

Barberis, Pierre, ed. *'René' de Chateaubriand*. Paris, 1973.

Baring-Gould, William S. and Ceil, eds. *Annotated Mother Goose*. New York, 1962.

Barnett, Louise R. "American Novelists and the Portrait of Beatrice Cenci." *New England Quarterly*, 53 (1980): 168–83.

Bart, Benjamin F., and Robert Francis Cook. *The Legendary Sources of Flaubert's Saint Julian*. Toronto, 1977.

Barth, Paul, and Albert Goedeckemeyer. *Die Stoa*. Stuttgart, 1941.

Barthes, Roland. *Sade, Fourier, Loyola*. Trans. Richard Miller. New York, 1976.

Basil, Saint. *Regulae brevius tractatae*. PG, 31: 1079–321.

Battenhouse, Roy W. "*Measure for Measure* and Christian Doctrine of the Atonement." *PMLA*, 61 (1946): 1029–59.

———. *Shakespearean Tragedy: Its Art and Its Christian Premises*. Bloomington, Ind., 1969.

Bayle, Pierre. *Dictionnaire Historique et Critique*. Rev. ed. with notes by Chaufepié, Joly, La Monnoie, Leduchat, Leclerc, Marchand, et al. 16 vols. Paris, 1820[–24].

Beaumont, Francis, and John Fletcher. *A King and No King.* Ed. Robert K. Turner. Lincoln, Nebr., 1963.

Beethoven, Ludwig van. Symphony No. 9 ("Chorale") in D Minor, op. 125. In *The Nine Symphonies of Beethoven in Score.* Ed. Albert Wier. [New York, 1935.]

Behn, Aphra. *The History of the Nun; or the Fair Vow Breaker.* London, 1689.

Belleforest, F. de. *Le Cinquiesme Tome des histoires tragiques.* Paris, 1582.

Benardete, Seth. "A Reading of Sophocles' *Antigone.*" *Interpretation,* 4 (1975): no. 3, 148–96; 5 (1975): no. 1, 1–56; 5 (1975): no. 2, 148–84.

Bennet, Josephine Waters. *"Measure for Measure" as Royal Entertainment.* New York, 1966.

Benrath, Karl. *Bernardino Ochino von Siena: Ein Beitrag zur Geschichte der Reformation.* Braunschweig, 1892. Rpt. Nieuwkoop, 1968.

Benrekassa, Georges. "Loi naturelle et loi civile: L'Idéologie des Lumières et al prohibition de l'inceste." *Studies on Voltaire and the Eighteenth Century,* 87 (1972): 115–44.

Bentham, Jeremy. *Bentham's Theory of Fiction.* Ed. C. K. Ogden. Paterson, N.J., 1959.

Bentley, Thomas. *Monument of Matrons.* London, 1582.

Berg, William J., Michel Grimmaud, and George Moskos. *Saint Oedipus: Psychocritical Approaches to Flaubert's Art.* Ithaca, N.Y., 1982.

Bernard of Clairvaux, Saint. *On the Song of Songs.* Trans. Kilian Walsh. Intro. M. Corneille Halflants. Cistercian Fathers series, nos. 4, 7, 31, 40. Vols. 2–5 of *The Works of Bernard of Clairvaux.* Spencer, Mass., 1970–.

Bernard of Pavia [Bernardus Balbus, Barnardus Papiensis]. *Summa.* Ed. E. A. T. Laspeyres. Ratisbon, 1860.

Bernard, Saint, of Vienne [France] et al. *Epistola S. Agobardi, Bernardi, et eaof episcoporum, ad eumdem imperatorum, de Judaicis superstitionibus.* PL, 104: 77–98.

Bernstein, Marcelle. *Nuns.* London, 1976.

Bertrand-Barraud, Daniel. *Les Idées philosophiques de Bernadrin Ochin, de Sienne.* Paris, 1924.

Bible. Except where indicated, English translations of the Bible are from the Authorized King James Version of 1611. Other citations are from:

1548. John Bale, Epistle Dedicatory and Conclusion to Princess Elizabeth, *Godley Medytacion.*

1560. *The Geneva Bible.* Facsimile ed. Intro. Lloyd E. Berry. Madison, Wis., 1969.

1952. Revised Standard Version.

Greek and Latin. *Novum Testamentum Graece et Latine.* Ed. August Merk. 6th ed. Rome, 1948.

Hebrew. *The Twenty-Four Books of the Old Testament.* Hebrew Text and English Version. Trans. rev. Alexander Harkavy. 4 vols. New York, 1928.

Bible Communism. A Compilation from the Annual Reports and Other Publications of the Oneida Association and Its Branches; Presenting, in Connection with Their History, a Summary View of Their Religious and Social Theories. Brooklyn, N.Y., 1853.

Bickerman, Elias J. *From Ezra to the Last of the Maccabees: Foundations of a Postbiblical Judaism.* New York, 1978.

Birch, William J. *An Inquiry into the Philosophy and Religion of Shakespeare.* London, 1848.

Bibliography

Birje-Patil, J. "Marriage Contracts in *Measure for Measure*," *Shakespeare Studies*, 5 (1970): 106–11.

Bischof, Norbert. "The Comparative Ethology of Incest Avoidance." In R. Fox, ed., *Bisocial Anthropology*. New York, 1975.

Black, W. H., ed. *The Life and Martyrdom of Thos. Beket*. Percy Soc., 19. London, 1845.

Blackmore, Simon Augustine. "Hamlet's Right to the Crown." In Blackmore, *The Riddles of Hamlet and the Newest Answers*. Boston, 1917.

Blake, William. *The Complete Writings*. Ed. G. Keynes. London, 1957.

Bloomfield, Morton. *The Seven Deadly Sins: An Introduction to the History of a Religious Concept, with Special Reference to Medieval English Literature*. East Lansing, Mich., 1967.

Boccaccio, Giovanni. *Decameron*. Trans. John Payne. [New York, 1947.]

Bolotin, David. *Plato's Dialogue on Friendship: An Interpretation of the Lysis, with a New Translation*. Ithaca, N.Y., 1979.

Bonaventure, Saint. *The Franciscan Vision*. Trans. J. O'Mahoney. London, 1937.

————. *The Soul's Journey into God*. Trans. Ewert Cousins. In *The Soul's Journey into God, the Tree of Life, and the Life of Saint Francis*. New York, 1978.

Borowitz, Eugene B. "Love." In *Encyclopaedia Judaica*.

Bourges, Elemir. *Crépuscule des dieux*. Paris, 1912.

Bowler, Peter J. "Preformation and Pre-existence in the Seventeenth Century: A Brief Analysis." *Journal of the History of Biology*, 4 (1971): 221–44.

Bradbrook, Muriel C. "Authority, Truth, and Justice in *Measure for Measure*." *Review of English Studies*, 17 (1941): 385–99.

————. *John Webster: Citizen and Dramatist*. New York, 1980.

Brain, Robert. *Friends and Lovers*. New York, 1976.

Brandeis, Arthur, ed. *Jacob's Well: An English Treatise on the Cleansing of Man's Conscience*. EETS, o.s. 115. London, 1900.

Brennan, Elizabeth. "The Relationship Between Brother and Sister in the Plays of John Webster." *Modern Language Review*, 58 (1963): 488–94.

Brewster, Paul G. *The Incest Theme in Folksong*. Helsinki, 1972.

Briggs, Katherine. *An Encyclopedia of Fairies: Hobgoblins, Brownies, Bogies, and Other Supernatural Creatures*. New York, 1976.

Brown, Norman O. *Love's Body*. New York, 1966.

Brown, Raymond E., trans. *The Gospel According to Saint John (i–xii)*. Vol. 29 of the Anchor Bible. Garden City, N.Y., 1966.

Brown, William Hill. *The Power of Sympathy; or, The Triumph of Nature*. Ed. Herbert Brown. Boston, 1961.

Buber, Martin. *I and Thou*. Trans. Ronald Gregor Smith. Edinburgh, 1937.

Buchanan, George. *Poetarum sui seculi facile principis, opera omnia*. Ed. Ruddiman. 2 vols. Edinburgh, 1715.

Bugge, John. *Virginitas: An Essay in the History of a Medieval Ideal*. The Hague, 1975.

Bullough, Geoffrey, ed. *Narrative and Dramatic Sources of Shakespeare*. Vol. 2: *The Comedies, 1597–1603*. London, 1958.

Burnet, Gilbert [Bishop of Salisbury]. *An Exposition of the Thirty-nine Articles of the Church of England*. London, 1699.

Burton, Robert. *The Anatomy of Melancholy*. Oxford, 1621.

Byerly, Greg, and Rick Rubin. *Incest: The Last Taboo—An Annotated Bibliography.* New York, 1983.

Byron, George Gordon, Lord. *Selected Verse and Prose Works.* Ed. Peter Quennell. London, 1959.

Callebaut, A. "Saint François et les privilèges, surtout celui de pauvreté concédé à sainte Claire par Innocent III." *Archivum Franciscanum Historicum,* 20 (1927): 182–93.

Calvin, John. *Contre la secte phantastique et furieuse des Libertins qui se nomment spirituels.* In his *Opera omnia,* 7: 145–248.

———. *Opera omnia.* Ed. J. W. Baum, E. Cunitz, E. Reuss, P. Lobstein, and A. Erichson. 59 vols. Brunsvigae/Berolini, 1863–1900.

Camden, William. *Annales. The True and Royal History of Elizabeth, Queen of England.* Trans. R. N[orton]. London, 1675.

Campbell-Jones, Suzanne. *In Habit: A Study of Working Nuns.* New York, 1978.

Caro, Joseph. *Eben Haäser: alle Gesetze über die Ehe.* In Caro, *Der Schulchen aruch; oder, Die vier jüdischen Gesetz-Bucher.* Trans. H. F. Löwe. 4 vols. in one. Hamburg, 1837–40.

Casolini, Fausta. "Sainte Claire et les Clarisses." Villier et al., eds., *Dictionnaire,* 5: 1401–22.

Cassian, John. *Conferences.* Ed. M. Petschenig. CSEL, 13 (1886).

Cassius Dio Cocceianus. *Dio's Roman History.* Trans. Earnest Cary. 9 vols. London, 1925.

Cavell, Stanley. *The Claim of Reason.* Oxford, 1979.

———. *Pursuits of Happiness: The Hollywood Comedy of Remarriage.* Cambridge, Mass., 1981.

———. "Recounting Gains, Showing Losses: Reading *The Winter's Tale.*" Forthcoming.

Ceccarelli, Fabio. *Il tabu dell'incesto: i fondamenti biologici del linguagio e della cultura.* Turin, 1978.

Chalmers, George. *A Supplemental Apology for the Believers in the Shakespeare Papers.* London, 1799.

Chamberlain, Frederick. *The Sayings of Queen Elizabeth.* London, 1923.

Chambers, R. W. "The Jacobean Shakespeare and *Measure for Measure.*" 27th Annual Shakespeare Lecture of the British Academy, 1937. London, 1938.

———. *Thomas More.* New York, 1936.

Chambrun, Clara [Longworth] de [Countess]. *Shakespeare: A Portrait Restored.* New York, [1957].

Champneis, John. *The Harvest is at hand wherein the tares shall be bound and cast unto the fyre.* London, 1548.

Chapman, George. *May-Day,* Vol. 2 of *Plays and Poems of George Chapman,* ed. T. M. Parrott. London, 1914.

———. *The Odyssey and the Lesser Homerica.* Vol. 2 of *Chapman's Homer,* ed. Allardyce Nicoll. London, 1967.

Charcot, Jean Martin. *Leçons du mardi à la Salpêtrière: Policlinique 1887–1888.* Paris, 1892.

Charlesworth, M. P. "Nero: Some Aspects." *Journal of Roman Studies,* 40 (1950): 69–76.

Charron, Pierre. *Of Wisdome.* Trans. Samson Lennard. London, [1606].

Chateaubriand, François Auguste René de. *Atala/René.* Trans. Irving Putter. Berkeley, 1952.

———. *Mémoires d'outre-tombe.* Ed. George Moulinier. 2 vols. Paris, 1951.

———. *Oeuvres romanesques et voyages.* Vol. 1. Ed. Maurice Regard. Paris, 1969.

———. *"René" de Chateaubriand: Un Nouveau Roman.* Ed. Pierre Barbéris. Paris, 1973.

Chateaubriand, Lucile de. *Lucile de Chateaubriand: Ses Contes, ses poèmes, ses lettres.* Ed. Anatole France. Paris, 1879.

Chaucer, Geoffrey. *The Canterbury Tales.* Ed. N. F. Blake. London, 1980.

———. *The works of Geoffrey Chaucer.* Ed. F. N. Robinson. 2d ed. Boston, 1957.

Cherry, C. L. *The Most Unvaluedst Purchase: Women in the Plays of Thomas Middleton.* Salzburg, 1973.

Chettle, Henry. *Englandes Mourning Garment: worne here by plaine Shepheardes; in memorie of their sacred Mistresse, Elizabeth, Queene of Virtue.* . . . London, 1603.

Chijs, A. van der. "Een bijdrage tot de kennis van de beteekenis van het incest en infantilisme in de schilderkunst" (A contribution to the knowledge of the significance of incest and infantilism in the art of painting). *Nederlandsch Tijdschrift voor Geneeskunde,* 1922, pp. 1460–69.

Cicero. *Laelius de amicitia.* Trans. Cyrus Edmonds. London, 1890.

Cimetier, F. "Parenté (Empêchements de)," Vacant et al., eds., *Dictionnaire,* vol. 11, pt. 2, 1995–2003.

Cinotti, Mia. *The Complete Paintings of Bosch.* Intro. Gregory Martin. New York, [1971].

Cirlot, Juan Eduardo. *A Dictionary of Symbols.* Trans. Jack Sage. New York, 1962.

Clare of Assisi, Saint. See Thomas of Celano.

Clarkson, Paul Stephen, and Clyde T. Warren. *The Law of Property in Shakespeare and Elizabethan Drama.* Baltimore, 1942.

Clement [Pseudo-]. *Epistolae ad virgines.* PG, 1 : 349–416.

Clement of Alexandria [Titus Clemens Alexandria]. *Stromata.* Ed. O. Stahlin. GCS, 3 (1909).

Clerke, William. *The Triall of Bastardie.* London, 1594.

Cleveland, Arthur. "Indictments for Adultery and Incest Before 1650." *Law Quarterly Review,* 29 (1913): 57–60.

Cockayne, Thomas Oswald, ed. *Hali Meidenhad, An Alliterative Homily of the Thirteenth Century.* EETS, o.s. 18. London, 1866.

Coghill, Nevill. "Comic Form in *Measure for Measure.*" *Shakespeare Survey,* 8 (1955): 14–27.

Cohen, Hermann. *Die Religion der Vernunft aus den Quellen des Judentums.* 2d ed. Frankfurt, 1929.

Cohen, Yehudi. "The Disappearance of the Incest Taboo." *Human Nature,* 1 (1978): 72–78.

Cohn, Norman. "The Cult of the Free Spirit: A Medieval Heresy Reconstructed." *Psychoanalysis and the Psychoanalytic Review,* 48 (1961): 51–68.

Coke, Edward. *Commentary upon Littleton.* 16th ed. Ed. Francis Hargrave and Charles Butler. London, 1809.

Cole, J. *Early Theories of Sexual Generation.* Oxford, 1930.

Coleccíon de canones de la iglesia española. Trans. Juan Tejeda y Ramiro. Madrid, 1849.

Coleridge, Samuel Taylor. *Biographia Literaria.* Ed. J. Engell and W. Jackson Bate. Vol. 7 of *Collected Works.*

——. *Collected Letters.* Ed. E. L. Griggs. 6 vols. London, 1956–71.
——. *Collected Works.* Ed. Kathleen Coburn. 16 vols. Princeton, 1969–.
——. *The Friend.* Ed. Barbara E. Rooke. Vol. 4 of *Collected Works.*
——. *Lectures and Notes on Shakespeare and Other English Poets.* Ed. T. Ashe. London, 1888.
——. *Letters.* Ed. E. H. Coleridge. London, 1895.
——. *Notebooks.* Vol. 1: *1794–1804.* Ed. Kathleen Coburn. Princeton, 1957.
——. *Shakespeare Criticism.* Ed. T. M. Rayser. 2 vols. 1936; rpt. Folcroft, Pa., 1969.
Collins, Adela Yarbro. "The Function of 'Excommunication' in Paul." *Harvard Theological Review,* 73 (1980): 251–63.
Connolly, Cyril. *The Unquiet Grave: A Word Cycle by Palinurus.* New York, 1945.
Conzelmann, Hans. *1 Corinthians.* Philadelphia, 1975.
Cook, Albert. "Metaphysical Poetry and *Measure for Measure*." *Accent,* 13 (1953): 122–27.
Cooper, J. M. "Incest Prohibitions in Primitive Culture." *Ecclesiastical Review,* 33 (1932): 4–7.
Cotgrave, Randle. *A Dictionarie of the French and English Tongues.* London, 1611.
Cousins, Ewert H. *Bonaventure and the Coincidence of Opposites.* Chicago, 1978.
Craster, H. H. E. "An Unknown Translation by Queen Elizabeth." *English Historical Review,* 29 (1914): 721–23.
Crawley, Ernest. *The Mystic Rose: A Study of Primitive Marriage and of Primitive Thought in Its Bearing on Marriage.* Ed. T. Bestermann. 2 vols. London, 1927.
Crosse, Robert. *The Lover, or Nuptial Love.* London, 1638.
Cyprian, Saint [Caecilius Cyprianus, Bishop of Carthage]. *Epistolae.* Vol. 2 of Cyprian, *Opera omnia,* ed. Guilemus Hartel. Vienna, 1868–71.
Daemmrich, Horst. "The Incest Motif in Lessing's *Nathan the Wise* and Schiller's *Braut von Messina*." *Germanic Review,* 42 (1967): 184–96.
Dagens, Jean. "Le 'Miroir des simples ames' et Marguerite de Navarre." In *La Mystique Rhénane: Colloque de Strasbourg, 16–19 mai 1961.* Bibliothèque des Centres d'Études Supérieres. Paris, 1963.
Dalke, Anne French. "'Had I known her to be my sister, my love would have been more regular': Incest in Nineteenth Century American Fiction." Ph.D. diss., Univ. of Pennsylvania, 1982.
Damasus I, Saint [Pope]. *Epigrammata Damasiana.* Ed. Antonius Ferrua. Vatican, 1942.
Damon, S. Foster. "Pierre the Ambiguous." *The Hound & Horn: A Harvard Miscellany,* 2 (1928): 107–18.
Dante Alighieri. *Divine Comedy.* Trans. John D. Sinclair. 3 vols. New York, 1961.
Daube, David. "Lex Talionis." In *Studies in Biblical Law.* Cambridge, 1947.
Defoe, Daniel. *A Treatise Concerning the Uses and Abuses of the Marriage Bed.* London, 1727.
Delaney, Samuel R. *The Jewel-Hinged Jaw: Notes on the Language of Science Fiction.* New York, 1977.
De Quincey, Thomas. *Autobiographical Sketches.* Vols. 1–2 of *The Collected Writings of Thomas de Quincey,* ed. David Masson, 14 vols. Edinburgh, 1889–90.
Desplandres, P. *L'Ordre des Trinitaires pour le rachat des captifs.* 2 vols. Toulouse, 1903.

Dewey, John. "The Historic Background of Corporate Legal Personality." *Yale Law Journal*, 35 (1926):655–73.

Dhont, R.-C. *Claire parmi ses soeurs*. Paris, 1973.

Diderot, Denis. *Le Fils naturel; ou les epreuves de la vertu*. Amsterdam, 1757.

———. *La Religieuse*. Paris, [1796].

Diels, H., ed. *Fragmente der Vorsokratiker*. 5th ed. Berlin, 1934.

Dinesen, Isak [Karen Blixen]. "The Caryatids, an Unfinished Tale." In *Last Tales*. New York, 1957.

Diogenes Laertius. *Lives of the Eminent Philosophers*. Trans. R. D. Hicks. 2 vols. Cambridge, Mass., 1979.

Disraeli, Benjamin. *Contarini Fleming*. New York, 1832.

Dixon, William Hepworth. *Spiritual Wives*. 2 vols. London, 1868.

Dodds, W. M. T. "The Character of Angelo in *Measure for Measure*." *Modern Language Review*, 41 (1946):246–55.

Doirion, S. Marilyn. "The Middle English Translation of the *Mirouer des simples ames*." In *Dr. L. Reypens Album*, pp. 131–52. Antwerp, 1964.

Dölger, F. "Brüderlichkeit der Fürsten." In *Reallexikon für Antike und Christentum*, ed. Theodor Klauser, vol. 2, cols. 641–46. Stuttgart, 1954.

Döllinger, I. I. von. *Beiträge zur Sektengeschichte des Mittelalters*. 2 pts. Munich, 1890.

Donne, John. *Bithanatos. A Declaration of that Paradox, or Thesis, that Self-homicide is not so naturally sin, that it may never be otherwise*. London, 1648.

Douglas, Mary. *Implicit Meanings: Essays in Anthropology*. Boston, 1975.

Dowden, Edward. *Shakespeare: A Critical Study of His Mind and Art*. London, 1875.

Downame, John. *Foure Treatises Tending to Disswade all Christians from foure no lesse hainous than Common Sinnes; namely, Swearing, Drunkennesse, Whoredome, and Briberie*. London, 1609.

Dreyfuss, H. *Symbol Sourcebook: An Authoritative Guide to International Graphic Symbols*. New York, [1972].

Drummond, William. *Notes of Ben Jonson's Conversations with William Drummond of Hawthornden*. Shakespeare Society. London, 1842.

Dryden, Edgar A. "The Entangled Text: Melville's *Pierre* and the Problem of Reading." *Boundary* 2, 7 (1979):145–73.

Dryden, John. *Don Sebastian*. Vol. 1 of *Dramatic Works*, ed. W. Gifford and A. Dyce, 3 vols. New York, 1965.

Du Cange [Charles du Fresne]. *Glossarium mediae et infimae latinitatis*. Graz, 1954.

DuChamps [Duchamp], Marcel. *The Bride Stripped Bare by Her Bachelors, Even*. A typographic version by Richard Hamilton of M. Duchamp's Green Box. Trans. George Heard Hamilton. London, 1960.

Duff, I. F. Grant. "Die Beziehung Elizabeth-Essex: eine psychoanalytische Betrachtung." *Psychoanalytische Bewegung*, 3 (1931):457–74.

Dugdale, Gilbert. *The Time Triumphant, Declaring . . . the Ariual of . . . King Iames into England*. London, 1604.

Dumm, Demetrius. *The Theological Basis of Virginity According to Saint Jerome*. Latrobe, Pa., 1961.

Durbach, Errol. "The Geschwister-Komplex: Romantic Attitudes to Brother-Sister Incest in Ibsen, Byron, and Emily Bronte." *Mosaic*, 12 (1979):61–73.

Durham, W. H. "What art thou, Angelo?" In B. H. Bronson et al., eds., *Studies in the Comic*. Berkeley, 1941.

Durkheim, Emile. *Incest: The Nature and Origin of the Taboo*. Trans. Edward Sagarin. New York, 1963.

Ebaugh, Helen Rose Fuchs. *Out of the Cloister: A Study of Organizational Dilemmas*. Austin, Tex., 1977.

Egido, Teófanes. "The Historical Setting of St. Teresa's Life." *Carmelite Studies*, 1980.

Ehrmann, Jacques. "Structures of Exchange in *Cinna*." *Yale French Studies*, 36/37 (1966): 169–99.

Eisenstadt, Shmuel N. "Ritualized Personal Relations." *Man*, 56 (1956): 90–95.

Eliot, T. S. *Essays in Elizabethan Drama*. New York, 1956.

Elizabeth, Princess [afterwards Queen]. *The Glasse of the Synnefull Soule*. Manuscript, 1544. Bodley. Ms. Cherry 36.

———. *The Mirror of the Sinful Soul*. Facsimile. Ed. Percy W. Ames. London, 1897.

———. *A Godley Medytacion of the Christen Sowle, concerninge a love towardes God and Hys Christe*, compyled in Frenche by lady Margarete quene of Naverre, and aptely translated into Englysh by the ryght vertuouse lady Elyzabeth daughter to our late soverayne kynge Henri the VIII. (Epistle Dedicatory and Conclusion by John Bale.) [Marburg?], 1548. EEB, reel 56; STC, no. 17320.

———. *A Godley Medytacion*. Ed. James Cancellar. London, 1568 [1570?]. Also in Thomas Bentley, *Monument of Matrones*, vol. 1, sigs. F2v–H4v. London, 1582.

———. *A Godley Medytacion*. Ed. John Bale [with a few minor changes]. London, 1590.

———. *Letters*. Ed. G. B. Harrison. New York, 1968.

———. *Queen Elizabeth's Englishings of Boethius, De Consolatione Philosophiae, A.D. 1593, Plutarch, De Curiositate, A.D. 1598, and Horace, De Arte Poetica (part), 1598*. Ed. Caroline Pemberton. EETS. London, 1899.

Ellis, John B. *Free Love and its Votaries, or American Socialism Unmasked, Being an Historical and Descriptive Account of the Rise and Progress of the Various Free Love Associations in the United States and of the Effects of their Vicious Teachings Upon American Society*. New York, [1870].

Else, Gerald F. *Aristotle's Poetics: The Argument*. Cambridge, Mass. 1956.

Elyot, Thomas. *The Image of Governaunce compiled by the actes and sentences notable of the most noble Emperor Alexandre Seuerus*. London, 1544.

Elze, Karl. *William Shakespeare*. Halle, 1876.

Empson, William. "Sense in *Measure for Measure*." *Southern Review*, 4 (1938): 340–50. Also in *The Structure of Complex Words* (Ann Arbor, Mich., 1967), and in Stead, ed., *Casebook*.

Encyclopaedia Judaica. 14 vols. Jerusalem, 1971–72.

Engels, Frederick. *The Origin of the Family, Private Property, and the State, in the Light of the Researches of Lewis H. Morgan*. Trans. Alec West. Intro. Eleanor Burke Leacock. New York, 1972.

Epictetus. *The Discourses, as Reported by Arrian; the Manual; and Fragments*. 2 vols. Trans. W. A. Oldfather. London, 1925.

Epstein, I., ed. *Babylonian Talmud*. London, 1935–48.

Epstein, Louis M. *Marriage Laws in the Bible and the Talmud*. Cambridge, Mass., 1942.

Erasmus. *Colloquies*. Trans. Craig R. Thompson. Chicago, 1965.

————. *The Dyalogue called Funus*. Trans. Gerrard. Ed. Robert R. Allen. Chicago, 1969.

————. *A ryght fruteful Epistle . . . in laude and prayse of matrimony*. Trans. Richard Taverner. London, 1532.

Erbstösser, M., and E. Werner. *Ideologische Probleme des mittelalterischen Pleberjetums. Die freigeistige Häresie und ihr sozialen Wurzeln*. Berlin, 1960.

Erikson, Erik. *Young Man Luther: A Study in Psychoanalysis and History*. New York, 1958.

Erikson, Joan Moinat. *Saint Francis and His Four Ladies*. New York, 1970.

Erlich, Gloria Chasson. "Race and Incest in Mann's 'Blood of the Walsungs.'" *Studies in Twentieth Century Literature*, 2 (1978): 113–26.

Estève, Edmond. "Le théâtre 'Monocal' sous la Révolution, ses précédents et ses suites." In *Etudes de littérature préromantique*. Paris, 1923.

Eusebius Pamphili of Caesarea. *The History of the Church from Christ to Constantine*. Trans. G. A. Williamson. New York, 1966.

Evans, Frederick Williams. *Autobiography of a Shaker, and Revelation of the Apocalypse*. 1888; repr. New York, 1973.

Evans-Pritchard, E. E. "Exogamous Rules among the Nuer." *Man*, 35 (1935): 11.

————. "The Nature of Kinship Extensions." *Man*, 32 (1932): 12–15.

————. "The Study of Kinship in Primitive Societies." *Man*, 29 (1929): 190–94.

Faber, M. D. *Culture and Consciousness: The Social Meaning of Altered Awareness*. New York, 1981.

Farr, Edward, ed. *Selected Poetry, Chiefly Devotional, of the Reign of Queen Elizabeth*. 2 pts. Parker Soc. Cambridge, 1845.

Febvre, Lucien. *Autour de l'Heptaméron: Amour sacré, amour profane*. 6th ed. Paris, 1944.

Feije, H. *De impedimentis et dispensationibus matrimonialibus*. Louvain, 1885.

Fiedler, Leslie. *Love and Death in the American Novel*. Rev. ed. New York, 1975.

Fiege, Marianus. *The Princess of Poverty*. 2d ed. Evansville, Ind., 1909.

Filmer, Robert. *Patriarcha and Other Political Works*. Ed. Peter Laslett. Oxford, 1949.

Fineman, Joel. "Fratricide and Cuckoldry: Shakespeare's Doubles." In Murray Schwartz and Coppélia Kahn, eds., *Representing Shakespeare*. Baltimore, 1980.

Finkelstein, Louis. *The Pharisees: The Sociological Background of Their Faith*. 2 vols. Philadelphia, 1983.

Fleetwood, William. *Sermon Against Clipping*. London, 1694.

Fletcher, John. *Women Pleased*. Ed. Hans Walter Gabler. In Fredson Bowers, ed., *The Dramatic Works in the Beaumont and Fletcher Canon*, vol. 5. Cambridge, 1982.

Ford, John. *'Tis Pity She's a Whore*. Ed. Derek Roper. London, 1975.

————. *'Tis Pity She's a Whore*. Ed. S. P. Sherman. Boston, 1915.

Ford, J. Massingberd. *A Trilogy on Wisdom and Celibacy*. Notre Dame, 1967.

Formaggio, Dino. *Basiliche di Assisi*. Novara, 1958.

Forward, Susan. *Betrayal of Innocence: Incest and Its Devastation*. New York, 1978.

Foucault, Michel. *Histoire de la sexualité*. Vol. 1: *La Volonté de savoir*. Paris, 1976.

Fowler, John Howard. "The Development of Incest Regulations in the Early Middle Ages: Family, Nurturance, and Aggression in the Making of the Medieval West." Ph.D. diss., Rice Univ., 1981.

Fox, Robin. *Kinship and Marriage: An Anthropological Perspective*. Harmondsworth, Middlesex, 1967.

———. *The Red Lamp of Incest*. New York, 1980.

Francis of Assisi, Saint. "Il Cantico di frate sole." In *St. Francis: Omnibus of Sources*, ed. Habig.

———. *Gli Scritti di San Francesco d'Assisi*. Società Editrice Vita e Pensiero. Milan, 1954.

———. *Saint Francis: Omnibus of Sources*. Ed. Marion A. Habig. Chicago, 1973.

Fränger, Wilhelm. *The Millennium of Hieronymus Bosch: Outlines of a New Interpretation*. Trans. Eithne Wilkins and Ernst Kaiser. London, 1952.

Frazer, James G. *The Golden Bough*. 12 vols. London, 1911–15.

———. *Totemism and Exogamy*. 4 vols. London, 1910.

Frederichs, J. "Un Luthérien français devenu libertin spirituel: Christophe Herault et les loïte d'Anvers (1490–1544)." *Bulletin de la societé de l'histoire du protestantisme français*, 41 (1892):250–69.

Freeburg, V. O. *Disguise Plots in Elizabethan Drama*. New York, 1915.

Freeman, Kathleen. *The Pre-Socratic Philosophers*. London, 1956.

Freud, Sigmund. "A Case of Successful Treatment by Hypnotism." SE, 1:115–30.

———. *Character and Culture*. Ed. Philip Rieff. New York, 1963.

———. *Civilization and Its Discontents*. Trans. J. Strachey, New York, 1962.

———. Footnotes to Charcot's *Tuesday Lectures*. SE, 1:137–46.

———. "Dostoevsky and Parricide." 1928. In CP, 5:222–42; and SE, 21:175–95.

———. *Group Psychology and the Analysis of the Ego*. Trans. J. Strachey. London and Vienna, 1922.

———. *Introductory Lectures on Psychoanalysis*. London, 1922.

———. "Obsessive Acts and Religious Practices." CP, 2:25–35.

———. "On the Psychical Mechanism of Hysterical Phenomena: A Lecture." SE, 3:25–42.

———. Preface to *Studies on Hysteria*, 2d ed. 1908. SE, 2:xxxi.

———. "The Taboo on Virginity." SE, 11:191–208.

———. *Totem and Taboo*. Trans. J. Strachey. New York, 1950.

———. "Two Artificial Groups: The Church and the Army." Pt. 5 of *Group Psychology and the Analysis of the Ego*; SE, 18:93–99.

Freud, Sigmund, and Joseph Breuer. "On the Psychical Mechanism of Hysterical Phenomena: Preliminary Communication." SE, 1:1–18.

Frey, Charles. "Shakespearean Interpretation: Promising Problems." *Shakespeare Studies*, 10 (1977):1–8.

Friedmann, Paul. *Anne Boleyn: A Chapter of English History, 1527–1536*. 2 vols. London, 1884. Repr. New York, 1973.

Frye, Northrop. *Fearful Symmetry*. Princeton, 1947.

Frye, Roland Mushat. *Shakespeare and Christian Doctrine*. Princeton, 1963.

Fuller, Lon L. *Legal Fictions*. Stanford, 1967.

Furness, Raymond. "The Androgynous Ideal: Its Significance in German Literature." *Modern Language Review*, 60 (1965):58–64.

Furnivall, F. J., and John Munro, eds. *"The Troublesome Reign of King John," Being the Original of Shakespeare's "Life and Death of King John."* Norwood, Pa., 1975.

Gardiner, Stephen. *Letters.* New York, 1933.

Garonne, S. E., ed. *J'ai connu Madame Sainte Claire: Le Procès de canonisation de Sainte Claire d'Assise.* Trans. by Marie de la Passion, with a preface by S. E. Garonne. Toulouse, Monastère des clarisses. Paris, 1961.

Geckle, George L., ed. *Twentieth Century Interpretations of "Measure for Measure."* Englewood Cliffs, N.J., 1970.

Genesis Rabba [Midrash]. In Julius Theodor and Chanoch Albeck, eds., *Bereschit Rabba mit kritischem Apparat und Kommentar.* 4 vols. Berlin, 1912–36.

Gesenius, William. *A Hebrew and English Lexicon of the Old Testament.* Trans. Edward Robinson. Ed. Francis Brown. Oxford, 1972.

Gibbon, Edward. *The History of the Decline and Fall of the Roman Empire.* 5 vols. London, 1776–88.

Gilberg, Arnold. "The Ecumenical Movement and the Treatment of Nuns." *International Journal of Psycho-Analysis*, 49 (1968):481–83.

Giraldi, Giovanni Battista [Cinthio]. *Hecatommithi.* 2 vols. Monreale, Italy, 1565.

Giraudoux, Jean. *Racine.* Paris, 1950.

Gless, Darryl J. *"Measure for Measure," the Law, and the Convent.* Princeton, 1979.

Goergen, Donald. *The Sexual Celibate.* New York, 1974.

Goethe, Johann Wolfgang von. *Elective Affinities.* Trans. R. J. Hollingdale. Baltimore, 1971.

———. *Faust, a Tragedy: Background, Criticism.* Trans. Walter Arndt. Ed. Cyrus Hamlin. New York, 1976.

———. *Goethes Werke.* 14 vols. Hamburg, 1949–60.

———. "The Roman Carnival." Trans. W. H. Auden and Elizabeth Mayer, in *Italian Journey.* New York, 1962.

———. "Das Römische Karneval." In *Hamburg Ausgabe*, 11:484–515.

Goldberg, Jonathan. *Endlesse Worke: Spencer and the Structures of Discourse.* Baltimore, 1981.

———. *James I and the Politics of Literature: Jonson, Shakespeare, Donne, and Their Contemporaries.* Baltimore, 1983.

———. "James I and the Theater of Conscience." *English Literary History*, 46 (1979):379–98.

Gollancz, Israel, ed. *The Sources of "Hamlet," with an Essay on the Legend.* London, 1926.

Gordan, Cyrus H. "Fratriarchy in the Old Testament." *Journal of Biblical Literature*, 54 (1935):223–31.

Gower, John. *Confessio Amantis.* Vols. 2 and 3 of *The Complete Works of John Gower*, ed. G. C. M. Macaulay. London, 1901.

Gratian. *Decretum.* Ed. A. L. Richter. Rev. A. Friedberg. In *Corpus iuris canonici*, vol. 1. Leipzig, 1879.

Gray, L. H. "Next-of-Kin Marriages in Iran." In James Hastings, ed., *Encyclopedia of Religion and Ethics*, 8:546–49. New York: 1924–27.

Greenberg, Joel. "Incest: Out of Hiding." *Science News*, April 5, 1980, pp. 218–20.

Greenberg, Moshe. "Incest." In *Encyclopaedia Judaica*.

Greenblatt, Stephen. Introduction to *The Forms of Power and the Power of Forms in the Renaissance*, an issue of *Genre*. *Genre*, 15 (1982):3–6.

Gregory of Nazianzus, Saint. *Epistolae*. Ed. and trans. P. Gallay. 2 vols. Paris, 1964–67. Also in PG, 35–38.

Gregory of Nyssa. *Vita S. Macrinae*. PG, 46:959–99.

Gregory the Great, Saint. *Moralium libri*. PL, 76:9–782.

———. *Vita S. Benedicti*. PL, 66:125–215.

Griffin, Mary. *The Courage to Choose: An American Nun's Story*. Boston, 1975.

Griffiths, E. *The Two Books of Homilies*. London, 1859.

Grillparzer, Franz. *Die Ahnfrau*. Vienna, 1817.

Grimm, Jakob and Wilhelm, *Deutsches Wörterbuch*. Leipzig, 1854–1960.

Groot, John Henry. *The Shakespeares and the Old Faith*. New York, 1946.

Gross, Manfred. *Shakespeares "Measure for Measure" und die Politik Jacobs I*. Neumünster, 1965.

Guarnieri, Romana. "Il movimento del libero spirito dalle origine al secolo XVI." *Archivio italiano per la storia della pietà*, 4 (1964).

Gudeman, S. "The Compadrazago as a Reflection of the Natural and Spiritual Person." In *Proceedings of the Royal Anthropological Institute of Great Britain and Ireland for 1971*, pp. 45–71. London, 1972.

Guyon, René. *Sex Life and Sex Ethics*. London, 1933.

Hall, Bill. *Breaking the Tabu*. Vancouver, 1955.

Hall, Lawrence Sargent. "Isabella's Angry Ape." *Shakespeare Quarterly*, 15 (1964):157–65.

Halley, Janet E. "Heresy, Orthodoxy, and the Politics of Religious Discourse: The Case of the English Family of Love." *Representations*, 15 (1986):98–120.

Halliwell-Phillipps, J. O. *Memoranda on Shakespeare's Comedy of "Measure for Measure."* 1880; repr. New York, 1974.

Hamilton, Gilbert. "Homosexuality as a Defense Against Incest." In R. E. L. Masters, *Patterns of Incest*.

Harding, Davis. "Elizabethan Brothels and *Measure for Measure*." *Journal of English and Germanic Philology*, 49 (1950):139–58.

Harding, Mary Esther. *Woman's Mysteries, Ancient and Modern*. London, 1935.

Harington, John. *Letters and Epigrams*. Ed. N. E. McClure. Philadelphia, 1930.

Harney, Martin P. *Brother and Sister Saints*. Paterson, N.J., 1957.

Harrington, William. *In this boke are conteyned the comendacions of matrymony the maner & fourme of contractyng solempnysynge and lyuying in the same*. London, 1528.

Harris, Jesse W. *John Bale: A Study in the Minor Literature of the Reformation*. Urbana, Ill., 1940.

Hartmann von Aue. *Gregorius: A Medieval Oedipus Legend*. Trans. Edwin H. Zeydel. Chapel Hill, N.C., 1955.

Haslip, J. *Lucrezia Borgia*. London, 1953.

Haugaard, William P. "Katherine Parr: The Religious Convictions of a Renaissance Queen." *Renaissance Quarterly*, 22 (1969):346–59.

Haupt, H. "Ein Beghardenprozess in Eichstadt vom Jahre 1381." *Zeitschrift für Kirchengeschichte*, 5 (1882):487–98.

Heckthorn, C. W. *The Secret Societies of All Ages and Countries*. London, 1897.

Hedde, R. "Libertins." In Vacant et al., eds., *Dictionnaire*, vol. 9, pt. 1, pp. 703–6.

Hefele, Carl Joseph von. *Conciliengeschichte*. 9 vols. Freiburg, 1855–87.

———. *Histoire des conciles*. Ed. H. LeClercq. Paris, 1907–.

Hegel, Georg Wilhelm Friedrich. *Werke*. 20 vols. Frankfurt, 1969–71.

Heilbrun, Carolyn H. *Toward a Recognition of Androgyny*. New York, 1973.

Helmholz, R. H. "Bastardy Litigation in Medieval England." *American Journal of Legal History*, 13 (1969): 360–83.

Henzen, Wilhelm, Eugene Bormann, et al., eds. *Inscriptiones urbis Romae Latinae*. Vol. 6 of CIL. Berlin, 1876.

Herman, Judith Lewis, with Lisa Hirschman. *Father-Daughter Incest*. Cambridge, Mass., 1981.

Herodotus. *Histories*. Trans. A. D. Godley. 4 vols. London, 1931–38.

Herrtage, J. H., ed. *The Early English Versions of the "Gesta Romanorum."* EETS, e.s. 33. London, 1879.

Hesse, Everett Wesley. "The Incest Motif in Tirso's 'La venganza de Tamar,'" *Hispania*, 47 (1964): 268–76.

Hesse-Fink, Evelyne. *Etudes sur le thème de l'inceste dans la littérature française*. Bern, 1971.

Heuscher, Julius E. *A Psychiatric Study of Myths and Fairy Tales: Their Origin, Meaning, and Usefulness*. 2d ed. Springfield, Ill., 1974.

Hexter, J. H. *More's Utopia: The Biography of an Idea*. New York, 1965.

Heymann, F. G. *George of Bohemia*. Princeton, 1965.

———. "The Hussite and Utraquist Church in the Fifteenth and Sixteenth Centuries." *Archiv für Reformationsgeschichte*, 52 (1961): 1–16.

———. *John Zizka and the Hussite Revolution*. Princeton, 1955.

Heywood, Thomas. *A Woman Killed with Kindness*. Ed. R. W. van Fossen. Cambridge, Mass., 1961.

Hill, Christopher. *Puritanism and Revolution*. London, 1962.

Hilpisch, P. Stephanus. *Die Doppelklöster: Entstehung und Organisation*. Beiträge zur Geschichte des alten Mönchtums und des Benediktinerordens, 15. Münster, 1928.

Hippolytus. *Philosophumena*. PG, vol. 16, pt. 3, 3009–454.

Hirsch, S. R. *Horeb: A Philosophy of Jewish Laws and Observances*. London, 1962.

Hitschmann, E. "Uber Nerven- und Geisteskrankheiten bein katholischen Geistlichen und Nonnen." *Internationale Zeitschruft für ärztliche Psychoanalyse*, 2 (1914): 270–72.

Homer. *Odyssey*. Trans. A. T. Murray. 2 vols. Cambridge, Mass., 1966.

Honigmann, E. A. J. *Shakespeare: The "Lost Years."* Manchester, Eng., 1985.

Hopkins, Keith. "Brother-Sister Marriage in Roman Egypt." *Comparative Studies in Society and History*, 22 (1980): 303–54.

Howard, Frank. *The Spirit of the Plays of Shakespeare Exhibited in a Series of Outline Plates*. 5 vols. London, 1827–33.

Hugh of St. Victor. *De beatae Mariae virginitate*. PL, 176: 857–76.

Hughey, Ruth. "A Note on Queen Elizabeth's 'Godly Meditation,'" *Library*, 4th ser., 25 (1935): 237–40.

Hunter, A. M. *Design for Life*. Gateshead on Tyne, 1954.

Hunter, George Kirkpatrick. "Six Notes on 'Measure for Measure,'" *Shakespeare Quarterly*, 15 (1964): 167–72.

Hunter, W. A. *A Systematic and Historical Exposition of Roman Law.* 4th ed. Edinburgh, 1903.

Huth, Alfred Henry. *The Marriage of Near Kin Considered with Respect to the Law of Nations, the Results of Experience, and the Teachings of Biology.* London, 1887.

Hutter, Horst. *Politics as Friendship: The Origins of Classical Notions of Politics in the Theory and Practice of Friendship.* Waterloo, Ont., 1978.

Ibsen, Henrik. *Ghosts.* In Ibsen, *Four Major Plays,* trans. Rolf Fjelde. New York, 1970.

Ignatius of Antioch, Saint. "The Epistle to the Ephesians." In *Corpus Ignatium: A Complete Collection of the Ignatian Epistles,* ed. William Cureton, pp. 15–38. Berlin, 1849. Also in PG, 5:729–56.

Irwin, John T. *Doubling and Incest / Repetition and Revenge: A Speculative Reading of Faulkner.* Baltimore, 1975.

Ivo Carnotensis. *Decretum.* PL, 161:47–1036.

Jackson, Bruce, with Diana Christian. *Out of Order.* Motion picture produced by Documentary Research, Inc. Buffalo, N.Y., 1982.

Jackson, Michael. "Ambivalence and the Last-Born: Birth Order Position in Convention and Myth." *Man,* n.s. 13 (1978):341–61.

Jacquemet, G., ed. *Catholicisme: Hier, aujourd'hui, demain.* 7 vols. Paris, 1947.

Jaffa, Harry V. "Chastity as a Political Principle: An Interpretation of Shakespeare's *Measure for Measure.*" In John Alvis and Thomas G. West, eds., *Shakespeare as Political Thinker.* Durham, N.C., 1981.

James I [James VI of Scotland]. *Basilicon Doron.* Ed. James Craigie. 2 vols. Edinburgh, 1944–50.

———. *The Political Works of James I.* Ed. and intro. Charles Howard McIlwain. Cambridge, Mass., 1918.

———. *The Trew Law of Free Monarchies: or The Reciprock and Mvtvuall Dvetie Betwixt a Free King, and his Naturall Subjects.* 1598. In *Political Works,* pp. 53–70.

James, M. R., ed. *Apocryphal New Testament.* Oxford, 1924.

Jameson, Anna Brownell. *Characteristics of Women, Moral, Poetical, and Historical.* 2 vols. London, 1832.

Jeanmaire, Henri. *Couroi et Courètes: Essai sur l'éducation spartiate et sur les rites d'adolescence dans l'antiquité hellénique.* Lille, 1939; repr. New York, 1975.

Jerome, Saint [Eusebius Hieronymus]. *Adversus Jovinianum.* PL, 23:221–350.

———. *Epistulae.* Ed. Isidorus Hilberg. CSEL, 54–56. Also in PL, 22:325–1224.

Jeshua ben Judah. *Sefer ha-Yashar: Das Buch von den verbotenen Verwandschaftsgraden.* (In Hebrew.) St. Petersburg, 1908.

John Chrysostom, Saint. *De virginitate.* PG, 48:533–96.

John of the Cross, Saint. *The Collected Works of St. John of the Cross.* Trans. Kieran Kavanaugh and Otilio Rodriguez. Intro. Kieran Kavanaugh. Washington, D.C., 1973.

Johnson, Paul. *Elizabeth I: A Study in Power and Intellect.* London, 1974.

Johnson, Samuel. *Johnson on Shakespeare.* Ed. Walter Alexander Raleigh. London, 1908. In Stead, ed., *Casebook.*

Jonas of Orleans. *De institutione laicali.* PL, 106:122–278.

Jones, Ernest. *Hamlet and Oedipus.* New York, 1976.

Josephus, Flavius [Joseph ben Matthias]. *Josephus Flavius.* Ed. and trans.

Bibliography

Henry St. J. Thackeray, R. Marcus, and L. H. Feldman. 9 vols. London, 1926–65.

Joyce, James. *Ulysses*. New York, 1961.

Julian of Norwich. *Revelations of Divine Love*. Ed. Grace Warrack. 13th ed. London, 1950.

Julius I, Saint [Pope]. *Decreta Julii papae decem*. PL, 8:967–71.

Jung, Carl. "Psychology of the Transference." In *The Practice of Psychotherapy: Essays on the Psychology of the Transference and Other Subjects*, trans. R. F. C. Hull. Vol. 16 of Jung, *Collected Works*, ed. Herbert Read, M. Fordham, and G. Adler. London, 1954.

Justice, Blair and Rita. *The Broken Taboo: Sex in the Family*. New York, 1979.

Justinian the Great. *Dialogue with Tryphon*. PG, 6:471–800.

———. *Digest*. Ed. T. Mommsen. 2 vols. Berlin, 1870.

Karras, M. Elizabeth Tucker. "Tragedy and Illicit Love: A Study of the Incest Motif in Cecilia Valdès and Os Maias." Ph.D. diss., Univ. of Colorado, 1973.

Kaslow, F., D. Haupt, A. A. Arce, and J. Werblowsky. "Homosexual Incest." *Psychiatric Quarterly*, 53 (1981):184–93.

Kaufmann, R. J. "Bond Slaves and Counterfeits: Shakespeare's *Measure for Measure*." *Shakespeare Studies*, 3 (1968 for 1967):85–97.

———. "Ford's Tragic Perspective." *Texas Studies in Language and Literature*, 1 (1960):522–37.

Kaula, David. *Shakespeare and the Archpriest Controversy: A Study of Some New Sources*. The Hague, 1975.

Kellman, Steven. *The Self-Begetting Novel*. New York, 1980.

Kelly, J. Thomas. *Thorns on the Tudor Rose: Monks, Rogues, Vagabonds, and Sturdy Beggars*. Jackson, Miss., 1977.

Kennard, Joseph Spencer. *The Friar in Fiction, Sincerity in Art, and Other Essays*. New York, 1923.

Kern, Louis J. *An Ordered Love: Sex Roles and Sexuality in Victorian Utopias—the Shakers, the Mormons, and the Oneida Community*. Chapel Hill, N.C., 1981.

Kingston, Maxine Hong. *The Woman Warrior: Memoirs of a Girlhood among Ghosts*. New York, 1977.

Klein, Jacob. *A Commentary on Plato's Meno*. Chapel Hill, N.C., 1965.

Knight, G. Wilson. *The Christian Renaissance*. New York, 1962.

———. *The Wheel of Fire*. London, 1930.

Knights, L. C. "The Ambiguity of *Measure for Measure*." *Scrutiny*, 10 (1942): 222–33.

———. "How Many Children Had Lady MacBeth?" In Knights, *Explorations*. New York, 1947.

Knowles, David, and R. N. Hadcock. *Medieval Religious Houses: England and Wales*. London, 1971.

Kohler, Kaufmann. "Brotherly Love." In Singer, ed., *Encyclopedia*.

Koran. Trans. George Sale. Intro. E. D. Ross. London, n.d.

Koschaker, Paul. "Fratriarchat, Hausgemeinschaft und Mutterrecht in Keilschriftexten." *Zeitschrift für Assyriologie*, 41 (1933):1–89.

Kott, Jan. "Die Austauschdienststruktur in *Measure for Measure*." In *Deutsche Shakespeare-Gesellschaft West Jahrbuch 1978/79*. Ed. Hermann Heuer. Heidelberg, 1978.

Krappe, Alexander Haggerty. "Uber die Sagen von der Geschwisterehe im Mittelalter." *Archiv für das Studium der neuren Sprachen*, 67 (1935):161–75.

Kretschmer, Paul W. "Die griechische Benennung des Brüders." In Kretschmer, *Einleitung in die Geschichte der griechischen Sprache*. Göttingen, 1896.

Kristeva, Julia. *Desire in Language: A Semiotic Approach to Literature and Art*. New York, 1980.

Kurath, Hans, Sherman M. Kuhn, and John Reidy, eds. *Middle English Dictionary*. Ann Arbor, Mich., 1956–.

Kyriakos, M. "Fiançailles et mariages à Moussoul." *Anthropos*, 6 (1911): 774–84.

[Lacy, John.] *A Middle English Treatise on the Ten Commandments*. Ed. James Finch Royster. *Studies in Philology*, 6 (1910).

Lang, A. *Social Origins*. London, 1903.

Lang, Andrew. "'Measure for Measure.'" Illus. E. A. Abbey. *Harper's New Monthly Magazine*, 84 (1891): 62–77.

Langer, Marie. "Isabel I, Reina de Inglaterra." *Revista de Psicoanalisis*, 12 (1955): 201–27.

Lascelles, Mary. *Shakespeare's "Measure for Measure."* 1953; repr. Folcroft, Pa., 1974.

———. "Sir Thomas Elyot and the Legend of Alexander Severus." *Review of English Studies*, n.s. 2 (1951): 305–18.

Laslett, Peter. "Comparing Illegitimacy over Time and Between Cultures." Intro. to Peter Laslett, K. Oosterveen, and R. M. Smith, eds., *Bastardy and Its Comparative History*. Cambridge, Mass., 1980.

Lawrence, D. H. *David*. In *The Complete Plays of D. H. Lawrence*. New York, 1965.

———. *Women in Love*. London, 1954.

Lawrence, Stephen, and Bruce Hart. "Sisters and Brothers." On *Free to Be . . . You and Me*, by Marlo Thomas and Friends. Arista Records.

Lawrence, W. W. "*Measure for Measure* and Lucio." *Shakespeare Quarterly*, 9 (1958): 443–53.

Layard, John. "The Incest Taboo and the Virgin Archetype." *Eranos Jahrbuch*, 12 (1945): 254–307.

Lazzeri, Z. "Die Geldfrage in der Regel der hl. Klara und in der Regel der Minderbrüder." *Chiara d'Assisi*, 1 (1953): 115–19.

Leach, Edmund R. "Magical Hair." In John Middleton, ed., *Myth and Cosmos: Readings in Mythology and Symbolism*. Garden City, N.Y., 1967.

———. "Virgin Birth." In *Genesis as Myth and Other Essays*. London, 1969.

Leander, Saint. *Regula, sive liber de institutione virginum et contemptu mundi, ad Florentinam sororem*. PL, 72: 874–94.

Leavis, F. R. "The Greatness of *Measure for Measure*." *Scrutiny*, 10 (1942): 234–47.

Leclerq, Jean. *Monks and Love in Twelfth-Century France: Psycho-Historical Essays*. Oxford, 1979.

———. *Otia monastica*. Etudes sur le vocabulaire de la contemplation au moyen âge. *Studia Anselmiana*, 51. Rome, 1963.

Leech, John. *John Webster: A Critical Study*. London, 1951.

Leff, Gordon. *Heresy in the Later Middle Ages: The Relation of Heterodoxy to Dissent, c. 1250 [to] c. 1450*. 2 vols. New York, 1967.

Lefranc, Abel. *À la découverte de Shakespeare*. Paris, 1950.

———. *Sous le masque de Shakespeare*. Paris, 1918.

Lemercier, Dom Grégoire. "Freud in the Cloister." *Atlas*, 13, no. 1 (January 1967): 33–37.

Lempp, E. "Die Anfänge des Clarissenordens." *Zeitschrift für Kirchengeschichte*, 13 (1892):181–245.

Leo, John. "'Cradle to Grave' Intimacy." *Time*, September 7, 1981, p. 69.

Leonard, Nancy. "Substitution in Shakespeare's Problem Comedies." *English Literary History*, 9 (1979):281–301.

Lesellier, J. "Deux Enfants naturels de Rabelais légitimés par le pape Paul III." *Humanisme et Renaissance*, 5 (1938):549–70.

Lessing, Gotthold Ephraim. *Lessings Werke*. Ed. J. Petersen, W. von Olhausen, et al. 25 vols. Berlin, 1925; repr. Hildesheim, 1970.

Levi-Bianchini, Mario. "La neurosi antifallica nell'ambito della vita sociale ed in quella religiosa cattolica romana." *Annali di neuropsichiatria e psicoanalisi*, 3 (1956):39–46.

Lévi-Strauss, Claude. *The Elementary Structures of Kinship*. Ed. Rodney Needham. Trans. James Harle Bell and John Richard von Sturmer. Boston, 1969.

———. "Language and the Analysis of Social Laws." In *Structural Anthropology*, trans. Claire Jacobson and Brooke Grundfest Schoepf. New York, 1967.

Levin, Richard. *New Readings vs. Old Plays: Recent Trends in the Reinterpretation of English Renaissance Drama*. Chicago, 1979.

Lewis, Matthew Gregory. *The Monk*. Ed. F. Peck. Intro. John Berryman. New York, 1952.

Lincoln, Victoria. *Teresa: A Woman. A Biography of Teresa of Avila*. Intro. Antonio T. de Nicholás. Albany, N.Y. 1984.

Lingard, John. *The History of England from the First Invasion by the Romans to the Accession of William and Mary in 1688*. 10 vols. London, 1883.

Lippard, George. *The Quaker City, or The Monks of Monk Hall; A Romance of Philadelphia Life, Mystery, and Crime*. Philadelphia, 1845. Edited as *The Monks of Monk Hall*, by Leslie Fiedler, with intro. by Fiedler. New York, 1970.

Little, Lester K. *Religious Poverty and the Profit Economy in Medieval Europe*. Ithaca, N.Y., 1978.

Livingstone, Frank B. "Genetics, Ecology, and the Origins of Incest and Exogamy." *Current Anthropology*, 10 (1969):45–61.

Locke, John. *Two Treatises on Civil Government*. Intro. W. S. Carpenter. London, 1924; rpr. 1953.

———. *Two Treatises on Government*. Preceded by Robert Filmer's *Patriarcha*. Intro. Henry Morley. London, 1884.

Longchamps, Pierre de. *Mémoires d'une religieuse écrits par elle-même*. Amsterdam, 1766.

Lope de Vega [Lope Felix de Vega Carpio]. *The Outrageous Saint*. Trans. Willis Barnstone. *Tulane Drama Review*, 7 (1962):58–104.

———. *El vaquero de Moraña*. Madrid, 1617.

Lupton, Thomas. *The Second Part and Knitting Up of the Boke entituled Too Good to Be True*. London, 1581.

Luther, Martin. "Against the Antinomians" (1539). Trans. Martin H. Bertram. LW, 47:101–20.

———. "The Estate of Marriage." Trans. Walther I. Brandt. LW, 45:17–49.

———. "Exhortation to All Clergy Assembled at Augsburg." Trans. Lewis W. Spitz. LW, 34:9–62.

———. "An Exhortation to the Knights of the Teutonic Order That They Lay Aside False Chastity and Assume the True Chastity of Wedlock." Trans. Albert T. W. Steinhaeuser, rev. Walther I. Brandt. LW, 45:141–58.

————. *Lectures on Genesis*. LW, 2.
————. "The Persons Related by Consanguinity and Affinity Who are Forbidden to Marry According to the Scriptures, Leviticus 18." Trans. Walther I. Brandt. LW, 45:7–9.
————. *Secular Authority: To What Extent It Should Be Obeyed.* In *Luther, Selections from His Writings*, ed. John Dillenberger. Garden City, N.Y., 1961.
————. *Tischreden.* 6 vols. Weimar ed. Weimar, 1912–21; repr. Weimar, 1967.
Macarius the Elder, Saint [of Egypt]. *Homiliae spirituales.* PG, 34:450–822.
McDonnell, Ernest W. *The Beguines and Beghards: With Special Emphasis on the Belgian Scene.* New York, 1969.
McGinn, Donald J. "The Precise Angelo." In J. G. M. Manaway, G. E. Dawson, and E. E. Willoughby, eds., *Joseph Quincy Adams Memorial Studies.* Washington, D.C., 1948.
Mackay, Alexander T. "Fate and Hybris in *Die Braut von Messina.*" *Forum for Modern Language Studies*, 6 (1970):214ff.
Mackay, Eileen. "*Measure for Measure.*" *Shakespeare Quarterly*, 14 (1963): 109–13.
McWilliams, Wilson C. *The Idea of Fraternity in America.* Berkeley, 1973.
Madan, Falconer. *A Summary Catalogue of Western Manuscripts in the Bodleian Library at Oxford.* Oxford, 1895.
Maimonides [Moses ben Maimon]. *Werke in Auswahl.* Ed. Otto Clemen et al. 4 vols. Bonn, 1912–13; Berlin, 1955–56.
Malinowski, Bronislaw. "Parenthood, the Basis of Social Structure." In V. F. Calverton and S. D. Schmalhausen, eds., *The New Generation.* New York, 1930.
Mangenot, E. "Inceste." In Vacant et al., eds., *Dictionnaire*, vol. 7, pt. 2, pp. 1539–57.
Mann, Thomas. *The Holy Sinner.* New York, 1951.
Manteuffel, Tadeusz. *Naissance d'une hérésie: Les Adeptes de la pauvreté volontaire au moyen âge.* Trans. Anna Posner. Paris, 1970.
Marguerite of Navarre [Marguerite d'Angoulême, Queen of Navarre]. *Correspondence.* Ed. Pierre Jourda. Paris, 1930.
————. *L'Heptaméron des nouvelles.* Ed. Le Roux de Lincy and Anatole de Montaiglon. 4 vols. Paris, 1880.
————. *Heptameron.* Trans. George Saintsbury. 5 vols. London, 1894.
————. *Le Miroir de l'âme pecheresse, et al.* Ed. Joseph L. Allaire. Munich, 1972.
————. *La Navire, ou consolation du Roi François I à sa soeur Marguerite.* Ed. Robert Marichal. Paris, 1956.
Martin du Gard, Roger. *La Sorellina.* Vol. 1 of *Oeuvres complètes.* Paris, 1969.
Martz, William J. *The Place of "Measure for Measure" in Shakespeare's Universe of Comedy.* Lawrence, Kans., 1982.
Masson, David. *Shakespeare Personally.* Ed. Rosaline Orme Masson. London, 1914.
Masters, R. E. L. *Patterns of Incest: A Psycho-social Study of Incest Based on Clinical and Historic Data.* New York, 1963.
Masters, R. E. L., and Donald Webster Cory. *Violation of Taboo: Incest in the Great Literature of the Past and Present.* New York, 1963.
Maura, Sister. *Shakespeare's Catholicism.* Cambridge, Mass., 1924.
Mauss, Marcel. *The Gift.* Trans. Ian Cunnison. Intro. E. E. Evans-Pritchard. New York, 1967.

Maynard, Theo. *Queen Elizabeth*. Milwaukee, 1940.

Mazon, André. *Contes slaves de la Macedonie sud-occidentale*. Paris, 1923.

Mead, Margaret. *Sex and Temperament in Three Primitive Societies*. New York, 1968.

Melcher, Marguerite F. *The Shaker Adventure*. Princeton, 1941.

Melville, Herman. *Billy Budd*. In *Selected Tales and Poems*, ed. with intro. Richard Chase. New York, 1950.

——. *Pierre, or, The Ambiguities*. Ed. Henry A. Murray. Foreword Lawrence Thompson. New York, 1964; rpr. of Melville's text as edited in the 1949 edition.

——. *Pierre, or, The Ambiguities*. Ed. Harrison Hayford, Hershel Parker, and G. Thomas Tanselle. Historical Note by Leon Howard and Hershel Parker. Evanston, Ill., 1971.

Middleton, Thomas. *The Family of Love*. Ed. Simon Shepherd. Nottingham, 1979.

Middletown, Russell. "Brother-Sister and Father-Daughter Marriage in Ancient Egypt." *American Sociological Review*, 27 (1962): 603–11.

Miles, Henry. *Forbidden Fruit: A Study of the Incest Theme in Erotic Literature*. London, 1973.

Miles, Rosalind. *The Problem of Measure for Measure*. London, 1976.

Miller, Lucien. *Masks of Fiction in 'Dream of the Red Chamber': Myth, Mimesis, and Persona*. Tucson, Ariz., 1975.

Millin, Aubin Louis. *Antiquités nationales*. 5 vols. Paris, 1790–99.

Milward, Peter. *Religious Controversies of the Elizabethan Age: A Survey of Printed Sources*. Lincoln, Nebr., 1977.

——. *Shakespeare's Religious Background*. London, 1973.

Mintz, Sidney W., and Eric R. Wolf. "An Analysis of Ritual Co-Godparentage." *Southwestern Journal of Anthropology*, 6 (1950): 341–68.

Mogan, Joseph J., Jr. "*Pierre* and *Manfred*: Melville's Study of the Byronic Hero." *Papers on English Language and Literature*, 1 (1965): 230–40.

Montaigne, Michel Eyquem de. *Essays*. Trans. Charles Cotten. 3 vols. London, 1738.

Montalembert, Charles Forbes René de Tyron [Count of]. *The Monks of the West from St. Benedict to St. Bernard*. 7 vols. Edinburgh, 1861–79.

Montesquieu, Charles de Secordat. *Lettres persanes*. In *Oeuvres complètes*, ed. Roger Caillois. Paris, 1949.

Montgomerie, William. "More an Antique Roman Than a Dane." *Hibbert Journal*, 59 (1960): 67–77.

Montrose, Louis Adrian. "'The Place of a Brother' in *As You Like It*." *Shakespeare Quarterly*, 32 (1981): 28–54.

——. "'Shaping Fantasies': Figurations of Gender and Power in Elizabethan Culture." *Representations*, 1 (1983): 61–94.

More, Thomas, Saint. *Confutacyon with Tindale*. Vol. 8, pt. 1 of *The Complete Works of St. Thomas More*, ed. Louis A. Schuster, Richard C. Marius, James P. Lusardi, and Richard J. Schoeck. New Haven, 1973.

——. *Utopia*. Ed. Joseph Hirst Lupton. Oxford, 1895.

Morison, Samuel Eliot. *The Oxford History of the American People*. New York, 1965.

Moulton, James Hope. *Early Zoroastrianism*. London, 1913.

Muir, Kenneth. *Shakespeare's Sources*. Vol. 1: *Comedies and Tragedies*. London, 1957. In Geckle, ed., *Interpretations*.

Muller, H. F. "A Chronological Note on the Physiological Explanation of the Prohibition of Incest." *Journal of Religious Psychology*, 6 (1913):294–95.

Müllner, Amand Gottfried Adolph. *Die Schuld*. Vienna, [1815].

Mumby, Frank A. *The Girlhood of Queen Elizabeth: A Narrative in Contemporary Letters*. London, 1909.

Munro, John. *The Shakespeare Allusion-Book*. London, 1909.

Murdock. G. P. *Social Structure*. New York, 1949.

Murry, John Middleton. "Shakespeare: The Redemption of Generation." In *Heaven—and Earth*, pp. 109–17. London, 1938.

Mutschmann, Heinrich, and Karl Wentersdorf. *Shakespeare and Catholicism*. New York, 1952.

Nabokov, Vladimir. *Ada, or Ardor: A Family Chronicle*. New York, 1969.

———. *Strong Opinions*. New York, 1973.

Nashe, Thomas. *The Anatomie of Absurditie*. London, 1590.

———. *The Works of Thomas Nashe*. Ed. R. B. McKerrow. 5 vols. London, 1910.

Nathan, Norman. "The Marriage of Duke Vincentio and Isabella." *Shakespeare Quarterly*, 7 (1956):43–45.

Naz, R., ed. *Dictionnaire de droit canonique*. Paris, 1935–.

Neale, J. E. *Elizabeth I and Her Parliaments, 1559–1581*. New York, 1958.

———. *Queen Elizabeth: A Biography*. 1935; repr. New York, 1957.

Needham, Rodney. *Primordial Characters*. Charlottesville, Va., 1978.

Nelson, Benjamin. *The Idea of Usury: From Tribal Brotherhood to Universal Otherhood*. Chicago, 1969.

Nelson, Gene, director. *Kissin' Cousins*. A motion picture starring Elvis Presley. MGM/Four Leaf, 1963.

Nemoy, Leon. *Karaite Anthology: Excerpts from the Early Literature, Translated from Arabic, Aramaic, and Hebrew Sources*. New Haven, 1952.

New Catholic Encyclopedia. 15 vols. New York, 1967.

Nichols, John. *The Progress and Public Processions of Queen Elizabeth*. 3 vols. London, 1823.

Nicolas of Cusa. *De ludo globi*. In Paul Wilpert, ed., *Quellen und Studien zür Geschichte der Philosophie*, vol. 6. Berlin, 1967.

Nicolson, Marjorie. "The Professor and the Detective." In Howard Hallcroft, ed., *The Art of the Mystery Story: A Collection of Critical Essays*, pp. 110–27. New York, 1946.

Nietzsche, Friedrich. *The Birth of Tragedy*. Trans. Francis Golffing. New York, 1956.

———. Excerpt from *The Birth of Tragedy*. Trans. Lebeck. In Thomas Woodard, ed., *Sophocles: A Collection of Critical Essays*. Englewood Cliffs, N.J., 1966.

———. *Die Geburt der Tragödie*. In *Werke in drei Bänden*, vol. 1. Munich, 1954.

Nigg, Walter. *The Heretics*. New York, 1962.

Nigrelli, R. F., ed. "Modern Ideas on Spontaneous Generation." *Annals of the New York State Academy of Sciences*, 69 (1957):257–376.

Nohrnberg, James. *The Analogy of the Faerie Queene*. Princeton, 1976.

Noonan, John T., Jr. *Contraception*. Cambridge, Mass., 1965.

Noyes, John. "An Essay on Scientific Propagation." [U.S.], 1875.

Onians, Richard Brocton. *The Origins of European Thought*. Cambridge, 1954.

Opie, Iona and Peter, eds. *The Classic Fairy Tales*. New York, 1974.

Optatus, Saint, Bishop of Milevi. *Contra Parmenianum Donatistam.* PL, 11: 759–1556, and CSEL, 56 (1893).

Ordinarye of Crysten Men. London, 1506.

Origen. *De oratione.* In *Origenes Werke,* ed. P. Koetschau, E. Klostermann, and E. Preuschen. GCS, 1899–1919.

Ovid. *Heroides and Amores.* Trans. Grant Showerman. 6 vols. 2d ed., rev. G. P. Goold. Cambridge, Mass., 1927.

Owen, D. D. R. *Noble Lovers.* London, 1975.

Oxford English Dictionary. 12 vols. Oxford, 1933.

Oxford Latin Dictionary. Since 1973, ed. P. G. W. Glare. Oxford, 1968–.

Paine, Thomas. *The Writings of Thomas Paine.* Ed. Moncure Daniel Conway. 2 vols. New York, 1902–6.

Paley, William. *Principles of Moral and Political Philosophy.* London, 1785.

Palladius. *Historia Lausiaca.* PG, 34:991–1262.

Parr, Katherine. *The Lamentacions of a Synner.* Nov. 5, 1547. STC, no. 4827. University Microfilms, no. 880. 2d ed., Mar. 28, 1548. STC, no. 4828. University Microfilms, no. 881.

Pater, Walter. Appreciations. London, 1910. Reproduced in Soellner and Bertsche, eds., *Shakespeare, Measure for Measure.*

Paul, Robert A. *The Tibetan Symbolic World: Psychoanalytic Explorations.* Chicago, 1982.

Pearlman, E. "Shakespeare, Freud, and the Two Usuries, or Money's a Meddler." *English Literary Renaissance,* 2 (1972):217–36.

Pearson, Jacqueline. *Tragedy and Tragicomedy in the Plays of John Webster.* Totowa, N.J., 1980.

Peers, E. Allison. *Studies of the Spanish Mystics.* Vol. 1. 2d ed., rev. London, 1951.

Perella, Nicolas J. *The Kiss, Sacred and Profane: An Interpretative History of Kiss Symbolism and Related Religio-Erotic Themes.* Berkeley, 1969.

Perkins, William. *Veniall Sinne.* In *Works.* 3 vols. London, 1617.

Perrens, F. T. *Les Libertins en France au XVIIe siècle.* 1896; repr. New York, 1973.

Peterkiewicz, Jerzy. *The Third Adam.* London, 1975.

Pfeil, Johann Gottlob Benjamin. *Der Wilde.* In *Versuch in moralischen Erzählungen.* Leipzig, 1757. Trans. by Louis Sebastian Mercier as *L'Homme sauvage.* Paris, 1767; Neuchâtel, 1784.

Pilcz, Alexander. "Uber Nerven- und Geisteskrankheiten bei katholischen Geistlichen und Nonnen." *Jahrbücher für Psychiatrie und Neurologie,* 34, 3H.

Pits, John. *Relationum Historicum de Rebus Anglica.* Paris, 1619.

Pitt-Rivers, Julian. "The Kith and the Kin." In Jack Goody, ed., *The Character of Kinship.* Cambridge, 1973.

———. "Pseudo-Kinship." In David L. Sills, ed., *International Encyclopedia of the Social Sciences,* 8:408–13. New York, 1966.

———. "Spiritual Kinship in Andalusia." In *The Fate of Schechem, or The Politics of Sex: Essays in the Anthropology of the Mediterranean.* Cambridge, 1977.

Pius XII [Pope]. "Sponsa Christi." *Acta Apostolicae Sedis,* 43 (1951):5–37.

Plato. *Cratylus, Parmenides, Great Hippias, Lesser Hippias.* Trans. H. N. Fowler. Cambridge, Mass., 1970.

———. *Euthyphro, Apology, Crito, Phaedo, Phaedrus.* Trans. H. N. Fowler. Cambridge, Mass., 1960.

————. *The Laws.* Trans. with intro. Trevor J. Saunders. Harmondsworth, Middlesex, 1975.

————. *Lysis, Symposium, Gorgias.* Trans. W. R. M. Lamb. Cambridge, Mass., 1975.

————. *Republic.* Trans. Francis M. Cornford. New York, 1961.

————. *Republic of Plato.* Trans. Allan Bloom. New York, 1968.

————. *Theaetetus and Sophist.* Trans. H. N. Fowler. Cambridge, Mass., 1970.

————. *Timaeus, Critias, Clitophon, Menexenus, Epistulae.* Trans. R. G. Bury. Cambridge, Mass., 1966.

Platt, Colin. *The Monastic Grange in Medieval England.* London, 1969.

Pomerius, Henry. "De origine monasterii Viridvallis." *Analecta Bollandiana,* 4 (1885–86): 263–322.

Ponton, Jeanne. *La Religieuse dans la littérature française.* Laval, Quebec, 1969.

Pope, Elizabeth. "The Renaissance Background of *Measure for Measure.*" *Shakespeare Survey,* 2 (1949): 66–82. In Geckle, ed. *Interpretations.*

Porete, Marguerite. *Le Mirouer des simples ames.* Ed. Romana Guarnieri. *Archivo italiano per la storia della pietà,* 4 (1964): 501–636.

Porter, Dennis. *The Pursuit of Crime: Art and Ideology in Detective Fiction.* New Haven, 1981.

Poulenc, Francis. *Dialogues des Carmelites.* Opera in three acts and twelve scenes. Text from the play of Georges Bernanos, inspired by a novelette by Gertrude von le Fort and a scenario by Philippe Agostini and the Rev. V. Bruckberger. English version by Joseph Machlis. N.p., 1957.

Poulet, Georges. *Études sur le temps humain.* Paris, 1949.

Prader, Florian. *Schiller und Sophokles.* Zurich, 1954.

Prat, Angel Valbuena. "A Freudian Character in Lope de Vega." *Tulane Drama Review,* 7 (1958): 44–55.

Preisendanz, Karl Lebrecht, ed. and trans. *Papyri graecae magicae. Die Griechische Zauberpapyri.* 2 vols. Leipzig, 1928.

Pye, Henry James. *Comments on the Commentators of Shakespeare.* London, 1807.

Quaife, G. R. *Wanton Wenches and Wayward Wives: Peasants and Illicit Sex in Early Seventeenth Century England.* London, 1979.

Rabanus [or Hrabanus] Maurus. *Concilium moguntium.* MANSI, 14: 900–912.

Rabelais, François. *Gargantua.* In *Oeuvres complètes,* ed. Jacques Boulanger, rev. Lucian Scheler. Paris, 1955.

————. *Gargantua and Pantagruel.* Trans. J. M. Cohen. Harmondsworth, Middlesex, 1955.

————. *Oeuvres complètes.* Ed. with intro. and notes P. Jourda. 2 vols. Paris, 1962.

Racine, Jean. *Oeuvres complètes.* Ed. Raymond Picard, preface Pierre Clarac. 2 vols. Paris, 1962.

Radcliffe-Brown, A. R. Introduction to A. R. Radcliffe-Brown and D. Forde, *African Systems of Kinship and Marriage.* Oxford, 1950.

Raglan, Lord. *Jocasta's Crime: An Anthropological Study.* London, 1933.

Ramey, James W. "Dealing with the Last Taboo." *SIECUS Report,* 7 (1979): 1.

Rank, Otto. *Das Inzest-Motiv in Dichtung und Sage.* Leipzig, 1912; repr. Darmstadt, 1974.

————. *The Myth of the Birth of the Hero and Other Writings.* Ed. Philip Freund. New York, 1932.

Rankin, H. D. "Catullus and Incest." *Eranos,* 74 (1976): 113–21.

Raybin, James B. "Homosexual Incest: Report of a Case of Homosexual Incest Involving Three Generations of a Family." *Journal of Nervous and Mental Disease*, 148 (1969): 105–10.

Recueil des historiens des Gaules et de la France. 24 vols. Paris, 1738–1904.

Redfield, James M. *Nature and Culture in the Iliad: The Tragedy of Hector*. Chicago, 1975.

Reid, Stephen A. "A Psychoanalytic Reading of *Troilus and Cressida* and *Measure for Measure*." *Psychoanalytic Review*, 57 (1970): 263–82.

Reik, Theodor. *Fragments of a Great Confession*. New York, 1949.

Reimer, Christian Josef. *Der Begriff der Gnade in Shakespeares "Measure for Measure."* Düren, 1937.

Remond, Jean-Pierre. "Il n'y a d'amour qu'incestueux donc impossible." *Quinzaine littéraire*, 245 (December 1–15, 1976): 7–8.

Renvoize, Jean. *Incest: A Family Pattern*. London, 1982.

Rice, George P. *The Public Speaking of Queen Elizabeth*. New York, 1951.

Riche, Barnabe. *The Adventures of Brusanus, Prince of Hungaria*. London, 1592.

Riquetti, Honoré Gabriel, Count de Mirabeau. *Des Lettres de cachet et des prisons d'état*. Hamburg, 1782.

————. *Errotika Biblion*. Rome, 1783.

————. *Lettres d'amour à Sophie*. Paris, 1924.

Rodenbach, Georges. *Le Carilloneur*. Paris, 1913.

Rodulphius, Petrus. *Historiarum seraphicae religionis Franciscanorum libri tres . . .* Venice, 1586.

Rofsky, Marvin. "Effects of Father-Daughter Incest on the Personality of Daughters." Ph.D. diss., United States International Univ., 1979.

Rogers, John. *The Displaying of an Horrible Secte of Grosse and Wicked Heretiques, naming themselves the Familie of Love*. N.p., 1578.

Rolandus [Orlando Bandinelli, Pope Alexander III]. *Summa*. Ed. Friedrich Thaner. Innsbruck, 1874.

Roscelli, William John. "Isabella, Sin, and Civil Law." *University of Kansas City Review*, 28 (1962): 215–27.

Rosenblatt, Jason P. "Aspects of the Incest Problems in *Hamlet*." *Shakespeare Quarterly*, 29 (1978): 349–64.

Rosset, François de. "Des Amours incestueuses d'une frère et d'une soeur, et de leur fin malheureuse et tragique." In *Les Histoires tragiques de nostre temps: où sont contenues les morts funestes et lamentables de plusieurs personnes*. 1615; repr. Geneva, 1980.

Rubin, Rick, and Greg Byerly. *Incest: The Last Taboo—An Annotated Bibliography*. New York, 1983.

Ruskin, John. *Proserpina*. Vols. 24–25 of *Works*, ed. E. T. Cook and Alexander Wedderburn, 39 vols. London, 1903–12.

Rymer, Thomas. *Critical Works*. Ed. Curt Zimansky. New Haven, 1956.

Sabatier, P. "Le Privilège de la pauvreté." *Révue d'histoire franciscaine*, 1 (1924): 1–54.

Sacks, Karen. *Sisters and Wives: The Past and Future of Sexual Equality*. Westport, Conn., 1979.

Sade, Donatien Alphonse François, Comte de. *La Philosophie dans le boudoir*. Preface by Matthieu Galey. Paris, 1972.

Saffady, William. "Fears of Sexual License During the English Reformation." *History of Childhood Quarterly*, 1 (1973): 89–97.

Saintsbury, George. *A Short History of English Literature*. London, 1898.

Salaman, Malcolm C. *Shakespeare in Pictorial Art*. Ed. Charles Holme. London, 1916.

Sandell, Sandra Dianne. "'A very poetic circumstance': Incest and the English Literary Imagination, 1770–1830." Ph.D. diss., Univ. of Minnesota, 1981.

Santiago, Luciano. *The Children of Oedipus: Brother-Sister Incest in Psychiatry, Literature, History, and Mythology*. New York, 1973.

Sawyer, Susan G. "Lifting the Veil on the Last Taboo." *Family Health*, June 1980, p. 43.

Sbaralea, Joannes Hyacinth, ed. *Bullarium Franciscanum*. Rome, 1799.

Schanzer, Ernest. "The Marriage Contracts in *Measure for Measure*." *Shakespeare Survey*, 13 (1960): 81–89. In *MM*, ed. Soellner and Bertsche.

———. *The Problem Plays of Shakespeare: A Study of "Julius Caesar," "Measure for Measure," "Antony and Cleopatra."* New York, [1963].

Schereschewsky, Ben-Zion [Benno]. "Mamzer." In Singer, ed., *Jewish Encyclopedia*.

Schiller, Friedrich von. *Bride of Messina*. Trans. Charles E. Passage. New York, 1967.

———. *Sämtliche Werke*. 5 vols. Munich, 1962.

Schlegel, August Wilhelm. *A Course of Lectures on Dramatic Art and Literature*. Trans. John Black. London, 1846. In Stead, ed., *Casebook*.

Schleiner, Einnifried. "*Divina virago*: Queen Elizabeth as an Amazon." *Studies in Philology*, 75 (1978): 163–80.

Schmitt, Clément. "Isabelle de France (Bienheureuse)." In Jacquemet, ed., *Catholicisme*, 6: 129.

Schneck, Jerome M. "Zooerasty and Incest Fantasy." *International Journal of Clinical and Experimental Hypnosis*, 22 (1974): 299–302.

Schneider, David M. *American Kinship: A Cultural Account*. Chicago, 1968.

Schneider, Gerhard. *Der Libertin: Zur Geistes- und Sozialgeschichte des Bürgertums im 16. und 17. Jahrhundert*. Stuttgart, 1970.

Schoenbaum, S. *William Shakespeare: A Compact Documentary Life*. New York, 1977.

Schroeder, Theodore. "Shaker Celibacy and Salacity Psychologically Interpreted." *New York Medical Journal*, 113 (1921): 800–805.

Schweizer, Eduard. *The Good News According to Matthew*. Atlanta, 1975.

Screech, M. A. *The Rabelaisian Marriage: Aspects of Rabelais's Religion, Ethics, and Comic Philosophy*. London, 1958.

Scriptorum illustrium maioris Brytanniae, quam nunc Angliam et Scotiam vocant. Basel, 1557, 1559.

See, Fred G. "Kinship of Metaphor—Incest and Language in Melville's *Pierre*." *Structuralist Review*, 1 (1978): 55–81.

Seemanov, Eva. "A Study of Children of Incestuous Matings." *Human Heredity*, 21 (1971): 108–28.

Séguy, Jean. "Une Sociologie des sociétés imaginées: Monachisme et utopie." *Annales: Economies, Societes, Civilisations*, 26 (1971): 328–54.

Seneca, Lucius Annaeus. *Ad Lucilium epistulae morales*. Trans. Richard M. Gummere. 3 vols. London, 1925.

———. *De beneficiis*. In *Moral Essays*, trans. John W. Basore. 3 vols. London, 1928–35.

———. *De beneficiis*. Trans. A. Golding. London, 1578.

Seters, John Van. *Abraham in History and Tradition*. New Haven, 1978.

Seymour, William. *Ordeal by Ambition: An English Family in the Shadow of the Tudors*. London, 1972.

Shakespeare, William. Complete works:

    Second Folio. London, 1632. Specimen expurgated by William Sankey under the authority of the Inquisition sometime between 1641 and 1651 for students in the English College at Valladolid, Spain. Folger Shakespeare Library.

    Bowdler, Thomas, ed. *The Family Shakespeare: in which nothing is added to the original text but those words and expressions are omitted which cannot with propriety be read*. 4 vols. London, 1807.

    Evans, G. Blakemore, ed. *The Riverside Shakespeare*. Boston, 1974.

    Harness, William, ed. *Dramatic Works*. 8 vols. London, 1825–30.

    Hudson, Henry N., ed. *The Works*. 11 vols. Boston, 1851–57.

    Johnson, Samuel, ed. *Plays of William Shakespeare*. 8 vols. 1765; repr. New York, 1968.

    Pope, Alexander, ed. *The Works of William Shakespear*. 6 vols. 1725; repr. New York, 1969.

    Singer, Samuel W., ed. *Dramatic Works of William Shakespeare*. 10 vols. London, 1826.

———. Individual plays. Plays are arranged alphabetically by abbreviation below. Except where otherwise noted, the first title to appear is the edition used for references in the text.

    ADO. *Much Ado About Nothing*. Ed. David L. Stevenson. New York, 1964.

    AWW. *All's Well That Ends Well*. Ed. Sylvan Barnett. New York, 1965.

    AYL. *As You Like It*. Evans, ed., *Riverside Shakespeare*.

    COR. *Coriolanus*. Ed. Reuben Brower. New York, 1966.

    CYM. *Cymbeline*. Ed. J. C. Maxwell. Cambridge, 1960.

    ERR. *Comedy of Errors*. Ed. Harry Levin. New York, 1965.

    1H4. *The First Part of King Henry the Fourth*. Ed. Maynard Mack. New York, 1965.

    2H4. *The Second Part of King Henry the Fourth*. Ed. A. R. Humphreys. London, 1967.

    H5. *King Henry the Fifth*. Ed. John H. Walter. London, 1954.

    2H6. *The Second Part of King Henry the Sixth*. Evans, ed., *Riverside Shakespeare*.

    3H6. *The Third Part of King Henry the Sixth*. Evans, ed., *Riverside Shakespeare*.

    H8. *King Henry the Eighth*. Ed. R. A. Foakes. London, 1968.

    HAM. *Hamlet*. Ed. Willard Farnham. Baltimore, 1957.

    ———. Ed. Harold Jenkins. London, 1982.

    KJ. *King John*. Ed. E. A. J. Honigmann. London, 1954.

    LLL. *Love's Labor's Lost*. Ed. Richard David. London, 1966.

    LR. *King Lear*. Ed. Tucker Brooke and William Phelps. New Haven, 1917.

    MM. *Measure for Measure*. Ed. J. W. Lever. London, 1965.

    ———. Ed. Mark Eccles. *A New Variorum Edition of Shakespeare*. New York, 1980.

    ———. Ed. Rolf Soellner and Samuel Bertsche. Boston, 1966.

    ———. Ed. A. T. Quiller-Couch, John Dover Wilson, et al. Cambridge, 1922.

    ———. Ed. William J. Rolfe. New York, 1905.

    ———. Ed. Robert Cecil Bald. Baltimore, 1956.

MND. *A Midsummer Night's Dream*. Ed. Wolfgang Clemen. New York, 1963.
MV. *The Merchant of Venice*. Ed. Brents Stirling. Baltimore, 1970.
PER *Pericles*. Ed. F. D. Hoeniger. London, 1969.
R2. *Richard the Second*. Ed. Peter Ure. London, 1966.
ROM. *Romeo and Juliet*. Evans, ed., *Riverside Shakespeare*.
SON. *Sonnets*. Ed. William Burto. New York, 1964.
TGV. *The Two Gentlemen of Verona*. Evans, ed., *Riverside Shakespeare*.
TN. *Twelfth Night*. Ed. J. M. Lothian and T. W. Craik. London, 1975.
TRO. *Troilus and Cressida*. Evans, ed., *Riverside Shakespeare*.
WT. *The Winter's Tale*. Ed. J. H. Pafford. London, 1968.
Shell, Marc. *The Economy of Literature*. Baltimore, 1978.
————. "The Family Pet." *Representations*, 15 (1986):121–53.
————. *Money, Language, and Thought: Literary and Philosophical Economies from the Medieval to the Modern Era*. Berkeley, 1982.
————. "The Mother Superior: Racine's *Brittanicus* and the Catholic Orders." Forthcoming.
————. "The Wether and the Ewe: Verbal Usury in *The Merchant of Venice*." *Kenyon Review*, n.s. 1 (1979):65–92.
Shelley, Percy Bysshe. *Poetical Works*. Ed. W. M. Rossetti. 3 vols. London, 1881.
Sidler, Nikolaus. *Zur Universalität des Inzesttabu: Eine kritische Untersuchung der These und der Einwände*. Stuttgart, 1971.
Siegel, Paul N. "*Measure for Measure*: The Significance of the Title." *Shakespeare Quarterly*, 4 (1953):317–20.
Silverman, Lloyd H., Jay S. Kwawer, Carol Wolitzky, and Mark Coron. "An Experimental Study of Aspects of the Psychoanalytic Theory of Male Homosexuality." *Journal of Abnormal Psychology*, 82 (1973):178–88.
Simonis, Yvan. *Claude Lévi-Strauss, ou "La Passion de l'inceste": Introduction au structuralisme*. Paris, 1968.
Simpson, Lucie. *The Secondary Heroes of Shakespeare, and Other Essays*. [London, 1951].
Singer, I., ed. *Jewish Encyclopedia*. 12 vols. London, 1925.
Skulsky, Harold. "Pain, Law, and Conscience in *Measure for Measure*." *Journal of the History of Ideas*, 25 (1964):147–68.
Skura, Meredith Anne. *The Literary Use of the Psychoanalytic Process*. New Haven, 1981.
Slater, Marian. "Ecological Factors in the Origin of Incest." *American Anthropologist*, 61 (1959):1042–59.
Slovenko, Ralph. "Incest." *SIECUS Report*, 7 (1979):4–5.
Smith, Charles Edward. *Papal Enforcement of Some Medieval Marriage Laws*. 1940; repr. Port Washington, N.Y., 1972.
Smith, Nigel, ed. *A Collection of Ranter Writings from the Seventeenth Century*. Foreword by John Carey. London, 1983.
Smith, Paul Edgar. "The Incest Motif and the Question of the Decadence of English Drama, 1603–1632." Ph.D. diss., Univ. of Pittsburgh, 1980.
Smith, T. V., and E. C. Lindeman. *The Democratic Way of Life*. New York, 1951.
Smith, William, W. Wayte, and G. E. Marindin, eds. *A Dictionary of Greek and Roman Antiquities*. 3d ed. 2 vols. London, 1890, 1891.
Snider, Denton J. "Shakespeare's *Measure for Measure*." *Journal of Speculative Philosophy*, 9 (1875):412–25.
Sophocles. *Antigone*. Trans. Elizabeth Wyckoff. In *Sophocles I: Oedipus at*

Colonus, and Antigone, trans. David Grene, Robert Fitzgerald, and Elizabeth Wyckoff. Chicago, 1954.

———. *Oedipus the King.* Trans. David Grene. In *Sophocles I.*

———. *The Plays and Fragments.* Ed. and trans. R. C. Jebb. Cambridge, 1881–96.

Southey, Robert. *The Life and Correspondence.* Ed. C. C. Southey. 6 vols. London, 1849–50.

Speiser, E. A. "The Wife-Sister Motif in the Patriarchal Narratives." In Alexander Altman, ed., *Biblical and Other Studies.* Cambridge, Mass., 1963. Also in *Oriental and Biblical Studies: Collected Writings of E. A. Speiser*, ed. J. J. Finkelstein and Moshe Greenberg. Philadelphia, 1967.

Speroni degli Alvarotti, Sperone. *Canace.* Florence, 1546.

Spiro, M. E. "Virgin Birth." *Man*, 7 (1972): 315–16.

———. "Virgin Birth, Parthenogenesis, and Physiological Paternity: An Essay in Cultural Interpretation." *Man*, 3 (1968): 242–61.

Stade, Bernard. *Geschichte des Volkes Israel.* 2 vols. Berlin, 1887–88.

Statius, Publius Papinus. *Thebais.* In *Works*, trans. J. H. Mozley. 2 vols. London, 1928.

Staves, Susan. *Players' Scepters: Fictions of Authority in the Restoration.* Lincoln, Nebr., 1979.

Stead, Christian K., ed. *Shakespeare: Measure for Measure, A Casebook.* London, 1971.

Steele, R. "English Books Printed Abroad, 1525–48." *Transactions of the Bibliographical Society.* o.s. 11 (1909): 189–236.

Steffen, Gustaf F. "Das Zölibat und seine Ursprunge bei den primitiven Völkern." *Politische-Anthropologische Revue*, 11 (1912–13): 235–39.

Steinberg, Leo. *The Sexuality of Christ in Renaissance Art and in Modern Oblivion.* New York, 1983.

Steiner, George. *After Babel.* New York, 1975.

Stendhal [Marie Henri Beyle]. *The Cenci.* In *The Shorter Novels of Stendhal*, trans. C. K. Scott-Moncrieff. New York, 1946.

Stephan of Tournai. *Summa decreti.* Ed. J. F. von Schulte. Giessen, 1891.

Stephen, James Fitzjames. *Liberty, Equality, Fraternity.* Ed. R. J. White. Cambridge, 1967.

Stevenson, David Lloyd. *The Achievement of Shakespeare's "Measure for Measure."* Ithaca, N.Y., 1966.

———. "Design and Structure in *Measure for Measure*: A New Appraisal." *English Literary History*, 23 (1956): 256–78.

———. "The Role of James I in Shakespeare's *Measure for Measure*." *English Literary History*, 26 (1959): 188–208.

Stone, Lawrence. *Crisis of the Aristocracy, 1558–1641.* Oxford, 1965.

———. *The Family, Sex, and Marriage: England 1500–1800.* New York, 1977.

Stow, John. *The Chronicles of England.* London, 1605.

Strabo. *The Geography of Strabo.* Trans. Horace Leonard Jones. 8 vols. London, 1928.

Strachey, Lytton. *Elizabeth and Essex.* London, 1928.

Strong, Roy. *The Cult of Elizabeth.* London, 1977.

Stubbes, Philip. *The Anatomie of Abuses.* London, 1583. Ed. F. J. Furnivall, New Shakespeare Society, London, 1877.

Suetonius, Tranquillus. *Lives of the Caesars.* Trans. J. C. Rolfe. Cambridge, Mass., 1950.
――――. *Nero.* Intro. B. H. Warmington. Bristol, 1977.
Sulpicius Severus. *Dialogues.* Ed. C. Halm. CSEL, 1 (1866).
Swinburne, Henry. *A Briefe Treatise of Testaments and Last Willes.* London, 1590.
――――. *Treatise of Spousals.* London, 1686.
Sypher, Wylie. *The Ethic of Time.* New York, 1976.
――――. "Shakespeare as Casuist: *Measure for Measure.*" *Sewanee Review,* 58 (1950): 262–80.
Szubin, Zvi H. "Mercy." In *Encyclopaedia Judaica.*
Tacitus. *Annals.* Trans. John Jackson. Cambridge, Mass., 1956.
Tanner, Tony. *Adultery and the Novel: Contract and Transgression.* Baltimore, 1979.
Taylor, Mark. *Shakespeare's Darker Purpose: A Question of Incest.* New York, 1982.
Tegnaeus, Harry. *Blood-Brothers: An Ethno-Sociological Study of the Institutions of Blood-Brotherhood with Special Reference to Africa.* Ethnographical Museum of Sweden, n.s. 10. Stockholm, 1952.
Telle, Emile V. "L'Île des alliances, ou l'Anti-Thélème." *Bibliotheque d'humanisme et renaissance,* 14 (1952): 159–75.
――――. *L'Oeuvre de Marguerite d'Angoulême, Reine de Navarre, et La Querelle des femmes.* Toulouse, 1937.
Tennenhouse, Leonard. "Representing Power: *Measure for Measure* in Its Time." *Genre,* 15 (1982): 139–56.
Teppe, Julien. *Chamfort: Sa Vie, son oeuvre, sa pensée.* Paris, 1950.
Teresa of Jesus, Saint. *The Complete Works of Saint Teresa of Jesus.* Trans. and ed. E. Allison Peers from the critical edition of P. Silverio de Santa Teresa. 3 vols. London, 1946.
Tertullian. *Ad uxorem libri duo.* PL, 1: 1385–416.
――――. *Apologeticus.* CC, 1: 85–171.
Teulet, Jean Baptiste Alexandre Theodore, ed. *Correspondence diplomatique de Bertrand de Salignac de la Mothe Fénélon.* 7 vols. Paris, 1838–40.
Thayer, James Bradley. *Preliminary Treatise on Evidence at the Common Law.* Boston, 1898.
Thevet, Andre. *The Newe Founde Worlde.* London, 1568.
Thierfelder, Helmut. *Die Geschwisterehe im hellenistischrömischen Ägypten.* Münster, 1960.
Thirlby, Styan. Manuscript notes in Pope's edition of Shakespeare's works. Beinecke Library, Yale University.
Thiselton, Alfred A. *Some Textual Notes on "Measure for Measure."* London, 1901.
Thomas Aquinas, Saint [Thomas of Aquino]. *Introduction to St. Thomas Aquinas.* Ed. Anton C. Pegis. New York, 1948.
――――. *Summa contra gentiles.* Trans. the English Dominican Fathers. 5 vols. London, 1923–29.
――――. *Summa theologica.* Trans. the Fathers of the English Dominican Province. 3 vols. New York, 1947.
Thomas of Celano(?). *The Legend and Writings of St. Clare of Assisi.* Franciscan Institute, St. Bonaventure, N.Y., 1953.
――――. *Sainte Claire d'Assise: Vie par Thomas de Celano; ses écrits.* Trans. P. Damien Vorreux. Paris, 1953.

Thomas, Brook. "The Writer's Procreative Urge in *Pierre*: Fictional Freedom or Convoluted Incest?" *Studies in the Novel*, 11 (1979):416–30.

Thompson, Alexander Hamilton. "Double Monasteries and the Male Element in Nunneries." Appendix 8 of *The Ministry of Women*, a Report by a Committee by His Grace the Lord Archbishop of Canterbury. London, 1919.

Thompson, Stith, ed. *Motif Index of Folk Literature*. 6 vols. Bloomington, Ind., 1955–58.

Thompson, W. Meredith, ed. *"Ye wohunge of Ure Lauerd"* . . . , *together with "On ure isun of Ure Louerde."* . . . Published for EETS by Oxford Univ. Press. London, 1958.

Thomson, George. *Aeschylus and Athens. A Study in the Social Origins of Drama.* 1940; repr. New York, 1967.

Thorslev, Peter, Jr. "Incest as Romantic Symbol." *Comparative Literature Studies*, 2 (1965):41–58.

Tilley, M. P. *Dictionary of Proverbs in England in the Sixteenth and Seventeenth Centuries*. London, 1950.

Tillyard, E. M. W. *Shakespeare's Problem Plays*. London, 1950. Also in Stead, ed., *Casebook*.

Torrey, C. C. *The Second Isaiah*. New York, 1928.

Tourneur, Cyril. *The Revenger's Tragedy*. Ed. Lawrence J. Ross. Lincoln, Nebr., [1966].

Traversi, Derek A. *An Approach to Shakespeare*. 2d ed. New York, 1956.

———. *"Measure for Measure."* *Scrutiny*, 11 (1942):40–58.

Trithemius, J. *Annales Hirsaugiensis*. 2 vols. St. Gall, 1690.

Tyrrel, William Blake. *Amazons: A Study in Athenian Mythmaking*. Baltimore, 1984.

Vacant, A., E. Mangenot, and E. Amann, eds. *Dictionnaire de théologie catholique*. 23 vols. Paris, 1923–72.

Valency, M., ed. *The Palace of Pleasure: An Anthology of the Novella*. New York, 1960.

Vaux, Roland de. *The Early History of Israel*. Trans. David Smith. Philadelphia, 1978.

Vega Carpio, Lope de. *El vaquero de Moraña*. Madrid, 1617.

Venable, E. "Kiss." In William Smith and Samuel Cheetham, eds., *Dictionary of Christian Antiquities*, vol. 2. 2 vols. London, 1875–80.

Verba seniorum. PL, 73:739–1066.

Vermes, Geza. "Essenes, Therapeutae, Qumran. Ancient Jewish Mysticism and the Dead Sea Scrolls." *Durham Journal*, 52, no. 3 (n.s. 21, no. 3) (1960): 97–115.

Vessie, P. R. "Psychiatry Catches Up with Shakespeare." *Medical Record*, August 5, 1936, pp. 141–45.

Vest, Walter E. "William Shakespeare, Syphilographer." *West Virginia Medical Journal*, 34, no. 1 (March 1938):130–37.

Villier, M., et al., eds. *Dictionnaire de spiritualité*. Paris, 1937–.

Wagenknecht, Edward. *Cavalcade of the American Novel*. New York, 1952.

Wagner, Richard. "Das Liebesverbot." In *Sämtliche Schriften und Dichtungen*, 5th ed. 12 vols. Leipzig, 1911.

Walker, Williston. *John Calvin: The Organizer of Reformed Protestantism*. New York, 1969.

Walpole, Horace. *The Mysterious Mother, A Tragedy.* Strawberry Hill, Middlesex, 1768.

Watkins, Floyd C. "Melville's Plotinus Plinlimmon and *Pierre.*" In William E. Walker and Robert L. Welker, eds., *Reality and Myth: Essays in American Literature in Memory of Richard Croom Beatty*, pp. 39–51. Nashville, 1964.

Webster, John. *The Devil's Law Case.* In *Three Plays*, ed. D. C. Gunby. Harmondsworth, Middlesex, 1972.

Weigand, Hermann. "*Oedipus Tyrannus* and *Die Braut von Messina.*" *Illinois Studies in Language and Literature*, 46 (1959): 171–202.

Weiss, Peter. *The Persecution and Assassination of Jean Paul Marat as Performed by the Inmates of the Asylum of Charenton under the Direction of the Marquis de Sade.* English version by Geoffrey Skelton. Verse adapt. by Adrian Mitchell. Intro. Peter Brook. New York, 1965.

Wentworth, Harold, and Stuart Berg Flexner, eds. *The Dictionary of American Slang.* New York, [1967].

Werder, Karl. *Vorlesungen über Shakespeare's Hamlet.* Berlin, 1875.

Westermarck, Edward. *The History of Human Marriage.* 2d ed. London, 1894. 5th ed. 3 vols. New York, 1922.

Whetstone, George. *An Heptameron of Ciuill Discourses.* London, 1582.

———. *The History of Promos and Cassandra.* London, 1578. Selections in *MM*, ed. Soellner and Bertsche.

White, Edward J. *Commentaries on the Law in Shakespeare.* St. Louis, Mo., 1913.

White, Richard G. *Shakespeare's Scholar.* New York, 1854.

Wilamowitz-Moellendorf, Ulrich von. *Aischylos Interpretationen.* Berlin, 1914.

Wilibald of Mainz. *Vita S. Bonifacii.* PL, 89:603–32.

Wilkins, David, ed. *Concilia Magnae Brittaniae et Hiberniae.* 4 vols. London, 1737.

Wilkinson, W. *A Supplication of the Family of love . . . Examined, and found derogatory in an hie degree.* London, 1606.

Williams, Neville. *Elizabeth, Queen of England.* London, 1967.

Wilson, James D. "Incest and American Romantic Fiction." *Studies in the Literary Imagination*, 7 (1974): 31–50.

Wilson, John Dover. *What Happens in Hamlet?* London, 1935.

Wolf, Arthur P. "Adopt a Daughter-in-Law, Marry a Sister: A Chinese Solution to the Problem of the Incest Taboo." *American Anthropologist*, 70 (1968): 864–74.

Workman, Herbert B. *The Evolution of the Monastic Ideal from the Earliest Times Down to the Coming of the Friars: A Second Chapter in the History of Christian Renunciation.* Boston, 1962.

Wrightston, Keith. "The Nadir of English Illegitimacy in the Seventeenth Century." In P. Laslett, K. Oosterveen, and R. M. Smith, eds., *Bastardy and Its Comparative History.* Cambridge, Mass., 1980.

Wycliffe, John. *Two Short Treatises Against the Orders of the Begging Friars.* Oxford, 1608.

Young, Benjamin S. *The Testimony of Christ's Second Coming.* Lebanon, Ohio, 1808.

Yudkin, Marcia. "Breaking the Incest Taboo: Those Who Crusade for Family 'Love' Forget the Balance of Family Power." *Progressive*, 45 (May 1981): 26–28.

Zeller, Edward. *Die Philosophie der Griechen in ihrer geschictlich Entwicklung.* 3 vols. Leipzig, 1880.

Zelnick, Stephen. "The Incest Theme in *The Great Gatsby*: An Exploration of the False Poetry of Petty Bourgeois Consciousness." In Norman Rudick, ed., *Weapons of Criticism: Marxism in America and the Literary Tradition.* Palo Alto, Calif., 1976.

Index

Library of Congress Cataloging-in-Publication Data

Shell, Marc.
    The end of kinship : "Measure for measure," incest, and the ideal of universal
siblinghood / Marc Shell.—Johns Hopkins pbk. ed.
        p.   cm.
    Includes bibliographical references and index.
    —ISBN 0-8018-5242-0 (pbk. : alk. paper)
    1. Shakespeare, William, 1564-1616.   Measure for measure.   2. Literature and
anthropology—England—History—17th century.   3. Kinship in literature.   4. Incest
in literature.   5. Family in literature.   6. Taboo in literature.   7. Sex in literature.
8. Lex talionis.   9. Kinship.   10. Incest.   I. Title.
PR2824.S48   1995
822.3´3—dc20   95-20440